A A T
DRAFTING FINANCIAL
STATEMENTS

Technician (NVQ/SVQ Level 4)

British Library Cataloguing-in-Publication Data

A catalogue record for this book is available from the British Library.

Published by
Kaplan Publishing Foulks Lynch
Unit 2, The Business Centre
Molly Millars Lane
Wokingham
RG41 2QZ

ISBN 10: 1 84710 129 1
ISBN 13: 978 1 84710 129 7

© FTC Kaplan Limited, July 2006

Printed and bound in Great Britain.

We are grateful to the Association of Accounting Technicians for permission to reproduce past assessment materials.
The solutions have been prepared by Kaplan Publishing Foulks Lynch.

CONTENTS

CONTENTS

WORKBOOK

PREFACE

This is a study text and workbook for Unit 11 (Drafting Financial Statements) of the Standards of Competence NVQ/SVQ Level 4 in Accounting.

STUDY TEXT

The study text is written in a practical and interactive style:
· key terms and concepts are clearly defined
· all topics are illustrated with practical examples with clearly worked solutions
· frequent practice activities throughout the chapters ensure that what you have learnt is regularly reinforced
· 'pitfalls' and 'examination tips' help you avoid commonly made mistakes and help you focus on what is required to perform well in your simulation.

WORKBOOK

The workbook comprises three main elements
(a) A question bank of key techniques to give additional practice and reinforce the work covered in each chapter. This comprises a series of short case studies which cover the major topics of the standards for this unit.
(b) A mock examination which closely reflects the type of examination students may expect.

STANDARDS OF COMPETENCE

Unit commentary

This unit is concerned with competence in drafting and interpreting the financial statements of limited companies. Students will have attained competence at levels 2 and 3 in the process of identifying and recording financial transactions in accounts and ledgers following the principles of double-entry book-keeping. They will also be able to draft the financial statements of sole traders and partnerships. Students will thus have some experience in measuring assets and liabilities at level 3. Unit 11 builds upon these competences and concentrates on the function of drafting financial statements of limited companies from the records and accounts prepared. It ensures that students understand what information is required to be provided, how it is to be presented to users of the financial statements and how the rules and principles established in financial reporting standards apply to the process of drafting financial statements. The unit also ensures that students grasp the reasons why financial statements are prepared and communicated so that their significance is understood. They need to understand who these users are and what use they make of this information. The unit also requires the student to grasp the techniques applied to financial statements that are used to assess the financial performance and the financial position of an entity.

The Standard is divided into two elements:
Element 11.1
Draft limited company financial statements
Element 11.2
Interpret limited company financial statements

Knowledge and Understanding

To perform this unit effectively you will need to know and understand

	The business environment	**Chapters**
1	The elements and purposes of financial statements of limited companies as set out in the conceptual framework for financial reporting (Element 11.2)	1, 2
2	The general legal framework of limited companies and the obligations of Directors in respect of the financial statements (Element 11.1)	1, 3, 4, 5
3	The statutory form of accounting statements and disclosure requirements (Element 11.1)	4, 5
4	The UK regulatory framework for financial reporting and the main requirements of relevant Financial Reporting Standards or The relevant requirements of the International Accounting Standards (Element 11.1)	9, 10, 11, 12, 13, 14, 15, 16
5	The forms of equity and loan capital (Element 11.1) 4	4
6	The presentation of Corporation Tax in financial statements (Element 11.1)	4, 5, 13

Accounting techniques:

7	Preparing financial statements in proper form (Element 11.1)	Throughout
8	Analysing and interpreting the information contained in financial statements (Element 11.2)	17
9	Computing and interpreting accounting ratios (Element 11.2)	17

Accounting principles and theory:

10	Generally accepted accounting principles and concepts (Element 11.1)	2
11	The general principles of consolidation (Element 11.1)	7, 8, 9

The organisation:

12	How the accounting systems of an organisation are affected by its roles, organisational structure, its administrative systems and procedures and the nature of its business transactions (Elements 11.1 & 11.2)	Throughout

KAPLAN PUBLISHING

Element 11.1 Draft limited company financial statements

Performance criteria

In order to perform this element successfully you need to:

A	Draft limited company financial statements from the appropriate information	3, 4
B	Correctly identify and implement subsequent adjustments and ensure that discrepancies, unusual features or queries are identified and either resolved or referred to the appropriate person	3, 4
C	Ensure that limited company financial statements comply with relevant accounting standards and domestic legislation and with the organisation's policies, regulations and procedures	4, 5
D	Prepare and interpret a limited company cash flow statement	6
E	Ensure that confidentiality procedures are followed at all times	Throughout

Range statement

Range Statement, element 11.1 makes it clear that the financial statements that are drafted under this element are the:

· Income statement
· Balance sheet
· Statement of total recognised income and expense
· Supplementary notes required by statute, SSAPs, FRSs and other relevant pronouncements

Element 11.1 requires that the financial statements be drafted from appropriate information. This might include a trial balance or an extended trial balance and might include other information about balances or transactions relating to the period under consideration. The range statement makes it clear that these financial statements might be unitary or consolidated. In other words, students may be asked to draft financial statements for single companies or consolidated group accounts. Performance criteria D makes it clear that the drafting of cash flow statements is also included in this element. These may be drafted from the other financial statements of a company in conjunction with further relevant information.

In drafting financial statements the knowledge and understanding required is set out in the Standards. Students will need to know and understand the general legal framework of limited companies and the obligations of directors in respect of the financial statements. This includes a grasp of the Companies Act accounting and reporting requirements. The student must thus be aware of the format of accounting statements and disclosure requirements in order that they can prepare the financial statements in proper form.

This includes an understanding of the content and form of published accounts of limited companies. Pro-formas for the income statement, statement of recognised income and expense, balance sheet consistent with the requirements of IAS 1 are provided in examinations as is a pro-forma for the cash flow statement in consistent with the requirements of IAS 7. Items required to be disclosed in notes to the accounts required by IAS 1 and the disclosure of directors' emoluments under Schedule 6 Part I and the requirements for disclosure of auditors' remuneration under Section 390A of the Companies Act must be grasped. Cash flow statements are to be drafted in accordance with the requirements of IAS 7.

There must be an understanding of the UK regulatory framework of financial reporting. This includes a grasp of which bodies are involved in the standard-setting process, the process by which standards are promulgated, the structure of regulation and the roles of the bodies involved and the process of enforcing standards. Drafting financial statements involves a grasp of generally accepted accounting principles and concepts as well as detailed knowledge of the main requirements of relevant International Accounting Standards (IAS). Only IASs will be assessed in the unit. The requirements of SSAPs and FRS's are not assessable. The extent to which IASs will be assessable under this unit is given below. This guidance will be updated as new Standards are promulgated. Drafting consolidated financial statements involves a grasp of the general principles of consolidation. Only simple consolidations will be assessed. This will involve minority interests and pre-acquisition profits. However, the consolidation of sub-subsidiaries or acquisitions where shares in subsidiary undertakings are acquired at different times will not be assessable. Simple equity accounting for associated companies is assessable. The forms of equity and loan capital and the presentation of Corporation Tax in financial statements must be understood for all companies.

Element 11.2   Interpret limited company financial statements

Performance criteria
In order to perform this element successfully you need to:

A	Identify the general purpose of financial statements used in limited companies	1
B	Identify the elements of financial statements used in limited companies	2
C	Identify the relationships between the elements within financial statements of limited companies	17
D	Interpret the relationship between elements of limited company financial statements using ratio analysis	17
E	Identify unusual features or significant issues within financial statements of limited companies	17

F	Draw valid conclusions from the information contained within financial statements of limited companies	17
G	Present issues, interpretations and conclusions clearly to the appropriate people	17

Range statement

This element requires students to understand the general purposes of limited company financial statements. The Range Statement makes clear that the financial statements in question are:

· the balance sheet
· income statement.

The objective of financial statements is set out in the IASB's Framework for the Preparation and Presentation of Financial Statements. A knowledge of the purposes of financial statements as set out in this document is required by the knowledge and understanding of this unit. The users of financial statements and the purposes for which they use financial statements are set out in the Framework.

The elements of financial statements are set out in the Range Statement. This follows the identification of elements given in the Framework. The elements are:

· assets
· liabilities
· ownership interest
· gains, losses
· contributions from owners and distributions to owners

Students need to understand how these elements relate to each other within financial statements. This involves a grasp of which financial statement they appear in and how they are related to each other within the statements. In the balance sheet the relationship between assets, liabilities and ownership interest need to be understood using the accounting equation. The effect of contributions from owners and distributions to owners on the balance of ownership interest needs to be grasped. How gains and losses are reflected in the income statement must be understood and how the income statement articulates with the balance sheet must be grasped.

Students must also be able to interpret the relationship between elements of limited company financial statements using ratio analysis. This involves computing and interpreting accounting ratios relating to profitability, liquidity, efficient use of resources and financial position. Unusual features or significant issues raised by the analysis should be identified. Valid conclusions should be drawn from this information and the issues, interpretations and conclusions should be clearly presented to appropriate people.

ASSESSMENT AND GUIDANCE

How the unit will be assessed

This unit is assessed by a three-hour examination with 15 minutes reading time. The examination is divided into two sections. The first section centres on drafting financial statements and assesses the performance criteria of element 11.1. This will comprise 70% of the total assessment. The second section centres on interpreting financial statements and assesses the performance criteria of element 11.2. This will comprise 30% of the total assessment. The tasks are generally of a practical nature designed to provide evidence that the performance criteria have been met and to ensure that the relevant knowledge and understanding is present. Guidance on the time allocation of tasks will be given in the examination paper.

Typical tasks in the first section might include:
· Preparing a consolidated profit and loss account for a limited company
· Preparing a consolidated balance sheet for a limited company
· Calculating the goodwill on acquisition and/or minority interest for a limited company
· Calculating the amount at which an interest in an associate is to be included in consolidated financial statements
· Making adjustments to the balances in a trial balance or extended trial balance of a company in accordance with the requirements of company law, accounting concepts and accounting standards
· Explaining the UK regulatory framework of financial reporting including the bodies involved and their respective roles
· Explaining the reason for the adjustments by reference to accounting concepts and accounting standards
· Drafting a profit and loss account and/or a balance sheet from a trial balance or extended trial balance in accordance with the format and requirements of accounting standards
· Explaining the requirements for the accounting treatment of items in company financial statements by reference to the requirements of accounting standards
· Drafting notes to the accounts as required by accounting standards
· Explaining the general legal framework of limited companies and the obligations of directors in respect of the financial statements
· Drafting a statement of total recognised gains and losses for a limited company
· Drafting a cash flow statement and/or a reconciliation between operating profit and cash flow from operating activities from the financial statements of a limited company
· Interpreting a cash flow statement

Typical tasks in the second section might include:
· Setting out the general purposes of financial statements and illustrating these in relation to users and their needs
· Identifying and explaining the elements of financial statements

- Explaining what is meant by the balance sheet equation and how the elements fit into the equation
- Explaining the articulation of the balance sheet with the profit and loss account
- Demonstrating the effect of contributions from owners and distributions to owners on ownership interest
- Calculating ratios for limited companies
- Interpreting the meaning of the ratios and of changes in the ratios of limited companies
- Comparing ratios of limited companies with industry averages
- Setting out the results of the computation and analysis of ratios in report format or in a letter and clearly setting out conclusions of the analysis therein

What is the Chief Assessor looking for?

Detailed guidance on the difficulties encountered by students and on the strengths and weaknesses in student's work is given by the Chief Assessor in the booklet published by the AAT Competency-based Financial Accounting Level 4. What is expected of competent students in this unit and some typical areas of weakness are set out below:

Section 1

1   Students need to have a clear grasp what is involved in drafting consolidated financial statements. This involves a clear understanding of when there is a parent/subsidiary undertaking relationship. The student must grasp the principles behind consolidated accounts and demonstrate a clear grasp of the techniques of producing consolidated profit and loss accounts and balance sheets. The lack of a clear technique often lies behind the failure to demonstrate competence in these tasks.

2   In order to show competence in the tasks of adjusting balances a clear grasp of the accounts affected by transactions or the requirements of company law, accounting concepts and accounting standards is required as well as a grasp of the mechanics of journal entries. Failure in this area would result from a lack of precision in identifying the accounts affected and through confusions as to when an account is debited or credited.

3   Students need to be able to draft financial statements in accordance with the requirements of accounting standards. This involves an ability to enter the balances and transactions correctly onto the pro-formas provided. Students who are not sufficiently familiar with the accounts that form part of the financial statement balances may encounter problems. The lack of knowledge of certain accounting standards may be reflected in uncertainty as to the treatment of certain accounting items. This is a particular problem for this unit and is made more acute by the proliferation of, and detail included in, accounting standards. Guidance is given on the extent to which accounting standards are assessable is given below. Students need to have regard to this guidance in preparing for the examination and ensure that a wide range of assessable standards are covered if ignorance of the requirements of accounting standards is not to undermine per-

formance in this unit. The lack of knowledge of these accounting standards undermines efforts to answer tasks that require an explanation of adjustments to account balances or an explanation of accounting treatment of certain items in the financial statements of companies.

4   The drafting of financial statements in accordance with IAS 1 may cause problems for students. An adequate familiarity with the requirements of this accounting standard is required.

5   Tasks which require the drafting of notes to the accounts may suffer from an occasional gap in knowledge. Once again, reference to the guidance on accounting standards and the notes required therein given below should be made to ensure adequate coverage.

6   Knowledge of the standard-setting process and the bodies involved in the promulgation and policing of accounting standards is required by the unit. A lack of precise knowledge of the bodies involved and their particular roles may result in a lack of competence in tasks in this area.

7   The drafting of cash flow statements and the reconciliation and notes required by IAS 7 is required by this unit. A clear grasp of the technique of drafting such a statement and reconciliation may prove problematic for some students. The interpretation of such statements may also present particular problems for students. It is important to try and relate the information presented in cash flow statements into a coherent whole. Part of the problem with such tasks is the potential failure of students to be explicit in stating what information the cash flow statement and the reconciliation are giving about the company. If figures are left to speak for themselves there is little in the way of interpretation of the information.

Section 2

1   Students must demonstrate an awareness of the overall purpose of financial statements and of the particular purposes of individual users of financial statements. Students may not be competent on these tasks because they do not pay sufficient attention to the requirements of the task. Students need to be able to distinguish external and internal users of financial information as well as appreciating the difference between the use of financial statements for the purposes of stewardship and other economic decisions.

2   The student must be able to identify the elements of financial statements and give appropriate definitions. Some students may not be competent because they do not set out definitions of the elements with sufficient precision. They might fail to adequately explain the elements in terms of the SOP definitions and give examples of elements rather than explanations of the sort of thing that they are.

3   Students must have a clear grasp of the accounting equation and be able to show how the equation reflects the equation through a numerical example. The articulation of the profit and loss account with the balance sheet needs to be grasped and students should be prepared to show how the profit for the year and any other gains reported in shown in the statement of recognised income and expense changes the ownership interest.

4   The calculation of the various ratios that show profitability, liquidity, efficient use of resources and financial position is required by the unit. This involves a grasp of the formulas. Guidance on the appropriate formulas is given in the booklet published by the AAT. In general, students must

demonstrate a grasp of the meaning of the ratios, the import of changes in the ratios from one year to the next or of the differences in ratios between two companies and/or the industry averages. The results of the analysis should be clearly set out and relevant conclusions drawn. Students may not demonstrate competence because their analysis is superficial and does not demonstrate a clear understanding of the ratios and the information they convey. Sometimes the ratios may be left to speak for themselves and little more is said than that the ratio went up or down, without any indication of the effect that this has on the company. Conclusions may be inadequately supported or not derived from a consideration of the preceding analysis. The presentation of answers to some of the tasks may not be in accordance with the requirements of the task. Credit for presentation would be accordingly lost.

AAT guidance notes on the assessability of IAS in Unit 11 Drafting Financial Statements

These notes indicate the extent to which international accounting standards are assessable in Unit 11 Drafting Financial Statements. The areas that are assessable are described under each Standard. The number in brackets that follows refers to the paragraph in the main body of the Standard where the accounting issues and treatment is set out. Reference should be made to the Standard to identify the information that is assessable in examinations under this Unit. Further explanations may be available about these issues and treatment in other sections of the Standard or the Guidance Notes accompanying the Standard. Knowledge of these explanations may be useful in understanding the requirements of the Standard, but will not be examined.

International Financial Reporting Standards

IFRS 3 *Business Combinations*
· Definition of a business combination (4)
· Ways in which a business combination comes about (5)
· Requirement to apply this IFRS in consolidated financial statements (6)
· Requirement for use of purchase method in accounting for business combinations and preclusion of pooling of interests method (14)
· Requirement to identify an acquirer for all business combinations and definition of acquirer as entity obtaining control of the other entity or business (17)
· Explanation of control (19)
· Measurement of cost of a business combination (24) [fair value defined by IAS 2 (6)]
· Requirement to allocate the cost of the business combination to the assets acquired and liabilities and contingent liabilities assumed and criteria for recognition (36 & 37)
· Requirement to recognise goodwill (51)
· Measurement of goodwill after initial recognition, the preclusion of amortisation of goodwill and the requirement for impairment review in accordance with IAS 36 (54 & 55)

IRFS 5 *Non-current Assets Held for Sale and Discontinued Operations*

- Requirement to classify a non-current asset as held for sale if its carrying amount will be recovered principally through a sale transaction rather than through continuing use (6)
- Measurement of non-current assets held for sale at lower or carrying amount and fair value less costs to sell (15)
- Disclosure of non-current assets held for sale separately from other assets on the balance sheet (38)
- Requirement to disclose post-tax profit or loss of discontinued operations in income statement (33)

IAS 1 *Presentation of Financial Statements*

- Purpose of financial statements (7)
- Components of financial statements (8)
- Requirement for financial statements to present fairly the financial position, financial performance and cash flows of an entity and its meaning including (13)
- Requirement to comply with IFRS (14) defined in the Standard (11)
- Circumstances in which departure from IFRS allowed and disclosure of departure (17 & 18)
- Requirement to assess going concern (23)
- Requirement for accrual accounting (27)
- Requirement for consistence of presentation and classification (27)
- Requirement to present each material class of similar items separately (29) and definition of material (11)
- Prohibition of offsetting elements (32)
- Requirement for comparative information (36)
- Requirement to identify clearly financial statements (44) and each component of financial statements (46)
- Reporting period (49)
- Requirement to separate current and non-current assets and liabilities (51)
- Criteria for current assets (57) and current liabilities (60)
- Information to be presented on face of the balance sheet (68), subclassifications on the face of the balance sheet or in notes (74 & 75) and disclosure of other items on the face of the balance sheet or in notes (76)

[A pro-forma for balance sheets will be provided for students in the examination and includes the items students will be expected to be able to deal with. Assessment of notes in paragraph 76 is restricted to notes (a) (i), (ii) & (iii).]

- Requirement to disclose all items of income and expense recognised in the period in the profit and loss account (78)
- Information to be presented on the face of the income statement (81,82 & 83)

[A pro-forma for income statements will be provided for students in the examination and includes the items students will be expected to be able to deal with.]

- Prohibition of extraordinary items (85)
- Separate disclosure of material items of income and expense (86)
- Requirement to analyse expenses based on nature of expenses or their function and criteria of choice (88 with examples of analysis in 92)

[Only the form of analysis in paragraph 92 will be assessed. A pro-forma for income statements using this analysis will be provided for students in the examination.]

· Requirement to present a statement of changes in equity (96)

[A pro-forma of the statement of changes in equity, in the form of a statement of recognised income and expense, will be provided in the examination.]

· General requirements for notes (103), cross referencing (104), disclosure of accounting policies (108), disclosure of dividends proposed (125)

IAS 2 *Inventories*

· Definition of inventories (6)
· Measurement of inventories (9) and definition of net realisable value (6)
· What is included in cost of inventories (10 & 15) and what is excluded (16)
· Formulas for determining the cost of inventories for interchangeable items i.e. FIFO and weighted average (25)
· Recognition as an expense when inventories sold (34)

IAS 7 *Cash Flow Statements*

· Requirement for an entity to prepare a cash flow statement in accordance with this Standard (1)
· Definitions of terms used in Standard (6)
· Requirement to report cash flows during the period classified by operating, investing and financing activities (10)
· Examples of cash flows from operating activities (14)
· Examples of investing activities (16)
· Examples of financing activities (17)
· Requirement to report cash flows from operating activities using either the direct method or the indirect method (18) [Only the indirect method will be assessed. An example of the indirect method is given in Appendix A of the Standard. This provides a model of the Cash Flow Statements that should be used in drafting such statements. A pro-forma will be given in the examination.]
· Requirement to report separately major classes of gross cash receipts and gross cash payments arising from investing and financing activities (21)
· Requirement to disclose separately cash flows from interest and dividends received and paid in a consistent manner from period to period as either operating, investing or financing activities (31)
· Requirement to disclose separately cash flows from taxes on income as cash flows from operating activities unless they can be specifically identified with financing and investing activities (35)
· Requirement to present separately aggregate cash flows from acquisitions and disposals of subsidiaries or other business units as investing activities (39)
· Disclosure of components of cash and cash equivalents and the reconciliation of the amounts in its cash flow statement with the equivalent items reported in the balance sheet (45)

IAS 8 *Accounting Policies, Changes in Accounting Estimates and Errors*

· Requirement to apply IRFSs (Standards and Interpretations defined in (5)) to transactions, other events or conditions to which they apply (7)

- Criteria to be used where judgement is required because there is no Standard or Interpretation (10,11 & 12)
- Requirement for consistency in applying accounting policies (13) as defined (in 5)
- Conditions that require a change in accounting policy
- Requirement to follow transitional arrangements arising from the initial application of a Standard or Interpretation where they are included in the Standard, otherwise retrospectively (23)
- Requirements of retrospective application of a change in accounting policy (22)
- Requirement to correct material prior period errors retrospectively (42) as defined (in 5)

IAS 10 *Events after the Balance Sheet Date*

- Definitions of events after the balance sheet date and adjusting and non-adjusting events (5)
- Requirement to adjust for adjusting events after the balance sheet date (8) with examples (9)
- Prohibition on adjustment of non-adjusting events after the balance sheet date (10) with examples (11)
- Prohibition on recognising dividends declared after the balance sheet date as a liability (12)
- Prohibition on preparing financial statements on a going concern basis if there is an intention to liquidate or cease trading (14)
- Requirement to disclose date when financial statements were authorised (17)
- Requirement to disclose material non-adjusting events (21) with examples (22)

IAS 12 *Income Taxes*

- Requirement for recognition of unpaid current tax (12)
- Requirement to recognise a deferred tax liability for all taxable temporary differences (15) including definitions of deferred tax liabilities and taxable temporary differences (5)
- Measurement rule for current tax liabilities (46)
- Disclosure of tax expense related to profit or loss from ordinary activities on face of income statement (77) and of current and deferred tax (81 (a))

[There will be no assessment of the computation of current tax or of deferred tax.]

IAS 14 *Segment Reporting*

- Application of Standard to entities whose equity or debt securities are publicly traded (3) or to those who voluntarily choose to disclose segment information
- Definition of business segment and geographical segment (9)
- Rule on whether the primary segment reporting format will be business segments or geographical segments (26)
- Requirement to prepare segment information (44)

[There will be no assessment involving the preparation of segment information.]

IAS 16 *Property, Plant and Equipment*
· Definition of property, plant and equipment (6)
· Recognition rule for items of property, plant and equipment (7)
· Recognition rules for subsequent expenditure (12, 13 and 14)
· Measurement rule at recognition (15) and of elements of cost (16, 17 & 19)
· Measurement rules after recognition (29) including explanation of cost model (30) and revaluation model (31)
· Definitions of fair value (6) and how it is computed (32 & 33)
· Rules on frequency of revaluations (34)
· Rule that all assets belonging to a class must be revalued if one item in that class is revalued (36) and examples of different classes (37)
· Treatment of revaluation surpluses or decreases (39 & 40)
· Requirement to depreciate each part of an item of property, plant and equipment separately (43)
· Depreciation charge for each period to be recognised in the profit and loss account (48)
· Depreciable amount to be allocated on a systematic basis over the asset's useful life (50)
· Requirement to review the residual value at least at the year-end and any change to be accounted for as a change in accounting estimate (51)
· Rule that depreciation required even if fair value exceeds carrying amount as long as the residual value does not exceed its carrying amount, in which case depreciation is zero, and not negated by repair and maintenance (52)
· Depreciable amount determined after deducting residual value (53)
· Factors determining useful life of an asset (56)
· Land not depreciated (58)
· Rule for determining depreciation method (60) with examples of methods (62) and need for review at least at the year-end (61)
· Derecognition rule (67)
· Treatment of gain and loss (68) and how computed (71)
· Disclosure relating to each class of property, plant and equipment (73), depreciation method and useful life or depreciation rates, depreciation and accumulated depreciation (75)

IAS 17 *Leases*
· Classification of leases as finance and operating leases (8) and examples of situations in which a lease would be classified as a finance lease (10 & 11)
· Application of distinction between operating and finance leases to leasing of land and buildings (14 & 15)
· Initial recognition of finance leases of lessees (20) including related definitions of fair value, minimum lease payments, interest rate implicit in lease & incremental borrowing rate (4)
· Subsequent measurement of finance leases of lessees (25)
· Requirement to depreciate assets on finance leases of lessees (27) including definition of useful life (4)
· Accounting requirements for operating leases of lessors (33)
· Initial recognition of finance leases as assets and liabilities in balance sheets of lessors (36)

- Subsequent measurement of finance leases of lessors (39)
- Requirements relating to recording assets on operating leases in the balance sheet of lessors (49)
- Recognition of income from operating leases of lessors (50)
- Depreciation requirements for assets leased on operating leases for lessors (53)

[There will be no computational questions relating to the accounting for leases.]

IAS 18 *Revenue*
- Scope of Standard (1)
- Definitions of revenue and fair value (7)
- Measurement of revenue (9)
- Conditions for recognising revenue from the sale of goods (14), rendering of services (20) and dividends (29 & 30)

IAS 23 *Borrowing Costs*
- Definitions of borrowing costs and qualifying assets (4)
- Recognition of borrowing costs for benchmark treatment (7) and allowed alternative treatment (10 & 11)
- Rules for determining the amount of borrowing costs (15 & 17)
- Commencement and cessation of capitalisation of borrowing costs (20 & 25)

IAS 27 *Consolidated and Separate Financial Statements*
- Scope of Standard (1 & 3)
- Definitions of terms used in Standard (4)
- Requirement to prepare consolidated financial statements (9
- Requirement to include all subsidiaries of the parent (12) and explanation of when control is presumed
- Consolidation procedures (22)
- Requirement to eliminate intragroup balances, transactions, income and expenses (24 & 25)
- Need to used uniform accounting policies in consolidation (28)
- Presentation of minority interests (33)
- Requirement to include investment in subsidiaries and associates at cost or fair value in accordance with IAS 39 when preparing separate financial statements (37)

[Assessment of the ability to account for business combinations is restricted to preparing simple consolidated balance sheets and profit and loss accounts taking into account pre- and post-acquisition profits, minority interest, fair value adjustments, calculation of goodwill and elimination of inter-company profit.]

IAS 28 *Investments in Associates*
- Definitions of terms used in Standard (2)
- Criteria for significant influence (6 & 7)
- Requirement to account for associates using the equity method (13) and description of that method (11)
- Need to used uniform accounting policies in applying the equity method (26 & 27)

IAS 33 *Earnings per Share*
- Scope of Standard (2 & 3)
- Definition of ordinary share (5)
- Measurement of basic earnings per share (9 & 10)
- Explanation of amounts attributable to ordinary equity holders of the parent entity (12 & 13)
- Need to use weighted average number of ordinary shares in calculating basic earnings per share (19 & 20)
- Presentation of basic earnings per share (66)

IAS 36 *Impairment of Assets*
- Scope of Standard (2 & 4)
- Requirement to assess whether there are indications that assets may be impaired and requirement to estimate recoverable amount where there are such indications (9) and definition of carrying amount and recoverable amount (6)
- Requirement to asset intangible assets meeting certain criteria and goodwill annually (10)
- Indications of impairment (12, 13 & 14)
- Explanations of how to determine fair value less costs to sell (25, 26, 27 & 28)
- Explanations of how to determine value in use (30 & 31)
- Explanations of the discount rate to be used in determining value in use (55)
- Recognising and measuring an impairment loss for in individual assets other than goodwill (59 & 60) including definition (6) and revision of depreciation charge (63) including definition of depreciation, depreciable amount and useful life (6)
- Requirement to determine recoverable amount for individual assets if possible but for asset's cash-generating unit if not possible (66) along with definition of cash-generating unit (6)
- Requirement to test goodwill allocated to cash-generating unit for impairment annually (96) by comparing the carrying amount of the unit, including the goodwill, with the recoverable amount of the unit (90)
- Requirement to allocate impairment loss first against goodwill and then against other assets of the unit (104)
- Disclosure of impairment loss in profit and loss account (126 (a))

IAS 37 *Provisions, Contingent Liabilities and Contingent Assets*
- Definitions (10)
- Distinction of provisions from other liabilities (11), idea of being contingent in the Standard (12) and distinction of provisions from contingent liabilities
- Requirement to recognise provisions and criteria (14)
- Prohibition on recognising contingent liabilities (27) and contingent assets (31)
- Measurement of provision (36)
- Determination of amount of provision where the effect of the time value of money is material (45)
- Requirement to review provisions at each balance sheet date to reflect

current best estimate (59)
- Use of provisions (61)
- Examples of events that amount to restructuring (70) and determination of constructive obligation to restructure (72) along with amounts to be included in restructuring provision (80)
- Disclosure of contingent liabilities (86) and contingent assets (89)

IAS 38 *Intangible Assets*
- Definition of an intangible asset (8)
- Identifiability criterion in definition of an intangible asset (12)
- Recognition criteria for intangible assets (21) including explanation of future economic benefits (17)
- Measurement rule for intangible assets (24)
- Prohibition on recognition of internally generated goodwill (48)
- Rules of recognition of internally generated intangible assets including the need to classify the generation of the asset into a research phase and a development phase (52) and the rules that prohibit the recognition of intangible assets from the research stage (54) and the rules governing the recognition of intangible assets arising from the development stage (57)
- Prohibition of the recognition of internally generated brands and similar items (63)
- Examples of directly attributable costs for internally generated intangible assets (66) and prohibited costs (67)
- Rule on measurement after recognition (72) and explanation of cost model (74) and revaluation model (75) with related definitions (8)
- Treatment of revaluation gains (85) and losses (86)
- Need to determine whether useful life of an intangible asset is finite or indefinite (88)
- Rules for depreciation of intangible assets with finite useful lives (97), residual value (100) and review of amortisation period (104)
- Prohibition of amortisation for intangible assets with indefinite useful life (107) and requirement for impairment review in accord with IAS 36 (108) and review of useful life assessment (109)

IAS 40 *Investment Property*
- Definitions (5)
- Examples of investment property (8)
- Recognition rule (16)
- Measurement rule at recognition (20)
- Requirement to choose as its accounting policy either the fair value model or the cost model after recognition (30)
- Explanation of requirements of fair value model (33) and treatment of gains or losses in fair value (35)
- Explanation of the requirements of the cost model in accordance with IAS 16 (56)
- Rule for derecognition of investment property (66) and treatment of gains or losses from retirement or disposal (69)
- Disclosure of whether the fair value or cost model is used (75 (a))

Other pronouncements

IASB's Framework for the Preparation and Presentation of Financial Statements
- Users and their information needs (9 &10)
- The objective of financial statements (12, 13 & 14)
- Underlying assumptions: accruals (22) and going concern (23)
- Qualitative characteristics of financial statements (24 – 42)
- True and fair/fair presentation (46)
- The elements of financial statements (47 – 81)
- Recognition principle (83)
- Measurement bases (99 –101)

Legislation
Under Schedule 6 of the Companies Act the following information, which is required to be disclosed by way of notes to the accounts, should also be covered:
- Directors' emoluments including Chairman's emoluments where necessary.

Under Sec. 390A of the Companies Act 1985 the following note should be covered:
- Auditor's remuneration.

THE REGULATORY FRAMEWORK

INTRODUCTION
In this initial chapter we will be covering background information that is essential for your understanding of the preparation of financial statements for many types of organisation, in particular for limited companies.

KNOWLEDGE & UNDERSTANDING

· The elements and purposes of financial statements of limited companies as set out in the conceptual framework for financial reporting (Element 11.2)
· The general legal framework of limited companies and the obligations of Directors in respect of the financial statements (Element 11.1)

CONTENTS

1 Introduction
2 The purpose of financial statements
3 The legal framework
4 Accounting standards

PERFORMANCE CRITERIA
· Identify the general purpose of financial statements used in limited companies (Element 11.2)

1   Introduction

1.1 Background knowledge

In Unit 5 your accounting studies took you from ledger accounts to a trial balance to an extended trial balance. On the extended trial balance you will have put through a number of adjustments for inventories, accruals, prepayments, depreciation and bad and doubtful debts. Each account on the extended trial balance was then balanced and extended into either the income statement columns or the balance sheet columns depending upon whether the balance was income, expenditure, an asset or a liability.

For this unit your accounting knowledge must be taken further.

1.2 Drafting financial statements

Element 1 of this unit involves the drafting of the relevant financial statements for limited companies. You must be able to prepare a balance sheet, income statement, statement of changes in equity and cash flow statement in accordance with all the applicable regulations (the Companies Act 1985, accounting standards, etc).

1.3 Interpretation of financial statements

Element 2 of this unit is entitled 'Interpret limited company financial statements'. It is concerned with being able to analyse and understand the structure and purpose of financial statements of limited companies. It requires a sound understanding of the elements of financial statements and an ability to interpret the relationships between these elements of financial statements by using ratio analysis.

In order to understand and interpret limited company financial statements you must be able to understand how they have been prepared. Therefore in the first few chapters of this text we will consider the preparation of simple accounts for a sole trader and then transfer these principles to gaining an understanding of how the financial statements of limited companies are prepared.

In this chapter and the next, however, we will consider the background to the preparation of financial statements for limited companies by considering the regulatory framework and then the conceptual framework within which these financial statements must be prepared.

2   The purpose of financial statements

2.1 Introduction

The main purpose of financial statements is to provide information to a wide range of users.

The balance sheet provides information on the financial position of a business (its assets and liabilities at a point in time).

The income statement provides information on the performance of a business (the profit or loss which results from trading over a period of time).

The statement of changes in equity provides information about how the equity of the company has changed over the period.

The cash flow statement provides information on the financial adaptability of a business (the movement of cash into and out of the business over a period of time).

2.2 Stewardship

Financial statements also show the results of the stewardship of an organisation. Stewardship is the accountability of management for the resources entrusted to it by the owners or the Government. This applies to the financial statements of limited companies as well as to central and local government and the National Health Service.

2.3 Needs of users

All users of financial statements need information on financial position, performance and financial adaptability. However, many different groups of people may use financial statements and each group will need particular information. Users of financial statements may include investors, management, employees, customers, suppliers, lenders, the government and the public. Investors need to be able to assess the ability of a business to pay dividends and manage resources. Management need information with which to assess performance, take decisions, plan, and control the business. Lenders, such as banks, are interested in the ability of the business to pay interest and repay loans. HM Revenue and Customs uses financial statements as the basis for tax assessments.

2.4 Legal requirements

The law requires limited companies to prepare financial statements annually. These financial statements must be filed with the Registrar of Companies and are then available to all interested parties. Most businesses, whether incorporated or not, are required to produce financial statements for submission to HM Revenue and Customs.

In the UK, the form and content of limited company accounts is laid down within the Companies Acts. The preparation of limited company accounts is also subject to regulations issued by the Accounting Standards Board if the company is still following UK standards or the International Accounting Standards Board if the company has adopted International standards.

3 The legal framework

3.1 Introduction

The financial statements of limited companies must be prepared within the legal framework of the Companies Acts. The Companies Act 1985 (CA85) contains guidance and rules on:

· Formats for the financial statements
· Fundamental accounting principles
· Valuation rules.

The Companies Act has been amended to take account of the companies who have adopted International Financial Reporting Standards (IFRSs). It allows companies to use the format of accounts set out in IAS 1 *Presentation of Financial Statements* if they have adopted IFRS or continue to use the format in the CA85 if they have not.

3.2 Fundamental accounting principles

The CA85 embodies five accounting principles:
· going concern
· consistency
· prudence
· accruals
· separate valuation.

In previous years going concern, consistency, prudence and accruals were known as the 'four fundamental concepts' and were to be considered in preparing accounts. In recent times, only going concern and accruals are seen as being key accounting concepts. These two are discussed in the next chapter.

Prudence is less important now as excessive prudence in accounting can cause financial statements to misrepresent the true picture. Consider a company that makes large non specific provisions. This would misrepresent the true results for the period as the profit should have been higher had the provisions not been made.

Consistency in terms of accounting means to use the same method and policies year on year. This would not necessarily be relevant if a business changed its key operations and needed to change its method of accounting to reflect this.

4 Accounting standards

4.1 IFRSs and IASs

Accounting standards give guidance in specific areas of accounting. The DFS syllabus follows International standards which consist of the following:

· *International Financial Reporting Standards (IFRSs)*
  These are issued by the International Accounting Standards Board. Many

countries have used IFRSs for some years. Back in 2002, the Council of Ministers of the European Union (EU) decided that any company which is listed on a European Stock Exchange must prepare their consolidated accounts in line with IFRSs with effect from 1 January 2005.

· *International Accounting Standards (IASs)*
IASs were created by a body known as the International Accounting Standards Committee (IASC) the predecessor of the IASB. When the IASB was formed it adopted the standards of the IASC which were called IASs. In recent times, the IASB has introduced many new standards so several IASs have now been superseded.

4.2 The structure of the IASC

The structure of the International Accounting Standards Committee Foundation (IASCF) and its subsidiary bodies is shown below:

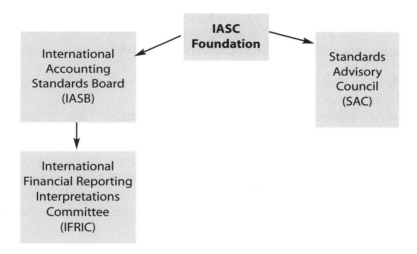

4.3 The International Accounting Standards Committee Foundation (IASCF)

The IASCF is an independent not-for profit foundation based in the US. The Trustees of the Foundation appoint the members of the International Accounting Standards Board, Standards Advisory Council and International Financial Reporting Interpretations Committee.

4.4 The International Accounting Standards Board

The IASB has sole responsibility for the setting of international accounting standards. The members of the IASB are independent experts in accounting.

The IASB's objectives are:
(a) to develop a single set of high quality, global accounting standards that require transparent and comparable information in general purpose financial statements;
(b) to promote the use and rigorous application of those standards; and
(c) to work actively with national standard setters to bring about convergence of national accounting standards and IFRSs.

IFRSs set out the recognition, measurement, presentation and disclosure requirements of transactions and events that are important in accounting. They apply to all general purpose financial statements and any limitation in scope of the standard is stated within the standard.

The IASB cooperates with other accounting standard setters with the aim of achieving harmony of accounting practice throughout the world. This has been the case in the UK as the Accounting Standards Board (ASB) has adopted recent IFRSs as UK standards so there will be minimal difference in accounting practice for companies who have adopted IFRS and those who haven't.

4.5 International Financial Reporting Interpretations Committee

The aim of the IFRIC is to assist the IASB in establishing and improving standards of financial accounting and reporting. It promotes the rigorous and uniform application of IFRS. This is achieved by the IFRIC providing timely guidance on:
1 newly identified financial reporting issues not specifically covered by an accounting standard; or
2 where unsatisfactory or conflicting interpretations have developed or may develop.

The guidelines the IFRIC publishes are called IFRIC Interpretations. If a company complies with IFRSs, then it is automatically presumed that this includes the IFRIC Interpretations as well as the relevant standards. Previously IFRIC Interpretations were called SICs and many of these are still relevant.

4.6 Standards Advisory Council

The SAC advises the IASB and sometimes the Trustees of the IASCF. The objectives of the SAC are:
1 to give advice to the IASB on priorities in the IASB's work
2 to inform the IASB of the implications of proposed standards for users and preparers of financial statements
3 to give other advice to the IASB or the Trustees.

4.7 The standard setting process

There are a number of steps in the process of developing and issuing a new accounting standard by the IASB. These are detailed below:
(a) The staff are asked to identify and review all the issues associated with the topic and to consider the application of the IASB Framework to the issues;

(b) Study of national accounting requirements and practice and an exchange of views about the issues with national standard-setters;

(c) Consulting the SAC about the advisability of adding the topic to the IASB agenda;

(d) Formation of an advisory group to give advice to the IASB on the project;

(e) Publishing for public comment a discussion document;

(f) Publishing for public comment an exposure draft approved by at least eight members of the IASB, including any dissenting opinions held by IASB members;

(g) Publishing within an exposure draft a basis for conclusions;

(h) Consideration of all comments received within the comment period on the discussion documents and exposure drafts;

(i) Consideration of whether to hold a public hearing and to conduct field tests and, if necessary, holding such hearings and conducting such tests;

(j) Approval of a standard by at least eight members of the IASB and inclusion in the published standard of any dissenting opinions; and

(k) Publishing within a standard a basis for conclusions, explaining, among other things the steps in the IASB due process and how the IASB dealt with public comments on the exposure draft.

5 Test your knowledge

1 What are the four statements that would be seen in a set of financial statements?

2 What is meant by the term 'stewardship'?

3 What is the main Act of Parliament governing the conduct and financial statements of companies in the UK?

4 What five accounting principles are required by this Act? Nowadays, which are the most important?

5 What is the role of the IASB?

6 What is the role of IFRIC?

[Answers on p. 8]

6 Summary

The regulatory framework for preparing financial statements under international standards consists of:

· The Companies Act which applies to all UK companies regardless of whether they follow UK or International accounting rules

· The International Accounting Standards Board and its associated bodies who are responsible for the setting of IFRSs.

Answers to 'test your knowledge' questions

Test your knowledge

1   Balance sheet, income statement, statement of changes in equity and cash flow statement.

2   Stewardship is the accountability of management for the resources entrusted to it by the owners or the Government.

3   The Companies Act 1985.

4   Going concern, consistency, prudence, accruals and separate valuation. Nowadays, the most important principles are seen to be going concern and accruals.

5   The role of the IASB is to set accounting standards. They are called International Financial Reporting Standards.

6   IFRIC assists the IASB by producing IFRIC Interpretations which guide on new accounting issues that are not covered by an accounting standard or guide on the correct interpretation of a standard if it is being applied incorrectly.

THE CONCEPTUAL FRAMEWORK

INTRODUCTION
This chapter provides some essential background knowledge of the principles and concepts that underlie the preparation of financial statements for limited companies. The IASB have produced a framework for the preparation and presentation of financial statements.

KNOWLEDGE & UNDERSTANDING

· The elements of financial statements of limited companies as set out in the conceptual framework for financial reporting (Element 11.2)
· Generally accepted accounting principles and concepts (Element 11.1)

CONTENTS

PERFORMANCE CRITERIA
· Identify the elements of financial statements used in limited companies (Element 11.2)

1 User groups

1.1 The purpose of accounting

The purpose of accounting is to provide information to users of financial state-ments. Legally, company financial statements are drawn up for the benefit of the shareholders, so that they can assess the performance of their Board of Directors. However, in practice many other groups will use these financial statements, and these groups will all have different needs. These groups, and their needs, are described below.

1.2 Management

Management will be interested in an analysis of revenues and expenses that will provide information that is useful when plans are formulated and deci-sions made. Once the budget for a business is complete, the accountant can produce figures for what actually happens as the budget period unfolds, so that they can be compared with the budget. Management will also need to know the cost consequences of a particular course of action to aid their deci-sion making.

1.3 Shareholders and potential shareholders

This group includes the investing public at large and the stockbrokers and commentators who advise them. The shareholders should be informed of the manner in which management has used their funds that have been invested in the business. This is a matter of reporting on past events. However, both share-holders and potential shareholders are also interested in the future perform-ance of the business and use past figures as a guide to the future if they have to vote on proposals or decide whether to sell their shares.

Financial analysts advising investors such as insurance companies, pension funds, unit trusts and investment trusts are among the most sophisticated users of accounting information, and the company contemplating a takeover bid is yet another type of potential shareholder.

1.4 Employees and their trade union representatives

These use accounting information to assess the potential performance of the business. This information is relevant to the employee, who wishes to discover whether the company can offer him safe employment and promotion through growth over a period of years, and also to the trade unionist, who uses past profits and potential profits in his calculations and claims for higher wages or better conditions. The viability of different divisions of a company is of interest to this group.

1.5 Lenders

This group includes some who have financed the business over a long period by lending money which is to be repaid at the end of a number of years, as well as short-term payables such as a bank which allows a company to overdraw its bank account for a number of months, and suppliers of raw materials, which permit a company to buy goods from them and pay in, say, four to twelve weeks' time.

Lenders are interested in the security of their loan, so they will look at an accounting statement to ensure that the company will be able to repay on the due date and meet the interest requirements before that date. The amount of cash available and the value of assets, which form a security for the debt, are of importance to this group. Credit rating agencies are interested in accounts for similar reasons.

1.6 Government agencies

These use accounting information, either when collecting statistical information to reveal trends within the economy as a whole or, in the case of the Inland Revenue, to assess the profit on which the company's tax liability is to be computed.

1.7 The business contact group

Customers of a business may use accounting data to assess the viability of a company if a long-term contract is soon to be placed. Competitors will also use the accounts for purposes of comparison.

1.8 The public

From time to time other groups not included above may have an interest in the company e.g. members of a local community where the company operates, environmental pressure groups, and so on.

◇ CONCLUSION

Financial statements serve a wide variety of user groups, who have different interests and also different levels of financial sophistication. This makes it particularly difficult to produce accounts that are intelligible to the layman but comprehensive for the expert.

The next section looks at how standards have been developed to try to meet these diverse needs.

---

2   A conceptual framework

A conceptual framework is a coherent system of inter-related objectives and fundamentals that can lead to consistent standards and that prescribes the nature, function and limits of financial accounting and financial statements. The IASB's conceptual framework is known as the Framework for the Preparation and Presentation of Financial Statements.

The basic objective of the conceptual framework is to provide a logical and sensible guide for preparing accounting standards and applying them. In effect it will be the constitution within which accountants work, while the standards themselves will be the detailed laws enacted to apply these constitutional principles.

3   Framework for the preparation and presentation of financial statements

The Framework is not an accounting standard. Nothing in the Framework over-rides a specific international accounting standard.

3.1 The matters dealt with in the Framework

The following topics are covered in the Framework:
·   The objective of financial statements.
·   Underlying assumptions.
·   Qualitative characteristics of financial statements.
·   Definition of elements of financial statements.
·   Recognition of the elements of financial statements.
·   Measurement of the elements of financial statements.
·   Concepts of capital and capital maintenance.

4   The objective of financial statements

4.1 Usefulness for particular purposes

The objective of financial statements is to provide information about the financial position, performance and changes in financial position of an entity that is useful to a wide range of users in making economic decisions. Financial statements may not provide all the information that users need to make economic decisions as they portray the effect of past events and do not always provide non-financial information.

The two most common 'economic decisions' made by users are:
·   to buy or sell shares, and
·   to re-elect or replace the Board of Directors.

Users need to be able to evaluate the ability of the entity to generate cash. They also need to be able to predict the timing and certainty of the cash being generated. To be able to do this users need historic information about:
· financial position
· performance
· cash flow of an entity.

The financial position of an entity is affected by:
· the economic resources it controls
· its financial structure
· its liquidity and solvency
· its capacity to adapt to changes in the environment in which it operates.

This information is normally found in the balance sheet.

(a) Information about the performance of an entity comprises the return obtained by the entity on the resources it controls. This can be found in the income statement and the statement of changes in equity.

(b) Information on cash flows of an entity is useful in providing the user with an additional perspective on the performance of an entity by indicating the amounts and principal sources of its cash inflows and outflows. This is provided by the cash flow statement.

Each statement reflects different aspects of the same transactions and events. A user should study all of the statements before making any decisions.

4.2 User groups

Traditionally financial statements were prepared for the benefit of the shareholders (the owners) and the creditors. The Framework recognises that other user groups may have a reasonable right to information, and that financial statements should take their needs into account. The Framework identifies the following users:

· equity investors (existing and potential)
· employees (existing, potential and past)
· lenders, existing and potential, including providers of short-term loans
· suppliers and other trade creditors
· customers
· government, including tax authorities
· the public.

5 Underlying assumptions

The underlying assumptions governing financial statements are:
· *The accrual basis*

The accrual basis of accounting means that the effects of transactions and other events are recognised as they occur and not as cash or its equivalent is received or paid.

· *Going concern*

The going concern basis assumes that the entity will continue in operation for the foreseeable future and has neither the need nor the intention to liquidate or curtail materially the scale of its operations.

6 The qualitative characteristics of financial statements

6.1 Overview

There are four primary qualitative characteristics of useful financial information:

· relevance
· reliability
· comparability, and
· understandability.

Additionally, the Framework provides guidance on the concept of materiality.

☐ **DEFINITIONS** ☐☐☐☐	
Relevance	Information is relevant when it influences the economic decision of users by helping them evaluate past, present or future events.
Reliability	Information is reliable when it is free from material error and bias and can be depended upon to represent faithfully what it claims to represent. Accounting standards and the audit are all means of ensuring that accounting information is reliable.
Materiality	Information is material if its omission or misstatement could influence the economic decisions of users of the financial statements. Materiality depends on the size of the item and the circumstances of its misstatement or omission. It acts as a threshold for determining whether information is useful as information that is not material will not affect the decisions of users.
Comparability	Information is comparable when it can be compared over time to identify trends in financial performance and position. It is also useful to be able to compare the performance of different entities. To achieve comparability an entity needs to apply accounting policies consistently over a period of time and also disclose those accounting policies so that users can see on

what basis the accounts have been prepared. Comparative figures must also be shown in the financial statements to assist with comparability.

Understandability Information provided in the financial statements should be readily understandable by users. The users are assumed to have a reasonable knowledge of business and economic activities and accounting and a willingness to study the information with reasonable diligence. Therefore the focus of financial statements is the informed user. Information in the financial statements should not be excluded because it may be too difficult for certain users to understand.

6.2 True and fair view/fair presentation

Financial statements are frequently described as giving a true and fair view, or presenting fairly the position, performance and changes in financial position of an entity. The Framework does not define the concept of a true and fair view, but by following accounting standards as well as the four qualitative characteristics above should provide financial statements which present a true and fair view.

7 The elements of financial statements

The Framework identifies five elements of financial statements:
· assets
· liabilities
· equity interest
· income
· expenses.

7.1 Assets

The Framework defines an asset as:

'A resource controlled by the entity as a result of past events and from which future economic benefits are expected to flow to the entity.'

'Controlled by the entity'
Control is the ability to obtain economic benefits from an asset through use or sale. It also includes the ability to restrict other people's access to an asset.

'Past events'
Assets arise from past events. For example land arises from a purchase and trade receivables from a sale.

'Future economic benefits'
Ultimately, an asset generates cash. A trade receivable should realise cash directly. A machine will make goods that will be sold, creating trade receivables that will realise cash.

7.2 Liabilities

The Framework defines a liability as:

'A present obligation of the entity arising from past events, the settlement of which is expected to result in an outflow from the entity of resources embodying economic benefits.'

'Obligations'
These may be legal or not. A trade payable is a legal obligation. A warranty provision arises from sales during the year, but won't become a legal liability until a customer makes a claim.

'Outflow of economic benefits'
This could be the transfer of cash or another asset, or the provision of a service. It also includes refraining from profitable activities.

'Past transactions or events'
For example, a tax liability arises from past profits.

Complementary nature of assets and liabilities
Assets and liabilities should normally be recognised separately. Sometimes they may be offset, e.g. issuing a credit note reduces the value of the trade receivable.

7.3 Equity interest

The Framework defines equity as:

'The residual interest in the assets of the entity after deducting all its liabilities.'

In other words, equity is what is left when all liabilities have been settled. This is essentially the net assets of a business.

Equity interest is usually analysed to distinguish between that arising from owners' contributions and that arising from profits, revaluations or other events.

Share capital and revaluation reserves are normally non-distributable.

7.4 Income

Income consists of both revenue and gains. Revenue arises from a business's ordinary activities such as the sale of goods. Gains represent increases in economic benefits such as a gain on disposal of a non current asset. Gains are usually shown separately from the revenue generated by the business often because they need to be disclosed separately to give a full understanding of the transaction. Note that contributions from shareholders are not income, they are part of equity.

7.5 Expenses

Expenses are losses as well as expenses that arise in the normal course of business such as cost of sales, wages and depreciation. Losses represent a decrease in economic benefits such as losses on disposal of non current assets or disasters such as fire or flood. As with gains, losses are often shown separately in the financial statements to give a full understanding of the situation. Note that distributions (dividends) to shareholders are not expenses.

8 The accounting equation

The performance criteria for Element 2 of this unit require that the elements of the financial statements should be identified and that the relationships between these elements are also identified.

Earlier in your studies you will have learned the accounting equation:

Assets - liabilities = Capital + profits - drawings

We can now restate this as:
Assets - liabilities = Equity; or
Assets - liabilities = Contributions from owners + Gains - Losses - Distributions to owners

9 Recognition of the elements of financial statements

9.1 General recognition criteria

An item should be recognised in the financial statements if:
· it meets one of the definitions of an element (asset, liability, equity, income, expense).
· it is probable that any future economic benefit associated with the item will flow to or from the entity (for example, income is recognised when a sale is made, not when an order is received).
· the item has a cost or value that can be measured with reliability.

Normally the monetary amount will come straight from the sale or purchase invoice. However, reasonable, reliable and prudent estimates can be recognised, for example, a property revaluation or a warranty provision.

The recognition process
Recognition is triggered where a past event indicates that there has been a measurable change in the assets or liabilities of the entity.

The effect of uncertainty
The more evidence there is for an item, the more reliable its recognition and measurement will be.

10 Measurement of the elements of financial statements

The Framework identifies four possible measurement bases:
· historical cost
· current cost
· realisable value
· present value.

10.1 Historical cost

Assets are recorded at the amount of cash paid to acquire them. Sometimes the terms, cash equivalents or fair value at acquisition will be used instead.

Liabilities are recorded at the proceeds received in exchange for the obligation.

10.2 Current cost

Assets are carried at their current purchase price.

Liabilities are carried at the undiscounted amount currently required to settle them.

10.3 Realisable value

Assets are carried at the amount, which could currently be obtained by an orderly disposal. Liabilities are carried at their settlement values – the amount to be paid to satisfy them in the normal course of business.

10.4 Present value

Assets are carried at the present discounted value of the future net cash inflows that the item is expected to generate in the normal course of business.

Liabilities are carried at the present discounted value of the expected cash outflows necessary to settle them.

Although historical cost is the most common basis, the others are often used to modify historical cost. For example, inventories are usually carried at the lower of cost and net realisable value, investments may be carried at market value and pension liabilities are carried at their present value.

11 The potential benefits and drawbacks of an agreed conceptual framework

Potential benefits

The potential benefits of a conceptual framework are:
- A framework for setting future accounting standards.
- A basis for resolving disputes as the elements of financial statements are clearly defined.
- Fundamental principles do not have to be repeated in accounting standards.
- There should be a reduction in pressure from vested interests who wish to pursue a particular policy out of self-interest rather than satisfying the general needs of users.

Potential drawbacks

Drawbacks to a conceptual framework include:
- Due to their general nature the principles may not, in practice, reduce the options available.
- There may be further disagreement as to the contents of the framework in addition to disagreement over the contents of standards.

12 IAS 8 *Accounting Policies*

Accounting policies are the specific principles, bases, conventions, rules and practices applied by an entity in preparing and presenting financial statements.

Management should select and apply appropriate accounting policies so that the financial statements comply with all international standards (IFRSs and IASs) and IFRIC Interpretations.

If there is no specific standard for a particular item then management should choose policies that are relevant and reliable. Management should refer to IFRSs, IASs and Interpretations dealing with similar issues and to the Framework.

All material accounting policies should be disclosed and explained in the notes to the financial statements.

An entity should select and apply accounting policies consistently for similar transactions.

13 Other key concepts

13.1 Substance over form

Under this concept, transactions and other events are accounted for and presented in financial statements in accordance with their economic substance and financial reality and not merely with their legal form.

For example, leasehold buildings are owned by the landlord rather than the occupier, but the occupier is using them for his business in the same way as if they were freehold. Thus it is appropriate to treat them as a fixed asset in the occupier's balance sheet, provided that it is made clear that the premises are leasehold.

13.2 The consistency concept

Like items are treated in a similar manner within each accounting period and from one period to the next. This aids comparison of results over time.

▷ **ACTIVITY 1**   ▷ ▷ ▷ ▷

Sabrina Ltd

Balance sheet as at 31 March 20X4

	£
Non-current assets	
Property, plant and equipment	20,500
Current assets	17,500
Current liabilities	(13,000)
Non-current liabilities	(5,000)
Net assets	20,000
Equity	
Share capital	12,000
Share premium	3,000
Retained earnings	5,000
	—————
	20,000

What are the monetary values of the equity, the assets and the liabilities in Sabrina Ltd as at 31 March 20X4 and how are they related in the accounting equation?

[Answer on p. 23]

▷ ACTIVITY 2

The framework for the preparation and presentation of financial statements states 'the objective of financial statements is to provide information about the financial position, performance and changes in financial position of an entity.'

Additionally it states 'financial statements also show the results of the stewardship of management, ...'

(a) What is meant by saying that financial statements show the results of 'stewardship of management'?

(b) What is meant by 'Equity'? How is it related to other elements in the accounting equation?

[Answer on p. 23]

▷ ACTIVITY 3

The accounting equation is:

Assets – Liabilities = Equity

(a) Define the following elements of financial statements:
  (i) Assets
  (ii) Liabilities
  (iii) Equity

(b) Explain why inventory is an asset of a company.

[Answer on p. 23]

14 Test your knowledge

1 Who are the main users of financial statements?

2 What does management require from financial information?

3 What would potential shareholders' interests be in the financial statements?

4 What is a conceptual framework?

5 What is meant by the relevance of information?

6 How does the IASB Framework define:
  · assets
  · liabilities?

7 What is the going concern concept?

8 What is the accruals concept?

[Answers on p. 24]

15 Summary

The framework for the preparation and presentation of financial statements sets out two fundamental accounting concepts:
· going concern
· accruals.

The objective of financial statements is to provide information about the reporting entity's financial performance and financial position that is useful to a wide range of users for assessing the stewardship of management and for making economic decisions.

The qualitative characteristics of financial information are:
· relevance
· reliability
· comparability
· understandability.

The elements of financial statements are:
· assets
· liabilities
· equity interest
· income
· expenses.

Answers to chapter activities & 'test your knowledge' questions

△ ACTIVITY 1   △△△△

Sabrina Ltd

The monetary values are as follows:

	£
Equity	20,000
Assets	38,000
Liabilities	18,000

The figures are related in the accounting equation as follows

Assets – Liabilities	= Equity
38,000-20,000	= 20,000

△ ACTIVITY 2   △△△△

(a) Management is accountable for the safe-keeping of the entity's resources and for their proper, efficient and profitable use. In other words, they are the 'stewards' of the resources of the entity and are responsible to share-holders for the management of the resources to ensure that they generate adequate profit and cash flows to give them a return and to ensure that lenders to the business are repaid.

(b) Equity is 'the residual amount found by deducting all of the entity's liabilities from all of the entity's assets'. The equity is related to the other elements in the accounting equation as follows:

Assets – Liabilities = Equity

△ ACTIVITY 3   △△△△

(a) The elements of financial statements are defined by the framework for the preparation and presentation of financial statements as follows:

   (i)   'Assets' are rights or other access to future economic benefits controlled by an entity as a result of past transactions or events.

   (ii)   'Liabilities' are obligations of an entity to transfer economic benefits as a result of past transactions or events.

   (iii)   Equity is 'the residual amount found by deducting all of the entity's liabilities from all of the entity's assets'.

(b) Inventory fits the definition of an asset in that:

   ·   the purchase of inventory for resale gives rise to a right to future economic benefits in that the entity can sell the inventory or to use the inventory to manufacture products that are sold to generate future economic benefits

   ·   this is as a result of a past transaction.

Test your knowledge △ △ △

1 Shareholders

2 Management will be interested in an analysis of revenues and expenses that will provide information that is useful when plans are formulated and decisions made. Once the budget for a business is complete, the account-ant can produce figures for what actually happens as the budget period unfolds, so that they can be compared with the budget. Management will also need to know the cost consequences of a particular course of action to aid their decision making.

3 The future performance of the business.

4 A conceptual framework is a coherent system of inter-related objectives and fundamentals that can lead to consistent standards and that prescribes the nature, function and limits of financial accounting and financial state-ments.

5 Information must be relevant to the decision-making needs of users.

6 An asset is a resource controlled by the entity as a result of past events and from which future economic benefits are expected to flow to the enterprise. A liability is a present obligation of the entity arising from past events, the settlement of which is expected to result in an outflow of economic bene-fits.

7 Going concern
   The going concern basis assumes that the entity will continue in operation for the foreseeable future and has neither the need nor the intention to liq-uidate or curtail materially the scale of its operations.

8 The accruals concept
   The accrual basis of accounting means that the effects of transactions and other events are recognised as they occur and not as cash or its equivalent is received or paid.

DRAFTING FINANCIAL STATEMENTS

INTRODUCTION

For Element 1 of this unit you need to be able not only to draft a set of limited company financial statements but also to understand the structure of income statements and to explain how these tie in with the balance sheet. This can only be achieved by a detailed knowledge of how to prepare a set of financial statements. Therefore in this chapter we will concentrate on the preparation of a set of financial statements initially for a sole trader and then in later chapters we will consider the preparation of financial statements for a limited company.

KNOWLEDGE & UNDERSTANDING

· The general legal framework of limited companies and the obligations of Directors in respect of the financial statements (Element 11.1)

CONTENTS

1 Types of profit making organisation
2 Types of non-profit making entities
3 Preparing final accounts
4 Making adjustments
5 The extended trial balance
6 From trial balance to final accounts

PERFORMANCE CRITERIA

· Draft limited company financial statements from the appropriate information (Element 11.1)
· Correctly identify and implement subsequent adjustments and ensure that discrepancies, unusual features or queries are identified and either resolved or referred to the appropriate person (Element 11.1)

1 Types of profit making organisation

1.1 Introduction

There are three main types of profit making business organisation:
· sole trader (sole proprietor)
· partnership
· limited company.

1.2 Sole trader

As the name suggests, this is an organisation owned by one person.

Accounting conventions recognise the business as a separate entity from its owner. However, legally, the business and personal affairs of a sole trader are not distinguished in any way. The most important consequence of this is that a sole trader has complete personal unlimited liability. Business debts which cannot be paid from business assets must be met from the sale of personal assets, such as a house or car.

Sole trading organisations are normally small because they have to rely on the financial resources of their owner.

The advantages of operating as a sole trader include flexibility and autonomy. A sole trader can manage the business as he or she likes and can introduce or withdraw capital at any time.

1.3 Partnership

A partnership is two or more persons associated for the purpose of a business or a profession. Like a sole trader, a partnership is not legally distinguished from its members. Personal assets of the partners may have to be used to pay the debts of the partnership business.

The advantages of trading as a partnership stem mainly from there being many owners rather than one. This means that:
· more resources may be available, including capital, specialist knowledge, skills and ideas;
· administrative expenses may be lower for a partnership than for the equivalent number of sole traders, due to economies of scale; and
· partners can substitute for each other.

Partners can introduce or withdraw capital at any time, provided that all the partners agree.

1.4 Limited company

A limited company is a distinct, artificial 'person' created in order to separate legal responsibility for the affairs of a business (or any other activity) from the personal affairs of the individuals who own and/or operate the business.

The owners are known as shareholders (or members) and the people who run the business are known as directors. In a small corporation, owners and directors are often the same people.

1.5 Limited liability

The concept of limited liability is based on the premise that the company's debts and liabilities are those of the company and not those of the members. Each member of a limited company is liable to contribute if called on to do so only the amount he has agreed to pay on his shares.

Limited liability refers to the liability of each shareholder being limited to any unpaid amount on their shares. Usually, all the shares are fully paid so the members have no liability.

1.6 Comparison of limited companies to sole traders and partnerships

The fact that a company is a separate legal entity means that it is very different from a sole trader or partnership in a number of ways.

· **Property holding**

The property of a limited company belongs to the company. A change in the ownership of shares in the company will have no effect on the ownership of the company's property. (In a partnership the firm's property belongs directly to the partners who can take it with them if they leave the partnership.)

· **Transferable shares**

Shares in a limited company can usually be transferred without the consent of the other shareholders. In the absence of agreement to the contrary, a new partner cannot be introduced into a firm without the consent of all existing partners.

· **Contracts with members**

A limited company can contract with its members and can sue and be sued on such contracts. A partner cannot enter into contracts with his own firm, nor can a sole trader.

· **Suing and being sued**

As a separate legal person, a limited company can sue and be sued in its own name. Judgements relating to companies do not affect the members personally.

· **Number of members**

There is no upper limit on the number of members in a company. In a partnership, except in certain restricted categories, such as accountants and stockbrokers, the maximum number of partners is 20. This limitation on numbers makes it difficult for a partnership to raise large amounts of capital.

· **Security for loans**

A company has greater scope for raising loans by, for example, borrowing on debentures (long-term borrowings) and may secure them with floating charges.

A floating charge is a mortgage over the constantly fluctuating assets of a company providing security for the lender of money to a company. It does not prevent the company dealing with the assets in the ordinary course of business. Such a charge is useful when a company has no non-current assets such as land, but does have a large and valuable inventories.

The law does not permit partnerships or individuals to secure loans with a floating charge.

· **Taxation**

Because a company is legally separate from its members, it is taxed separately from its members. Tax payable by companies is known as corporation tax. Partners and sole traders are personally liable for income tax on the profits made by their businesses.

1.7   Disadvantages of incorporation

The disadvantages of being a limited company arise principally from the restrictions imposed by the Companies Act 1985.

· **Formalities, publicity and expenses**

When they are being formed, companies have to register and to file a Memorandum and Articles of Association (formal constitution documents) with the Registrar. Registration fees and legal costs have to be paid.

The accounts of larger limited companies are subject to an annual audit inspection (this requirement has been lifted for small companies). The costs associated with this can be high. Partnerships and sole traders are not subject to this requirement unless as members of professional bodies whose own rules apply.

A registered company's accounts and certain other documents are open to public inspection. The accounts of sole traders and partnerships are not open to public inspection.

·   **Capital maintenance**

Limited companies are subject to strict rules in connection with the introduction and withdrawal of capital and profits.
·   **Management powers**

Members of a company may not take part in its management unless they are directors, whereas all partners are entitled to share in management, unless the partnership agreement provides otherwise.

2   Types of non-profit making entities

2.1   Introduction

The main types of non–profit making entity are:
·   clubs and societies
·   charities
·   public sector organisations (including central government, local government and National Health Service bodies).

2.2   Objectives of profit making and 'not for profit' entities compared

The main objective of sole traders, partnerships and limited companies is normally assumed as being to make a profit.

The main objective of charities, clubs and societies is to carry out the activities for which they were created. In order to do this, they need to attract or generate sufficient income to cover their expenditure, including administration costs. A large surplus of income over expenditure in the accounts of a charity is normally regarded as a bad sign, as it suggests that donors' money is not being used for the purpose for which it was intended.

The main objective of public sector organisations is to provide services to the general public. Like charities, their long term aim is normally to break even, rather than to generate a surplus. Most public sector organisations aim to provide value for money which is usually analysed into the three Es – economy, efficiency and effectiveness.

2.3 Other differences between profit making and non-profit making entities

These are summarised in the table below:

	Profit making	Clubs, societies, charities	Public sector
Managed by:	Sole traders, part-ners, directors (who may also be shareholders)	Depends on constitution/other internal regula-tions	Elected officials, e.g. MPs, council-lors
Main sources of finance	Personal capacity, equity, debt	Donations, membership fees	Taxation
Stewardship responsibilities to: (likely to be main users of financial state-ments)	Shareholders	Members, donors, beneficiaries	The general public
Financial state-ments used to assess:	Financial performance, whether to hold or sell investment	Whether resources have been used effi-ciently to achieve objectives	Level of spending in relation to services provided, whether services provide value for money, whether services have been provided economically effi-ciently, effec-

2.4 Accounts of non-profit making entities

Most non–profit making entities prepare a statement of financial performance (the equivalent of a income statement for a profit making entity) and a balance sheet. Many entities also prepare a cash flow statement. Increasingly, non–profit making entities are adopting commercial style accounting prac-tices, so that the basic principles used to prepare accounts are very similar to those used by a profit making entity. This is particularly true of the public sector. Many charities are companies and must therefore comply with the accounting requirements of the Companies Act.

3 Preparing final accounts

3.1 Introduction

Final accounts are the end result of a process of summarising, classifying and structuring large quantities of data. The objective of preparing final accounts is to turn individual transactions into useful information.

3.2 Process of preparing final accounts

Whether the accounts are being prepared for a sole trader, a partnership or a limited company, the steps in the process are basically the same.

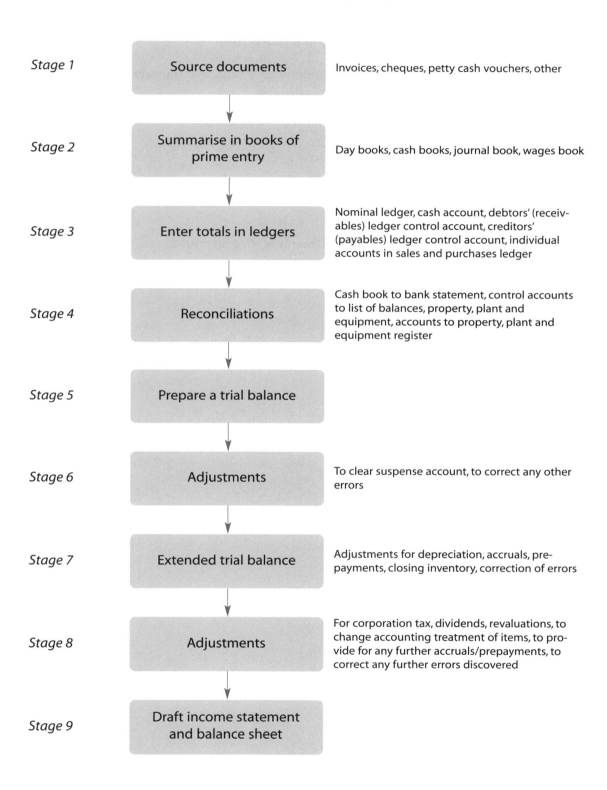

Stage 1	Source documents	Invoices, cheques, petty cash vouchers, other
Stage 2	Summarise in books of prime entry	Day books, cash books, journal book, wages book
Stage 3	Enter totals in ledgers	Nominal ledger, cash account, debtors' (receivables) ledger control account, creditors' (payables) ledger control account, individual accounts in sales and purchases ledger
Stage 4	Reconciliations	Cash book to bank statement, control accounts to list of balances, property, plant and equipment, accounts to property, plant and equipment register
Stage 5	Prepare a trial balance	
Stage 6	Adjustments	To clear suspense account, to correct any other errors
Stage 7	Extended trial balance	Adjustments for depreciation, accruals, prepayments, closing inventory, correction of errors
Stage 8	Adjustments	For corporation tax, dividends, revaluations, to change accounting treatment of items, to provide for any further accruals/prepayments, to correct any further errors discovered
Stage 9	Draft income statement and balance sheet	

The first few stages should be familiar to you as you have covered them in your earlier studies. In this chapter we will concentrate on the later stages, in particular:

· making final adjustments
· drafting the final accounts.

3.3   The income statement of a sole trader

The income statement is a summary of a business' transactions for a given period.

Pro forma income statement for the year ended ...

	£	£
Revenue		X
Less: Cost of sales		
Inventories, at cost on 1 January (opening inventories)	X	
Add: Purchases of goods	X	
	—	
	X	
Less: Inventories, at cost on 31 December (closing inventories)	(X)	
	—	
		(X)
		—
Gross profit		X
Sundry income:		
Discounts received	X	
Commission received	X	
Rent received	X	
	—	
		X
		—
		X
Less: Other expenses:		
Rent	X	
Rates	X	
Lighting and heating	X	
Telephone	X	
Postage	X	
Insurance	X	
Stationery	X	
Office salaries	X	
Depreciation	X	
Accountancy and audit fees	X	
Bank charges and interest	X	
Bad and doubtful debts	X	
Delivery costs	X	
Van running expenses	X	
Advertising	X	
Discounts allowed	X	
	—	
		(X)
		—
Net profit		X
		—

3.4 Explanations

- The top half discloses the gross profit generated by the business by comparing revenue with the cost of those revenues. This is sometimes called the trading account as it shows the results of the business's trade. A shopkeeper, for example, will purchase for resale items from various suppliers (wholesalers); by adding a profit margin to this cost, the selling price of the goods will be computed and this margin is the gross profit.

- Cost of sales is calculated by taking the cost of the goods available for sale during the year (ie opening inventories plus purchases) and deducting the cost of the goods which were unsold (i.e. closing inventories). Revenue and cost of goods sold relate to the same number of units.

- The income statement shows other items of income and expenditure earned or incurred by the business, in order to arrive at net profit.

- In a manufacturing industry, further analysis is needed of the figure for cost of sales.

3.5 The balance sheet of a sole trader

The balance sheet is a statement of the financial position of a business at a given date, usually the end of the period covered by the income statement. It is a snapshot at one given moment.

Pro forma balance sheet at ...

	Cost £	Depreciation £	£
Non-current assets			
Freehold factory	X	X	X
Machinery	X	X	X
Motor vehicles	X	X	X
	X	X	X
Current assets			
Inventories		X	
Trade receivables	X		
Less: Allowance for doubtful debts	(X)	X	
Prepayments		X	
Cash at bank		X	
Cash in hand		X	
		X	
Current liabilities			
Trade payables	X		
Accrued charges	X		
		(X)	

	Cost £	Depreciation £	£
Net current assets			X
			────
		X	
Non-current liabilities			
12% loan			(X)
			────
Net assets			X
			────
Representing:			
Capital at 1 January			X
Profit for the year			X
			────
			X
Less: Drawings			(X)
			────
Proprietor's funds			X
			────

3.6 Explanations

· *Non-current assets:* Assets acquired for use within the business on a continuing basis with a view to earning profits, but not for resale. They are normally valued at cost less accumulated depreciation.

· *Current assets:* Assets acquired for conversion into cash in the ordinary course of business; they should not be valued at a figure greater than their realisable value.

· *Current liabilities:* Amounts owed by the business, payable within one year.

· *Net current assets:* Funds of the business available for day-to-day transactions. This can also be called *working capital.*

· *Non-current liabilities:* Funds provided for the business on a medium to long-term basis by an individual or organisation other than the proprietor. Long-term liabilities are repayable in more than one year.

4 Making adjustments

4.1 Introduction

Adjustments to the initial trial balance, the extended trial balance and the draft accounts are made by drawing up and posting a journal entry.

4.2 Journals

In practice, journals may be used in several ways:
· to record major or unusual transactions;
· to record period-end adjustments (e.g. depreciation, inventory, doubtful debts); and
· to facilitate the correction of errors, and to explain the nature of the errors.

Journals are recorded in the journal book. This is a book of prime entry and is not part of the double entry. From the journal book, the journals are posted to the relevant accounts in the nominal ledger.

○ **EXAMPLE**   ○○○○

On 31 March 20X5 a company purchased a new motor vehicle for £20,000 in cash. How would this be recorded in the journal?

Solution

The double entry for this would be:

Debit: Motor vehicles   £20,000
Credit: Cash   £20,000

This statement of the double-entry is itself known as a journal.

In the journal book, the transaction would be recorded as follows:

Journal number	Date	Narrative	Account No	Dr £	Cr £
1	31.3.X5	Dr Motor Vehicles Cr Cash	M1 C41	20,000	20,000
		Purchase of new motor vehicle (registration YY56 BLR)			

4.3   Posting the journal

When period-end adjustments are made, the journal is drawn up and the trial balance or draft accounts are adjusted. These journals are not normally posted to the nominal ledger until the accounts have been finalised. The nominal ledger accounts are then balanced off and the new balances brought down for the start of the next accounting period.

○ EXAMPLE   ○ ○ ○ ○

Flagg extracted the following trial balance from his ledgers at 31 March 20X4:

	£ Dr	£ Cr
Petty cash	48	
Capital		3,830
Drawings	3,360	
Revenue		49,457
Purchases	37,166	
Purchases returns		504
Inventories (1 April 20X3)	5,057	
Fixtures and fittings	1,704	
Trade receivables	4,366	
Sundry creditors		4,987
Carriage on purchases	262	
Carriage on sales	442	
Rent and rates	1,104	
Light and heat	180	
Postage and telephone	204	
Sundry expenses	456	
Cash at bank	4,328	
	58,677	58,778

The trial balance did not agree. On investigation, Flagg discovered the following errors:

(1) In extracting the schedule of trade receivables, the credit side of a trade receivables account had been overcast by £24.

(2) An amount of £10 for carriage on sales had been posted in error to the carriage on purchases account.

(3) A credit note for £41 received from a trade payable had been entered in the purchase returns book but no entry had been made in the trade payable account.

(4) £84 charged for repairs to Flagg's private residence had been charged, in error, to the sundry expenses account.

(5) A payment of a telephone bill of £51 had been entered correctly in the cash book but had been posted, in error, to the postage and telephone account as £15.

Required:

Show the journal entries to correct the errors and set up the suspense account and show how it is cleared. Finally show the corrected trial balance.

Solution

Step 1

The trial balance is repeated with a suspense account added to balance the columns.

	£ Dr	£ Cr
Petty cash	48	
Capital		3,830
Drawings	3,360	
Revenue		49,457
Purchases	37,166	
Purchases returns		504
Inventories (1 April 20X3)	5,057	
Fixtures and fittings	1,704	
Trade receivables	4,366	
Sundry creditors		4,987
Carriage on purchases	262	
Carriage on sales	442	
Rent and rates	1,104	
Light and heat	180	
Postage and telephone	204	
Sundry expenses	456	
Cash at bank	4,328	
Suspense account	**101**	
	58,778	58,778

Step 2

The adjustments are as follows:

	Dr £	Cr £
1 Debit Trade receivables	24	
Credit Suspense account		24
Being correction of undercast in trade receivables account		
2 Debit Carriage on sales	10	
Credit Carriage on purchases		10
Being correction of wrong posting		
3 Debit Trade payables	41	
Credit Suspense account		41
Being correction of omitted entry		
4 Debit Drawings	84	
Credit Sundry expenses		84
Being payment for private expenses		
5 Debit Postage and telephone	36	
Credit Suspense account		36
Being correction of transposition error		

Step 3

Journals 1, 3 and 5 clear the suspense account:

Suspense account

	£		£
Difference per trial balance	101	Trade receivables	24
		Trade payables	41
		Postage	36
	101		101

Step 4

The trial balance is then corrected:

	Original TB		Adjustments		Adjusted TB	
	Dr	Cr	Dr	Cr	Dr	Cr
	£	£	£	£	£	£
Petty cash	48				48	
Capital		3,830				3,830
Drawings	3,360		84		3,444	
Revenue		49,457				49,457
Purchases	37,166				37,166	
Purchases returns		504				504
Inventories (1 April 20X3)	5,057				5,057	
Fixtures and fittings	1,704				1,704	
Trade receivables	4,366		24		4,390	
Sundry creditors		4,987	41			4,946
Carriage on purchases	262			10	252	
Carriage on sales	442		10		452	
Rent and rates	1,104				1,104	
Light and heat	180				180	
Postage and telephone	204		36		240	
Sundry expenses	456			84	372	
Cash at bank	4,328				4,328	
Suspense account	101			101		
	58,778	58,778			58,737	58,737

Note: In a full extended trial balance, the adjustment columns that are shown here with the entries to clear the suspense account, would also hold the other year end adjustments such as depreciation, bad debts, closing inventories, etc. There would then not be an 'adjusted TB' column. The entries would be extended directly into the income statement and balance sheet columns.

5 The extended trial balance

5.1 Introduction

A trial balance is simply a list of all the balances on the ledger accounts before year-end adjustments are made. These adjustments need to be made before

the preparation of the income statement and balance sheet and they normally include the following:
- correction of errors
- recognition of accruals and prepayments
- depreciation charge for the year
- review of the charge for bad and doubtful debts
- inclusion of closing inventories.

The **extended trial balance** is a worksheet which takes us from the trial balance to the income statement and balance sheet.

Layout of a typical extended trial balance

Account	Trial balance		Adjustments		Income statement		Balance sheet	
	Dr	Cr	Dr	Cr	Dr	Cr	Dr	Cr
	£	£	£	£	£	£	£	£

The names of the ledger accounts and the corresponding amounts per the trial balance are entered into the first three columns.

The adjustments columns are used for all of the year-end adjustments mentioned above.

○ EXAMPLE ○○○○

Trial balance at 31 December 20X6

	Dr £	Cr £
Shop fittings at cost	2,000	
Depreciation provision at 1 January 20X6		100
Leasehold premises at cost	12,500	
Depreciation provision at 1 January 20X6		625
Inventories at 1 January 20X6	26,000	
Trade receivables at 31 December 20X6	53,000	
Allowance for doubtful receivables at 1 January 20X6		960
Cash in hand	50	
Cash at bank	2,250	
Trade payables		65,000
Proprietor's capital at 1 January 20X6		28,115
Drawings to 31 December 20X6	2,000	
Purchases	102,000	
Revenue		129,000
Wages	18,200	
Advertising	2,300	
Rates for 15 months to 31 March 20X7	1,500	
Light and heat	1,800	
Bank charges	200	
	223,800	223,800

The following adjustments are to be made:

(1) Depreciation of shop fittings   £100

Depreciation of leasehold premises   £625

(2) A debt of £500 is irrecoverable and is to be written off; the allowance for doubtful receivables is to be increased to the equivalent of 2% of the remaining trade receivables.

(3) Advertising fees of £200 have been treated incorrectly as wages.

(4) The proprietor has withdrawn goods costing £1,000 for his personal use; these have not been recorded as drawings.

(5) Inventories at 31 December 20X6 are valued at £30,000.

(6) The electricity charge for the last three months of 20X6 is outstanding and is estimated to be £400.

Prepare the extended trial balance at 31 December 20X6.

Solution

Step 1
The balances per the trial balance are recorded in the correct columns and the total of the debit balances is agreed to the total of the credit balances.

Step 2
We shall now deal with the adjustments (apart from accruals and prepayments).

· **Correction of errors**
Two errors need to be corrected. One of the errors concerns the drawings of the proprietor, ie the fact that some of the purchases were bought for his own use. To correct this, we should decrease the purchases and increase the drawings, ie:

		£	£
Debit	Drawings	1,000	
Credit	Purchases		1,000

The other error concerns the mis-classification of advertising fees as wages. To correct this, the following adjustment is necessary:

Debit	Advertising	200	
Credit	Wages		200

· **The depreciation charge for the year**
The charge for the year is £725 and we need to charge this to the depreciation expense account and also to increase the accumulated depreciation carried forward. The double-entry is:

Debit	Depreciation expense: shop fittings	100	
Debit	Depreciation expense: leasehold premises	625	
Credit	Accumulated depreciation: shop fittings		100
Credit	Accumulated depreciation: leasehold premises		625

We will need to set up the depreciation expense account as none exists.

Allowance for doubtful trade receivables

The trade receivables amount to £52,500 after the write-off of the bad receivable of £500. An allowance of £1,050 (£52,500 2%) is therefore required at 31.12.X6. The allowance brought forward at the beginning of the year was £960; therefore it should be increased by £90 (1,050 – 960). The total charge to the income statement is £590 (the receivable written off of £500 plus the increase in the allowance of £90). The double-entry is:

		£	£
Debit	Bad and doubtful receivables expense	590	
Credit	Allowance for doubtful receivables		90
Credit	Trade receivables		500

An expense account will need to be created for bad and doubtful receivables.

Inclusion of closing inventories

Closing inventories appears in both the income statement and the balance sheet.

- In the income statement, it is a reduction of cost of goods sold and hence is a credit.
- In the balance sheet, it is an asset and hence is a debit.

Accordingly we set up two accounts for inventories: one for the balance sheet and one for the income statement. The adjustment is:

Debit	Inventories (balance sheet)	30,000	
Credit	Inventories (income statement)		30,000

If you turn to the extended trial balance on the next page, you will see that each of these pairs of double-entry has been recorded in the adjustment columns. As the debit entries should always equal the credit entries, it is a useful check to cast the debit and credit adjustment columns to see that the totals are equal.

Step 3

We now have to deal with the last adjustments, i.e. the accruals and prepayments.

Electricity

The income statement charge for the year needs to be increased by £400 and a creditor for £400 must be established. The double-entry is:

Debit	Light and heat	400	
Credit	Accruals		400

The accruals account will need to be set up.

Rates

The income statement charge for the year should be £1,200 (12/15 £1,500), and therefore there should be a prepayment of £300. The double-entry is:

		£	£
Debit	Prepayments	300	
Credit	Rates		300

Step 4

We have now recorded all of the adjustments and we need to prepare the income statement and balance sheet columns. This is achieved by the following:

· Cross-cast each account and enter the total in the appropriate column of the income statement or balance sheet columns. Some examples are as follows:

  – Fittings (2,000 + 0 = £2,000) are recorded in the debit column of the balance sheet.

  – Accumulated depreciation on fittings (100 + 100 = £200) is recorded in the credit column of the balance sheet.

  – Purchases (102,000 – 1,000 = £101,000) is recorded in the debit column of the income statement.

Note: Accruals are added to the original trial balance amount whereas prepayments are subtracted.

· Add the debit and credit sides of the income statement. The difference between these two columns is a profit (if the credits exceed the debits) or a loss (if the debits exceed the credits). The difference is recorded in the correct column of the income statement (so that the two sides now balance) and the double-entry is with the balance sheet.

· Add the debit and credit columns of the balance sheet. These should agree unless you have made any errors.

Step 5

The income statement and balance sheet are then prepared from the relevant columns.

The completed extended trial balance is shown overleaf:

Extended trial balance at 31 December 20X6

Account	Trial balance Dr £	Trial balance Cr £	Adjustments Dr £	Adjustments Cr £	Income statement Dr £	Income statement Cr £	Balance sheet Dr £	Balance sheet Cr £
Shop fittings	2,000						2,000	
Accumulated depreciation 1.1.X6		100		100				200
Leasehold premises	12,500						12,500	
Accumulated depreciation 1.1.X6		625		625				1,250
Inventories 1.1.X6	26,000		30,000	30,000	26,000	30,000	30,000	
Trade receivables	53,000			500			52,500	
Allowance for doubtful debts 1.1.X6		960		90				1,050
Cash in hand	50						50	
Cash at bank	2,250						2,250	
Trade payables		65,000						65,000
Capital		28,115						28,115
Drawings	2,000		1,000				3,000	
Purchases	102,000			1,000	101,000			
Revenue		129,000				129,000		
Wages	18,200			200	18,000			
Advertising	2,300		200		2,500			
Rates	1,500			300	1,200			
Light and heat	1,800		400		2,200			
Bank charges	200				200			
Depreciation – shop fittings			100		100			
Depreciation – leasehold premises		625			625			
Bad debts expense		590			590			
Prepayments		300					300	
Accruals				400				400
					152,415	159,000		
Net profit					6,585			6,585
223,800	223,800	33,215	33,215	159,000	159,000	102,600	102,600	102,600

The income statement and balance sheet are now drafted from the extended trial balance. (For the purpose of this example, we are assuming that there are no further adjustments to the extended trial balance; in practice, this might not be the case. Any further adjustments would be made by drawing up and posting journal entries, exactly as before.)

Income statement for the year ended 31 December 20X6

	£	£
Revenue	129,000	
Less: Cost of sales		
Opening inventories	26,000	
Purchases	101,000	
	127,000	
Closing inventories	(30,000)	
		(97,000)
Gross profit	32,000	
Less: Expenses		
Wages	18,000	
Advertising	2,500	
Rates	1,200	
Light and heat	2,200	
Bank charges	200	
Depreciation (100 + 625)	725	
Bad debts	590	
		(25,415)
Net profit		6,585

Balance sheet at 31 December 20X6

		Cost value £	Accumulated depreciation £	Net book
£				
Non-current assets				
Shop fittings		2,000	200	1,800
Leasehold premises	1	2,500	1,250	11,250
		14,500	1,450	13,050
Current assets				
Inventories			30,000	
Trade receivables (52,500 – 1,050)			51,450	
Prepayments			300	
Cash at bank			2,250	
Cash in hand			50	
			84,050	
Current liabilities				
Trade payables		65,000		
Accruals		400		
			(65,400)	
Net current assets				18,650
				31,700
Represented by: Capital				28,115
Add: Net profit for the year				6,585
				34,700
Less: Drawings				(3,000)
				31,700

▷ ACTIVITY 1   ▷ ▷ ▷ ▷

Sandro Venus

Data

You have been asked by Sandro Venus to assist in the preparation of the year end financial statements of his business. He is a sole trader who runs a trading business which specialises in ornaments decorated with sea shells. The extended trial balance as at 31 March 20X7 is set out below.

Description	Trial balance		Adjustments		Income statement		Balance sheet	
	Dr £	Cr £	Dr £	Cr £	Dr £	Cr £	Dr £	Cr £
Wages and National Insurance Contributions	28,996		348		29,344			
Capital as at 1 April 20X6		83,696						83,696
Postage and stationery	524				524			
Accumulated depreciation – Motor vehicles		8,125		6,094				14,219
Accumulated depreciation – Office equipment		1,375		1,375				2,750
Accumulated depreciation – Fixtures & fittings		2,780		2,780				5,560
Purchases	103,742				103,742			
Trade payables		17,725						17,725
Carriage inwards	923				923			
Motor vehicles (cost)	32,500						32,500	
Office equipment (cost)	13,745						13,745	
Fixtures & fittings (cost)	27,800						27,800	
Revenue		187,325				187,325		
Returns outwards		1,014				1,014		
Trade receivables	18,740						18,740	
Drawings	14,400						14,400	
Depreciation – Motor vehicles			6,094		6,094			
Depreciation – Office equipment			1,375		1,375			
Depreciation – Fixtures & fittings			2,780		2,780			
Prepayments			320				320	
Accruals				1,131	1,131			
Inventories	27,931		30,229	30,229	27,931	30,229	30,229	
Returns inwards	1,437				1,437			
Cash at bank	9,473						9,473	
Cash in hand	166						166	
Bank deposit interest		972				972		
Carriage outwards	657				657			
Rent, rates and insurance	8,041			320	7,721			
Bad debts	830				830			
Discounts allowed	373				373			
Bank charges	693				693			
Telephone	3,524		783		4,307			
Lighting and heating	3,755				3,755			
Motor expenses	4,762				4,762			
Profit					22,292			22,292
	303,012	303,012	41,929	41,929	219,540	219,540	147,373	147,373

You are given the following further information.

1   An allowance for doubtful receivables is to be set up at 5% of the year end debtors' balance.

2   During the year Sandro Venus took goods which had cost £500 for his own personal use in decorating his flat.

3   At the end of the year, one of the motor vehicles which had cost £5,500 and on which there was accumulated depreciation of £2,400 was sold for £3,500. Payment for the vehicle sold has not yet been received by Sandro Venus and no entry to reflect the sale has been made in the extended trial balance.

Task 1
Make additional adjustments you feel necessary to the balances in the extended trial balance as a result of the matters set out in the further information above. Set out your adjustments in the form of journal entries.

Note: Narratives are not required.

Task 2
Draft an income statement for the year ended 31 March 20X7.

Task 3
Sandro Venus is considering whether to incorporate the business and has said that he will telephone you tomorrow for advice.

Prepare notes for the telephone conversation that will enable you to explain the difference between the legal status of a sole trader and that of a company in respect of:
(i)   the liability of the owners for the debts of the business;
(ii)   the legal identity of the business;
(iii) the regulation of the production of the financial statements for the business.

[Answer on p. 56]

6   From trial balance to final accounts

6.1   Introduction

In the last paragraphs we saw how to prepare a income statement and balance sheet from an extended trial balance. However it is more likely in an assessment that you will be required to prepare a set of final accounts from a trial balance (not an extended trial balance) and a given set of adjustments to the trial balance figures.

6.2   Additional problems

There are no major additional problems in doing this as the adjustments are the same as those encountered with an extended trial balance. However there are two aspects that you must be able to deal with:

· you must be able to work out which balances from the trial balance appear in the income statement and which appear in the balance sheet;

· you must be able to put through the adjustments required without the adjustment column of the extended trial balance. You can do this by opening up ledger accounts for each of the accounts that are affected by the adjustments. This is a safe but very slow way of doing things. It is quicker to do your working on the face of the income statement and balance sheet as we shall see, with additional workings for any difficult items.

○ EXAMPLE   ○ ○ ○ ○

Set out below is the trial balance of Lyttleton, a sole trader, extracted at 31 December 20X5.

	Dr £	Cr £
Capital account		7,830
Cash at bank	2,010	
Non-current assets at cost	9,420	
Accumulated depreciation at 31 December 20X4		3,470
Trade receivables	1,830	
Inventories at 31 December 20X4	1,680	
Trade payables		390
Revenue		14,420
Purchases	8,180	
Rent	1,100	
Electricity	940	
Rates	950	
	———	———
	26,110	26,110
	———	———

On examination of the accounts, the following information is obtained.

1   Depreciation for the year of £942 is to be charged.

2   An allowance for doubtful receivables of 3% of total trade receivables is to be set up.

3   Purchases include £1,500 of goods which were bought for the proprietor's personal use.

4   Inventories at 31 December 20X5 were £1,140.

5   The rent account shows the monthly payments of £100 made from 1 January to 1 November 20X5 inclusive. Owing to an oversight the payment on 1 December 20X5 was not made.

6   The rates account shows the prepayment of £150 brought forward at the beginning of 20X5 (and representing rates from 1 January 20X5 to 31 March 20X5) together with the £800 payment made on 1 April 20X5 and relating to the period from 1 April 20X5 to 31 March 20X6.

7   The electricity charge for the last three months of 20X5 is outstanding and is estimated to be £400.

Required:

Prepare an income statement for the year ended 31 December 20X5 and a balance sheet as at that date.

Step by step approach

Step 1
Read the requirements at the end of the question to see what it is you are required to do.

Step 2
Draft out working papers as per the requirements, one complete page for each including a working paper.

Income statement	Balance sheet as at	Working Paper

Step 3
Go through the trial balance in the question and write each of the amounts against the relevant account on the proformas. Do not at this stage enter anything in the final columns.

Lyttleton income statement for year ended 31 December 20X5

	£	£
Revenue 14,420		
Cost of sales		
Opening inventories 1,680		
Purchases 8,180		
	_____	
Less: Closing inventories		
	_____	
		_____
Gross profit		
Less: Expenses		
Rent 1,100		
Electricity 940		

	£	£
Rates	950	
Depreciation		
Bad and doubtful debts		
	———	
		———
Net profit		———

Lyttleton balance sheet as at 31 December 20X5

			Cost	Depn	
			£	£	£
Non-current assets	Cost	9,420			
	Depreciation	3,470			
			———	———	
Current assets					
Inventories					
Trade receivables	1,830				
Allowance for doubtful receivables					
			———		
Prepayments					
Cash	2,010				
				———	
Current liabilities					
Trade payables	390				
Accruals					
			———		
Net current assets				———	
				———	
				———	
Capital as at 1.1.X5	7,830				
Profit for the year					
				———	
Less: Drawings					
				———	
				———	

Notes:

1   The opening inventories at 31.12.20X4 are entered in the trading account, not the balance sheet.
2   The non-current assets and depreciation need to be kept separate under non-current assets in the balance sheet.
3   It is a good idea to tick the items in the question as you write them onto the proforma to make sure you haven't forgotten any.

Step 4

Now go through each of the additional bits of information in the question and either:

(a)   enter it directly onto the relevant line on the face of the proformas in Step 3 (not in the 'final columns') if it is straightforward; or

(b)   open up a working for tricky items to calculate the required amount, and then enter the number on the proformas.

Notes:

1   In the proformas below, (P1) after a number indicates that it is 'point 1' of the additional information in the question; (W1) after a number indicates that it is a working which follows the proforma.

2   Again, you should tick the additional points in the question to show that you have used them.

Lyttleton income statement for year ended 31 December 20X5

		£	£
Sales 14,420			
Cost of sales			
Opening inventories 1,680			
Purchases 8,180 – 1,500 (P3)			
		_____	
Less: Closing inventories 1,140 (P4)			
		_____	_____
Gross profit			
Less: Expenses			
Rent 1,100 + 100 (P5)			
Electricity 940 + 400 (P7)			
Rates 950 – 200 (W1)			
Depreciation 942 (P1)			
Bad and doubtful receivables			
(3% x 1,830) (P2)			
		_____	_____
Net profit			_____

Lyttleton balance sheet as at 31 December 20X5

		Cost £	Depn £	£
Non-current assets:	Cost 9,420			
	Depreciation			
	3,470 + 942 (P1)			
		_____	_____	
Current assets				
Inventories 1,140 (P4)				
Trade receivables 1,830				
Allowance for doubtful receivables				
(3% x 1,830) (P2)				
			_____	
Prepayments 200 (W1)				
Cash 2,010				
			_____	
Current liabilities				
Trade payables 390				
Accruals (100 + 400) (P5 + P7)				
			_____	

	Cost £	Depn £	£
Net current assets			
			————
			————
Capital as at 1.1.X5 7,830			
Profit for the year			
			————
Less: Drawings 1,500 (P3)			
			————

Working 1

Point 6 of question – rates

Rates

	£		£
b/d	150	Income statement	750
1.4X5	800	c/d 1.1.X6 – 31.3.X6	200
	————		————
	950		950
	————		————
b/d	200		

The prepayment is for three months (1.1.X6 to 31.3.X6) and is $^3/_{12}$ £800 = £200.

This is shown as a deduction on the proforma, reducing the charge for the year by £200 to £750.

Very important note:
Note how the adjustments that have to be made for the 'additional information' in the question require two entries to be made in the accounts. For example, the prepayment for rates (£200) is entered in the income statement to reduce the rates charge and is also entered in the balance sheet as a prepayment. This double entry is required because this is a new piece of information and has to follow normal double entry rules.

Contrast this with the entries from the original trial balance. These were entered on the proforma with a single entry. This is because they are the balances of the various accounts which have resulted from all the double entry that has already taken place.

Step 5
Take each line on the proformas in turn and extend the numbers you have written into the 'final columns'.

Lyttleton income statement for year ended 31 December 20X5

	£	£
Revenue 14,420		14,420
Cost of sales		
Opening inventories 1,680	1,680	
Purchases 8,180 – 1,500 (P3)	6,680	
	8,360	
Less: Closing inventories 1,140 (P4)	(1,140)	
		(7,220)
Gross profit		7,200
Less: Expenses		
Rent 1,100 + 100 (P5)	1,200	
Electricity 940 + 400 (P7)	1,340	
Rates 950 – 200 (W1)	750	
Depreciation 942 (P1)	942	
Bad and doubtful debts (3% x 1,830) (P2)	55	
		4,287
Net profit		2,913

Lyttleton balance sheet as at 31 December 20X5

	Cost £	Depn £	£
Non-current assets 9,420	9,420		
3,470 + 942 (P1)		4,412	5,008
Current assets			
Inventories 1,140 (P4)		1,140	
Trade receivables 1,830	1,830		
Allowance for doubtful receivables			
(3% x 1,830) (P2)	(55)		
		1,775	
Prepayments 200 (W1)		200	
Cash 2,010		2,010	
		5,125	
Current liabilities			
Trade payables 390	390		
Accruals (100 + 400) (P5 + P7)	500		
		(890)	
Net current assets			4,235
			9,243

	Cost	Depn	
	£	£	£
Capital as at 1.1.X5 7,830			7,830
Profit for the year (from income statement)			2,913
			———
			10,743
Less: Drawings 1,500 (P3)			(1,500)
			———
			9,243
			———

▷ ACTIVITY 2   ▷ ▷ ▷ ▷

Given below is the trial balance of a sole trader's business as at 31 March 20X5:

	£	£
Motor vans	25,700	
Motor vans - accumulated depreciation		6,460
Revenue		106,080
Purchases	58,760	
Trade receivables	8,840	
Trade payables		4,940
Capital		20,740
Opening inventories	5,460	
Discount received		130
Discount allowed	160	
Carriage inwards	570	
Carriage outwards	800	
Rent	1,250	
Heat, light and power	1,400	
Loan		5,000
Telephone	1,670	
Wages	25,220	
Motor expenses	1,700	
Drawings	10,400	
Bank	1,420	
	———	———
	143,350	143,350
	———	———

You also have the following additional information:
· the motor vans are being depreciated at a rate of 15% per annum straight line
· the inventories at 31 March 20X5 are £6,100
· a bad debt of £240 is to be written off
· an allowance for doubtful receivables of 3% is to be set up
· purchases include £400 of goods which the owner has used for personal purposes
· the rent in the trial balance is for the 15 months ending 30 June 20X5
· a £200 bill for electricity was received just after the year end and has not been accounted for.

You are required to prepare the income statement for the year ending 31 March 20X5 and the balance sheet at that date.

[Answer on p. 57]

▷ ACTIVITY 3   ▷ ▷ ▷ ▷

Given below is the trial balance at 30 June 20X4 for a sole trader.

	£	£
Motor vehicles at cost	75,000	
Fixtures and fittings at cost	18,400	
Motor vehicles - accumulated depreciation		26,000
Fixtures and fittings - accumulated depreciation		4,160
Bank	4,960	
Electricity	1,490	
Loan		12,500
Loan interest paid	550	
Capital		79,100
Carriage outwards	500	
Discount received		1,730
Revenue		272,800
Opening inventories	14,880	
Trade receivables	24,800	
Allowance for doubtful receivables		400
Wages	64,400	
Discount allowed	2,720	
Trade payables		14,880
Rent	3,750	
Insurance	1,980	
Carriage inwards	990	
Drawings	22,000	
Purchases	175,150	
	411,570	411,570

You are also given the following information:

· closing inventories have been valued at £19,800

· £50 of loan interest is to be accrued

· no depreciation charge has yet been accounted for for the year. The rates of depreciation are:

- motor vehicles 20% reducing balance

- fixtures and fittings 10% straight line

- a bad debt of £1,800 is to be written off and the allowance for doubtful receivables is to remain at 2% of debtors

- the rent is £250 per month payable quarterly in advance

- there is an insurance prepayment at the end of the year of £280

You are required to prepare the income statement for the year ended 30 June 20X4 and a balance sheet at that date.

[Answer on p. 59]

7 Test your knowledge

1   Is a limited company a separate legal entity?

2   What is meant by limited liability?

3   Give four examples of current assets.

4   What is represented in the two most right-hand columns of an extended trial balance?

[Answers on p. 61]

8   Summary

The journal is used to record period-end adjustments. Each journal entry must be accompanied by a narrative stating the nature of the transaction.

The extended trial balance is simply a worksheet showing the adjustments made to the figures in the trial balance to lead to the income statement and balance sheet.

Procedure:
·   Set out initial trial balance.
·   Deal with adjustments.
·   Deal with accruals and prepayments.
·   Add the columns across into the 'income statement' and 'balance sheet' columns.
·   Add the columns down and determine the net profit for the period.
·   Prepare the income statement and balance sheet from the relevant columns.

You must be ready to be required to prepare financial statements from a trial balance with a number of required adjustments. The trick here is to recognise which balances appear in the income statement and which in the balance sheet.

Answers to chapter activities & 'test your knowledge' questions

△ **ACTIVITY 1**   △△△△

Sandro Venus

Task 1

			£	£
1	DR	Doubtful receivables expense	937	
	CR	Allowance for doubtful receivables (5% x ?18,740)		937
2	DR	Drawings	500	
	CR	Purchases		500
3	DR	Motor vehicles – accumulated depreciation	2,400	
	DR	Sundry receivables	3,500	
	CR	Motor vehicles – cost		5,500
	CR	Profit on sale of motor vehicle		400

Task 2

Sandro Venus
Income statement for the year ended 31 March 20X7

	£	£
Revenue	187,325	
Less Returns inwards	1,437	
		185,888
Less Cost of sales		
Opening inventories	27,931	
Purchases (103,742 – 500)	103,242	
Carriage inwards	923	
Less Returns outwards	(1,014)	
	131,082	
Less Closing inventories	(30,229)	
		100,853
Gross profit		85,035
Plus Profit on the sale of motor vehicle		400
Interest on bank deposit		972
Less Expenses		
Wages and NIC	29,344	
Rent, rates and insurance	7,721	
Depreciation – Motor vehicles	6,094	
– Office equipment	1,375	
– Fixtures and fittings	2,780	
Receivables written off	830	
Increase in allowance for doubtful debts	937	
Motor expenses	4,762	

Bank charges	693	
Lighting and heating	3,755	
Postage and stationery	524	
Telephone	4,307	
Carriage outwards	657	
Discounts allowed	373	
	———	
		(64,152)
		———
Net profit		22,255
		———

Task 3

Notes

(i) A sole trader is liable for all of the debts of the business and his personal possessions can be used to meet the debts of the business. A company normally has limited liability and hence the owners of the business, once they have paid the full value of their shares, cannot be forced to contribute more money to pay for the liabilities of the business.

(ii) In law, there is no distinction between the owner of the business and the business itself for a sole trader. However, a company is a separate legal entity and can sue and be sued in its own right.

(iii) The production of financial statements of a company is regulated by the Companies Act. By law, a company must prepare financial statements in accordance with the requirements of the Companies Acts, send them to members and file them with the Registrar of Companies who makes them available to members of the public. Sole traders are not regulated as to production of financial statements, although they may be required to be produced for taxation and other purposes.

△ ACTIVITY 2   △△△△

Income statement for the year ended 31 March 20X5

		£	£
Revenue			106,080
Less:	Cost of sales		
	Opening inventories	5,460	
	Purchases (58,760 – 400)	58,360	
	Carriage inwards	570	
		———	
		64,390	
Less:	Closing inventories	6,100	
		———	
			58,290
			———
Gross profit			47,790
Discount received			130
			———
			47,920

Less:	Expenses		
	Motor van depreciation (25,700 x 15%)	3,855	
	Bad debt write off	240	
	Doubtful debts allowance ((8,840 – 240) x 3%)	258	
	Discount allowed	160	
	Carriage outwards	800	
	Rent (1,250 x 12/15)	1,000	
	Heat, light and power (1,400 + 200)	1,600	
	Telephone	1,670	
	Wages	25,220	
	Motor expenses	1,700	
		_____	
			36,503
			_____
Net profit			11,417
			_____

Note that carriage inwards is treated as part of cost of sales as it is a cost of getting inventories to their current location and condition. Carriage outwards, however, is treated as an expense.

Balance sheet as at 31 March 20X5

	£	£
Non-current assets:		
Motor vans at cost		25,700
Less: Accumulated depreciation (6,460 + 3,855)		10,315
		_____
Net book value		15,385
Current assets:		
Inventories		6,100
Trade receivables (8,840 – 240 – 258)	8,342	
Prepayment – rent (1,250 x 3/15)	250	
Bank	1,420	
	_____	
	16,112	
	_____	
Current liabilities:		
Trade payables	4,940	
Accruals – electricity	200	
	_____	
	5,140	
	_____	
Net current assets		10,972
		_____
		26,357
Loan		(5,000)
		_____
		21,357
		_____

Capital at 1 April 20X4		20,740
Profit for the year		11,417
		———
		32,157
Less: Drawings (10,400 + 400)		10,800
		———
		21,357
		———

△ ACTIVITY 3   △ △ △ △

Income statement for the year ended 30 June 20X4

	£	£
Revenue		272,800
Less: Cost of sales		
Opening inventories	14,880	
Purchases	175,150	
Carriage inwards	990	
	———	
	191,020	
Less: Closing inventories	19,800	
	———	
		171,220
		———
Gross profit		101,580
Discount received		1,730
		———
		103,310
Less: Expenses		
Motor vehicle depreciation		
(20% x (75,000 – 26,000))	9,800	
Fixtures and fittings depreciation		
(10% x 18,400)	1,840	
Electricity	1,490	
Loan interest (550 + 50)	600	
Carriage outwards	500	
Bad debt	1,800	
Increase in allowance for		
doubtful debts (W1)	60	
Wages	64,400	
Discount allowed	2,720	
Rent (12 x 250)	3,000	
Insurance (1,980 – 280)	1,700	
	———	
		87,910
		———
Net profit		15,400
		———

Balance sheet as at 30 June 20X4

	£	£	£
Non-current assets:			
Motor vehicles	75,000	35,800	39,200
Fixtures and fittings	18,400	6,000	12,400
	93,400	41,800	51,600
Current assets:			
Inventories			19,800
Trade receivables (24,800 – 1,800)	23,000		
Less: Allowance for doubtful debts	460		
		22,540	
Prepayment - insurance		280	
- rent (3,750 – 3,000)		750	
Bank		4,960	
		48,330	
Current liabilities:			
Trade payables		14,880	
Accruals - loan interest		50	
		14,930	
Net current assets		33,400	
			85,000
Loan			12,500
			72,500
Capital at 1 July 20X3			79,100
Net profit for the year			15,400
			94,500
Less: Drawings			22,000
			72,500

Workings

(W1)	£
Allowance for doubtful debts required (£24,800 – 1,800) x 2%	460
Opening allowance	400
Increase in allowance	60

Test your knowledge △ △ △

1 Yes.

2 The shareholders are only liable for the company's debts to the amounts unpaid on their shares.

3 Inventories, debtors, prepayments, bank balance.

4 The balance sheet of the business.

PREPARING LIMITED COMPANY ACCOUNTS

INTRODUCTION

For Element 1 of this Unit you need to be able to draft the financial statements of a limited company. In this chapter we will consider the preparation of financial statements for limited companies and consider the legal and regulatory requirements for the presentation of those financial statements.

KNOWLEDGE & UNDERSTANDING

· The general legal framework of limited companies and the obligations of Directors in respect of the financial statements (Element 11.1)
· The statutory form of accounting statements and disclosure requirements (Element 11.1)
· The forms of equity and loan capital (Element 11.1)
· The presentation of Corporation Tax in financial statements (Element 11.1)

CONTENTS

1 Distinctive features of limited companies
2 Key differences between a sole trader's accounts and limited company accounts
3 Introduction to company accounts
4 The balance sheet
5 The income statement
6 Notes to the accounts
7 Preparing company accounts
8 Statement of changes in equity
9 Drafting a full set of company accounts

PERFORMANCE CRITERIA

· Draft limited company financial statements from the appropriate information (Element 11.1)
· Correctly identify and implement subsequent adjustments and ensure that discrepancies, unusual features or queries are identified and either resolved or referred to the appropriate person (Element 11.1)
· Ensure that limited company financial statements comply with relevant accounting standards and domestic legislation and with the organisation's policies, regulations and procedures (Element 11.1)

1 Distinctive features of limited companies

1.1 Differences between a sole trader and a limited company

A limited company is a separate legal entity and is distinct from its owners. This is in contrast to a sole trader who in law is not a separate entity from his business, even though he is treated as such for accounting purposes.

The key advantage of this is the limited liability that an investment in shares offers the shareholder. While a sole trader has unlimited liability for the debts of his business, shareholders have limited liability for the debts of the company in which they hold shares.

1.2 Types of limited company

There are two types of limited company, public and private. A public company must include in its name the letters 'plc' standing for public limited company. Private companies must include Limited or Ltd in their name. The main difference is that a private company may not offer its shares to the public and so all companies listed on the Stock Exchange are public companies.

1.3 Advantages and disadvantages of incorporated status

There are certain advantages and disadvantages associated with trading as a company rather than as a sole trader.

The advantages are as follows:

·   If a company goes into liquidation the owners of the company (the shareholders) are only liable to pay any amounts that they have not yet paid for the shares that they hold. A sole trader would be personally liable for any outstanding debts of the business.

·   The shareholders can share in the profits of the business without necessarily having to work day-to-day for the business.

·   Companies are in a better position when borrowing money; for example they can issue debentures.

·   The company will continue in existence even if shareholders die. If a sole trader dies the business will only continue if the business is sold.

The disadvantages are as follows:

·   A large company must normally have an audit of its accounts and therefore must pay auditors' fees. However an audit also offers benefits to the company.

·   A company must prepare its accounts in a format prescribed by legislation.

·   A company suffers a greater administrative burden than a sole trader. For example, it must file its accounts each year with the Registrar of Companies and must hold an Annual General Meeting of its shareholders.

1.4 Accounting distinctions between a limited company and a sole trader

There are three main differences between the final accounts of a company and those of a sole trader:
·   the way in which profit and tax are dealt with in the income statement
·   the composition of capital in the balance sheet
·   the statutory requirements of the Companies Act 1985.

We will look first at the non-statutory requirements, i.e. the accounts of a company ignoring the statutory formats. The accounts prepared by a company for its own internal use can be in any format that the managers choose. It is only the accounts filed publicly with the Registrar of Companies each year that have to follow the statutory formats. The statutory formats will be considered later in the following chapter.

1.5 Proforma accounts

Proforma income statement for a limited company (for internal use)

	£	£
Revenue		X
Opening inventories	X	
Add: Purchases of goods/transfers from factory	X	
	———	
	X	
Less: Closing inventories	(X)	
	———	
Cost of sales		(X)
		———
Gross profit		X
Sundry income		X
		———
		X
Expenses (classified/listed as appropriate)		(X)
		———
Profit from operations		X
Finance costs		(X)
		———
Profit before taxation		X
Taxation		(X)
		———
Profit after taxation		X

Proforma balance sheet for a limited company (for internal use)

	Cost	Depreciation	
	£	£	£
Non-current assets			
Freehold factory	X	X	X
Machinery	X	X	X
Motor vehicles	X	X	X
	X	X	X
Current assets			
Inventories		X	
Trade receivables	X		
Less: Allowance for doubtful receivables	(X)		
		X	
Prepayments		X	
Cash and cash equivalents		X	
		X	
Current liabilities			
Trade payables	X		
PAYE, NIC and VAT	X		
Corporation tax	X		
Accruals	X		
		(X)	
Net current assets			X
Total assets less current liabilities			X
Non-current liabilities			
Debenture loans			(X)
			X
Equity			
Share capital	X		
Share premium account			X
Other reserves		X	
Retained earnings			X
			X

2 Key differences between a sole trader's accounts and limited company accounts

There are a few differences between the format and content of a sole trader's accounts and the published financial statements of a limited company. The key differences are explained below.

2.1 Capital and accumulated profits

The capital introduced by the shareholders is classified separately in the balance sheet. It is split between nominal value and share premium. The nominal value is defined by law. The premium is any extra money received by the company when the shares were first issued.

Accumulated profits consist of the brought forward accumulated retained profits, plus the net profit for the year, less dividends. The movement on accumulated profits is reported in the statement of changes in equity.

2.2 Dividends

Dividends for limited companies are the equivalent of drawings for a sole trader. Dividends are reported in the statement of changes in equity. Dividends are recognised on a cash basis when they are paid. Dividends declared but not paid at the year end are disclosed in the notes to the financial statements.

2.3 Taxation

Tax does not appear in a sole trader's income statement. However, limited companies pay their own income tax, and this will be charged to the income statement. The tax will not be paid until after the year-end, and so the charge for the year will be a liability at the year-end. The closing liability is an estimate, and any over or under estimate is reversed out through the following year's income statement.

2.4 Cost of sales and other expenses

Cost of sales and other expenses can be reported in two ways.

The most common way is the **function of expenditure** method. This groups together expenses under three headings: cost of sales, distribution costs and administrative expenses.

Some manufacturing industries use the **nature of expenditure** method. This itemises out expenditure according to its nature, e.g. depreciation, staff costs.

2.5 Non-current assets

Non-current assets such as buildings, machinery or vehicles are analysed out in a note to the accounts. Only the total net book value appears in the balance sheet.

2.6 Notes and workings

Notes are printed and published as part of the financial statements. Their contents are normally specified by an accounting standard.

Workings are confidential. They will not be published.

3 Introduction to company accounts

3.1 The content of company accounts

The financial statements of a company comprise the following elements.
· Balance sheet and notes
· Income statement and notes
· Statement of changes in equity
· Cash flow statement and notes
· Accounting policies note
· Comparative figures

3.2 Regulations governing company accounts

The main sources of regulations are the Companies Act 1985 (CA 85) and accounting standards.

IAS 1 (Presentation of Financial Statements) is the main sources for the required formats and disclosures in the published income statement, balance sheet and statement of changes in equity.

Relevant accounting standards include IAS 7 (requirement for cash flow statement) and additional disclosures are specified by other standards.

4 The balance sheet

Company balance sheet as at 31 December 20XX

Non-current assets

	£000
Goodwill	X
Other intangible assets	X
Property, plant and equipment	X
Investments in subsidiaries	X
Investments in associates	X
	X

Current assets

Inventories	X
Trade and other receivables	X
Cash and cash equivalents	X
Total assets	X

Current liabilities

Trade and other payables	X
Tax liabilities	X
Bank overdrafts and loans	X
Net current assets	X

Non-current liabilities

Bank loans	(X)
Long-term provisions	(X)
Total liabilities	X
Net assets	X

Equity

Share capital	X
Share premium account	X
Revaluation reserve	X
Retained earnings	
Total equity	X

As well as the balance sheet figures for this year, comparative figures as at the previous year-end must also be shown in a statutory balance sheet. Any line item with a nil value this year and the previous year need not be shown in the balance sheet.

5   The income statement

Company Income Statement for the year ended 31 December 20XX

	£000
Continuing operations	
Revenue	(X)
Cost of sales	(X)
Gross profit	X
Distribution costs	(X)
Administrative expense	X
Profit from operations	(X)
Finance costs	X
Profit before tax	(X)
Tax	X
Profit for the period from continuing operations	
Discontinued operations	
Loss for the period from discounted operations	(X)
Profit for the period attributable to equity holders	X

6   Notes to the accounts

6.1 Accounting policies

The notes to the accounts must state the accounting policies adopted by the company for all material items in the financial statements, for example, depreciation of property, plant and equipment and valuation of inventories.

6.2 Notes to the balance sheet – non-current assets

Classification of non-current assets

Assets are classified as non-current assets if they are intended for use on a continuing basis in the company's activities.

Non-current assets are subdivided as follows:

Intangible non-current assets	These are assets that have no physical form, such as patents and goodwill.
Tangible assets (property, plant and equipment)	These assets have physical form, such as buildings.

Investments

This relates to long-term investments in other companies. It includes shares and loans made to other companies.

Property, Plant and Equipment

The property, plant and equipment note analyses the total net book value shown in the balance sheet by category, and by cost and cumulative depreciation.

The movements for the year (by category, cost and depreciation) are disclosed as follows:

· Opening balance
· Additions/charges for the year
· Effect of revaluations
· Disposals
· Closing balance

Intangible assets

The notes to the accounts will detail the total in the balance sheet.

	20XX
	£000
Development costs	X
Concessions, patents, licences and trade marks	X
Goodwill	X
	——
	X
	——

An example of a property, plant and equipment note is shown below.

	Land and buildings	Plant and machinery	Fixtures, fittings, tools and equipment	Payments on account and assets in course of construction	Total
	£000	£000	£000	£000	£000
Cost or valuation:					
At 1 January 20XX	X	X	X	X	X
Additions	X	X	X	X	X
Disposals	–	(X)	(X)	–	(X)
	——	——	——	——	——
At 31 December 20XX	X	X	X	X	X
	——	——	——	——	——

	Land and buildings	Plant and machinery	Fixtures, fittings, tools and equipment	Payments on account and assets in course of construction	Total
	£000	£000	£000	£000	£000
Accumulated depreciation:					
At 1 January 20XX	X	X	X	–	X
Provision for year	X	X	X	X	X
Disposals	–	(X)	(X)	–	(X)
At 31 December 20XX	X	X	X	X	X
Net book amount:					
at 31 December 20XX	X	X	X	X	X
at 31 December 20XX	X	X	X	X	X

Non-current asset investments

These are investments that the company intends to keep for more than 12 months from the balance sheet date. They will normally be stated at cost.

6.3 Notes to the balance sheet – current assets

Classification of current assets

Current assets are assets that are expected to be converted into cash within 12 months. For example, inventories will be sold and converted into cash or receivables. Receivables in turn will settle their debts in cash. If it becomes apparent that the amount of cash that will be received will be less than the book value of the asset, then the asset should be written down to its recoverable amount. This is the basis for valuing inventories at the lower of cost and net realisable value, and for making allowances for doubtful receivables.

Inventories

Inventories are stated at the lower of cost and net realisable value. They will be analysed as follows:

	20XX £000
Raw materials and consumables	X
Work in progress	X
Finished goods and goods for resale	X
	X

6.4 Liabilities

Non-current liabilities do not have to be repaid within the next 12 months.

Current liabilities are payable within the next 12 months.

Liabilities include provisions. Provisions are made for liabilities of uncertain timing or amount.

6.5 Notes to the balance sheet – capital and reserves

Called Up Share Capital

	20XX
	£000
Allotted and fully paid:	
Ordinary shares of £1 each	X
Ordinary shares of 50p each	X
	———
	X
	———

Any movement in the share capital of the company should be disclosed. This is done in the statement of changes in equity. The authorised share capital should also be disclosed.

Reserves

The movement in reserves is analysed out in the statement of changes in equity.

6.6 Notes to the income statement

Revenue

The IAS 14 Segment Reporting requires disclosure of the analysis of revenue by class of business and by geographical market.

Operating costs and revenues

Disclose all material items of income and expense e.g.
· Disposals of non-current assets
· Cost associated with discontinued operations etc.

Auditors' remuneration (all remuneration to the auditor, whether for audit or other services) - per CA85

○ EXAMPLE   ○○○○

Profit from operations

Profit is stated after charging the following.

	£000	£000
Loss on sale of property plant and equipment		X
Auditors' remuneration		X
In capacity as auditor	X	
In other capacities	X	
	——	
		X
Exceptional write off of receivable		X

Directors (all CA85 disclosure)

Disclose the aggregate of directors' emoluments*.
·   Include salary, fees, bonuses, benefits in kind.
·   Exclude share options, pensions, long-term incentive schemes.

Disclose gains on exercise of share options (listed companies only)*.

Disclose assets (excluding share options and, for non-listed companies, shares) receivable under long-term incentive schemes*.

Disclose pension contributions paid by the company.

Disclose the number of directors covered by each of two types of pension schemes.
·   Money purchase schemes
·   Defined benefit schemes

For non-listed companies only, disclose the number of directors who:
·   exercised share options
·   received or became entitled to shares under a long-term incentive scheme.

Where the items marked * total more than £200,000 the following additional disclosures are required in relation to the highest paid director.
·   How much of the above amounts are attributable to him
·   If covered by a defined benefit pension scheme, the amount of accrued retirement benefits (excluding money purchase benefits or those from his own voluntary contributions)
·   Whether he exercised share options or received or became entitled to shares under a long-term incentive scheme (non-listed companies only)

Finally, disclose excess retirement benefits paid to directors or past directors, and compensation for loss of office, including payments in connection with breach of contract.

○ **EXAMPLE**   ○ ○ ○ ○

Directors	£000
Emoluments	X
Gains made on exercise of share options	X
Company contributions to money purchase pension schemes	X
Compensation for loss of office	X

All X directors are accruing pension benefits under money purchase schemes.

X directors exercised share options during the year.

The above details include the following amounts in respect of the highest paid director:

	£000
Emoluments	X
Gains on exercise of share options	X
Company contributions to money purchase pension scheme	X

Tax on profit on ordinary activities

There are three elements to the tax charge, all of which are disclosed in the tax note:

	20XX
	£000
Taxation on the profit for the year:	
Income tax	356
Under (over) provision in previous year	12
Deferred tax	18
	———
	386
	———

7   Preparing company accounts

7.1 Introduction

We now show how all of this information is brought together.

○ **EXAMPLE**   ○ ○ ○ ○

The following trial balance at 30 September 20X2 relates to V Ltd, a manufacturing company.

	£000	£000
Revenue		382
Inventories at 1 October 20X1	10	
Purchases	75	
Advertising	15	
Administrative salaries	14	
Manufacturing wages	60	
Interest paid	14	

	£000	£000
Audit fee	7	
Bad debts	10	
Taxation	37	
Grant received		30
Premises (cost)	450	
Plant (cost)	280	
Premises (depreciation)		40
Plant (depreciation)		160
Investments (long-term)	100	
Trade receivables	23	
Bank	169	
Trade payables		7
Deferred taxation		62
Debenture loans at 10%		140
Share capital		100
Retained earnings at 1 October 20X1		343
	1,264	1,264

Further information

(a)   Inventories were worth £13,000 on 30 September 20X2.

(b)   Premises consist of land costing £250,000 and buildings costing £200,000. The buildings have an expected useful life of 50 years.

(c)   Plant includes an item purchased during the year at a cost of £70,000. A government grant of £30,000 was received in respect of this purchase. These were the only transactions involving property, plant and equipment during the year.

Depreciation of plant is to be charged at 10% per annum on a straight-line basis.

(d)   The balance on the corporation tax account comprises the under provision for corporation tax brought forward from the year ended 30 September 20X1.

(e)   The provision for deferred tax is to be reduced by £17,000.

(f)   The directors have estimated that corporation tax of £57,000 will be paid on the profits of the year, based on a tax rate of 30%.

Required:

Prepare an income statement for V Ltd for the year ended 30 September 20X2 and a balance sheet at that date. These should be in a form suitable for presentation to the shareholders in accordance with the requirements of IAS 1 and be accompanied by notes to the accounts so far as is possible from the information given above.

You are not required to prepare the note relating to accounting policies.

Solution

Bear in mind the following points of assessment technique.

Get yourself organised: you will need to prepare a sheet for the profit and loss account and a separate sheet for the balance sheet

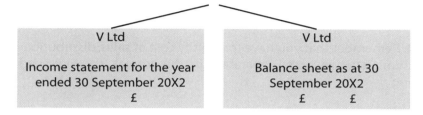

V Ltd	V Ltd
Income statement for the year ended 30 September 20X2	Balance sheet as at 30 September 20X2
£	£ £

You will also need a sheet for notes to the accounts and a sheet for workings.

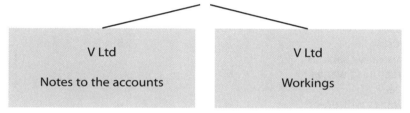

V Ltd	V Ltd
Notes to the accounts	Workings

Note

Some of the numbers you require for this answer will come straight out of the question. Some will require a working which is not a note to the accounts. Finally, some will be calculated as part of a note to the accounts. We will go through the answer line by line and indicate how the amount is calculated.

You must let the statutory format dictate the order of working.

Below we show the answer as it will appear in the statutory format, and the workings and notes will follow.

V Ltd – Income statements for the year ended 30 September 20X2

Notes	£000
Revenue (Step 1)	382
Cost of sales (W1) (Step 2)	161
	———
Gross profit	221
Distribution costs (W1) (Step 2)	(25)
Administrative expenses (W1) (Step 2)	(21)
	———
Profit from operations	175
Finance costs (Step 3)	(14)
	———
Profit on before tax	161
Tax (Step 4)	(77)
	———
Profit for the period from continuing operations	84

Step 1

The revenue figure is taken directly from the question.

Step 2

Cost of sales

This is found by a working.

(**Note:** Remember that you have to identify cost of sales, distribution costs and administrative costs separately in the format, so you need this working.)

(W1)   Cost of sales etc

	Cost of sales	Distribution costs	Administrative expenses
	£000	£000	£000
Opening inventories	10		
Purchases	75		
Advertising		15	
Administrative salaries			14
Manufacturing wages	60		
Audit fee			7
Receivables written-off		10	
Grant (see below)	(3)		
Closing inventories	(13)		
Depreciation – buildings (200/50)	4		
Depreciation – plant (280 x 10%)	28		
	——	——	——
	161	25	21
	——	——	——

Treatment of capital grant

The treatment of the capital grant requires that the grant is treated as a deferred credit and brought into the income statement over the expected useful life of the asset which it was used to buy.

The plant has an expected life of ten years and the grant will therefore be brought into the income statement over ten years. In the current year we transfer £3,000 (£30,000 ÷ 10 = £3,000) to the income statement; the remainder (£27,000) is deferred income.

Step 3

Finance costs come straight from the question.

Step 4

When you get as far as taxation, you can then turn your attention to any required notes to the accounts.   We shall produce the notes in their correct order even though some cannot be produced because of lack of information.

(a) *Note 1* usually deals with accounting policies but we are told not to provide this note in the present question.

(b) *Note 2* (analysis of revenue) cannot be completed as we are given no information.

(c) *Note 3* (operating costs and revenues) There are no material items to disclose however we must disclose the audit fee.

(d) 1 *Profit from operations*

Profit is stated after charging the following:

	£000
Auditors' remuneration	7

(e) There are detailed disclosure requirements on directors but we do not have the relevant information

(f) The next note is Tax.

2 *Tax on profit* (this is the first note we can produce)

	£000
Corporation tax (at 30%) based on profits of the year	57
(Over)/under provision for corporation tax in previous year	37
Transfer to/(from) deferred tax	(17)
	77

·   The corporation tax charge for the year is given in the additional information in the question. This is however only an estimate of the tax for the year – the final figure will be determined by HM Revenue and Customs after the year-end and this figure may be different to this estimated charge of £57,000.

·   We still have a debit balance on the taxation account of £37,000, being an under-provision from last year. This must be included in this year's tax charge.

·   Finally the deferred tax provision is being reduced. As the provision is a credit balance, to reduce it we debit the deferred tax account and credit the income statement with £17,000.

(g) The income statement is now complete.

Step 5

You are now in a position to prepare the balance sheet using exactly the same approach. Allow the format to take you through the question.

As before we will show the answer below in the correct format and indicate where the numbers come from.

V Ltd – Balance sheet as at 30 September 20X2

Note		£000
	Non-current assets	
2	Property, plant and equipment (Step 6)	498
	Investments (Step 7)	100
		598
	Current assets	
	Inventories (Step 7)	13
	Trade and other receivables (Step 7)	23
	Cash and cash equivalents (Step 7)	169
	Total assets	205
		803
	Current liabilities	
	Trade and other payables (Step 8)	34
	Tax liabilities (charge for the year)	57
		91
	Net current assets	114
	Non-current liabilities (Step 9)	
	Debenture loans	140
	Deferred tax	45
		185
	Total liabilities	276
	Net assets	527
	Equity (Step 11)	
	Share capital	100
	Retained earnings	427
		527

Step 6

We will continue the balance sheet notes directly on from the profit and loss notes. Note 4 will therefore be non-current assets — Property, plant and equipment. This note will also form the working for the figure on the balance sheet.

Note 2 Property plant and equipment

	Land and buildings £000	Plant and machinery £000	Total £000
Cost at 1 October 20X1	450	210	660
Additions	-	70	70
Cost at 30 September 20X2	450	280	730
Depreciation at 1 October 20X1	40	160	200
Charge for year	4	28	32
Depreciation at 30 September 20X2	44	188	232
NBV at 1 October 20X1	410	50	460
NBV at 30 September 20X2	406	92	498

This can then be taken to the balance sheet and cross referenced to Note 2.

Step 7

Investments, inventories, trade receivables and cash all come directly from the question.

Step 8 Current liability workings

(1) You will need a working for trade and other payables

Trade payables	7
Cost grant (30 – 3)	27
	34

(2) Working for tax

Corporation tax estimate for year	57

Add this in to the balance sheet and continue to work down.

Step 9

Debenture loans come directly from the question.

Deferred tax (62-17)	45

Step 10

You are now in a position to complete the balance sheet with equity.
(a)   The called up share capital comes directly from the question.
(b)   The retained earnings figure comes from the retained earnings brought forward at 1/10/X1 of 343 and profit for the period of 84 from the income statement.

You should now have completed:
· an income statement
· a balance sheet
· notes to the accounts
· your working paper.

8 Statement of changes in equity

The statement of changes in equity brings together all the gains and losses for the period, including items which do not pass through the income statement.

The most common example of an item which does not pass through the income statement is a gain on the revaluation of a non-current asset. Revaluation gains cannot be taken to the income statement because they are unrealised, but nevertheless, they may form an important part of a company's overall performance. The statement changes in equity highlights the effect of revaluations and other items such as prior period adjustments and helps users of the financial statements to appreciate their impact upon the company's overall financial performance.

Example plc
Statement of changes in equity

	Share capital £000	Share premium £000	Revaluation £000	Other reserves £000	Retained earnings £000	Total £000
At 1 January 20X4	X	X	X	X	X	X
Revaluation			X		X	
Transfer between reserves				X	(X)	–
Profit for the year					X X	
Dividends paid at						
31 December 20X4				–	(X)	(X)
	X	X	X	X	X	X

9 Drafting a full set of company accounts

9.1 Introduction

The example below allows you to apply all your knowledge of company accounting learnt to date, to prepare a full set of accounts for a company (do not prepare an accounting policies note).

○ EXAMPLE   ○○○○

The following is the trial balance of Transit Ltd at 31 March 20X8.

	£	£
Issued share capital (ordinary shares of £1 each)		42,000
Leasehold properties, at cost	75,000	
Motor vans, at cost (used for distribution)	2,500	
Accumulated depreciation on motor vans to		
31 March 20X7		1,000
Administration expenses	7,650	
Distribution expenses	10,000	
Inventories at 31 March 20X7	12,000	
Purchases	138,750	
Revenue		206,500
Directors' remuneration (administrative)	25,000	
Rents receivable		3,600
Investments at cost (short-term)	6,750	

	£	£
Investment income		340
7% Debentures		15,000
Debenture interest	1,050	
Bank interest	162	
Bank overdraft		730
Trade receivables and payables	31,000	23,000
VAT control		1,100
Interim dividend paid	1,260	
Retained earnings, 31 March 20X7		17,852
	———	———
	311,122	311,122
	———	———

You are given the following additional information.

· All the motor vans were purchased on 1 April 20X5. Depreciation has been, and is to be, provided at the rate of 20% per annum on cost from the date of purchase. On 31 March 20X8 one van, which had cost £900, was sold for £550, as part settlement of the price of £800 of a new van, but no entries with regard to these transactions were made in the books. Depreciation is charged on assets in the year of their disposal.

· The estimated corporation tax liability for the year to 31 March 20X8 is £12,700.

· It is proposed to pay a final dividend of 10% for the year to 31 March 20X8.

· Inventories valued at the lower of cost and net realisable value on 31 March 20X8 are £16,700.

Required:

Prepare:
(a) an income statement for the year ended 31 March 20X8
(b) a balance sheet at that date
(c) a statement of changes in equity
(d) all relevant notes.

Solution

Step 1

Get yourself organised. The requirements are an income statement balance sheet and statement of changes in equity for Transit Limited and the relevant notes. Draft proformas for each main statement, leaving plenty of space to slot in detail and any missed headings. You will also probably need a page for notes and a page for workings.

Transit limited
Income statement for the year ended 31 March 20X8

	£	£
Revenue		
Cost of sales		
Gross profit		
Investment income		
Rental income		
Distribution costs		
Administrative expenses		
Finance costs		
Profit before tax		
tax		
Profit for the period from continuing operations		

Balance sheet at 31 March 20X8

	£	£	£
Non-current assets			
Property, Plant and Equipment			
Investments held for sale			
Current assets			
Inventories			
Trade and other receivables			
Total assets			
Current liabilities			
Trade and other payables			
tax liabilities			
Bank overdraft and loans			
Net current assets			
Non-current liabilities			
Debentures			
Total liabilities			
Net assets			
Equity			
Share capital			

Statement of changes in equity for the year ended 31 March 20X8

	Share capital	*Retained earnings*	*Total*
Balance at 31 March 20X7			
Profit for the period			
Dividends			
Balance at 31 March 20X8			

Workings

(W1)   *Expenses*

	Cost of sales £000	Distribution costs £000	Administration expenses £000

Step 2

Read the question to establish the information available.

Step 3

Start with the Income statement and let the proforma guide you through the information you require.

Start with revenue. Slot the figure in the proforma and tick it off on the trial balance.

Cost of sales will come from the expenses working so you will need to enter the cost of sales items from the information into the table.

Transit limited
Income statement for the year ended 31 March 20X8

		£
Revenue	206,500	
Cost of sales (W1)		134,050
		———
Gross profit		72,450
Investment income		340
Rental income	3,600	
Distribution costs (W1)		(10,310)
Administrative expenses (W1)		(32,650)
		———
Profit from operations	33,430	
		———
		33,430
Finance costs	(1,212)	
		———
Profit before tax	32,218	
Tax		12,700
		———
Profit for the period from continuing operations		19,518
		———

Step 4

Repeat the process for the balance sheet.

Balance sheet at 31 March 20X8

		£
Non-current assets		
Property, plant and equipment		76,440
Investments held for re-sale		6,750
		83,190
Current assets		
Inventories	16,700	
Trade and other receivables		31,000
		47,700
Total assets	130,890	
Current liabilities		
Trade and other payables (W5)		(23,250)
Tax liabilities	(13,800)	
Bank overdraft		(730)
		37,780
Net current assets		93,110
Non-current liabilities		
7% Debentures		(15,000)
Net assets		78,110
Capital and reserves		
Ordinary shares of £1 each	42,000	
Retained earnings (see statement of changes in equity)		36,110
		78,110

Step 5

Now complete the statement of changes equity.

Retained earnings

Statement of changes in equity for the year ended 31 March 20X8

	Share capital	Retained earnings	Total
Balance at 31 March 20X7	42,000	17,852	59,852
Profit for the period	-	19,518	19,518
Dividends	-	(1,260)	(1,260)
Balance at 31 March 20X8	42,000	36,110	78,110

Step 6

Now complete the notes.

Notes to the accounts

(1) Profit from operations includes
     profit from sale of property, plant and equipment   190
(2) Corporation tax for the year   12,700
(3) Directors' remuneration   25,000
(4) Property, plant and equipment

	Leasehold properties	Motor vans	Total
Cost at 31 March X7	75,000	2,500	78,400
Additions	-	800	-
Disposals	-	(900)	-
At 31 March X8	75,000	2,400	77,400
Accumulated depreciation at 31 March 20X7	-	1,000	1,000
Charge for year	-	500	500
Disposals	-	(540)	(540)
	-	960	960
NBV at 31 March 20X8	75,000	1,440	76,440
NBV at 31 March 20X9	75,000	1,500	77,400

(5) Dividends
There are dividends proposed of £4,200.

(Note that when a dividend expressed as a percentage the amount of the dividend is the percentage of the nominal value of the share capital i.e. 10% x £42,000.)

Workings

(W1) *Expenses*

	Cost of sales £	Distribution costs £	Administration expenses £
Opening inventories	12,000		
Purchases	138,750		
Closing inventories	(16,700)		
Distribution costs		10,000	
Administration expenses			7,650
Depreciation (W2)		500	
Directors' remuneration			25,000
Profit from sale of van		(190)	
	134,050	10,310	32,650

(W2) *Depreciation*

Motor vans cost	2,500
Disposal at cost	(900)
	1,600
Charge at 20%	320
Depreciation on disposed asset	

	£
(£900 x 20%)	180
Total charge for year	500

Disposal account

	£		£
Motor van cost	900	Accumulated depreciation (£900 x 20%) x 3 years	540
Profit on disposal	190	Cash	550
	1,090		1,090

(W3) *Profit on disposal of fixed assets*

(W4) *Accumulated depreciation*

	£
Balance b/d	1,000
Disposed asset (W3)	(540)
	460
Charge for year (W2)	500
	960

(W5) *Trade payables*

	£
Trade payables	23,000
Balance due on new motor vehicle (£800 – £550)	250
	23,250

▷ ACTIVITY 1   ▷ ▷ ▷ ▷

Oscar plc

The following trial balance has been extracted from the books of account of Oscar plc as at 31 March 20X8.

	£000	£000
Called up share capital (ordinary shares of £1 fully paid)		600
Trade receivables	400	
Prepayments	70	
Bank overdraft		260
Listed non-current asset investments	560	
Plant and machinery		
At cost	750	
Accumulated depreciation (at 1 April 20X7)		145
Retained earnings (at 1 April 20X7)		180
Trade payables		260
Profit for the year (subject to any items appearing in the following notes)		335
	1,780	1,780

Additional information

(1) Inventories at 31 March 20X8 were valued at £150,000 and have been valued consistently at the lower of cost and net realisable value.
(2) Annual depreciation on plant and machinery is to be calculated at the rate of 10% on cost.
(3) The corporation tax charge based on the profit on ordinary activities is estimated to be £74,000.
(4) The company's authorised ordinary share capital consists of 1,000,000 ordinary shares of £1 each.
(5) A final dividend of 50p per share is proposed.
(6) Additions have been made to plant costing £10,000.
(7) The market value of the listed non-current asset investments as at 31 March 20X8 was £580,000. There were no purchases or sales of such investments during the year.

Required:

Insofar as the information permits, prepare the company's published balance sheet at 31 March 20X8. (Relevant notes are required, including a statement of accounting policies.)

[Answer on p. 95]

▷ ACTIVITY 2   ▷ ▷ ▷ ▷

Suzanne plc

Suzanne plc is a quoted company with an authorised share capital of £500,000 consisting of ordinary shares of £1 each. The company prepares its accounts as at 31 March each year and the trial balance extracted on 31 March 20X5 before final adjustments is as follows.

	£000	£000
Ordinary share capital, issued and fully paid		400
Retained earnings on 1 April 20X4		122
6% debenture stock (secured on leasehold factory)		120
Leasehold factory	400	
Accumulated depreciation at 1 April 20X4		152
Plant and machinery	180	
Accumulated depreciation at 1 April 20X4		60
Trade and other payables		340
Trade receivables	200	
Prepayments	160	
Bank	180	
Loss for the year (subject to any items in the following notes)	98	
Sale proceeds of plant		
		24
	_____	_____
	1,218	1,218
	_____	_____

Additional information

1   Plant was acquired in the year costing £20,000. This is included in the trial balance figure for plant and machinery.

2   Annual depreciation has been calculated as follows (but not yet put through the T.B.)
     Leasehold factory   2% on cost   £8,000
     Plant and machinery   20% reducing balance   £18,880
     A full year's charge is to be made on additions in the year with no charge in the year of disposal.

3   Plant was sold in the year. It had originally cost £32,000. Depreciation charged at the date of disposal was £6,400.

4   Inventories at 31 March 20X5 are £320,000 and have been valued at the lower of cost and net realisable value.

5   A final dividend of 20% is proposed.

Required:

Prepare a balance sheet as at 31 March 20X5, in a form suitable for publication. Notes to the accounts (including a statement of accounting policies) are required.

[Answer on p. 97]

▷ ACTIVITY 3 ▷▷▷▷

Readycut Toys plc

The draft accounts of Readycut Toys plc, a toy manufacturer, have been prepared for the year ended 30 September 20X2 and are shown below.

The authorised share capital is 6,000,000 8% preference shares of 50p each and 36,000,000 ordinary shares of 25p each.

Extract from the trial balance for the year ended 30 September 20X2:

	£000	£000
Revenue		318,000
Increase in allowance for bad debts	131	
Auditors' remuneration	93	
Loan interest	405	
Dividends		
– interim preference	120	
– interim ordinary	370	
Corporation tax (over-provision)		20
Directors' emoluments	400	
Administration costs	7,500	
Distribution costs	29,250	
Inventories at 1 October 20X1	9,000	
Purchases	267,662	
Trade payables		2,160
Retained earnings at 1 October 20X1		5,467
Loan		6,000
Preference shares (50p)		3,000
Ordinary shares (25p)		4,500
Plant and machinery	2,580	
Depreciation – plant and machinery		774
Land	2,400	
Buildings	3,900	
Depreciation – buildings		462
Fixtures and fittings	720	
Depreciation – fixtures and fittings		144
Trade receivables	6,315	
Bank	9,681	
	———	———
	340,527	340,527
	———	———

The following information was available at the time the accounts were drafted.

(1) The policy of the company is to provide depreciation at the following rates.

Buildings	2% per annum on cost	£78,000
Plant and machinery	20% per annum on cost	£516,000
Fixtures and fittings	10% per annum on cost	£72000

(2) The loan is unsecured and repayable in the year 20X4. It carries interest at 9% per annum.

(3) The charge for corporation tax for the year is estimated to be £4,360,000. An over-provision of £20,000 had been made in the previous year.

(4) The directors' emoluments of £400,000 comprise the following.

	Salary	Fees
	£	£
Managing director	146,000	10,000
Chairman	120,000	-
Four other directors, each receiving	25,000	6,000

M Leggo, one of the four other directors, was based in Paris and only returned to London for board meetings.

(5) The following dividends are proposed.
Preference shares   Payment of second half year's dividend
Ordinary shares   Payment of a dividend of 24%

(6) The closing inventories are £9,828,000 when valued at the lower of cost and net realisable value.

Required:

Prepare the income statement and the statement of changes in equity for the year ended 30 September 20X2 and the relevant notes for publication.

[Answer on p. 99]

▷ ACTIVITY 4   ▷ ▷ ▷ ▷

KL plc

KL plc is a manufacturing company. On 31 December 20X4 the following trial balance was extracted from the records of the company.

KL plc trial balance at 31 December 20X4	£000	£000
Revenue		7,000
Purchase of raw materials	1,280	
Wages		
Manufacturing	800	
Administration	420	
Distribution	340	
Administrative costs	400	
Selling and advertising	480	
Manufacturing overhead	1,118	
Opening inventories		
Raw materials	370	
Work in progress	410	
Finished goods	640	
Interim dividend	36	
Dividends received		6
Taxation	14	
Factory building		
Cost	1,200	
Accumulated depreciation		464

KAPLAN PUBLISHING

Plant and machinery		
Cost	1,770	
Accumulated depreciation		894
Disposal profit		4
Investments (short-term)	28	
Bank		280
Overdraft interest	34	
UJ Division	350	
Trade receivables	580	
Bad debts	44	
Audit fee	14	
Non-executive directors salaries (£12K each)	36	
Trade payables		340
Accruals		50
Deferred taxation		110
Share capital		600
Share premium		200
Retained earnings		416
	10,364	10,364

Notes

(1)   Inventories at 31 December 20X4 were valued as follows.

	£000
Raw materials	390
Work in progress	255
Finished goods	615

(2)   In the year a machine with a cost of £50,000 and accumulated depreciation of £30,000 was sold for £24,000, giving a profit on disposal of £4,000. All accounting has been correctly processed. The depreciation charge relating to plant and equipment for the year was £354,000 and this has already been accounted for. The opening balance of accumulated depreciation was £570,000.

(3)   On 31 December 20X4 the factory building was valued at £1,500,000 by S and J, a firm of Chartered Surveyors. The directors have decided to bring this valuation into the balance sheet. The depreciation charge relating to property for the year was £24,000 and this has already been accounted for. The opening balance of accumulated depreciation was £440,000.

(4)   The production director's salary of £27,000 is included in manufacturing overhead.

(5)   The sales director's salary of £24,000 is included in selling and advertising.

(6)   The managing director's salary of £32,000 and the chairman's salary of £18,000 are included in administrative costs.

(7)   The balance on the UJ Division account is the cost of liquidating a loss-making division which had manufactured an obsolete product line which was unrelated to the rest of KL plc's business.

(8)   The balance on deferred tax is to be increased by £27,000.

(9) Corporation tax of £920,000 is to be provided in respect of the total taxable profit earned during the year.

(10) The directors have proposed a final dividend of £72,000.

Required:

Prepare an income statement for KL plc for the year ended 31 December 20X4, a balance sheet at that date and a statement of changes in equity. These should be in a form suitable for publication.

The accounting policies note is not required.

[Answer on p. 102]

10 Test your knowledge ▷ ▷ ▷

1 What is the difference between a private company and a public company?

[Answer on p. 105]

11 Summary

In order to prepare limited company financial statements you need:
· a detailed knowledge of the disclosure requirements IAS 1
· the ability to get the knowledge onto paper quickly and neatly.

Therefore, you must learn the requirements and test that knowledge by practising questions.

'Published accounts' is primarily a practical subject, so take the opportunity to learn from financial statements which you come across in practice.

Answers to chapter activities & 'test your knowledge' questions

△ **ACTIVITY 1** △△△△

Oscar Plc

Balance sheet as at 31 March 20X8

	Notes	£000	£000
Non-current assets			
Property, plant and equipment	2		530
Investments	3		560
			1,090
Current assets			
Inventories			150
Trade and other receivables		470	
			620
Total assets			1,710
Current liabilities (Step 6)			260
Trade and other payables			74
Tax			260
Bank overdrafts and loans			594
Net current assets			26
Net assets			1,116
Equity			
Called up share capital	4		600
Retained Earnings (w1)			516
			1,116

Note 1 to the accounts

1   Statement of accounting policies
   (i)   The accounts have been prepared in accordance with applicable accounting standards.
   (ii) Depreciation
        Plant and machinery depreciation is charged at 10% per annum on cost.
   (iii) Inventories
        Inventories have been valued at the lower of cost and net realisable value.

Note 2 to the accounts

2   Plant property and equipment

Cost	Plant and machinery £000	Total £000
Cost at 1 April 20X7	740	740
Additions	10	10
Cost at 31 March 20X8	750	750

Accumulated depreciation		
At 1 April 20X7	145	145
Charge for year (750 x 10%)	75	75
Accumulated depreciation at 31 March 20X8	220	220
Net book value at 1 April 20X7	595	595
Net book value at 31 March 20X8	530	530

Note 3 to the accounts

3   *Investments*

	£000
Listed investments at cost	560
Market value of listed investments	580

Note 4 to the accounts

4   *Called up share capital*

	Authorised	Allotted and fully paid
Ordinary shares of £1 each	1,000,000	600,000

5   There are proposed dividends of ?300,000.

Workings

(W1) *Retained earnings*	£000
Retained earnings as at 1 April 20X7	180
Profit for the year (W2)	336
Retained earnings as at 31 March 20X8	516

(W2)   *Profit for the year*

	£000
As per trial balance	335
Add closing inventories	150
Less: Depreciation charge	(75)
Tax	(74)
Profit for the year	336

△ ACTIVITY 2   △ △ △ △

Suzanne plc

Balance sheet as at 31 March 20X5

	Notes	£	£
Non-current assets			
Plant, property and equipment	2		315,520
Current assets			
Inventories			320,000
Trade and other receivables			360,000
Cash and cash equivalents			180,000
Total assets			860,000
			1,175,520
Current liabilities			
Trade and other payables			340,000
Net current assets		520,000	
Non-current liabilities			
Debentures			(120,000)
Net assets			715,520
Equity			
Called up share capital	3		400,000
Retained earnings			315,520
			715,520

Notes to the accounts

1   *Statement of accounting policies*
    (a)   The accounts have been prepared in accordance with the historical cost convention and applicable accounting standards.

(b) Depreciation is charged at the following rates.
1   Leasehold factory
Depreciation is calculated at 2% per annum on cost.
2   Plant and machinery
Depreciation is calculated on the reducing balance method at 20% per annum. Assets acquired in the year are charged a full year's depreciation.
(c) Inventories have been valued at the lower of cost and net realisable value.

2   *Plant property and equipment*

	Long leasehold property	Plant and machinery	Total
	£	£	£
Cost			
At 1 April 20X4	400,000	160,000	560,000
Additions	-	20,000	20,000
Disposals	-	(32,000)	(32,000)
At 31 March 20X5	400,000	148,000	548,000
Accumulated depreciation			
At 1 April 20X4	152,000	60,000	212,000
Eliminated on disposal	-	(6,400)	(6,400)
Charge for year	8,000	18,880	26,880
At 31 March 20X5	160,000	72,480	232,480
Net book value at 31 March 20X4	248,000	100,000	348,000
Net book value at 31 March 20X5	240,000	75,520	315,520

3   *Called up share capital*

	Authorised	Allotted and fully paid
Ordinary shares of £1 each	£500,000	£400,000

4   *Dividends*

There are dividends proposed of £80,000.

Workings

(W1)   *Retained earnings*

	£
Retained earnings as at 1 April 20X4	122,000
Add: retained profit for the year (W3)	193,520
Retained earnings as at 31 March 20X5	315,520

(W2)   *Disposal of plant*

Disposal account

	£		£
Cost	32,000	Proceeds	24,000
		Depreciation	6,400
		Loss on disposal	1,600
	32,000		32,000

(W3)   *Retained profit for the year*

	£
Per trial balance	(98,000)
Add back closing inventories	320,000
Less depreciation (£8,000 + £18,880)	(26,880)
Loss on sale (W2)	(1,600)
	193,520

△ **ACTIVITY 3**   △ △ △ △

Readycut Toys plc

Income statement for the year ended 30 September 20X2

	Notes	£000
Revenue	1	318,000
Cost of sales (W1)		(267,428)
Gross profit		50,572
Distribution costs (W1)		(29,381)
Administrative expenses (W1)		(8,065)
Profit from operations	2	13,126
Finance costs		(540)
Profit before tax		12,586
Tax	4	(4,340)
Profit for the period from continuing operations		8,246

Statement of changes in equity for the year ended 30 September 20X2

	Share capital £000	Retained earnings £000
Balance as at 31 October 20X1	4,500	5,467
Earnings for the year		8,246
Dividends paid during the year		(490)
Balance as at 31 October 20X2	4,500	13,223

Note 1 to the accounts (this does not produce a number in the profit and loss account, but it is the first statutory note)

1   Accounting policies
   (a)   Depreciation is charged on a straight line basis to write off the cost of each asset over its expected useful life.
         The following rates are used.

Buildings	2% pa
Plant and machinery	20% pa
Fixtures and fittings	10% pa

   (b)   Turnover represents sales for the year.
   (c)   Inventories are valued at the lower of cost and net realisable value.

(W1) *Cost of sales, distribution costs and administrative expenses*

	Direct cost of sales £000	Selling and distribution costs £000	General and admin expenses £000
Allowance for bad debts		131	
Auditors' remuneration			93
Depreciation (W2)			
Buildings	78		
Plant and machinery	516		
Fixtures and fittings			72
Directors' emoluments			400
Admin expenses			7,500
Distribution costs		29,250	
Opening inventories	9,000		
Purchases	267,662		
Closing inventories	(9,828)		
	267,428	29,381	8,065

Note 2 to the accounts

2   Profit from operations is stated after charging the following

	£000
Directors' emoluments	
Fees	34
Other emoluments	366
Auditors' remuneration	93

Note 3 to the accounts (this note does not produce a number for the profit and loss account, but it is a statutory note)

3   *Directors' emoluments*
Highest paid director   £156,000

(*Tutorial note:* This disclosure is required since the aggregate emoluments exceed £200,000.)

Note 4 to the accounts

4 *Taxation*	£000
Estimated tax charge for the year	4,360
Over provision for corporation tax in prior period	(20)
	4,340

Note 5 to the accounts

5   *Dividends proposed*
The following dividends were proposed after the year end:
8% preference shares proposed dividend of £120,000
Ordinary dividend proposed of £1,080,000

△ ACTIVITY 4 △△△△

KL plc

(a)

KL plc
Profit and loss account for the year ended 31 December 20X4

	Note	£000	£000
Revenue			7,000
Cost of sales (W1)			(3,354)
Gross profit			3,646
Investment income			6
Distribution costs (W1)			(864)
Administrative expenses (W1)			(870)
Profit from operations	1		1,918
Finance costs	3		(34)
Profit before tax			1,884
Tax	4		(961)
Profit for the period from continuing operations			923
Discontinued operations:			
Loss for the period from continued operations			(350)
Profit for the financial year			573

KL plc
Balance sheet as at 31 December 20X4

	Note	£000	£000	£000
Non-current assets				
Plant, property, and equipment	5			2,376
Investments held for re-sale				28
				2,404
Current assets				
Inventories			1,260	
Trade and other receivables				580
				1,840
Total assets				4,244

Current liabilities

Trade and other payables	390
Tax liabilities	920
Bank overdrafts and loans	280
	———
	1,590
	———
Net current assets	250
	———

Non-current liabilities

Deferred taxation	137
	———
Total liabilities	1,727
	———
Net assts	2,517
	———

Equity

Called up share capital	600
Share premium account	200
Revaluation reserve	764
Retained earnings	953
	———
	2,517
	———

KL plc
Statement of changes in equity for the year ended 31 December 20X4

	Share capital	Share premium	Revaluation reserve	Retained earnings	Total
	£000	£000	£000	£000	£000
1 January 20X4	600	200	–	416	1,216
Profit for the year	–	–	–	573	573
Dividends	–	–	–	(36)	(36)
Revaluation	–	–	764	–	764
	———	———	———	———	———
31 December 20X4	600	200	764	953	2,517
	———	———	———	———	———

Notes to the accounts

1   *Operating profit*

Profit from operations is stated after accounting for:

	£000	£000
Audit fee		14
Directors' emoluments		
– Fees	36	
– Other emoluments	101	
	——	
		137

2 Loss on discontinued operations
  This loss arose on the sale of the UJ division.

3 Tax

	£000
Corporation tax based on the profit on ordinary activities for the year	920
Under provision in previous year	14
Transfer to deferred taxation	27
	961

4 *Tangible fixed assets*

	Property £000	Plant £000	Total £000
Cost at 1 January 20X4	1,200	1,820	3,020
Revaluation	300	-	300
Disposals	-	(50)	(50)
Cost or valuation at 31 Dec 20X4	1,500	1,770	3,270
Depreciation at 1 January 20X4	440	570	1,010
Revaluation	(464)	-	(464)
Disposals		(30)	(30)
Charge for the year	24	354	378
	-	894	894
Net book value at 31 December 20X4	1,500	876	2,376
Net book value at 1 January 20X4	760	1,250	2,010

The freehold property was revalued at 31 December 20X4 by S and J, Chartered Surveyors. Their valuation amounted to £1,500,000.

5 The directors have proposed a final dividend of £72,000.

Workings

(W1)   *Expenses in income statement*

	Cost of sales £000	Distribution costs £000	Administrative expenses £000
Purchases	1,280		
Wages	800	340	420
Administration costs			400
Selling and advertising		480	
Manufacturing overhead	1,118		

Opening inventories			
Raw materials	370		
Work in progress	410		
Finished goods	640		
Bad debts		44	
Closing inventories			
Raw materials	(390)		
Work in progress	(255)		
Finished goods	(615)		
Profit on disposal	(4)		
Audit fees			14
Directors' fees			36
	——	——	——
	3,354	864	870
	——	——	——

Test your knowledge

1   Public companies can offer their shares to the public.

PREPARING LIMITED COMPANY ACCOUNTS: ADDITIONAL INFORMATION

INTRODUCTION

The previous chapter is the key chapter to concentrate on with regards to company accounts. This chapter provides additional detail with regards to share issues and different types of reserves. Additionally this chapter considers the directors report and abbreviated accounts.

KNOWLEDGE & UNDERSTANDING

· The general legal framework of limited companies and the obligations of Directors in respect of the financial statements (Element 11.1)
· The statutory form of accounting statements and disclosure requirements (Element 11.1)
· The presentation of Corporation Tax in financial statements (Element 11.1)

CONTENTS

1   Company finance
2   Types of share issue
3   Types of reserves
4   Finance costs, tax and dividends
5   The directors' report and other matters
6   Summary financial statements
7   Abbreviated accounts

PERFORMANCE CRITERIA

· Ensure that limited company financial statements comply with relevant accounting standards and domestic legislation and with the organisation's policies, regulations and procedures (Element 11.1)

1 Company finance

1.1 Introduction

The way in which the assets of a company (non-current assets, inventories, receivables and cash) are financed will vary from one company to another. Part of the finance may be provided by the owners or proprietors of the company (referred to as shareholders), while part may be provided by outsiders including suppliers, banks and other lenders of funds.

Companies will also normally be partly financed by their own accumulated profits known as retained earnings.

1.2 The nature and purpose of share capital and reserves

> **□ DEFINITION** □□□□
>
> Share capital represents the capital invested in the company by its share-holders by the purchase of shares.

> **□ DEFINITION** □□□□
>
> Reserves represent the balance of net assets belonging to the shareholders. These may include part of past issues of share capital (known as share pre-mium), retained trading profits and revaluation gains on the revaluation of fixed assets.

The total of share capital and reserves represents the book value of the net assets of the company.

1.3 Distinction between nominal value and market value of share capital

> **□ DEFINITION** □□□□
>
> The nominal value of a share is its face value e.g. £1 ordinary shares or 50p ordinary share.

Each share has a stated nominal (or par) value. This has little practical signifi-cance except as a base line price below which further shares may not general-ly be issued. The nominal value is also used as a means of calculating dividends to shareholders.

> **□ DEFINITION** □□□□
>
> The market value of a share is the price at which that share could be bought or sold.

The market value of a share is not fixed at any particular date. The market value is related to the market value of the business of the company. For example, if a business is worth £100,000 and there are 1,000 £1 shares in issue in the com-pany, the market value of each share is £100 whereas the nominal value is £1. If the company is listed on a stock exchange then a price will be quoted for the shares based upon recent transactions between purchasers and sellers of shares. This is also referred to as the market value of a share, but this may not be the same value that would apply if the entire business was sold and thus all the shares were sold as one transaction.

1.4 Why companies are concerned with the value of their shares

Companies are concerned with the value the stock market places on the shares for two main reasons:

(a) Shareholders will look at a steadily rising price of the shares as evidence of sound management of the company by the directors. It would indicate additional profits being made every year.

(b) If the company wishes to raise further finance through the issue of shares, the current market price will be used as a basis for issuing more shares. The higher the price, the fewer shares will need to be issued and the less dilution there will be of the existing shareholders' effective interest in the company.

It is important to appreciate that the market value of a share quoted on the stock exchange has no direct relationship to the nominal value.

1.5 Share capital

The share capital of a company may be divided into various classes. The company's internal regulations (the articles of association) define the respective rights attached to the various shares e.g. as regards dividend entitlement or voting at company meetings. The various classes of share capital are dealt with below. In practice it is usually only larger companies which have different classes of share capital.

1.6 Ordinary shares

> **□ DEFINITION**　□□□□
>
> Ordinary shares are the normal shares issued by a company. The normal rights of ordinary shareholders are to vote at company meetings and to receive dividends from profits.

Ordinary shares are often referred to as equity shares. A special class of ordinary share is the redeemable ordinary share where the terms of issue specify that it is repayable by the company.

There are various accounting terms to describe share capital: authorised, issued, called up and paid up.

(a) When a company is first established it must prepare a Memorandum of Association which will state the maximum amount of shares which the company is allowed to issue to its shareholders. This is the authorised share capital of the company.

(b)   There is nothing to compel the company to issue to shareholders all of the shares which it is authorised to issue. The number of shares actually issued is known as the issued share capital.

(c)   Once the company has asked its shareholders to pay for the shares it has issued to them, the shares are said to be called up.

(d)   Once those shareholders have paid the company for the shares, the shares are said to be paid up.

1.7 Share premium account

Each share in the UK has a nominal value, e.g. a company might have in issue 1,000 £1 shares. The share premium is the amount for which a share is issued over and above its nominal value. Thus if a share has a nominal value of £1 and it is issued for £1.50, 50p will be the share premium.

The amounts of share premium received by a company must be credited to a share premium account on the balance sheet.

○ EXAMPLE   ○ ○ ○ ○

Enterprise Limited makes an issue of 10,000 £1 ordinary shares for £1.60 each. What are the accounting entries?

Solution

Debit	Cash account £16,000
Credit	Share capital account £10,000
Credit	Share premium account £6,000.

The share capital account is only ever credited with the nominal value of the shares issued. Any excess over this nominal value must be credited to the share premium account.

1.8 Preference shares

□ DEFINITION   □ □ □ □

Preference shares are shares carrying a fixed rate of dividend, the holders of which have a prior claim to any company profits available for distribution.

The rights and advantages of the shares will be specified in the articles of association.

Special categories of preference shares include:

(i)   **Participating preference shares** - where shareholders are entitled to participate together to a specified extent in distributable profits and surpluses on liquidation. Again, the rights of the shareholders are set out in the articles.

(ii) **Redeemable preference shares** - the terms of issue specify that they are repayable by the company.

Redeemable preference shares are more like debt than equity.

1.9 Ordinary and preference shares compared

Aspect	Ordinary shares	Preference shares
Voting power	Carry a vote	Do not carry a vote
Distribution of profits (dividends)	A dividend which may vary from one year to the next after the preference shareholders have received their dividend.	A fixed dividend (fixed percentage of nominal value) in priority to ordinary dividend.
Liquidation of the company	Entitled to surplus assets on liquidation after liabilities and preference shares have been repaid.	Priority of repayment over ordinary shares but not usually entitled to surplus assets on liquidation.

1.10 Debentures or loan stock

☐ DEFINITION ☐☐☐☐

A debenture is a written acknowledgement of a loan to a company, given under the company's seal, which carries a fixed rate of interest.

A debenture may relate to a loan from one person. Debenture stock, on the other hand, rather like shares, may be held by a large number of individuals. The conditions and regulations are set out in a debenture trust deed.

Debentures are not part of a company's share capital - they are third party liabilities. Debenture interest is therefore a charge against profit and must be paid whether or not the company makes a profit.

Debentures are shown as liabilities in the balance sheet, just like any other loan.

1.11 Gearing and risk

Companies with borrowings (such as long-term loans or debentures) or preference shares in their capital structure are said to have 'gearing'. This means that they have raised loans (i.e. borrowed money or raised capital from preference shares) and thereby taken on a degree of financial risk. The risk comes from the fact that even if the company's financial performance deteriorated badly, the company would still have to pay the annual interest charge and the preference dividend each year. If it was unable to pay these amounts, the company could be wound up.

There is less risk associated with ordinary share capital, since there are no penalties directly associated with not paying an ordinary dividend in one year. If a dividend is not paid on the ordinary shares, this simply means that the owners of the business (the ordinary shareholders) have decided not to pay themselves a dividend – this is their choice.

Gearing is looked at in more detail in the later chapter covering the interpretation of financial statements.

2 Types of share issue

2.1 Introduction

Once the initial shares in a company have been issued the company may, at a later date, wish to make further share issues.

2.2 Bonus issues

Sometimes, extra shares may be issued to existing shareholders without any more money having to be paid for them. Such an issue of shares is known as a bonus issue (or capitalisation issue). The extra shares will be issued to existing shareholders in proportion to their present shareholdings. Since no cash changes hands, the exercise is merely a bookkeeping one.

The accounting entries are as follows.
Debit   Reserves
Credit   Ordinary share capital

With the nominal value of the bonus shares issued.

Advantages of a bonus issue are:
· As the market price of a share will fall after a bonus issue it can make the shares more marketable and so promote share purchases.
· Issued share capital is increased giving creditors greater protection.

The disadvantage of a bonus issue is that no cash is raised.

2.3 Rights issues

A rights issue differs from a bonus issue in that the company actually raises cash through an additional issue of shares at a favourable price to the existing shareholders.

Existing shareholders are given the exclusive right to take up a new issue of shares at a specific price. The number of shares that they are entitled to take up will be in proportion to their existing holdings; for example, with a one for five rights issue, a shareholder with one hundred shares has the right to subscribe for twenty new shares. The issue price will normally be below the market price in order to encourage the shareholders to take up their rights and pay the cash to the company.

Advantages of a rights issue are:
· it is the cheapest way for a company to raise new finance using a share issue
· it has a greater guarantee of acceptance than issuing to the public.

The disadvantage of a rights issue is the possibility that the issue may not raise all the capital required if the shareholders choose not to take up their rights.

○ EXAMPLE ○○○○

Z Ltd has 400,000 50p ordinary shares in issue and makes the following issues:

(i) Bonus issue of 100,000 50p ordinary shares.
   The only available reserve is the retained earnings of £460,000.

(ii) A rights issue of 100,000 50p ordinary shares at 80p per share. The issue is fully taken up.

Required:
Show the entries in the relevant ledger accounts.

Solution

Share capital

	£		£	
c/f	300,000	b/f (400,000 x 50p)	200,000	
	300,000	Retained Earnings (100,000 x 50p)	50,000	(W1)
		Bank (100,000 x 50p)	50,000	(W2)
			300,000	
		b/f	300,000	

Retained earnings

	£		£
Share capital (100,000 x 50p)	50,000	b/f	460,000
c/f	410,000		
	460,000		460,000
		b/f	410,000

Bank

	£		£
Share capital	50,000		
Share premium	30,000		

Share premium

	£		£	
c/f	30,000	Bank (100,000 x 30p)	30,000	(W2)
Share premium	30,000		30,000	
		b/f	30,000	

Workings

(W1) Bonus issue: 100,000 shares at £0.50 = £50,000; transferred from the retained earnings

(W2) Rights issue: 100,000 x £0.50 = £50,000 is entered in the share capital account.
   100,000 x £0.30 = £30,000 is entered in the share premium account.

○ EXAMPLE

XYZ plc has 2,000,000 25p ordinary shares in issue and its summarised balance sheet is given below.

	£000
Net assets	2,300
Equity	
Share capital	500
Retained earnings	1,800
	2,300

The company decides to make a rights issue of one for every five held at £1 each.

Required:

Show the balance sheet after the rights issue is complete.

Solution

The rights issue will be 400,000 shares at £1 each and will raise cash of £400,000 which can be split between nominal value and premium as follows.

	£
Nominal value 400,000 x 25p	100,000
Share premium (75p each)	300,000
Cash	400,000

The accounting entries to record the transaction are as follows:

DR Cash   £400,000

    CR Share capital   £100,000

    CR Share premium   £300,000

The new balance sheet will be as follows.

	£000
Net assets (2,300 + 400)	2,700
Equity	
Share capital (500 + 100)	600
Share premium	300
Retained earnings	1,800
	2,700

3 Types of reserves

3.1 Introduction

Having looked at share capital we will now consider the different types of reserves a company might have.

3.2 Reserves

The assets and liabilities are shown on the top half of a balance sheet; the share capital and reserves are shown on the bottom half. For example:

	£000
Net assets	500
Equity	
Share capital	300
Share premium	50
Retained earnings	100
Revaluation reserves	50
	500

Equity comprise:
·   Share capital
·   Retained earnings
·   Capital reserves

3.3 Retained earnings

These comprise the cumulative total of the company's retained profits. In respect of each accounting period the profit attributable to equity holders (at the bottom of the income statement) will be added to retained earnings; the double entry will be as follows.

Debit	Income statement
Credit	Retained earnings

The company may well have more than one revenue reserve depending on the purpose for which the fund is intended, e.g. plant replacement reserve, general reserve etc. However, they all have one feature in common, namely that they represent the retention of an amount of profit by the company, as opposed to the distribution of that amount by way of dividend to its shareholders.

Appropriation of profits in a limited company

This shows the appropriation of profits firstly to shareholders then to specific named reserves and then finally the retained profits which go to the retained earnings.

The heading 'retained earnings' among the reserves on a balance sheet refers to the unappropriated profits balance to date.

3.4 Capital reserves

Some reserves are established in certain circumstances by law, for example:
(a) share premium account
(b) revaluation reserve.

These may also be referred to as statutory reserves.

The balances on these capital or statutory reserves cannot legally be paid out in dividends, as opposed to retained earnings which could legally be paid out in dividends if the directors wished.

4   Finance costs, tax and dividends

4.1 Finance costs

If a company has debentures or preference shares in issue then the company usually must pay interest to the debenture or preference share holder. Effectively the company is paying interest on the money it has borrowed. Usually the rate is fixed when the debenture or share is purchased e.g. 10% debentures. This means the company must pay 10% of the issued debentures as interest. The double entry is

Dr Interest payable (finance costs)
    Cr Trade and other payables (current liabilities)

When the interest is paid

Dr Trade and other payables
    Cr Cash

4.2 Corporation tax

The figure for the corporation tax charge in a company's income statement is a provision for tax based on the profits for the year. It does not represent the tax paid because, as you will see later in your studies, corporation tax is not payable immediately but nine months or more after the year end.

The accounting entries for the corporation tax payable for the year are as follows:

Debit   Income statement
   Credit   Corporation tax account (shown as a current liability in the balance sheet)

In the next year, when the tax is paid, the entry will be as follows:

Debit   Corporation tax account
   Credit   Cash

4.3 Under or over provision for corporation tax

The tax charge for the year is an estimate of the tax charge that is due to be paid next year. If the amount actually paid in the following year is different to the estimate then there will be an under or over provision which remains on the corporation tax account and must be dealt with in the following year.

O EXAMPLE   OOOO

For the year ended 31 December 20X1 the estimated corporation tax charge was £20,000. The actual payment made in 20X2 was only £18,000. Show the accounting entries relevant to this.

Solution

The estimate of corporation tax is recognised in the accounts with the following entry:

		£	£
DR	Corporation tax expense (income statement)	20,000	
CR	Corporation tax liability		20,000

When the cash was paid, the following entry was made:

		£	£
DR	Corporation tax liability	18,000	
CR	Cash		180,000

Corporation tax

	£			£
20X2 Bank	18,000	31 Dec 20X1 P&L		20,000
Bal c/d	2,000			
	20,000			20,000
		Bal b/d		2,000

This was an over provision in 20X1 which will be used to reduce the 20X2 tax charge. The double entry being

		£	£
DR	Corporation tax liability	2,000	
CR	Tax expense - income statement		2,000

The reverse entry would be made for an under provision.

4.4 Dividends

As far as a sole trader is concerned, when they drew money from the business, the double-entry was as follows:

Debit	Drawings account
Credit	Cash

However for a company, where there may be many hundreds of shareholders, it would be far from practical for each one of them to have a drawings account. A system of dividend payments is therefore used. The actual amount of dividend to be paid by a company will be determined by many factors, the main one being the need to retain sufficient profits to provide for the future working capital and fixed assets requirements of the company.

4.5 Interim dividend

Some companies pay an amount on account of the total dividend before the end of the year. This is known as an interim dividend. The bookkeeping entry is as follows:

Debit	Dividend account
Credit	Cash

(The dividend account is a deduction from accumulated profits in the statement of changes in equity.)

4.6 Final dividend

It will only be at the end of the year, when the company's results for the whole accounting period are known, that the directors can declare a final dividend. The dividend is usually declared after the year end and therefore is not a liability at that point in time and so cannot be accounted for until the next period. Any dividends that are proposed but not approved by the year end are disclosed in the financial statements.

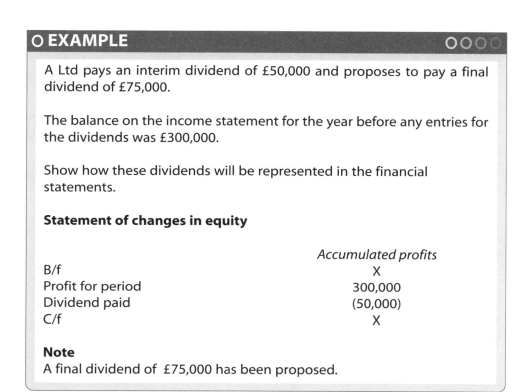

○ **EXAMPLE**   ○○○○

A Ltd pays an interim dividend of £50,000 and proposes to pay a final dividend of £75,000.

The balance on the income statement for the year before any entries for the dividends was £300,000.

Show how these dividends will be represented in the financial statements.

Statement of changes in equity

	Accumulated profits
B/f	X
Profit for period	300,000
Dividend paid	(50,000)
C/f	X

Note
A final dividend of £75,000 has been proposed.

5   The directors' report and other matters

5.1 Introduction

In addition to a balance sheet, income statement and statement of changes in equity, shareholders must also receive a report prepared on behalf of the directors. Although the Companies Act specifies the contents of this report no formal layout is included in the Act.

Remember that in assessments the term financial statements does not include the directors' report. If a directors' report is required the assessor will ask for it specifically.

Directors' Report - Drake Limited

The directors present herewith their report and accounts of Drake Limited for the year ended 31 December 20X4.

Activities and business review of the company

The principal activity of the company is that of manufacturing television and video equipment. Both the level of business and the year end financial position were satisfactory and the directors expect that the level of activity will continue to grow for the foreseeable future.

Events after the balance sheet date

Subsequent to the 31 December 20X4 balance sheet date, the company has purchased a large retail outlet, and intends to sell a substantial proportion of its manufacture to the public direct.

Research and development

Company policy is to invest in product innovation and manufacturing improvement to enable it to retain and enhance its market position. Such research and development expenditure is written off in the year in which it is incurred.

Non-current assets

Details of the company's non-current assets are set out in Notes 12 and 13 to the accounts. The market value of the freehold land and buildings at 31 December 20X4 was estimated by the directors at £150,000.

Directors

The company's directors during the year were as follows:
    M R Worbbs
    F E Gines
    D G Thimms
    G A Tison
    C G Donker (appointed 1 July 20X4)

Their interests, including those of their family in the ordinary shares of the company were as follows:

M R Worbbs	31,000	30,000
F E Gines	30,000	30,000
D G Thimms	20,000	20,000
G A Tison	31,300	30,000
C G Donker	16,500	Nil*

*At date of appointment.

In addition to the above holdings, Mr M R Worbbs was the non-beneficial holder of 1,000 ordinary shares (20X3 1,000 shares). No director held any interest in the company's debenture stock.

Dividends

The directors recommend the payment of a final ordinary dividend of 15p per share for the year ended 31 December 20X4 (20X3 13.25p) which, together with the interim dividend of 5p (20X3 5p) already paid, makes a total of 20p per share. A full preference dividend is recommended.

Transfers to reserves

The directors recommend a transfer to the debenture redemption reserve of £50,000 (20X3 £50,000).

Disabled persons

The policy of the company is to recruit disabled persons on a fair basis, to provide training and career development facilities on the same basis as for other staff, and to make every effort to retain and assist any individuals disabled in the course of their employment.

Political and charitable contributions

During the year, charitable contributions by the company were £4,290 (20X3 £2,550). No political contributions were made.

6 Summary financial statements

The Companies Act 1989 introduced summary financial statements. These may be produced by public limited companies which have a full Stock Exchange Listing as an alternative to publishing full accounts.

This recognises that the vast amount of detail as required by full Companies Act formats and disclosures may not be of relevance or interest to all shareholders.

Public limited companies must always file a full set of accounts with the Registrar of Companies.

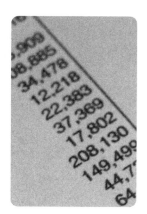

If the company decides to produce summary financial statements, the company must ascertain whether its shareholders wish to receive full or summary financial statements. This will usually be achieved by writing to each shareholder. Once a shareholder's preference has been ascertained, it is up to the shareholders to notify the company of any change in future years. The shareholders will always have the right to demand a full set of accounts.

The contents of the summary financial statements must be derived from the full accounts. No additional information can be included which is not in the full accounts.

The summary financial statements must carry a 'health warning' to advise shareholders not to take investment decisions based on the contents of these statements.

7 Abbreviated accounts

Certain small and medium-sized companies can take advantage of accounting exemptions in section 247 of Companies Act 1985 permitting them to prepare two sets of accounts, normal full accounts for their shareholders and abbreviated accounts which are filed at Companies House. The benefit of preparing abbreviated accounts is that companies can keep details, for example profit margins, secret from their competitors. In 2004, the Department for Trade and industry (DTI) increased the thresholds for small and medium sized companies so that more companies can take advantage of filing simplified accounts.

7.1 Qualifying conditions for abbreviated accounts

· At least two out of the three criteria to be satisfied for the current and immediately preceding financial years.

		Small	Medium
1	Revenue not more than:	£5,600,000	£22,800,000
2	Assets not more than:	£2,800,000	£11,400,000
3	Average number of employees not more than:	50	250

· If the qualifying conditions are met, the company will be entitled to the same status in the following financial year irrespective of whether the criteria are met.
· If the qualifying conditions are met in the company's first financial year, it can file abbreviated accounts in that year.
· Whatever their size there are some companies which can never file abbreviated accounts. These are as follows:
  (i) public companies;
  (ii) banking and insurance companies;
  (iii) companies authorised to carry out investment business;
  (iv) companies in a group which contains a public company, a banking or insurance company, or a company authorised to carry out investment business.

7.2 Exemptions permitted for medium-sized companies

· No requirement to state whether the accounts have been prepared in accordance with applicable accounting standards.

This exemption applies regardless of whether abbreviated accounts are prepared.

- **Income statement**
    - (i) Start with gross profit (i.e. no figures for revenue and cost of sales need to be disclosed).
    - (ii) No analysis of revenue by class of business or geographical destination.

7.3 Exemptions permitted for small-sized companies

- No requirement to state whether the accounts have been prepared in accordance with applicable accounting standards.

  This exemption applies regardless of whether abbreviated accounts are prepared.

- **Income statement**
  Not required.

- **Balance sheet**
  Only the figures for the main headings (non-current assets, current assets, etc).

- **Notes to the accounts**
  Only the following notes are required:
    - (i) accounting policies;
    - (ii) share capital;
    - (iii) trade receivables recoverable after more than one year;
    - (iv) trade payables due after more than five years;
    - (v) secured creditors;
    - (vi) the movements (in total) on intangible assets, property, plant and equipment and non-current asset investments.

- **Directors' report**
  Not required.

7.4 Other exemptions for small companies

Regardless of whether a small company (as previously defined) has chosen to file abbreviated accounts, it may take advantage of certain additional exemptions when preparing full accounts for distribution to shareholders.
These exemptions result in a simplified balance sheet format, with some of the more minor items being combined – for example:
- (a) property, plant and equipment have only two sub-categories
- (b) all categories of inventory are combined, with the exception of payments made on account;
- (c) the separate headings under current liabilities are reduced.

The income statement remains the same.

There is also a considerable reduction in the number of notes required, e.g. particulars of staff, emoluments of directors, taxation notes are all not required.

8   Test your knowledge

1   What are the accounting entries for an issue of shares at their nominal value?

2   What are the accounting entries for an issue of 1,000 ordinary £1 shares for £3 each?

3   What are the accounting entries for a rights issue that involves issuing 10,000 new £1 ordinary shares raising a total of £18,000?

4   Does the directors' report have to name all directors who held office at any time during the year?

5   A company has turnover of £6m, total assets of £2m and 20 employees. Is it a small company?

[Answers on p. 125]

9   Summary

You need to understand how to calculate finance costs, debenture interest and dividends in order to make adjustments to company account questions.

You need to have a basic understanding of shares and debentures.

Although in your syllabus the Directors' report and abbreviated accounts etc is not mainstream knowledge. You must concentrate on preparing financial statements as seen in Chapter 4.

Answers to 'test your knowledge' questions

Test your knowledge

1 Debit cash, Credit share capital.

2 Debit cash   £3,000

    Credit share capital   £1,000
    Credit share premium   £2,000

3 Debit cash   £18,000
    Credit share capital   £10,000
    Credit share premium   £8,000

4 Yes.

5 Yes. It satisfies the criteria for assets and employees.

CASH FLOW STATEMENTS

INTRODUCTION

A typical task in the second section of a Central Assessment might be to draft a cash flow statement from information provided in the balance sheets, income statement and additional information.

CONTENTS

1 IAS 7 *Cash Flow Statements*
2 The elements of a cash flow statement
3 Preparing a cash flow statement
4 More complex areas
5 Interpretation of a cash flow

PERFORMANCE CRITERIA

· Prepare and interpret a limited company cash flow statement (Element 11.1)

1 IAS 7 *Cash Flow Statements*

1.1 The need for a cash flow statement

IAS 7 requires all financial statements (except those of small companies as defined in the CA 85) to include a cash flow statement, showing the generation of cash and cash equivalents and the uses of cash and cash equivalents in the period.

One reason why a cash flow statement is considered necessary is that final profit figures are relatively easy to manipulate. There are many items in an income statement involving judgement, including:
· Valuation of inventories
· Depreciation policy
· Allowance for doubtful debts

This makes it difficult to interpret a company's results with confidence. An IAS 7 statement showing merely inflows and outflows of cash and cash equivalents is easier to understand and more difficult to manipulate.

Cash flows, including net present value calculations, have always been a popular management accounting tool and the requirement to produce a cash flow statement as part of the financial statements helps to form a basis for any future decision making process.

1.2 The IAS 7 proforma

The standard headings shown in the IAS 7 cash flow statement are as follows.
· Cash flows from operating activities
· Cash flows from investing activities
· Cash flows from financing activities
· Net increase/decrease in cash and cash equivalents
· Cash and cash equivalents at beginning of period
· Cash and cash equivalents at end of the period

The key to producing an accurate cash flow statement in the examination is to know which cash flows go under which heading. Below is a typical IAS 7 statement showing many of the cash flows one would normally expect to see.

Proforma cash flow statement for the year ended 31 December 20X6

Cash flows from operating activities	£000	£000
Profit before tax	X	
Adjustments for:		
Depreciation charges	X	
Investment income	X	
Interest expense	X	
	X	

Increase in trade and other receivables	(X)	
Decrease in inventories	X	
Decrease in trade payables	(X)	
Cash generated from operations	X	
Interest paid	(X)	
Tax paid	(X)	
Net cash from operating activities		X
Cash flows from investing activities		
Purchase of property plant and equipment	(X)	
Proceeds from sale of equipment	X	
Interest received	X	
Dividends received	X	
Net cash used in investing activities		(X)
Cash flows from financing activities		
Proceeds from issue of shares	X	
Proceeds from long-term borrowing	X	
Dividends paid	(X)	
Net cash used in financing activities		(X)
Net increase in cash and cash equivalents		X
Cash and cash equivalents at beginning of period		X
Cash and cash equivalents at end of period		X

The composition of cash and cash equivalents is analysed in a note. A proforma example is set out below.

1.3 Proforma note to the cash flow statement

Cash and cash equivalents

Cash on hand and balances with banks	X
Short term investments	X
Cash and cash equivalents as previously reported	X

2 The elements of a cash flow statement

2.1 Net cash flow from operating activities

This is the first heading of the cash flow statement in the proforma shown above. It can be derived by adjusting the profit before tax figure shown in the income statement. The profit figure is adjusted for any transactions not involving the movement of cash, e.g. depreciation or profit/loss on disposal of fixed assets.

Note the increase/decrease in inventories, trade receivables and trade payables. An increase in inventories involves an outflow of cash and is, hence, a negative figure. Likewise, if the payables balance has reduced then cash has been spent paying our suppliers and hence this is also a cash outflow which is a negative figure. The main problem here is to get the signs right.

Note that any dividends received would be included here whilst dividends paid are disclosed separately, lower down the cash flow statement (although they could in fact be shown here as well).

Interest paid and tax paid also appear here. This is the amount *paid* during the year, not the amount *charged* in the income statement.

2.2 Cash flows from investing activities

This shows the extent to which the business has spent cash investing in the future of the business. An example is the purchase of non-current assets such as plant and machinery which will be used to generate cash and profits in the future.

2.3 Cash flows from financing

This includes any or all of the following elements.
· Proceeds of share issues
· Proceeds on taking out a new loan or debenture
· Payments to redeem a loan or debenture
· Dividends paid

2.4 Increase/decrease in cash and cash equivalents

This is the net amount of the cash flows from operating, investing and financing activities. It reconciles the opening and closing balances for cash and cash equivalents.

3   Preparing a cash flow statement

3.1 Direct and indirect methods

In principle, there are two methods of preparing a cash flow statement. The indirect method and the direct method. You will only need to prepare cash flows using the indirect method.

○ EXAMPLE   ○○○○

The summarised balance sheets of Grasmere Ltd at 31 December 20X4 and 20X5 were as follows. Note that 20X5 is on the right.

	20X4 £	20X5 £
Plant property and equipment, at cost	15,000	16,500
Less depreciation	8,000	10,000
	7,000	6,500
Inventories	20,000	23,500
Trade receivables	10,000	15,000
Cash	5,000	2,000
	42,000	47,000
Share capital	20,000	20,000
Retained earnings	17,000	21,000
Trade payables	5,000	6,000
	42,000	47,000

No fixed assets have been sold during the period under review. Depreciation provided for the year amounted to £2,000. There is no interest paid, dividends paid or taxation paid.

Required:

Prepare a cash flow statement for the year ended 31 December 20X5 using the indirect method.

Solution

IAS 7 questions usually appear in the same format: you are given two balance sheets plus additional information.

We shall work through the question using a step by step approach.

Step 1

The first thing to do is to layout the cash flow statement and calculate the increase/decrease in cash and cash equivalents figure.

Then you now need to go through the rest of the proforma cash flow statement line by line and enter any relevant items from the question. We include the full proforma below to remind you of the sorts of things that you will be looking for in a larger question, and have filled in the only numbers that are relevant to this question.

Cash flows from operating activities	£	£
Profit before tax (21,000-17,000)	4,000	
Adjustments for:		
Depreciation charges (10,000-8,000)	2,000	
Investment income	X	
Interest expense	X	
	6,000	
Increase in trade and other receivables (15,000-10,000)	(5,000)	
Increase in inventories (23,500-20,000)	(3,500)	
Increase in trade payables (6,000-5,000)	1,000	
Cash generated from operations	(1,500)	
Interest paid	(X)	
Tax paid	(X)	
Net cash from operating activities		
		(1,500)
Cash flows from investing activities		
Purchase of property plant and equipment	(1,500)	
Proceeds from sale of equipment	X	
Interest received	X	
Dividends received	X	
Net cash used in investing activities		(1,500)
Cash flows from financing activities		
Proceeds from issue of shares	X	
Proceeds from long-term borrowing	X	
Dividends paid	X	
Net cash used in financing activities		(X)
Net decrease in cash and cash equivalents		(3,000)
Cash and cash equivalents at beginning of period		5,000
Cash and cash equivalents at end of period		2,000

The numbers above are all found by simply subtracting the 20X4 value of an item from the 20X5 value. This gives the increase/decrease in the year.

You should tick the numbers on the balance sheets as you use them to keep track of what you have dealt with.

Remember that an increase in an asset (inventories, trade receivables) means that cash has been reduced. An increase in a liability (trade payables) means that cash has been gained.

O EXAMPLE

The following information relates to X plc. The company's accounting year ends on 30 September. Note that 20X7 is on the right.

Balance sheets	30 September 20X6		30 September 20X7	
	£000	£000	£000	£000
Plant property and equipment (Note 1)		945		1,662
Current assets				
Inventories	1,225		1,488	
Trade receivables	700		787	
Short-term liquid investments	175		262	
Cash at bank	184		186	
		2,284		2,723
Current liabilities				
Bank overdraft	52		105	
Trade and other payables	534		745	
Taxation	280		403	
		(866)		(1,253)
Non-current liabilities				
Long-term loan		(525)		(700)
Net assets		1,838		2,432
Equity				
Called up ordinary share capital		1,225		1,400
Share premium account		-		87
General reserve		525		787
Retained earnings		88		158
		1,838		2,432

Summary income statement for the year ended 30 September 20X7

	£000
Profit on ordinary activities before taxation	735
Corporation tax	(403)
Profit on ordinary activities after taxation	332
Transfer to general reserve	(262)
Retained earnings for the year	70

Note 1   Plant property and equipment

	Freehold premises	Plant and machinery	Freehold premises	Plant and machinery
	20X6		*20X7*	
	£000	£000	£000	£000
At cost	560	455	560	718
Additions during the year	-	263	280	700
	560	718	840	1,418
Less depreciation	35	298	53	543
Net book value	525	420	787	875

Required:

Prepare a cash flow statement and the related Note for X plc for the year ended 30 September 20X7, conforming to the requirements of IAS 7, in so far as this is possible from the information given.

Solution

Step 1

As before we start by producing the cash flow statement and calculating the increase in cash and cash equivalents.

Start to work down the proforma cash flow statement. We produce the whole answer below and then give the steps needed to reach that answer.

Cash flows from operating activities	£000	£000
Profit before tax	735	
Adjustments for:		
Depreciation charges (W1)	263	
Investment income	X	
Interest expense	X	
	998	
Increase in trade and other receivables (787 – 700)	(87)	
Increase in inventories (1,488 – 1,225)	(263)	
Increase in trade payables (745 – 534)	211	
Cash generated from operations	859	
Interest paid	(X)	
Tax paid (W2)	(280)	
Net cash from operating activities		579

Cash flows from investing activities

Purchase of property plant and equipment (W2)	(980)	
Proceeds from sale of equipment	X	
Interest received	X	
Dividends received	X	

Net cash used in investing activities

		(980)

Cash flows from financing activities

Proceeds from issue of shares (W2)	262	
Proceeds from long-term borrowing (W2)	175	
Dividends paid	X	

Net cash used in financing activities

		437
Net increase in cash and cash equivalents		36
Cash and cash equivalents at beginning of period		307
Cash and cash equivalents at end of period		343

Note 1

(1)

Cash and cash equivalents	X7	X6
Cash on hand and balances with banks	81	132
Short-term investments	262	175
Cash and cash equivalents as previously reported	343	307

(W1) Depreciation

You have to go to the note to the balance sheet to calculate the depreciation charge as we are not given a detailed income statement. You need to calculate the difference between the accumulated depreciation at the end of the current year and at the end of the previous year. Be careful to find the right line and pick up the right figures.

Freehold premises (53 – 95)	18
Plant and machinery (543 – 298)	245
	263

(W2) The other figures are calculated by simply comparing the two balance sheets and calculating the increase or decrease in the relevant items.

The main thing to be careful of is whether the result is an increase or decrease in cash. Remember that if an asset (say inventories) increases in the second year compared to the first year, this means that extra cash has been spent, i.e. a decrease in cash. If a liability (say trade payables) increases, this means that cash has been conserved so that cash has increased.

Note Remember to tick the numbers you have used in the question.

Taxation

The 20X7 corporation tax (£403,000 in the summary profit and loss account) has not been paid and is a creditor in the balance sheet.

The 20X6 corporation tax (£280,000) has been paid and that is the cash that is entered in the cash flow statement.

Payments to acquire plant property and equipment

You have to go to Note 1 in the balance sheet to find the information for this. In the line 'additions during the year' the amounts are given (280 + 700) = 980.

Issue of ordinary share capital

The ordinary share capital has increased, as has the share premium account. Clearly shares have been issued at a premium. The total amount issued = £(1,400,000 + 87,000 − 1,225,000) = £262,000.

Loans

Long-term loans have increased. New loans raised = £(700,000 − 525,000) = £175,000.

Increase in cash and cash equivalents

We can use the note required to produce this. Short-term investments plus cash less overdrafts. (262+186-105)-(175+184-52)

4 More complex areas

4.1 Introduction

In many cases the figures for the cash flow statement can be found simply by comparing the opening and closing balance sheets. However in other instances a slightly more involved approach is required.

4.2 Interest paid

Care must be taken as the interest charge in the profit and loss account may not always be the amount of cash paid in interest. If there are accruals for interest payable in the balance sheet then a T account working will be required in order to determine the interest paid.

○ **EXAMPLE** ○ ○ ○ ○

The interest charge in a company's income statement is £300. The balance sheet shows the following figures under current liabilities.

	Opening balance sheet	Closing balance sheet
	£	£
Interest payable	120	150

What is the amount of interest paid in the year?

Solution

Open up a T account putting in the opening and closing balance sheet figures and the profit and loss account charge for interest. The balancing figure is the cash paid for interest in the year.

Interest payable

£	£		£
Cash paid (bal fig)	270	Opening balance	120
Closing balance	150	Income statement	300
	___		___
	420		420

The amount to appear in the cash flow statement for interest paid is therefore £270.

4.3 Tax paid

A similar method is used in order to determine the amount of tax paid during a year.

A T account is opened for tax. The opening and closing creditors for tax and are entered together with the relevant income statement figures and the amount of cash paid is the balancing figure. If you see a deferred tax balance in the balance sheet then the opening and closing balance must also be included in your T account working. Usually, this is a liability so is shown in the same way as the corporation tax creditor.

○ **EXAMPLE** ○ ○ ○ ○

Given below are extracts from the income statement and balance sheets for a business.

Profit and loss account

	£000
Profit before tax	1,300
Tax	400
	___
Profit after tax	900

	Opening balance sheet £000	Closing balance sheet £000
Current liabilities		
Corporation tax	360	400

What figures should appear in the cash flow statement for tax paid?

Solution

Corporation tax

	£000		£000
Cash paid (bal fig)	360	Opening balance	360
Closing balance	400	Charge for year	400
	760		760

4.4 Non-current assets and depreciation

Further calculation problems can arise when trying to find the relevant figures for non-current assets and depreciation.

The depreciation charge for the year is required in order to add back to operating profit. Any additions to fixed assets are also cash outflows and they may also have to be calculated.

Again the technique is to use a T account for fixed assets at cost and for accumulated depreciation and to enter into these accounts all of the relevant figures from the question.

○ EXAMPLE   ○ ○ ○ ○

Given below are extracts from the opening and closing balance sheets for a company.

	Opening balance sheet £000	Closing balance sheet £000
Non-current assets at cost	1,000	1,100
Accumulated depreciation	400	480
Net book value	600	620

You are also told that an asset which had cost £150,000 and on which £90,000 of accumulated depreciation had been charged was sold during the year for £50,000.

What are the figures for depreciation, profit or loss on disposal and additions to fixed assets for the cash flow statement?

Solution

Open up a T account for non-current assets at cost. Enter the opening and closing balances and the cost of the asset disposed of. The additions will then be the balancing figure.

Fixed assets at cost

	£000		£000
Opening balance	1,000	Disposals	150
Cash paid (bal fig)	250	Closing balance	1,100
	1,250		1,250

Now to find the depreciation charge for the year by using the same technique with an accumulated depreciation T account.

Accumulated depreciation

	£000		£000
Disposals	90	Opening balance	400
Closing balance	480	Income statement (bal fig)	170
	570		570

Therefore the depreciation charge for the year is £170,000 to be added back to operating profit.

Finally any profit or loss on disposal can be found using a disposal account.

Disposal account

	£000		£000
Non-current assets at cost	150	Accumulated depreciation	90
		Cash proceeds	50
		Loss on disposal (bal fig)	10
	150		150

4.5 Fixed assets at net book value

In some tasks you are only given the net book value of the non-current assets rather than separate cost and accumulated depreciation information. In such questions you may need to find either the depreciation charge for the year or the additions. Again this is done by drawing up a T account showing all of the non-current asset entries as follows:

Non-current assets at NBV

	£		£
Opening NBV	X	Disposals @ NBV	X
Additions	X	Depreciation charge	X
		Closing NBV	X
	X		X

○ **EXAMPLE**   ○ ○ ○ ○

Given below is an extract from the opening and closing balance sheets of a company.

	Opening balance sheet £000	Closing balance sheet £000
Non-current assets at net book value	3,000	3,200

During the year assets with a net book value of £100,000 were sold and assets costing £650,000 were purchased. What is the depreciation charge for the year?

Solution

Non-current assets at NBV

	£000		£000
Opening NBV	3,000	Disposals @ NBV	100
Additions	650	Depreciation charge (bal fig)	350
		Closing NBV	3,200
	3,650		3,650

4.6 Provisions

In some tasks you might find a provision in the balance sheet. Any increase or decrease in a provision is not a cash flow and therefore the increase or decrease should be dealt with by adjusting the operating profit.

An increase in provision will be added back to profit and a decrease will be deducted.

5 Interpretation of a cash flow

5.1 Introduction

A common exam question is to be asked to prepare a cash flow statement and then have to comment on what it tells us about a company's performance. This is relatively straightforward to do and is a way the Examiner can be sure that candidates understand what the cash flow shows.

The best approach to take when interpreting a cash flow is to work through each of the headings in the cash flow in turn. You need to look for large changes in the balances compared to the previous year or any figure that seems to stand out.

5.2 Net cash from operating activities

Operating cash flow is very important to a business as this reflects how well it is generating cash from its day to day activities. A negative operating cash flow is not good and would suggest that the business is not operating efficiently. This would lead you to look at the cash flow from working capital – inventories, receivables and payables.

Also, compare the operating cash flow to the profit from operations to establish the quality of profits. The higher the cash from operations in relation to profit from operations, the better quality of profits as most of it is being converted into cash. This can be expressed as a ratio as follows:

Quality of profit = $\dfrac{\text{Operating cash flow}}{\text{Profit from operations}}$

5.3 Working capital

Another easy comment to make is the effect of working capital on the company's cash position. If a company has moved from being cash positive in the previous period to cash negative in the current period then look at the movements on working capital.

For example, you may see that inventories have risen as the company has increased inventory levels, thus spending cash. It may be that receivables have increased which suggests potential inefficiency in credit control procedures. If trade payables have increased then this suggests that the company has not paid its suppliers which is good for cash flow but potentially harmful for supplier relations.

5.4 Purchase of non-current assets

This section of the cash flow deals with the company's investments for the long term. A huge cash outflow now may bring benefits in the future.

If a company has made an investment in non current assets, then they are obviously planning for the future which is a positive move. You must also comment on how they have financed this investment. If they are cash rich they may manage to purchase the assets out of cash. Watch out for an increasing overdraft as this is an expensive form of finance and should not be used in the long term.

Other methods of financing the purchase could be an issue of share capital which is a cheap method of raising finance and encourages new investors into the business. Alternatively, the business may take out a loan. This is a common method of financing assets, but the business will now need to pay the interest on the loan.

5.5 Sale of non-current assets

A company may sell non-current assets because they are old or obsolete. Often the cash flow will show the sale of assets and the purchase of new assets as the business is updating its facilities.

However, if the company's cash flow is looking severely depleted, the sale of non current assets may be a desperate measure to raise cash. Whilst this will get cash into the business it is not a good idea in the long term as the business will not have the assets to continue operating.

5.6 Financing

In the financing section you can comment on issues of new shares and loan transactions. A share issue is a means of raising finance for expansion of the business. You may be able to relate this to non-current asset purchases in the investing section.

As with the share issue, if you see that there has been increased loan finance, then try and establish why the loan has been taken out. This may point you in the direction of non-current asset purchases or perhaps to fund the expansion of the business. You can also look at the level of interest payable to see the effect of an increase in the income statement.

If debt has decreased then the business may have had surplus cash and decided to reduce interest payments by repaying the debt. This is a strong position to be in.

Dividend payments will also be seen in the financing section of the cash flow. You must ensure that there is sufficient cash available to pay the dividend without the company having to rely on overdrafts. Many companies are not keen on reducing dividend payments to shareholders as it sends a sign that the business is not performing well.

▷ **ACTIVITY 1**   ▷ ▷ ▷ ▷

Fallen plc

Fallen plc has prepared the following draft accounts for the year ended 31 December 20X8.

Income Statement	£000
Revenue	11,019
Cost of sales	(5,502)
Gross profit	5,517
Distribution costs	(402)
Administrative expenses	(882)
Finance costs	(152)
Profit before tax	4,081
Taxation	(1,531)
Profit after tax	2,550

Balance sheets

	31 December	
	20X8	20X7
	£000	£000
Property plant and equipment (net)	11,640	9,480
Short-term investments at cost	2,406	2,208
Inventories	2,880	1,986
Trade receivables	2,586	1,992
Bank	-	576
	———	———
	19,512	16,242
	———	———
Share capital (25p ordinary)	2,280	1,800
Share premium	2,112	1,800
Retained earnings	9,498	6,948
Debentures (10%)	1,240	1,800
Trade and other payables	2,228	1,718
Overdraft	222	-
Taxation	1,932	2,176
	———	———
	19,512	16,242
	———	———

The following data is relevant.

1   The 10% debentures redeemed during the year were redeemed at par.
2   Plant and equipment with a written down value of £276,000 was sold for £168,000 giving a loss on disposal of £108,000. New plant was purchased for £2,500,000.
3   Depreciation charged for the year was £1,364,000
4   Leasehold premises costing £1,300,000 were acquired during the year.

Required:
Prepare the cash flow statement and supporting notes for 20X8 in accordance with IAS 7.

[Answer on p. 146]

△ ACTIVITY 2 △△△△
Oxford Ltd

Oxford Ltd has been trading for five years using a patented recipe for apple sauce. You are given the following information.

	30 June 20X8			30 June 20X7		
	Cost	Depn	NBV	Cost	Depn	NBV
	£	£	£	£	£	£
Property plant and equipment						
Freehold factory	142,000	–	142,000	142,000	–	142,000
Plant and machinery	121,800	(47,500)	74,300	99,000	(48,300)	50,700
Patents	2,000	–	2,000	2,000	–	2,000
	265,800	(47,500)	218,300	243,000	(48,300)	194,700
Current assets						
Inventories		11,100			10,000	
Trade receivables		11,000			7,500	
Short-term investments		13,000			–	
Balance at bank		7,100			2,100	
			42,200			19,600
Total assets			260,500			214,300
Current liabilities						
Trade payables		13,400			12,600	
Taxation		900			700	
			(14,300)			(13,300)
Non-current liabilities *(8% debentures)*			(40,000)			(40,000)
Net assets			206,200			161,000
Equity						
Called up share capital			115,000			100,000
Share premium account			15,000			10,000
Retained earnings			76,200			51,000
			206,200			16,100

Summary income statement for the year ended 30 June 20X8

	£
Revenue	244,400
Cost of sales	(160,900)
Gross profit	83,500
Administrative expenses	(53,800)
Finance costs	(3,200)
Profit before taxation	26,500
Taxation	(1,300)
Profit after taxation	25,200

During the year the company disposed of five apple-bashing machines for a total of £4,200 and replaced them with more modern machinery. The old machines were standing in the books at a cost of £14,000 with accumulated depreciation of £12,600. The profit made on the sale has been credited to the profit and loss account.

All purchases and disposals of plant and machinery were settled in cash during the year.

The short-term investment is a one-month bank deposit.

Required:

Prepare a cash flow statement for the year ended 30 June 20X8.

[Answer on p. 147]

6 Test your knowledge ▷ ▷ ▷

1 What does a cash flow statement show?
2 Do we add or subtract an increase in receivables and inventory to the operating profit?
3 What are the two methods that can be used to prepare a cash flow statement?
4 In 20X1 a company has an overdraft of £50,000, in 20X2 it has cash of £30,000 and short-term investments of £10,000. What is the increase in cash and cash equivalents?

[Answers on p. 148]

7 Summary

A cash flow statement provides information additional to that contained in the income statement and balance sheet. It is an obligatory disclosure for all except small companies.

The content of a cash flow statement is governed by IAS 7.

Answers to chapter activities & 'test your knowledge' questions

△ ACTIVITY 1   △△△△

Fallen plc

Cash flow statement for the year ended 31 December 20X8

	£000	£000
Cash from operating activities		
Profit before tax	4,081	
Adjustments for:		
Depreciation charges	1,364	
Loss on disposal	108	
	———	
Increase in trade and other receivables	(594)	
Increase in inventories	(894)	
Increase in trade payables	510	
	———	
Cash generated from operations	4,575	
Tax paid	(1,775)	
	———	
Net cash from operating activities		2,800
Cash flows from investing activities		
Purchase of property, plant and equipment	(3,800)	
Proceeds from sale of equipment	168	
	———	
Net cash used in investing activities		(3,632)
Cash flows from financing activities		
Proceeds from issue of shares	792	
Redemption of loan	(560)	
	———	
Net cash used in financing activities		232
		———
Net decrease in cash and cash equivalents		(600)
Cash and cash equivalents at beginning of period		2,784
		———
Cash and cash equivalents at end of period		2,184
		———

Taxation

	£000		£000
Cash (balance)	1,775	Balance brought forward	2,176
Carried forward	1,932	Profit and loss account	1,531
	———		———
	3,707		3,707
	———		———

△ ACTIVITY 2   △ △ △ △

Oxford Ltd

Cash flow statement for the year ended 30 June 20X8

	£000	£000
Cash from operating activities		
Profit before tax	26,500	
Adjustments for:		
Depreciation charges (W1)	11,800	
Profit on disposal (W2)	(2,800)	
	———	
Increase in trade and other receivables (£11,000 - £7,500)	(3,500)	
Increase in inventories (£11,100 - £10,000)	(1,100)	
Increase in trade payables (£13,400 - £12,600)	800	
Cash generated from operations	31,700	
	———	
Tax paid (W3)	(1,100)	
Net cash from operating activities		30,600
Cash flows from investing activities		
Purchase of property, plant and equipment (W4)	(36,800)	
Proceeds from sale of equipment	4,200	
	———	
Net cash used in investing activities		(32,600)
Cash flows from financing activities		
Proceeds from issue of shares (W5)	20,000	
	———	
Net cash used in financing activities		20,000
		———
Net decrease in cash and cash equivalents		18,000
Cash and cash equivalents at beginning of period		2,100
		———
Cash and cash equivalents at end of period		20,100
		———

Workings

(1)

Accumulated depreciation

	£		£
Depreciation on disposals	12,600	b/d	48,300
c/d	47,500	Depreciation charge for the year	11,800
	———	(balancing figure)	———
	60,100		60,100
	———		———

(2)

Disposal account

	£		£
Plant and machinery (cost)	14,000	Provision for depreciation	12,600
Profit on disposal (balancing fig)	2,800	Cash proceed	4,200
	———	(balancing figure)	———
	16,800		16,800
	———		———

(3)

Tax liability

	£		£
Tax paid (balancing figure)	1,100	b/d	700
c/d	900	Charge for year (balancing figure)	1,300
	2,000		2,000

(4)

Plant and machinery (cost)

	£		£
Brought forward	99,000	Disposal (cost)	14,000
Additions (balancing figure)	36,800	Carried forward	121,800
	135,800		135,800

(5) *Issue of shares for cash*

	£
Nominal value of shares issued	15,000
Increase in share premium	5,000
Proceeds of share issue	20,000

Test your knowledge △ △ △

1   The cash flow shows the cash inflows and outflows for the accounting period. It totals down to the decrease or increase in cash and cash equivalents. (Therefore it may be a better indicator to use regarding a companies position than profit because profit can be manipulated.)

2   Subtract (e.g. extra cash is used to increase inventories therefore we have less cash).

3   Direct and Indirect.

4   Increase of £90,000.

CONSOLIDATED ACCOUNTS – BALANCE SHEET

INTRODUCTION

For this Unit you may have to draft a consolidated balance sheet using the financial statements of a parent and a subsidiary undertaking.

KNOWLEDGE & UNDERSTANDING

· The general principles of consolidation
  (Element 11.1)

CONTENTS

1 Group accounts
2 The mechanics of consolidation
3 Minority interests
4 Accounting for reserves
5 Fair values
6 Other considerations

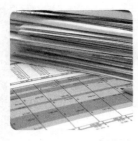

1 Group accounts

1.1 Introduction

Until now, we have only dealt with the accounts of a single company. In this and the following chapters, we cover the major topic of group accounts.

In this chapter, we meet the basic principles of consolidation whilst preparing a consolidated balance sheet. This will provide us with the foundation for studying the area in more detail in later chapters. In studying these chapters, you should always keep in mind these basic principles.

1.2 Groups

A group comprises a parent company and the undertakings (usually companies) under its control, which are called subsidiaries. The full legal definitions of a parent and subsidiaries are dealt with later and are not important at this stage. For now, we shall assume that a parent has control of another company if it holds more than 50% of that company's ordinary shares.

1.3 Group accounts

The Companies Act 1985 requires a parent company to produce group accounts which show a true and fair view of the group to the parent's shareholders. The group accounts provide the parent's shareholders with information about the parent and the investments which it has made. Group accounts are intended for the parent's shareholders and are therefore prepared from the perspective of the parent company.

The parent's own individual balance sheet shows the investment in the subsidiary, usually at cost, and its income statement shows dividend income from the subsidiary in investment income. Where the investing company has a controlling interest in another company, it is not sufficient merely to show the investment in this way as this does not reflect the substance of the relationship between a parent and its subsidiaries.

1.4 Control

As the parent has control, it can decide how a subsidiary's assets are used to generate income in the same way that it can decide how to manage its own resources. Hence, the Companies Act requires group accounts to be in the form of consolidated accounts, which combine the results and net assets of the group members into a single set of figures.

Group accounts comprise the following:

·   a consolidated balance sheet, which is presented in addition to the parent's own balance sheet as an individual company
·   a consolidated income statement, which is usually presented instead of the

parent's own individual income statement, although the parent may choose to publish its own individual income statement as well

· a consolidated cash flow statement and statement of changes in equity (preparation of these for group accounts is beyond the scope of this Unit)

· notes to the accounts, including accounting policies.

The requirement to produce group accounts is subject to exemptions, which are dealt with later.

Note that, although the parent does not need to publish its own income statement as an individual company since it is publishing a consolidated income statement instead, it must still publish its own individual balance sheet, in addition to the consolidated balance sheet.

1.5 Single entity concept

Group accounts consolidate the results and net assets of the individual group members to present the group to the parent's shareholders as a single economic entity.

This contrasts with the legal form that each company is a separate legal person. This is called the single entity concept and is an example of reflecting economic substance in financial statements rather than strict legal form.

Single entity concept

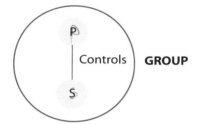

The group is viewed as a single entity.

To present the group as a single entity, the net assets and results of subsidiaries are added to those of the parent line by line to show the group's financial position and performance.

2   The mechanics of consolidation

2.1 Introduction

A standard group accounting assessment task will present you with the accounts of the parent company and the accounts of the subsidiary and will require you to prepare consolidated accounts.

To tackle tasks of this kind we will use a formal pattern of five workings. These are listed below. In a complex example all five of these workings may be needed, but we will begin with simpler cases.

2.2 Standard workings

We are going to use this formal pattern of workings to illustrate the approach to these questions, starting with basic examples and gradually building in complications.

(W1) **Establish the group structure**

This working enables us to see the structure we are working with. We can be clear about the percentage holding the parent has in the subsidiary and whether there are any minority shareholders.

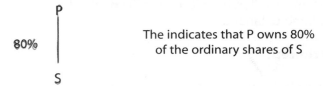

80%

The indicates that P owns 80% of the ordinary shares of S

(W2) **Set out the net assets of S**

We need the net assets for two points in time. Firstly, the date we gained control of the subsidiary which is the date of acquisition so we can establish the net assets we bought into. Secondly, the balance sheet date which is our reporting date.

	At date of acquisition	At the balance sheet (B/S) date
	£	£
Share capital	X	X
Retained earnings	X	X
	X	X

(W3) **Calculate the goodwill on acquisition**

Goodwill is the difference between the price we paid for the subsidiary and the fair value of the net assets we acquired. It represents the premium we paid over and above the value of the assets in the business.

	£
Cost of shares acquired	X
Less share of net assets at acquisition (see W2)	(X)
	X

(W4) **Calculate the minority interest**

The minority interests represent the shareholders that are not part of the group. In this case, P owns 80% of S, so other shareholders own the remaining 20%.

	£
Share of net assets at balance sheet date (see W2)	X

(W5) **Calculate the retained earnings**

We have to calculate the retained earnings for the group. We can only include the group's share of the retained earnings of the subsidiary from the date of acquisition.

	£
P Ltd retained earnings (100%)	X
S Ltd – group share of post-acquisition profits	X
	X

2.3 Buying shares in another company

When one company buys shares in another company the cash paid is recorded as an investment in the acquiring company's balance sheet (DR Investment CR Cash). When the consolidated balance sheet is prepared this investment is substituted by the net assets of the subsidiary which are included in the consolidated balance sheet on a line by line basis.

○ EXAMPLE   ○ ○ ○ ○

Draft balance sheets of Polar and Squirrel on 31 December 20X1 are as follows.

	Polar Ltd	Squirrel Ltd
	£000	£000
Property, plant and equipment	90	80
Investment in Squirrel at cost	110	
Current assets	50	30
	250	110
Current liabilities	(30)	(10)
	220	100
Equity		
Share capital	100	100
Retained earnings	120	-
	220	100

Polar Ltd has just bought 100% of the shares of Squirrel on the balance sheet date.

Required:

Prepare a consolidated balance sheet as at 31 December 20X1.

Solution

Step 1

· Get organised
· Always present the answer first, supported by workings
· Set up two sheets of A4 paper.

| **Polar group** **Consolidated Balance Sheet** £000 £000 | **Polar group** **Working Paper** |

· Start with the workings. Then use your workings to construct the balance sheet.

Step 2

The starting point is to establish the group structure. We are told that Polar owns 100% of Squirrel and therefore (W1) will look like this.

(W1)   *Group structure*

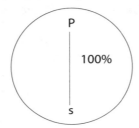

(Tutorial note. P controls S and therefore we need to prepare group accounts.)

Step 3

Our next step is to focus on the net assets of the subsidiary. We calculate net assets by remembering that:

Net assets = Share capital + reserves

Squirrel Ltd has no reserves and so net assets = share capital. The balance sheet date is the same as the date of acquisition.

(W2) will look like this.

Net assets of Squirrel Ltd

	At date of acquisition £000	*At balance sheet date* £000
Share capital	100	100

The reason for preparing (W2) is so that we can go on to calculate the goodwill arising on consolidation. This is a key mark-earning calculation.

Step 4

The difference between the amount P paid to acquire S ('the purchase consideration') and the share of the net assets acquired is the amount P paid for goodwill. This is normally, but not always, a positive figure. In other words, P usually pays an amount greater than the value of the tangible net assets, the excess being the amount paid for the intangible asset 'goodwill'.

We use (W3) to calculate the goodwill.

(W3) Goodwill	£000
Purchase consideration (from P's balance sheet)	110
For 100% of net assets (£100,000) acquired (W2)	(100)
Goodwill	10

The positive goodwill is a further asset which P has paid for. It will appear as a non-current asset in the consolidated balance sheet and will be reviewed for impairment annually per IAS 36 (see later chapter).

Step 5

As Polar owns 100% of Squirrel, there is no minority interest. Squirrel has no retained earnings so there is no need for that working either.

We are now in a position to produce a consolidated balance sheet.

Watch out for the following key points.

· The investment in S at cost will never appear in the consolidated balance sheet.
· The share capital of S will never appear in the consolidated balance sheet.
· The investment in S has been cancelled against the share capital on consolidation and it is only the difference between the two (i.e. goodwill) which appears in the consolidated balance sheet as a non-current asset.

We include 100% of the assets and liabilities of both the parent and subsidiary in a consolidated balance sheet because by definition we control these net assets. They belong to the group and must be disclosed in full in the consolidated balance sheet.

You can now produce an answer which is cross-referenced to the workings.

Polar Group consolidated balance sheet as at 31 December 20X1

	£000	£000
Goodwill (W3)		10
Property, plant and equipment (90 + 80) 100% P + S		170
		———
		180
Current assets (50 + 30) 100% P + S	80	
Current liabilities (30 + 10) 100% P+S	(40)	
	———	
Net current assets		
		40
		———
Net assets		220
		———
Equity		
Share capital (100% P only)		100
Retained earnings (100% P)		120
		———
		220
		———

Workings

(W1)   *Group structure*

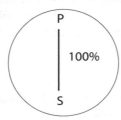

(W2) *Net assets of S*

	At date of acquisition £000	At balance sheet date £000
£1 shares	100	100
	———	———

(W3) *Goodwill*

	£000
Purchase consideration	110
For 100% net assets acquired	(100)
	———
Goodwill	10
	———

▷ ACTIVITY 1   ▷ ▷ ▷ ▷

Puffin (I)

Draft balance sheets of Puffin and Seagull on 31 December 20X1 are as follows.

	Puffin Ltd £000	Seagull Ltd £000
Property, plant and equipment	146	35
Investment in Seagull at cost	90	
Current assets	24	15
	260	50
Current liabilities	(30)	(10)
	230	40
Equity		
Share capital	100	40
Retained earnings	130	–
	230	40

Puffin Ltd has just bought 100% of the shares of Seagull on the balance sheet date.

Required:

Prepare a consolidated balance sheet as at 31 December 20X1.

[Answer on p. 171]

3   Minority interests

3.1 Control

We said earlier that we can 'control' a company without necessarily owning it 100%. In fact any holding of more than 50% of the equity shares is usually sufficient to give control. If we own more than 50%, but less than 100%, of the equity shares of another company we need an additional working: (W4) minority interest. This calculation is necessary to reflect the third-party owner-ship in the net assets of the subsidiary.

○ EXAMPLE   ○ ○ ○ ○

Suppose that Polar's investment in Squirrel represents only 80% of Squirrel's equity, not 100%. All other details remain the same.

Required:

Prepare a consolidated balance sheet as at 31 December 20X1.

Solution

We use exactly the same technique as before, following our standard pattern of workings.

Step 1

(W1)   *Group structure*

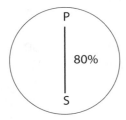

Step 2

(W2) *Net assets of Squirrel*	At date of acquisition	At balance sheet date
	£000	£000
£1 shares	100	100
	———	———

Step 3

(W3) *Goodwill*	£000
Purchase consideration	110
For 80% of net assets (£100,000) acquired	(80)
	———
Goodwill	30
	———

Note that the application of the 80% in (W3) gives us a different goodwill figure.

Step 4

We now move on and calculate the third-party ownership in the net assets of Squirrel. Again, (W2) is a sub-working which will feed into (W4), minority interest. This time however it is the net assets at the balance sheet date which concern us.

(W4) *Minority interest*	£000
20% of net assets at balance sheet date (£100,000) (W2)	20
	———

Tutorial note. If we own 80% of the shares of Squirrel, third parties own the rest (20%). In other words 20% of Squirrel's net assets at the balance sheet date are 'owned' by third parties and this will need to be reflected in the consolidated balance sheet.

Step 5

We are now in a position to prepare a consolidated balance sheet. Note the position of the minority interest figure.

Polar Group consolidated balance sheet as at 31 December 20X1

	£000	£000
Non-current assets		
Goodwill (W3)		30
Property, plant and equipment (90 + 80)		170
		———
		200
Current assets (50 + 30)	80	
Current liabilities (30 + 10)	(40)	
	———	
Net current assets		40
		———
Net assets		240
		———
Equity		
£1 shares (100% P only)		100
Retained profits (100% P)		120
		———
Equity attributable to equity holders of the parent		220
Minority interest (W4)		20

▷ ACTIVITY 2

Puffin (II)

Using Activity 1, facts as before, but now assume that Puffin's investment in Seagull represents only a 90% interest.

Required:

Prepare a consolidated balance sheet as at 31 December 20X1

[Answer on p. 172]

4 Accounting for reserves

4.1 Pre-acquisition reserves

The reserves which exist in a subsidiary company at the date when it is acquired are called its 'pre-acquisition' reserves. These are capitalised at the date of acquisition by including them in the goodwill calculation.

To see what this means, remember that we calculate the value of net assets acquired not by totalling the value of individual assets, but instead (as a short cut) by referring to the other side of the balance sheet (Equity). Thus the value of net assets acquired is the value of share capital acquired plus the value of (pre-acquisition) profits acquired. By comparing this total with the amount of the purchase consideration we arrive at the value of goodwill.

○ **EXAMPLE**   ○ ○ ○ ○

Draft balance sheets of Piper and Swans on 31 December 20X1 are as follows.

	Piper Ltd £000	Swans Ltd £000
Property, plant and equipment	90	100
Investment in Swans at cost	110	
Current assets	50	30
	250	130
Current liabilities	(30)	(10)
	220	120
Equity		
Share capital	100	100
Retained earnings	120	20
	220	120

Piper Ltd had bought 80% of the shares of Swans on 1 January 20X1 when the retained earnings of Swans had stood at £15,000.

Required:

Prepare a consolidated balance sheet as at 31 December 20X1.

Solution

We use our standard workings as before, but when we calculate net assets at the date of acquisition we include share capital and reserves at the date of acquisition.

(W2) will look like this.

Net assets of Swans Ltd	At date of acquisition £000	At balance sheet date £000
£1 shares	100	100
Retained earnings	15	20
	115	120

If we follow our standard workings our answer will be as follows.

Piper Group consolidated balance sheet as at 31 December 20X1

	£000	£000
Non-current assets		
Goodwill (W3)		18
Property, plant and equipment (90 + 100)		190
		208
Current assets (50 + 30)	80	
Current liabilities (30 + 10)	(40)	
Net current assets		40
Net assets		248
Equity		
£1 shares (100% P only)		100
Retained earnings (W5)		124
Equity attributable to holders of the parent		224
Minority interest (W4)		24
Total equity		248

Workings

(W1)   *Group structure*

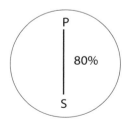

(W2) *Net assets of Swans*	At date of acquisition £000	At balance sheet date £000
Share capital	100	100
Retained earnings	15	20
	115	120

(W3) *Goodwill*	£000
Purchase consideration	110
For 80% of net assets (£115,000) acquired	(92)
Goodwill	18

(W4) *Minority interests*	
20% of net assets at balance sheet date (£120,000)	24

(W5)   *Group retained earnings*

Profits earned by the subsidiary after the date of acquisition are called 'post-acquisition reserves'. We include the group's share of the subsidiaries' post-acquisition reserves in the consolidated balance sheet, which gives us our final standard working (W5): the group retained earnings

	£000
100% Parent	120

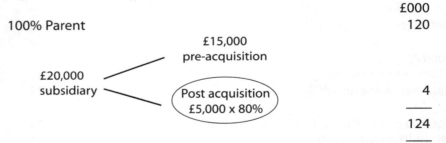

	£000
	4
	124

If the subsidiary has other reserves (e.g. a revaluation reserve, a share premium, a general reserve) we use the same basic calculation for each reserve separately.

▷ ACTIVITY 3   ▷ ▷ ▷ ▷

Pluto

Draft balance sheets of Pluto and Snoopy on 31 December 20X8 are as follows.

	Pluto Ltd £000	Snoopy Ltd £000
Property, plant and equipment	120	150
Investment in Snoopy at cost	140	–
Current assets	40	50
	300	200
Current liabilities	(40)	(30)
	260	170
Equity		
Share capital	100	100
Retained earnings	160	70
	260	170

Pluto purchased 75% of the shares of Snoopy on 1 January 20X7, when the retained earnings of Snoopy stood at £40,000.

Required:

Prepare a consolidated balance sheet as at 31 December 20X8.

[Answer on p. 173]

▷ ACTIVITY 4   ▷ ▷ ▷ ▷

Dublin

The following are the summarised balance sheets of Dublin and Shannon at 31 December 20X9.

	Dublin Ltd £	Shannon Ltd £
Non-current assets		
Property, plant and equipment	100,000	60,000
Investments:		
24,000 shares in Shannon Ltd	50,000	
Current assets	215,000	50,000
	365,000	110,000
Current liabilities	(150,000)	(20,000)
	215,000	90,000

Equity

Called up share capital (£1 ordinary)	190,000	40,000
Retained Earnings	25,000	50,000
	215,000	90,000

Dublin Ltd purchased its shares in Shannon Ltd on 1 January 20X9, when Shannon's retained earnings were £40,000.

Required:

Prepare the consolidated balance sheet as at 31 December 20X9.

[Answer on p. 174]

▷ ACTIVITY 5

Prince plc

On 1.1.20X4 Prince plc acquired 100% of the share capital of Madonna Ltd and Jackson Ltd, paying £60,000 and £40,000 respectively.

The balance sheets of the three companies are as follows at 31.12.X4:

	Prince £	Madonna £	Jackson £
Non-current assets			
Property, plant and equipment	60,000	40,000	32,000
Investments	100,000	–	–
	160,000	40,000	32,000
Current assets	90,000	86,000	52,000
Current liabilities	(50,000)	(41,000)	(40,000)
Net current assets	40,000	45,000	12,000
Total assets less current liabilities	200,000	85,000	44,000
Non-current liabilities	(18,000)	(30,000)	(10,000)
Net assets	182,000	55,000	34,000
Share capital	60,000	50,000	30,000
Retained earnings	122,000	5,000	4,000
	182,000	55,000	34,000

Profit for the year:

	£
Jackson Ltd	3,000
Madonna Ltd	1,000

Required:

Show how the consolidated balance sheet would look at 31 December 20X4.

[Answer on p. 176]

5 Fair values

5.1 Introduction

Goodwill is determined by comparing the value of the business as a whole with the aggregate of the fair values of its identifiable net assets. In our consolidation examples to date we have assumed that the fair value of the subsidiary's assets was equal to their book values. This approach is fine for assessment tasks where you are not given any information about the fair values.

If the fair value of the subsidiary's net assets, at the date of acquisition, is different from their book value, the book amounts should be adjusted to fair value on consolidation. The fair value is the amount the asset could be exchanged or sold in an arms length transaction.

○ **EXAMPLE**   ○ ○ ○ ○

Hardy Ltd acquired 80% of the share capital of Woolf Ltd for £54,000 on 31 December 20X7. The draft balance sheets of the two companies have been drawn up on that date.

	Hardy Ltd £	Woolf Ltd £
Non-current assets		
Property, plant and equipment	75,000	35,000
Investment in Woolf Ltd	54,000	–
Current assets	35,000	39,500
Current liabilities	(42,000)	(16,000)
	————	————
	122,000	58,500
	————	————
Share capital – £1 ordinary shares	60,000	20,000
Retained Earnings	62,000	38,500
	————	————
	122,000	58,500
	————	————

You are given the following additional information:

The fair value of the net assets of Woolf Ltd, on 31 December 20X7, was £66,000. This increase in value over the book value of the assets can be attributed to freehold land.

Required:

Prepare the consolidated balance sheet of Hardy Ltd as at 31 December 20X7.

Solution

Fair value adjustment

Looking at the net assets of Woolf Ltd:

	£
Fair value at 31 December 20X7	66,000
Book value at 31 December 20X7	58,500
Revaluation to fair value	7,500

We must increase the book value of Woolf Ltd's freehold land by ?7,500. The necessary journal entry is:

	£	£
Dr Non-current assets – freehold land	7,500	
Cr Pre acquisition revaluation reserve		7,500

Putting through this adjustment Woolf Ltd's balance sheet becomes:

Woolf Ltd: Balance sheet at 31 December 20X7

	£
Property, plant and equipment at valuation	42,500
Current assets	39,500
Current liabilities	(16,000)
	66,000
Share capital – £1 ordinary shares	20,000
Revaluation reserve	7,500
Retained earnings	38,500
	66,000

The increase in the value of Woolf Ltd's land occurred over time up to the date of takeover. The revaluation reserve is therefore a pre-acquisition reserve and is treated in the same way as pre-acquisition profits. This revaluation reserve will not be included in the group balance sheet.

We will now prepare the consolidated balance sheet.

Hardy Ltd: Consolidated balance sheet at 31 December 20X7

	£
Non-current assets	
Goodwill (W3)	1,200
Property, plant and equipment (75 + 42.5)	117,500
Current assets (35 + 39.5)	74,500
Current liabilities (42 + 16)	(58,000)
Net assets	135,200
Share capital – £1 ordinary shares	60,000
Retained earnings (W5)	62,000

Equity attributable to equity holders of the parent	122,000
Minority interest (W4)	13,200
	————
Total equity	135,200
	————

Consolidation workings

(W1) *Group structure*

Hardy Ltd

80%

Woolf Ltd

(W2) *Net assets of Woolf at 31 December 20X7*

	£
Share capital	20,000
Retained earnings	38,500
	————
	58,500
Fair value adjustment (revaluation reserve)	7,500
	————
Fair value of net assets	66,000
	————

(W3) *Goodwill schedule*

	£
Cost of shares in Woolf	54,000
Net assets acquired (80% x 66,000) (W2)	52,800
	————
	1,200
	————

(W4) *Minority interest schedule*

	£
20% x 66,000 (W2)	13,200
	————

(W5) *Retained earnings schedule*

	£
Hardy Ltd	62,000
	————

(Note that there are no post-acquisition profits for the subsidiary, since the acquisition has only just taken place.)

6   Other considerations

6.1 Other reserves

In many cases, there is only one reserve, retained earnings, in the subsidiary's balance sheet. The pre-acquisition retained earnings are taken to the goodwill computation and the parent's share of the subsidiary's post-acquisition retained earnings are included in the group retained earnings calculation.

A subsidiary may have other reserves in its balance sheet, such as a revaluation reserve. On consolidation, we treat these in exactly the same way as retained earnings. Hence, the reserves at acquisition are taken to the goodwill computation and the parent's share of any post-acquisition reserves is added to the parent's own reserves. However, it is important not to mix up the different categories of reserve. Therefore, if a subsidiary has a post-acquisition revaluation reserve, for example, the parent's share goes in the consolidated balance sheet under 'revaluation reserve' not 'retained earnings'.

6.2 Accounting policies

All balances included in consolidated accounts should be based on the same accounting policies. If a subsidiary uses different accounting policies in preparing its own accounts from those adopted by the group as a whole (e.g. regarding development costs), the subsidiary's accounts should be adjusted prior to consolidation for consistency. We should make any necessary adjustment to the subsidiary's retained earnings in the net assets working prior to calculating goodwill, minority interests and group reserves.

▷ ACTIVITY 6   ▷ ▷ ▷ ▷

Loittede plc (December 2003)

Loittede plc has one subsidiary undertaking Chetou Ltd, which it acquired on 1 October 20X2. The balance sheets of Loittede plc and Chetou Ltd as at 30 September 20X3 are set out below.

Balance sheet as at 30 September 20X3

	Loittede plc		Chetou Ltd	
	£000	£000	£000	£000
Property, plant and equipment		47,407		26,320
Investment in Chetou Ltd		21,000		
Current assets	19,843		8,914	
Current liabilities	(9,624)		(4,034)	
	————		————	
Net current assets		10,219		4,880
Long-term loan		(32,000)		(8,400)
		————		————
		46,626		22,800
		————		————
Equity				
Called up share capital		10,000		4,000
Share premium		4,000		2,000
Retained earnings		32,626		16,800
		————		————
		46,626		22,800
		————		————

You also have the following information.

- The share capital of Chetou Ltd consists of ordinary shares of £1 each. There have been no changes to the balances of share capital and share premium during the year. No dividends were paid by Chetou Ltd during the year.
- Loittede plc acquired 3,000,000 shares in Chetou Ltd on 1 October 20X2 at a cost of £21,000,000.
- At 1 October 20X2 the balance of retained earnings of Chetou Ltd was £14,320,000.
- The fair value Chetou Ltd's property, plant and equipment at 1 October 20X2 was £32,400,000. The book value of these assets at 1 October 20X2 was £28,720,000. The revaluation has not been reflected in the books of Chetou Ltd.

Required:

Prepare the consolidated balance sheet of Loittede plc and its subsidiary undertaking as at 30 September 2003.

[Answer on p. 177]

7 Test your knowledge

1   P Ltd acquires 90% of S Ltd for £100,000 on a date when S Ltd's net assets total £80,000. What is the goodwill arising on consolidation?

2   P Ltd owns 80% of S Ltd. S Ltd's net assets total ?100,000 on the balance sheet date. What figure for minority interests will appear in the consolidated balance sheet?

3   What accounting treatment does IAS 36 require for purchased goodwill?

4   S Ltd has net assets of £60,000 at the date of acquisition. However the Land of S Ltd has been revalued by £30,000. this has not been included on S Ltds balance sheet. What is the fair value of S Ltds net assets?

[Answers on p. 178]

8 Summary

In this chapter, we have met the basic principles of preparing a consolidated balance sheet. Make sure that you understand the concept of the group as a single entity and the distinction between control and ownership.

To reflect the fact that the parent controls the subsidiary and its operating policies, all of the subsidiary's assets and liabilities are consolidated in to the group balance sheet. Even if the parent only holds 60% of the shares, this is enough to give it control and all of the assets and liabilities are consolidated.

To reflect the ownership of the subsidiary in the group balance sheet, in the equity section of the balance sheet the share capital and reserves are effectively split into reserves of the group and the minority interest. The group can only take its share of the post acquisition reserves, whilst the minority interest shows its share of net assets. This reflects the fact that whilst the group controls all of the assets and liabilities it does not own them all.

This last point is summarised in the following proforma:

Consolidated balance sheet

		£
Net assets		X
P + S (100%)		
		—
CONTROL		X
		—
OWNERSHIP:		
Equity:		
Share capital	(P only)	X
Reserves	(P + P% x S post-acq)	X
		—
Owned by P's shareholders		X
Minority interests		X
(MI% x S's net assets consolidated)		
		—
Total equity		X
		—

Key

P	= parent
S	= subsidiary
P%	= parent share of subsidiary
MI%	= Minority interest share of subsidiary

If you remember the single entity concept and use the five standard workings then assessment tasks should be achievable.

Answers to chapter activities & 'test your knowledge' questions

△ **ACTIVITY 1** △ △ △ △

Puffin (I)

Consolidated balance sheet as at 31 December 20X1

	£000
Non-current assets	
Goodwill (W3)	50
Property plant and equipment (146 + 35)	181
Current assets (24 + 15)	39
	270
Current liabilities (30 + 10)	(40)
	230
Equity	
Share capital	100
Retained earnings	130
	230

Workings

(W1)   *Group structure*

(W2)   *Net assets of Seagull Ltd*

	At date of acquisition £000	At balance sheet date £000
Share capital	40	40
Reserves	-	-
	40	40

(W3)

	Goodwill £000
Purchase consideration	90
For 100% of net assets acquired	(40)
Goodwill	50

△ ACTIVITY 2   △ △ △ △

Puffin (II)

Consolidated balance sheet as at 31 December 20X1

	£000
Non-current assets	
Goodwill (W3)	54
Property, plant and equipment (146 + 35)	181
Current assets (24 + 15)	39
	274
Current liabilities (30 + 10)	(40)
	234
Equity	
Share capital	100
Retained earnings	130
Equity attributable to equity holders of the parent	230
Minority interest (W4)	4
Total equity	234

Workings

(W1) *Group structure*

(W2) *Net assets of Seagull Ltd*

	At date of acquisition £000	At balance sheet date £000
Share capital	40	40
Reserves	-	-
	40	40

(W3) *Goodwill*

	£000
Purchase consideration	90
For 90% of net assets acquired [40] (W2)	(36)
Goodwill	54

(W4) *Minority interests*

10% of net assets at balance sheet date [40] (W2)	4

△ ACTIVITY 3   △ △ △ △

Pluto

Consolidated balance sheet as at 31 December 20X8

	£000
Non-current assets	
Goodwill (W3)	35
Property, plant and equipment (120 + 150)	270
Current assets (40 + 50)	90
	395
Current liabilities (40 + 30)	(70)
	325
Equity	
Share capital	100
Retained earnings (W5)	182.5
Equity attributable to equity holders of the parent	282.5
Minority interest (W4)	42.5
Total equity	325

Workings

(W1)   *Group structure*

(W2)   *Net assets - Snoopy Ltd*

	At date of acquisition £000	At balance sheet date £000
Share capital	100	100
Retained earnings	40	70
	140	170

(W3)   *Goodwill*

	£000
Purchase consideration	140
For 75% of net assets acquired (140)	(105)
Goodwill	35

Minority interest

	£000
25% of net assets at balance sheet date (170)	42.5

(W5) *Group retained earnings*

	£000
100% Pluto Ltd	160

£40,000
Pre-acquisition

£70,000
Snoopy

Post acquisition
£30,000 x 75%

	22.5
	182.5

△ ACTIVITY 4   △ △ △ △

Dublin

Consolidated balance sheet as at 31 December 20X9

	£
Non-current assets	
Goodwill (W3)	2,000
Property, plant and equipment (100,000 + 60,000)	160,000
	162,000
Current assets (215,000 + 50,000)	265,000
Current liabilities (150,000 + 20,000)	(170,000)
	257,000
Equity	
Called up share capital	190,000
Retained earnings (W5)	31,000
Equity attributable to equity holders of the parent	221,000
Minority interest (W4)	36,000
Total equity	257,000

Workings

(W1)   *Group structure*

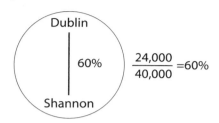

$$\frac{24,000}{40,000} = 60\%$$

(W2)   *Net assets - Shannon*

	At date of acquisition £	At balance sheet date £
Share capital	40,000	40,000
Retained earnings	40,000	50,000
	80,000	90,000

(W3)   *Goodwill*

	£
Purchase consideration	50,000
For 60% net assets acquired (80,000)	(48,000)
Goodwill	2,000

(W4)   *Minority interest*

40% (90,000)	£36,000

(W5)   *Group reserves*

	£
100% Dublin	25,000

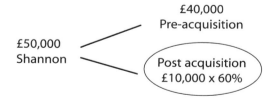

£40,000
Pre-acquisition

£50,000
Shannon

Post acquisition
£10,000 x 60%

	6,000
	31,000

△ ACTIVITY 5   △△△△

Prince plc

Consolidated balance sheet at 31 December 20X4

	£	£
Non-current assets		
Goodwill (W3)		15,000
Property, plant and equipment (60 + 40 + 32)		132,000
		147,000
Current assets (90 + 86 + 52)	228,000	
Current liabilities (50 + 41 + 40)	(131,000)	
Net current assets		97,000
Non-current liabilities (18 + 30 + 10)		(58,000)
Net assets		186,000
Equity		
Called-up share capital		60,000
Retained earnings (W4)		126,000
Equity attributable to holders of the parent		186,000

Workings

(W1)   *Group structure*

(W2)   *Net assets at acquisition*

	Madonna	Jackson
	£	£
Share capital	50,000	30,000
Retained earnings (5 - 1, 4 - 3)	4,000	1,000
	54,000	31,000

(W3)   *Goodwill schedule*

	Madonna	Jackson
	£	£
Cost of investment	60,000	40,000
Net assets acquired (W2)	(54,000)	(31,000)
Goodwill	6,000	9,000

Total at balance sheet date = 6,000+9,000 = 15,000

(W4) *Group retained earnings*

	£
P	122,000
M's post-acquisition profit	1,000
J's post-acquisition profit	3,000
	126,000

△ ACTIVITY 6   △ △ △ △

Loittede plc

Loittede plc
Consolidated balance sheet as at 30 September 20X3

	£000	£000
Non-current assets		
Goodwill (W4)		3,000
Property, plant and equipment		77,407
Current assets	28,757	
Current liabilities	(13,658)	
Net current assets		15,099
Non-current liabilities		
Long-term loan		(40,400)
Net assets		55,106
Equity		
Called up share capital		10,000
Share premium		4,000
Retained earnings		34,486
Earnings attributable to equity holders of the parent		48,486
Minority interest		6,620
Total equity		55,106

Workings

(W1) *Loittede plc holding in Chetou Ltd:*

$$\frac{3,000,000}{4,000,000} = 75\%$$

(W2) Revaluation of assets in Chetou Ltd to fair value at date of acquisition:

Dr	Property, plant and equipment (32,400 - 28,720)	£3,680,000
Cr	Revaluation reserve	£3,680,000

(W3)   *Net assets of Chetou Ltd*

	At balance sheet date	At acquisition date	Post acquisition date
	£000	£000	£000
Share capital	4,000	4,000	-
Share premium	2,000	2,000	-
Revaluation reserve (W2)	3,680	3,680	-
Retained earnings	16,800	14,320	2,480
	26,480	24,000	

(W4)   *Goodwill*

	£000
Cost of shares	21,000
Less fair value of net assets acquired (75% x 24,000)	(18,000)
	3,000

(W5)   *Minority interest*

	£000
25% x 26,480	6,620

(W6)   *Retained earnings - group*

100% of L	32,626
75% x 2,480	1,860
	34,486

Test your knowledge

1   Goodwill = £100,000 - 90% x £80,000 = £28,000.

2   Minority interests = 20% x £100,000 = £20,000.

3   Purchased goodwill should be capitalised as a non-current asset and reviewed for impairment annually.

4   £90,000.

CONSOLIDATED ACCOUNTS – INCOME STATEMENT

INTRODUCTION

For this Unit you may have to draft a consolidated income statement from the financial statements of a parent and a subsidiary undertaking. In this chapter therefore we will build on the consolidation principles from the previous chapter and prepare a consolidated income statement.

KNOWLEDGE & UNDERSTANDING

· The general principles of consolidation (Element 11.1)

CONTENTS

1 Basic principles

1 Basic principles

1.1 Introduction

In this chapter, we switch our attention to the consolidated income statement. This is prepared on the same basis as the consolidated balance sheet and thus most of the key principles will already be familiar. In particular, the single entity concept and the distinction between control and ownership are as important to the consolidated income statement as they are to the consolidated balance sheet.

The parent's own income statement as an individual company will show dividend income from the subsidiary. The consolidated income statement shows the incomes generated from the group's resources. Those resources are shown by the net assets in the consolidated balance sheet.

1.2 Control and ownership

When we prepared the consolidated balance sheet, we added together the net assets of the parent and subsidiary line by line to show the resources under the parent's control. We apply exactly the same principle in preparing the consolidated income statement by adding together the parent's and subsidiary's income and expenses line by line from revenue down to profit after tax. This will give us the profit after tax generated from the resources under the group's control.

In the consolidated balance sheet, we showed the ownership of the group's net assets on the equity side, where we showed the minority interests separately from the equity attributable to the parent's shareholders.

In the consolidated income statement, the parent's and minority's share of the profit after tax is shown in a note beneath the income statement.

1.3 Intra-group items

We need to cancel out any intra-group trading i.e. sales from the parent to the subsidiary and vice versa and also intra group interest e.g. if the parent has loaned the subsidiary money and is charging interest etc. If we are showing the results of the group as a single entity, then we cannot include transactions between the companies. If this were allowed, group companies might make sales between them in order to generate profit which would not give a true and fair view of the results. Therefore, we show the results of transactions which the group as a whole has made to third parties.

The journal to cancel out intra group trading is therefore:
Dr   Revenue   X
    Cr   Cost of sales   X

with the value of inter-company sales.

We shall now see in more detail how to prepare the consolidated income statement.

1.4 Proforma consolidated income statement

Work your way through the pro forma, referring to the tutorial notes which are referenced by letters in brackets.

Consolidated income statement for the year ended....

	£
Revenue (a)	X
Cost of sales (a)	(X)
Gross profit	X
Distribution costs	(X)
Administrative expenses	(X)
Other income(b)(c)	X
Profit from operations	X
Finance costs (b)	(X)
Profit before taxation (Note 1)	X
Income tax	(X)
Profit for the period (d)	X
Attributable to:	
Equity holders of the parent	X
Minority interests (e)	X
	X

Tutorial notes:

(a)   Intra-group sales must be eliminated from both the revenue of the selling company and the cost of sales of the buying company.

(b)   Any intra-group interest must be eliminated from interest receivable and interest payable respectively (single entity concept).

(c)   Similarly, dividends from subsidiaries must be eliminated since the whole of the profits of those subsidiaries are being consolidated and it would be double counting to include the dividends as well.

(d)   Profit after taxation – Up to this point, 100% of all items for the parent company and all subsidiaries have been aggregated (subject to intra-group adjustments). It is now necessary to compute the amount of the profit after taxation that is attributable to outside (minority) shareholders.

(e)   Minority interests – This is calculated by taking the minority interest's share of the subsidiary's profit after taxation.

○ EXAMPLE ○○○○

Set out below are the draft income statements of Smiths plc and its subsidiary company Flowers Ltd for the year ended 31 December 20X7.

On 31 December 20X5 Smiths plc purchased 75,000 ordinary shares and £10,000 10% debentures in Flowers Ltd. At that date the retained earnings of Flowers Ltd were £3,000.

The issued share capital of Flowers Ltd is 100,000 £1 ordinary shares, and it had £30,000 10% debentures outstanding on 31 December 20X7. Flowers Ltd pays its debenture interest on 31 December each year.

	Smiths plc £	Flowers Ltd £
Revenue	600,000	300,000
Cost of sales	(427,000)	(232,000)
Gross profit	173,000	68,000
Distribution costs	(41,000)	(14,000)
Administrative expenses	(52,000)	(31,000)
Income from shares in subsidiary	7,500	–
Income from other fixed asset investments (dividends from UK quoted companies)	3,000	1,000
Other interest receivable – from group companies	1,000	–
Finance costs	–	(3,000)
Profit before taxation (Note)	91,500	21,000
Tax	(38,500)	(8,000)
Profit after taxation	53,000	13,000

The following additional information is relevant:

(1) During the year Smiths plc sold goods to Flowers Ltd for £20,000, making a profit of £5,000. These goods were all sold by Flowers Ltd before the end of the year.

Required:

Prepare for presentation to members the consolidated income statement for the year ended 31 December 20X7.

Solution

Following through the pro forma, we will take the problems one at a time. Where you are uncertain of the treatment, refer back to the earlier tutorial notes.

Step 1

Group structure

Smiths plc

75%

Flowers Ltd

Step 2

Revenue and cost of sales

The total revenue is £900,000 but the intra-group sale of £20,000 has been included as part of Smiths plc's revenue. It must be eliminated, leaving £880,000.

Similarly, total cost of sales is £659,000 but the intra-group purchase of £20,000 has been included in cost of sales for Flowers Ltd. Eliminating it leaves £639,000.

Step 3

Investment income and interest payable

·   **Income from shares in group companies** of £7,500 represents the dividend receivable from the subsidiary (75% x £10,000). It must be excluded from the consolidated income statement.

·   **Interest receivable from group companies** of £1,000 is Smiths plc's share of the debenture interest paid by Flowers Ltd (10% x £10,000). It must be cancelled against the finance cost in Flowers Ltd's income statement to leave the net finance cost to people outside the group of £2,000.

Step 4

Minority interests

The minority interest is 25% of Flowers Ltd's profit after tax figure (i.e. 25% x £13,000 = £3,250).

Step 5

Prepare the consolidated income statement.

Smiths plc
Consolidated income statement for the year ended 31 December 20X7

	£
Revenue (600,000 + 300,000 – 20,000)	880,000
Cost of sales (427,000 + 232,000 – 20,000)	(639,000)
	———
Gross profit	241,000
Distribution costs (41,000 + 14,000)	(55,000)
Administrative expenses (52,000 + 31,000)	(83,000)
Income from other fixed asset investments (3,000 + 1,000)	4,000
Finance costs(3,000 - 1,000)	(2,000)
	———
Profit before taxation	105,000
Tax (38,500 + 8,000)	(46,500)
	———
Profit for the period	58,500
	———
Attributable to:	
Equity holders of the parent	55,250
Minority interests (25% x 13,000)	3,250
	———
	58,500
	———

▷ ACTIVITY 1

Pulp plc

Given below are the draft income statements of Pulp plc and Saxon Ltd for the year ending 31 March 20X2. Pulp plc purchased 60% of the share capital of Saxon Ltd on 1 April 20X0 at which date Saxon Ltd had a balance on its retained earnings of £20,000.

	Pulp plc £000	Saxon Ltd £000
Revenue	650	380
Cost of sales	320	180
	———	———
Gross profit	330	200
Expenses	(190)	(90)
Dividend from Saxon Ltd	24	-
	———	———
Profit before tax	164	110
Tax	(50)	(30)
	———	———
Profit for the period	114	80
	———	———

During the year Pulp plc sold goods costing £80,000 to Saxon Ltd and all of these had been sold outside the group by the end of the year.

You are required to prepare the consolidated income statement for the Pulp plc group for the year ending 31 March 20X2.

[Answer on p. 187]

▷ ACTIVITY 2   ▷ ▷ ▷ ▷

Aswall plc

Income Statement for the year ended 31 March 20X4

	Aswell plc	Unsafey Ltd
	£000	£000
Revenue	32,412	12,963
Cost of sales	(14,592)	(5,576)
Gross profit	17,820	7,387
Distribution costs	(5,449)	(1,307)
Administrative expenses	(3,167)	(841)
Dividends received from Unsafey Ltd	1,500	-
Profit from operations	10,704	5,239
Finance costs	(1,960)	(980)
Profit before taxation	8,744	4,259
Tax	(2,623)	(1,063)
Profit for the year	6,121	3,196

Further information:

· Aswall plc owns 75% of the ordinary share capital of Unsafey Ltd.
· During the year Unsafey Ltd sold goods which had cost £1,200,000 to Aswall plc for £1,860,000. All of these goods had been sold by Aswall plc by the end of the year.
· All operations are continuing operations.

Required:

Draft a consolidated income statement for Aswall plc and its subsidiary undertaking for the year ended 31 March 20X4.

[Answer on p. 187]

2 Test your knowledge ▷ ▷ ▷

1   P Ltd owns 80% of S Ltd. During 20X4, P Ltd reported revenue of £100,000 while S Ltd reported revenue of £50,000. What revenue will be reported in the consolidated income statement?

2   What is the journal entry for the consolidation adjustment to eliminate intra-group sales?

3   P Ltd owns 80% of S Ltd. S Ltd has profit after tax of £60,000. What is the minority interest reported in the consolidated income statement?

[Answers on p. 188]

3   Summary

The key thing to remember is that the consolidated income statement gives the results of the group trading with third parties.

Therefore the following adjustments are necessary:

·   Eliminate any intra-group sales from revenue and cost of sales.
·   Exclude dividends and interest received from the subsidiary.
·   Include minority interest, being the minority interest's share of the subsidiary company's profit after tax.

Answers to chapter activities & 'test your knowledge' questions

△ ACTIVITY 1 △△△△

Pulp plc
Consolidated income statement for the year ending 31 March 20X2

	£000
Revenue (650 + 380 - 80)	950
Cost of sales (320 + 180 - 80)	420
Gross profit	530
Expenses (190 + 90)	280
Profit before tax	250
Tax (50 + 30)	80
Profit for the period	170
Attributable to:	
Equity holders of the parent	138
Minority interest (40% x 80)	32
	170

△ ACTIVITY 2 △△△△

Aswall plc

Aswall plc
Consolidated income statement for the year ended 31 March 20X4

	£000
Revenue (W1)	43,515
Cost of sales (W2)	(18,308)
Gross profit	25,207
Distribution costs (5,449 + 1,307)	(6,756)
Administrative expenses (3,167 + 841)	(4,008)
Profit from operations	14,443
Finance costs (1,960 + 980)	(2,940)
Profit before taxation	11,503
Tax (2,623 +1,063)	(3,686)
Profit for the year	7,817
Attributable to:	
Equity holders of the parent	7,018
Minority interest (W3)	799
	7,817

Workings

(W1) *Revenue:*

	£000
Aswall plc sales	32,412
Unsafey Ltd sales	12,963
Less Inter-company sale	(1,860)
	43,515

(W2) *Cost of sales:*

	£000
Aswall plc cost of sales	14,592
Unsafey Ltd cost of sales	5,576
Less Inter-company purchase	(1,860)
	18,308

(W3) *Minority interest:* 25% x 3,196 =   799

Test your knowledge △ △ △

1 £100,000 + £50,000 = £150,000.

2 Debit group turnover, Credit group cost of sales.

3 MI = 20% X £60,000 = £12,000

CONSOLIDATED ACCOUNTS – LEGAL AND PROFESSIONAL REQUIREMENTS

INTRODUCTION

For this Unit you need to have an awareness of the legal factors and IFRSs that affect the preparation of consolidated accounts, namely IFRS 3 *Business Combinations*, IAS 27 *Consolidated and Separate Financial Statements* and *IAS 28 Investments in Associates.* In this final chapter on consolidated accounts we will cover the areas that are required knowledge.

KNOWLEDGE & UNDERSTANDING

· The UK regulatory framework for financial reporting and the main requirements of relevant International Financial Reporting Standards (Element 11.1)
· The general principles of consolidation (Element 11.1)

CONTENTS

1 IFRS 3 *Business Combinations*
2 IAS 27 *Consolidated and Separate Financial Statements*
3 IAS 28 *Investments in Associates*

1 IFRS 3 *Business Combinations*

1.1 Definition of a business combination

IFRS 3 defines a business combination as the bringing together of separate entities into one reporting entity. In most cases, when this occurs, one entity (the parent or acquirer) acquires control of the other entities (subsidiaries or acquirees).

There are different ways a business combination can be effected. In the examples we have seen so far, one company purchases the shares in another company. Other ways a business combination can occur include the purchase of the net assets of a business rather than the equity, or a reorganisation where a new company is created to control the newly acquired subsidiaries. However they are arranged, all business combinations are accounted for using the purchase method of accounting which is the method we have already seen in the previous two chapters.

1.2 Definition of parent and subsidiary

When a parent acquires a subsidiary it is said to control that subsidiary once more than 50% of the share capital has been acquired. Control is defined in IFRS 3 as:

'the power to govern the financial and operating policies of an entity so as to obtain benefits from its activities'.

However, IFRS 3 allows for situations where a parent may not own more than half of a entity's share capital but does exercise control (as demonstrated by the list below). In this case if the parent exercises control then it should consolidate the entity as a subsidiary regardless of the shareholding. Therefore the definition of control is the key factor when determining group structure.

An undertaking is the parent of another (a subsidiary) if any of the following apply:

· It holds a majority of voting rights.
· Power over majority of voting rights through agreement with other investors

· Power to govern the financial or operating policies of the entity under statute or an agreement

· Power to appoint/remove majority of members of the board of directors or equivalent governing body.

· Power to cast the majority of votes at meetings of the board of directors or equivalent.

2 IAS 27 *Consolidated and Separate Financial Statements*

2.1 Requirement to prepare group accounts

A company must prepare group accounts if it is a parent company at its year-end (i.e. it has one or more subsidiaries, unless it qualifies for exemption from this requirement). The consolidated accounts must include all of the subsidiaries of the parent.

2.2 Other points

IAS 27 details the consolidation procedures that we have already seen in the previous chapters, such as the requirement to eliminate inter company trading.

IAS 27 also states that uniform accounting policies should be used for amounts included in the group accounts. All companies within the group need to follow the same policies otherwise the group accounts will be prepared with many differing policies which would not be useful to the users of those accounts.

3 IAS 28 *Investments in Associates*

3.1 Introduction

We have seen that, if a company has an investment in another company, the accounting treatment of that investment depends upon whether or not that investment gives control.

- If the investment gives control, the investment is treated as a subsidiary and group accounts are prepared.
- If the investment does not give control, it is treated as a simple investment.

3.2 Significant influence

In practice, there is a third possibility.

An associate is an entity (usually a company) over which the group exerts significant influence but not control. A holding of 20% to 50% usually indicates significant influence. Significant influence involves active participation in management, not simply a passive role, as would be the case with a simple trade investment.

We need to distinguish an associate from a subsidiary and from a simple trade investment because, whilst the group does not have control over the associate, it does have more than a passive interest. Hence, we need a treatment in between full consolidation and leaving the investment at cost in the group accounts.

3.3 Relationship with group

As we saw in the first chapter on group accounts, a group comprises a parent and its subsidiaries. As an associate is neither a parent nor a subsidiary, it is not part of the group. Instead, the group has an investment in the associate. When we identify the group structure, we include the associate, even though it is not part of the group, as this helps us to identify its status and the actual percentage interest which, as we shall see, is important.

For example:

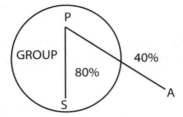

The associate is not part of the group.

3.4 Treatment in investing company's own accounts

In the balance sheet the investment in an associate is included under non-current assets as an investment, usually at cost which is the same way a subsidiary is dealt with.

In the individual company income statement we include dividend income from the associate which is also the same way a subsidiary is dealt with.

3.5 Treatment in group accounts

In the group accounts, we use a technique called equity accounting for an associate.

As we do not control an associate we cannot bring all of the associate's net assets and profits into the group accounts. Instead, we only include the group share of the associate's net assets and profits.

3.6 Balance sheet

In non-current asset investments, we replace the investment as shown in the investing company's own individual balance sheet with the group share of the associate's net assets at the balance sheet date, in one line, Investment in associate.

In group reserves, we include the parent's share of the associate's post-acquisition reserves (calculated in the same way as for a subsidiary).

We cancel the investment in the associate as shown in the investing company's own individual balance sheet against the group share of the associate's net assets at the date of acquisition (at fair value). The difference is the goodwill which is included in the consolidated balance sheet carrying value for the associate.

○ EXAMPLE   ○○○○

P Ltd owns 80% of S Ltd and 40% of A Ltd. Balance sheets of the three companies at 31 December 20X8 are:

	P Ltd £	S Ltd £	A Ltd £
Investment: Shares in S Ltd	800	-	-
Investment: Shares in A Ltd	600	-	-
Sundry net assets	3,600	3,800	4,400
	5,000	3,800	4,400
Share capital - £1 ordinary shares	1,000	400	800
Retained earnings	4,000	3,400	3,600
	5,000	3,800	4,400

P Ltd acquired its shares in S Ltd when S Ltd's retained earnings were £520 and P Ltd acquired its shares in A Ltd when A Ltd's retained earnings were £400.

Required:

Prepare the consolidated balance sheet at 31 December 20X8.

Solution

P Ltd: Consolidated balance sheet as at 31 December 20X8

	£
Goodwill	64
Investment in associate(4,400 x 40% + 120)	1,880
Sundry net assets (3,600 + 3,800)	7,400
	9,344
Share capital	1,000
Retained earnings (W5)	7,584
	8,584
Minority interests (W4)	760
	9,344

Workings

(W1) *Group structure*

(W2) *Net assets working*

S Ltd

	Acquisition	Balance sheet date
	£	£
Share capital	400	400
Retained earnings	520	3,400
	920	3,800

A Ltd

	Acquisition	Balance sheet date
	£	£
Share capital	800	800
Retained earnings	400	3,600
	1,200	4,400

(W3) *Goodwill*

S Ltd

	£
Cost of investment	800
Net assets acquired (80% x 920 (W2))	(736)
	64

A Ltd

	£
Cost of investment	600
Net assets acquired (40% x 1,200 (W2))	(480)
	120

(W4) *Minority interests*

	£
S Ltd only - (20% x 3,800)	760

(W5) Retained earnings

	£
P Ltd - from question	4,000
Share of S Ltd [80% x (3,400 x 520)]	2,304
Share of A Ltd [40% x (3,600 x 400)]	1,280
	———
	7,584

▷ ACTIVITY 1 ▷▷▷▷

A, B and C Ltd

Given below are the balance sheets of three companies at 31 March 20X2. A Ltd owns 60% of the share capital of B Ltd and 30% of the share capital of C Ltd.

	A Ltd £	B Ltd £	C Ltd £
Investment: Shares in B Ltd	1,000		
Investment: Shares in C Ltd	750		
Other net assets	5,250	4,000	3,000
	———	———	———
	7,000	4,000	3,000
	———	———	———
Share capital - ?1 ordinary shares	3,000	1,000	1,000
Retained earnings	4,000	3,000	2,000
	———	———	———
	7,000	4,000	3,000
	———	———	———

A Ltd acquired its shares in B Ltd when B Ltd's retained earnings were £400 and acquired its shares in C Ltd when C Ltd's retained earnings were £1,000.

Prepare the consolidated balance sheet at 31 March 20X2.

[Answer on p. 199]

3.7 Income statement

The treatment of an associate in the consolidated income statement is consistent with its treatment in the consolidated balance sheet.

We replace the dividend income from the investment in the associate, as shown in the investing company's own income statement, with the group share of the associate's profit after tax, in one line, as 'Share of profit of associates'.

Do not add in the associate's revenue or expenses line by line.

O EXAMPLE   O O O O

P Ltd has owned 80% of S Ltd and 40% of A Ltd for several years. Income statements for the year ended 31 December 20X8 are:

	P Ltd £	S Ltd £	A Ltd £
Revenue	14,000	12,000	10,000
Cost of sales	(9,000)	(4,000)	(3,000)
Gross profit	5,000	8,000	7,000
Administrative expenses	(2,000)	(6,000)	(3,000)
	3,000	2,000	4,000
Income from associates	400	-	-
Profit before taxation	3,400	2,000	4,000
Tax	(1,000)	(1,200)	(2,000)
Profit after taxation	2,400	800	2,000

Required:

Prepare the consolidated income statement for the year ended 31 December 20X8.

Solution

P Ltd: income statement for the year ending 31 December 20X8

	£
Revenue (14,000 + 12,000)	26,000
Cost of sales (9,000 + 4,000)	(13,000)
Gross profit	13,000
Administrative expenses (2,000 + 6,000)	(8,000)
Profit from operations	5,000
Share of profit of associate (40% x 2,000)	800
Profit before taxation	5,800
Tax (1,000 + 1,200)	(2,200)
Profit for the period	3,600
Attributable to:	
Equity holders of the parent	3,440
Minority interests (20% ? 800)	160
	3,600

Workings

(W1) *Group structure*

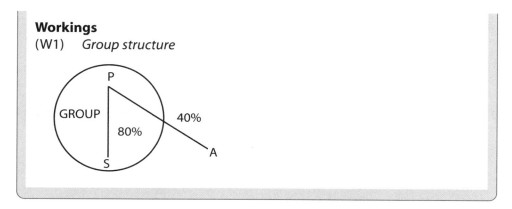

▷ ACTIVITY 2 ▷▷▷▷

D, E and F Ltd

Given below are the income statements for D Ltd, its 75% owned subsidiary E Ltd, and F Ltd its 30% owned associate for the year ended 30 June 20X1. Both E Ltd and F Ltd were acquired by D Ltd a number of years ago.

	D Ltd £	E Ltd £	F Ltd £
Revenue	440,000	180,000	250,000
Cost of sales	210,000	80,000	160,000
Gross profit	230,000	100,000	90,000
Administrative expenses	(80,000)	(30,000)	(25,000)
Income from associates	6,000	–	–
Profit before tax	156,000	70,000	65,000
Tax	46,000	20,000	18,000
Profit for the year	110,000	50,000	47,000

Prepare the consolidated income statement for the year ended 30 June 20X1.

[Answer on p. 200]

4 Test your knowledge ▷ ▷ ▷

1   P Ltd owns 40% of S Ltd but has the power to appoint all of S Ltd's directors. Is S Ltd a subsidiary of P Ltd?

2   P Ltd owns 80% of S Ltd and 30% of A Ltd. How should A Ltd be accounted for in the group accounts prepared for P and S?

[Answers on p. 200]

5   Summary

The main legal and professional requirements in respect of group accounts are set out in:

·   IFRS 3 *Business Combinations*
·   IAS 27 *Consolidated and Separate Financial Statements*
·   IAS 28 *Investments in Associates*

An undertaking is the parent of another (a subsidiary) if any of the following apply:

·   It holds a majority of voting rights.
·   Power over majority of voting rights through agreement with other investors.
·   Power to govern the financial or operating policies of the entity under statute or an agreement.
·   Power to appoint/remove majority of members of the board of directors or equivalent governing body.
·   Power to cast the majority of votes at meetings of the board of directors or equivalent.

If a parent company with subsidiaries has an associate then this must be accounted for using the equity accounting method in the consolidated financial statements.

Answers to chapter activities & 'test your knowledge' questions

△ ACTIVITY 1   △△△△

A, B and C Ltd

Consolidated balance sheet as at 31 March 20X2

	£
Goodwill	160
Interest in associated undertakings (3,000 x 30% + 150)	1,050
Other net assets (5,250 + 4,000)	9,250
	10,460
Share capital	3,000
Retained earnings (W5)	5,860
	8,860
Minority interest (W4)	1,600
	10460

Workings

(W1) *Group structure*

(W2) *Net assets working*

B Ltd

	At acquisition	At balance sheet date
	£	£
Share capital	1,000	1,000
Retained earnings	400	3,000
	1,400	4,000

C Ltd

	£	£
Share capital	1,000	1,000
Retained earnings	1,000	2,000
	2,000	3,000

(W3) *Goodwill*

		£
B Ltd	Cost	1,000
	Net assets acquired 60% x 1,400 (W2)	840
		160

		£
C Ltd	Cost	750
	Net assets acquired 30% x 2,000 (W2)	600
		150

(W4) *Minority interest*

	£
B Ltd only - 40% x 4,000 (W2)	1,600

(W5) *Retained earnings*

	£
A Ltd	4,000
B Ltd 60% x (3,000 - 400)	1,560
C Ltd 30% x (2,000 - 1,000)	300
	5,860

△ ACTIVITY 2 △△△△

D, E and F Ltd
Consolidated income statement for the year ended 30 June 20X1

	£
Revenue (440,000 + 180,000)	620,000
Cost of sales (210,000 + 80,000)	290,000
Gross profit	330,000
Administrative expenses (80,000 + 30,000)	(110,000)
Share of profit of associate (30% x 47,000)	14,100
	234,100
Tax (46,000 + 20,000)	(66,000)
Profit for the year	168,100

Attributable to:	
Equity holders of the parent	155,600
Minority interest (25% x 50,000)	12,500
	168,100

Test your knowledge △ △ △

1   Yes. P controls S.

2   A is an associate, so should be included in the group's accounts using equity accounting.

PROPERTY, PLANT AND EQUIPMENT

INTRODUCTION

For Unit 11 you need to be able to draft limited company year end financial statements and for that purpose you need to be aware of the main requirements of relevant accounting standards. In this chapter we will consider the detailed requirements of IAS 16 *Property, Plant and Equipment*. For this IFRS all aspects are assessable but the emphasis is on discursive rather than computational tasks. We will also consider IAS 40 *Investment Property* and IAS 23 *Borrowing Costs*.

KNOWLEDGE & UNDERSTANDING

· The UK regulatory framework for financial reporting and the main requirements of relevant International Financial Reporting Standards (Element 11.1)

CONTENTS

1   IAS 16 *Property, Plant and Equipment*

1.1 Introduction

IAS 16 Property, Plant and Equipment considers recognition of assets, determination of carrying amount and the depreciation charges and impairment losses to be recognised in relation to them.

1.2 Initial measurement

Initial measurement of property, plant and equipment (whether acquired or self-constructed) should be at its cost.

Cost should include all costs directly attributable to bringing the asset into working condition for its intended use. Cost can include finance costs – see 1.3.

If the carrying amount of the property, plant or equipment exceeds its recoverable amount (defined as the higher of net realisable value and value in use) then the asset is impaired and it should be written down to its recoverable amount – see IAS 36 in the next chapter.

1.3 IAS 23 *Borrowing Costs*

Finance costs (such as interest payable) directly attributable to the construction of a tangible non-current asset may be capitalised as part of the cost of the asset. Such capitalisation is optional.

Conditions:

·   Finance costs may only be capitalised if the entity adopts a policy of capitalising them. If such a policy is adopted, all qualifying finance costs must be capitalised.

·   Finance costs capitalised in a period must not exceed finance costs incurred in the period.

·   Capitalisation should begin when:
  -    finance costs are being incurred; and
  -    expenditure for the asset is being incurred; and
  -    work has begun on the asset or on getting it ready for use

·   Capitalisation should cease when:
  -    substantially all the activities necessary to get the asset ready for use are complete

○ **EXAMPLE**   ○○○○

AB plc incurs the following costs in constructing a new non-current asset:

	£
Site clearance	2,000
Cost of materials used in asset	30,000
Legal fees to secure a licence	1,000
Interest at 10% pa on £40,000	
loan raised to finance the asset's construction:	
3-month construction period (10% x £40,000 x $^{3}/_{12}$)	1,000
Cost of materials wasted in a flood	500
Cost of labour used in asset	8,000
Cost of industrial dispute	1,500

Which of the above costs can be capitalised into the initial cost of the non-current asset?

Solution

The directly attributable costs are:

	£
Site clearance	2,000
Cost of materials in asset	30,000
Necessary legal fee	1,000
Interest during construction period	1,000
Cost of labour in asset	8,000
	──────
	42,000
	──────

The cost of the wasted materials and the industrial dispute are not direct costs and must be written off to the income statement as incurred. Note that capitalisation of the interest cost (£1,000 in the example) is not compulsory, but is permitted by IAS 23.

1.4 Subsequent expenditure

Subsequent expenditure should be capitalised if it enhances the economic benefits of the asset in excess of its previously assessed standard of performance. Otherwise, subsequent expenditure that helps to maintain the asset's standard of performance (e.g. routine repairs and maintenance) should be charged to the income statement as it is incurred.

1.5 Valuation

Revaluation of property, plant and equipment is allowed if a policy of revaluation is adopted. Just as with the capitalisation of interest, revaluation is optional rather than mandatory.

Conditions:

· All assets of the same class must be revalued. For example, if certain land and buildings were to be revalued, this would not require the revaluation of plant and machinery, but would require the revaluation of all land and buildings held.

· Once revalued, the carrying amount in each balance sheet must be current value. This is fair value at date of valuation less any subsequent accumulated depreciation and subsequent accumulated impairment losses.

· Revaluations should be made regularly to ensure carrying value does not differ materially from fair value at balance sheet date. (some items may require annual revaluation others only every three to five years)

1.6 Reporting valuation gains and losses

· Gains
  - These are recorded in equity as a revaluation reserve. They can be seen in the statement of changes in equity (SOCE). If the increase reverses a previous loss which was recognised in the income statement, then it can be taken to the income statement to the extent that it reverses a previous revaluation loss on the same asset.

· Losses
  - These are recognised in the income statement unless there is already a balance in the revaluation reserve for that asset. In this case, the loss is taken to the revaluation reserve to the extent of any previous surplus and is also seen in the statement of changes in equity.

○ EXAMPLE ○○○○

A building costing £200,000 was purchased on 1 January 20X1. It is being depreciated over its useful life of 20 years on a straight line basis down to a nil residual value. At 31 December 20X1 the building was revalued at £247,000 and at 31 December 20X2 it was revalued at £150,000.

Show how these revaluations should be dealt with in the financial statements as at 31 December 20X1 and 20X2.

Solution

In the year ended 31 December 20X1, depreciation of $\frac{£200,000}{20} = £10,000$

would originally be charged so the net book value at the date of revaluation is £190,000.

The revaluation gain is £57,000 (from a net book value of £190,000 up to £247,000). This gain would be reported in the SOCE and would be shown in the balance sheet as a revaluation reserve.

The double entry for the revaluation is:

	£	£
DR Building (247 – 200)	47,000	
DR Accumulated depreciation	10,000	
CR Revaluation reserve		57,000

As the asset is being used, it is possible to transfer some of the revaluation reserve to retained earnings. The amount that is transferred is the amount of the revaluation reserve for the asset divided by the remaining life or alternatively the difference between the original depreciation based on cost and the depreciation based on the revaluated amount. In our example the journal would be:

	£	£
DR Revaluation reserve (57,000 ÷ 19)	3,000	
CR Retained earnings (13,000 – 10,000)		3,000

The journal above shows both methods of calculating this transfer. This realises a proportion of the revaluation reserve each year the asset is being depreciated.

In the year ended 31 December 20X2, depreciation of $\frac{£200,000}{20} = £13,000$

would originally be charged, so the net book value at the date of the second revaluation is £234,000. Once the asset has been revalued it is depreciated over its remaining useful life, hence the depreciation was over a period of 19 years and not 20.

The revaluation loss is ?84,000 (from a net book value of £234,000 down to £150,000).

This loss can be offset against the previous revaluation gain, to the extent that there is enough gain available. The previous revaluation surplus is now £54,000 (£57,000 - £3,000 transfer) so this part of the loss can be offset reducing the revaluation reserve to zero.

The remainder of the loss is £30,000 and this must be charged to the income statement.

The double entry for the revaluation is:

	£	£
DR Accumulated depreciation	13,000	
DR Income statement	30,000	
DR Revaluation reserve	54,000	
CR Building (150 – 247)		97,000

1.7 Gains and losses on disposal

Gains and losses on disposal of tangible non-current assets are shown in the income statement and are calculated as the difference between proceeds and carrying amount at the date of sale.

1.8 Depreciation

The depreciable amount (cost or valuation, less residual value) of a tangible non-current asset should be allocated on a systematic basis over its useful economic life. The following factors need to be considered when determining the useful economic life, residual value and depreciation method of an asset:

· Expected usage
· Expected physical wear and tear
· Economic or technological obsolescence
· Legal or similar limits on use, such as the expiry dates of related leases

Note that land is not depreciated. This is because it is not expected to have a finite life, whereas other assets such as buildings or machinery will have a finite life.

IAS 16 does not stipulate a particular method of depreciation. It is up to the directors to choose the fairest method possible.

1.9 Useful economic lives and residual values

The length of a non-current asset's life is clearly a very important number in a depreciation calculation. However, it is an estimate, as it is necessary to make predictions about the future.

Both the useful economic life and the residual value (if material) of a tangible non-current asset should be reviewed at the end of each reporting period. They should be revised 'if expectations are significantly different from previous estimates'.

▷ ACTIVITY 1   ▷ ▷ ▷ ▷

Ford plc

The following property, plant and equipment balances have been extracted from the books of Ford plc as at 31 December 20X7.

	£000	£000
Freehold factory cost at 1 January 20X7	1,440	
Freehold factory revaluation	760	
Freehold factory additions	500	
Freehold factory depreciation at 1 January 20X7		144
Freehold factory revaluation adjustment	144	
Freehold factory depreciation charge		60
Plant and machinery cost at 1 January 20X7	1,968	
Plant and machinery additions	75	
Plant and machinery depreciation at 1 January 20X7		257
Plant and machinery depreciation charge		233
Motor vehicles cost at 1 January 20X7	449	
Motor vehicles additions	35	

Motor vehicles depreciation at 1 January 20X7		194
Motor vehicles depreciation charge		87
Office equipment and fixtures cost at 1 January 20X7	888	
Office equipment and fixtures additions	22	
Office equipment and fixtures depreciation at 1 January 20X7		583
Office equipment and fixtures depreciation charge		182

You are given the following information for the year ended 31 December 20X7:

(1) The factory was acquired in March 20X2 and is being depreciated over 50 years.

(2) At 1 January 20X7, depreciation was provided on cost on a straight-line basis. The rates used were 20% for office equipment and fixtures, 25% for motor vehicles and 10% for plant and machinery.

(3) Early in the year the factory was revalued to an open market value of £2.2 million and an extension was built costing £500,000.

(4) It is the company's policy to charge a full year's depreciation in the year of acquisition.

Required:

Prepare the accounting policy and property, plant and equipment notes for the year ended 31 December 20X7 as required by IAS 16 and IAS 1 in so far as the information permits.

[Answer on p. 210]

2 IAS 40 *Investment Property*

2.1 Definition

An investment property is property held to earn rentals or for capital appreciation or both Investment property is not:

(a) Property intended for sale in the ordinary course of business
(b) Property being constructed on behalf of third parties
(c) Owner occupied property or property occupied by the parent or subsidiary company
(d) Property being constructed for future use as an investment property
(e) Property that is leased to another entity under a finance lease.

○ **EXAMPLE**   ○○○○

Which of the following are investment properties?

(a) Land which is leased out at an arm's length rental to a third party for use as a car park.

(b) A building used by the owning company as the company head office.

(c) A building leased to a subsidiary at an arm's length rental.

Solution

(a) This is an investment property.

(b) This is not an investment property, since it is occupied by the owning company for its own purposes.

(c) This is not an investment property, since it is let to a group company (i.e. a company in the same group of companies, a group comprising the parent company and the various subsidiaries).

2.2 Accounting treatment

Investment properties should be measured initially at cost After initial recognition an entity must choose either the fair value model or the cost model to value its investment property.

Fair value model – After initial recognition, all investment property is recognised at fair value. Fair value is the price the property could be exchanged between willing knowledgeable parties in an arms length transaction. Any gains or losses arising from a change in fair value shall be recognised in the income statement for period in which it arises.

Cost model - The asset is measured at cost and depreciated as per IAS 16 Property, Plant and Equipment.

The method used, whether the fair value or cost model, must be disclosed.

▷ ACTIVITY 2

X Ltd (part of Question 1 June 2004)

X Ltd owns the freehold of a building which they constructed for investment purposes. The building is currently rented to another company on commercial terms. The property is not recorded at its historical cost and has not been depreciated.

What is the correct accounting treatment for this property?

[Answer on p. 211]

3 Test your knowledge

1 Is the capitalisation of finance costs into the cost of tangible non-current assets mandatory or optional?

2 How should directors choose the depreciation method to be used?

3 At what value should investment properties be shown in the balance sheet?

[Answers on p. 211]

4   Summary

IAS 16 covers the accounting for property, plant and equipment. Property, plant and equipment should initially be shown at cost. Interest may be capitalised into the cost of non current asset in accordance with IAS 23 Borrowing costs.

Subsequently they may either be shown at cost less depreciation, or revalued to fair value. Where revalued, all similar items should be revalued and the revaluation must be kept up to date.

IAS 40 requires that investment properties should be valued using either the fair value model or cost model.

Answers to chapter activities & 'test your knowledge' questions

△ **ACTIVITY 1**   △ △ △ △

Ford plc

Accounting policy note

(1) Property, plant and equipment
Interests in buildings are stated at a valuation.

Other property, plant and equipment are stated at cost, together with any incidental expenses of acquisition.

Depreciation is calculated so as to write off the net cost or valuation of property, plant and equipment over their expected useful economic lives. A full year's charge is provided in the year of acquisition. The rates and bases used are as follows:

Buildings – on the straight-line basis	2% pa
Plant and machinery – on the straight-line basis	10% pa
Office equipment and fixtures – on the straight-line basis	20% pa
Motor vehicles – on the straight line basis	25% pa

(2) Property, plant and equipment

	Freehold land and buildings	Plant and machinery	Motor vehicles	Fixtures, fittings, tools and equipment	Total
	£000	£000	£000	£000	£000
Cost or valuation					
At 1 January 20X7	1,440	1,968	449	888	4,745
Additions	500	75	35	22	632
Revaluations	760	–	–	–	760
At 31 December 20X7	2,700	2,043	484	910	6,137
Depreciation					
At 1 January 20X7	144	257	194	583	1,178
Revaluation adjustment	(144)				(144)
Charge for year	60	233	87	182	562
At 31 December 20X7	60	490	281	765	1,596
Net book value					
At 31 December 20X7	2,640	1,553	203	145	4,541
At 1 January 20X7	1,296	1,711	255	305	3,567

△ ACTIVITY 2   △ △ △ △

X Ltd

Assuming that the other company is not a member of the same group as X Ltd then this property is an investment property as defined by IAS 40. Its is rented out on commercial terms and should therefore be classified in the balance sheet as a non-current asset under the heading Investment property.

The property shall be valued using either the fair value model or the cost model.

The fair value model is the price that could be achieved if the asset was sold to a knowledgeable willing party at an arms length transaction.

The cost model is initial construction cost less accumulated depreciation.

The valuation model chosen must be disclosed.

Test your knowledge △ △ △

1   Optional.

2   The depreciation method should reflect the pattern in which the asset's economic benefits are consumed.

3   Fair value or cost less depreciation.

INTANGIBLE FIXED ASSETS

INTRODUCTION

For Unit 11 you need knowledge of aspects of IAS 38 *Intangible Assets* and of IAS 36 *Impairment of Assets*.

KNOWLEDGE & UNDERSTANDING

· The UK regulatory framework for financial reporting and the main requirements of relevant International Financial Reporting Standards (Element 11.1)

CONTENTS

1 IAS 38 *Intangible Assets*
2 IAS 36 *Impairment of Assets*

1 IAS 38 *Intangible Assets*

1.1 Introduction

In the previous chapter you studied the accounting for property, plant and equipment such as buildings, cars and computers. Property, plant and equipment have physical form, so you can see what the company has paid for. Sometimes a company will pay money to acquire an intangible asset which has no physical form.

1.2 Criteria of an Intangible asset

An intangible asset is an identifiable, non-monetary asset without physical substance.

To be identified as an intangible asset, an asset must either:

· be capable of being separated or divided from the entity and sold, transferred, licensed, rented or exchanged either individually or together with a related contract, asset or liability or
· arise from contractual or other legal rights.

The definition requires an intangible asset to be identifiable to distinguish it from goodwill. In an acquisition, goodwill represents the payment made by the acquirer in anticipation of future benefits from the assets purchased. These benefits may result from cost savings when the businesses are combined, but cannot be separately identified as an asset.

Internally generated goodwill should not be recognised as an asset as it is not a separable asset or arise from contractual rights as seen above and it cannot be measured reliably.

1.3 Recognition and measurement

An intangible asset shall only be recognised if:

· it is probable that the expected future economic benefits that are attributable to the asset will flow to the entity; and
· the cost of the asset can be measured reliably.

Future economic benefits includes revenue from sale of products or services, cost savings, or other benefits resulting from use of the asset by the entity.

An intangible asset shall initially be measured at cost.

1.4 Internally generated intangible assets

To assess whether an internally generated intangible asset meets the criteria for recognition , an entity classifies the generation of the asset into:

· research phase
· development phase.

No intangible asset arising from research or from the research phase shall be recognised. Expenditure on the research phase is recognised as an expense in the income statement when it is incurred.

An intangible asset arising from the development or the development phase shall be recognised if an entity can demonstrate all of the following:

(a) technical feasibility of completing the intangible asset so it is available for use or sale

(b) intention to complete the intangible asset and use or sell it.

(c) ability to use or sell the intangible asset

(d) how the intangible asset will generate probable future economic benefits. E.g. how the entity can demonstrate the existence of a market for the output of the intangible asset or the intangible asset itself.

(e) availability of adequate technical, financial and other resources to complete the development and to use or sell the intangible asset.

(f) ability to measure reliably the expenditure attributable to the intangible asset during its development.

Internally generated brands, publishing titles, customer lists and similar items shall not be recognised as intangible assets.

1.5 Cost of an internally generated intangible asset

Cost comprises all directly attributable cost necessary to create, produce and prepare the asset for use. This will include the following:

· Costs of materials and services used or consumed in generating the intangible asset
· Costs of employee benefits arising from the generation of the intangible asset
· Fees to register a legal right
· Amortisation of patents and licences that are used to generate the intangible asset.

The following are not components of cost:

· Selling, administrative, and other general overhead expenses
· Identified inefficiencies and initial operating losses incurred before the asset achieves planned performance
· The cost of training staff to operate the asset.

1.6 Measurement after recognition

An entity shall choose either the cost model or revaluation model as its accounting policy

Cost model: The asset is carried at cost less any accumulated depreciation and any accumulated impairment losses

Revaluation model: The asset is carried at its revalued amount. This is its fair value at the date of revaluation less any subsequent accumulated amortisation and any subsequent impairment losses. The valuation must be reviewed regularly.

1.7 Revaluation gains or losses

A revaluation gain should be credited to the revaluation reserve. It will be recognised in the statement of changes in equity.

A revaluation loss will be debited to the income statement (unless reversing a previous gain in which case the loss will be debited to the relevant revaluation reserve).

1.8 Useful life

An entity needs to determine whether the useful life of an intangible asset is finite or indefinite.

Finite life

If finite then the entity must determine the length of the life. Amortisation shall begin when the asset is available for use and cease when the asset is either classified as held for sale or the date the asset is derecognised.

The amortisation method chosen should reflect the pattern in which the assets' future economic benefits are expected to be consumed by the entity. If this cannot be reliably measured then the straight-line method shall be used. The amortisation charge for each period shall be recognised in the income statement.

The residual value of an intangible asset shall be deemed to be zero unless:
·   there is a commitment by a third party to purchase the asset at the end of its useful economic life or
·   there is an active market for the asset and a residual market can be determined and the active market will still exist at the end of the assets useful economic life.

The amortisation period and method shall be reviewed at each financial year end.

Indefinite life

If an asset has an indefinite life it shall not be amortised.

The asset must be tested for impairment in accordance with IAS 36 Impairment of Assets.

An entity must compare the recoverable amount with the carrying amount of the asset. This must be done annually and whenever there is an indication that the asset may be impaired.

The useful life must be reviewed each period to ensure events and circumstances still support an indefinite useful life assessment for that asset.

▷ ACTIVITY 1

(a) Describe the difference between purchased and non-purchased goodwill, stating how each is created and how it should be accounted for.

(b) Explain the criteria in IAS 38 for capitalising research and development expenditure.

[Answer on p. 222]

---

2 IAS 36 *Impairment of Assets*

2.1 Introduction

We have already met impairment in this text:

· IAS 16 requires property, plant and equipment to be written down to their recoverable amounts when it is known that the carrying amount exceeds the recoverable amount.

· IAS 38 requires annual impairment reviews to be carried out whenever an intangible asset is deemed to have an infinite useful economic life.

□ DEFINITION

Impairment is the reduction in the recoverable amount of a non-current asset or goodwill below its carrying amount.

Recoverable amount is the higher of net selling price and value in use. Net selling price is the amount at which an asset could be disposed of, less any direct selling costs.

Value in use is the present value of the future cash flows arising from an asset's continued use, including those resulting from its ultimate disposal.

○ EXAMPLE   ○○○○

A machine has a net book value of £5,000 in the draft balance sheet as at 31 December 20X3. It could be sold now for £4,000, or retained in the business where it is expected to earn cash inflows of £1,800 pa for each of the next three years after which it will expire worthless. Current interest rates are 10% pa.

Assess whether the machine is impaired at 31 December 20X3.

Solution

Current book value (= carrying amount) = £5,000
Compare this with the recoverable amount, i.e. the higher of NRV and value in use.

NRV = £4,000
$$\text{Value in use} = \frac{£1,800}{1.1} + \frac{£1,800}{(1.1)^2} + \frac{£1,800}{(1.1)^3} = \frac{£4,476}{}$$

∴ Recoverable amount = £4,476

∴ the machine has a book value of £5,000 but a recoverable amount of only £4,476. It is impaired and should be written down to £4,476 in the balance sheet. An impairment loss of £5,000 − £4,476 = £524 must be recognised.

2.2 Identifying an asset that may be impaired

An entity shall assess at each reporting date whether there is any indication that an asset may be impaired.

Regardless of any indication an entity shall also:

· test an intangible asset with an indefinite useful economic life for impairment (this may be performed at any time during the year, provided it is performed at the same time each year)
· test goodwill acquired in a business combination for impairment annually.

2.3 Indicators of impairment

Examples of indications that an impairment may have occurred are as follows:

· a current period operating loss or net cash outflow from operating activities
· a significant decline in a fixed asset's market value during the period
· obsolescence or physical damage to a fixed asset
· a significant adverse change in the business or the market in which the fixed asset or goodwill is involved

· a management commitment to undertake a significant reorganisation
· a major loss of key employees, or
· a significant increase in market interest rates.

2.4 Determining fair value

The best evidence of an assets fair vale is a price in a binding sale agreement in an arm's length transaction.

If no binding sale agreement exists but the asset is traded on the active market then this value (less sales cost) could be used.

If neither of these exist then fair value less costs to sell is based on the best available information e.g. look at recent transactions for similar assets within the industry etc.

2.5 Determining value in use

The following shall be reflected in determining value in use:
(a) estimate of the future cash flows the entity hopes to derive from the asset
(b) expectations about possible changes of those future cash flows
(c) time value of money
(d) price for bearing the uncertainty inherent in the asset
(e) other factors (such as illiquidity) that market participants would reflect in pricing the future cash flows the entity expects to derive from the asset.

Estimating value in use involves:
(a) estimating future cash flows to be derived from the continuing use of the asset
(b) applying the appropriate discount rate to these cash flows. (The discount rate shall be pre-tax and reflect the time value of money and the specific risks to that asset.)

2.6 Accounting for impairment losses

Impairment losses must be recognised in the income statement, unless they arise on a previously revalued asset. Impairment losses on revalued assets are recognised in the Statement of changes in equity. After recognition of the impairment loss the depreciation (amortisation) charge for the asset shall be adjusted to allocate the asset's revised carrying amount over its useful economic life.

2.7 Cash generating units

If there is an indication that an asset has been impaired, then the recoverable amount shall be estimated for that individual asset. If this is not possible to do for an individual asset, then an entity shall determine the recoverable amount of the cash generating unit to which the asset belongs.

2.8 Timing of impairment tests for goodwill

The annual impairment test for a cash generating unit to which goodwill has been allocated may be performed at any time during an annual period, provided the test is performed at the same time each year.

If an impairment loss is found for a cash generating unit then the loss shall be allocated firstly to any assets that are specifically impaired and then as follows:
(a) to reduce the carrying amount of goodwill
(b) to reduce the carrying amount of the other assets in the unit on a pro rata basis.

2.9 Disclosure requirements

An entity shall disclose the amount of the impairment losses recognised during the period and the line item(s) of the income statement in which those impairment losses are included.

▷ **ACTIVITY 2**   ▷ ▷ ▷ ▷

Jasmine plc (part of Question 1 Dec 2004)

(a)   When would an impairment review of non-current assets be necessary?
(b)   What would you do in an impairment review?

[Answer on p. 223]

---

3   Test your knowledge ▷ ▷ ▷

1   What is purchased goodwill?

2   What is the required accounting treatment for costs during the research phase?

3   What is the accounting treatment of goodwill?

4   Explain how the recoverable amount of an asset is estimated.

[Answers on p. 223]

4   Summary

This chapter has covered two important accounting standards:

·   IAS 38 *Intangible Assets*

This requires intangibles to be capitalised and amortised over their useful economic lives.

It discusses the treatment of costs in the research and development phases of a product.

- IAS 36 *Impairment of Assets*

IAS 36 requires impaired assets (those for which the carrying value exceeds the recoverable amount) to be written down to their recoverable amount. The impairment loss is normally recognised in the income statement.

Answers to chapter activities & 'test your knowledge' questions

△ ACTIVITY 1   △△△△

Purchased goodwill is goodwill which is established as a result of a purchase of a business. Under these circumstances goodwill is measured as the difference between the value of the business as a whole and the aggregate value of the separable tangible and intangible assets. This represents a valuation of goodwill at the time of acquisition.

All other forms of goodwill are considered to be non-purchased goodwill. Whilst it is possible to speculate about how such goodwill has come into existence, (e.g. from the reputation of the business as a supplier of quality goods, good customer and/or staff relations, advantageous location etc) any list such as the foregoing cannot be considered either complete or definitive. Any expenditure incurred in creating circumstances where goodwill may arise cannot be directly related to the value of the resulting goodwill, and indeed may be completely unrelated to any goodwill in the business. Purchased positive goodwill should be capitalised. Goodwill is regarded as having an indefinite useful economic life and therefore, it should not be amortised.

An annual impairment review must be performed in order to identify any fall in value. The value of the goodwill should then be written down if necessary. Purchased goodwill should be capitalised for the following reasons.

· Including goodwill in the balance sheet means that users of the financial statements recognise that it is part of the cost of an investment, a cost for which management remains accountable.
· There is consistency between the treatment of goodwill and other assets.

Non-purchased goodwill should not be capitalised.

It can be argued that goodwill meets the definition of an asset in the IASB's Framework for the preparation and presentation of financial statements. However, only where the historical costs of creating or acquiring an asset are known is it capable of being measured with sufficient reliability to be recognised in the financial statements.

Where goodwill has been purchased, the cost of the goodwill has been established by an actual transaction, and is a matter of fact. Where goodwill has been generated internally any valuation can only be subjective. For this reason non-purchased goodwill cannot be included in the balance sheet.

(b) Expenditure on the research phase must be recognised as an expense in the income statement when it is incurred and can never be capitalised.

An intangible arising from the development or development phase shall be recognised if an entity can demonstrate all of the following:

(a) technical feasibility of completing the intangible asset so it is available for use or sale

(b) intention to complete the intangible asset and use or sell it.

(c) ability to use or sell the intangible asset

(d) how the intangible asset will generate probable future economic benefits e.g. how the entity can demonstrate the existence of a market for the output of the intangible asset or the intangible asset itself

(e) availability of adequate technical, financial and other resources to complete the development and to use or sell the intangible asset

(f) ability to measure reliably the expenditure attributable to the intangible asset during its development.

△ ACTIVITY 2   △ △ △ △

Jasmine plc

(a) An impairment review should be carried out if events or changes in circumstances indicate that the carrying amount of non-current assets may not be recoverable.

Regardless of any indication an entity shall also:

(i) test an intangible asset with an indefinite useful economic life for impairment (this may be performed at any time during the year, provided it is performed at the same time each year)

(ii) test goodwill acquired in a business combination for impairment annually.

(b) An impairment review comprises a comparison of the carrying value of the asset with its recoverable amount, which is the higher of its net realisable value and its value in use.

Test your knowledge △ △ △

1 Purchased goodwill arises when the cost of purchasing a company is greater than the aggregate of the fair values of the net assets it acquires.

2 Costs during the research phase must be written off as incurred.

3 Purchased goodwill is capitalised. Annual impairment reviews must be carried out. Internally generated goodwill can never be capitalised.

4 Recoverable amount is the higher of net selling price and value in use.

INVENTORIES

KNOWLEDGE & UNDERSTANDING

· The UK regulatory framework for financial reporting and the main requirements of relevant International Financial Reporting Standards (Element 11.1)

CONTENTS

1   Valuation of inventories
2   Methods of costing inventories

1   Valuation of inventories

1.1 The basic rule

Inventories should be stated at the **lower of cost and net realisable value.**

1.2 Cost

IAS 2 defines cost as comprising: 'all costs of purchase, costs of conversion and other costs incurred in bringing the inventories to their present location and condition'.

 Specifically excluded are:

(a)   abnormal amounts of wasted materials, labour and other production costs
(b)   storage costs, unless necessary in the production process before a further production stage
(c)   administrative overheads that do not contribute to bringing inventories to their present location and condition
(d)   selling costs.

This means that two identical items may have different costs if they are in different locations. For example, the cost of an item which has been shipped to a distribution centre in France will include the normal transport costs to France and hence will have a higher cost than a similar item held in the factory in England.

Note that only costs incurred in the normal course of business should be included. If the lorry taking items to France broke down, the costs of the break-down would not be included as part of the transport costs since they are considered abnormal.

○ **EXAMPLE**   ○○○○

The Standard Company plc has inventories at 31 December 20X7 and has gathered the following information together in order to determine its cost.

	£
Cost of original materials	16,000
Cost of work on material:	
Labour 1,000 hours @ £2.50	2,500
Variable overhead	700
Fixed production overhead during the period 1 October to 31 December 20X7	40,000
Number of hours worked in the period 1 October to 31 December 20X7	18,000 hours

You also discovered that 2,000 hours of work were lost during December due to an industrial dispute over the holiday work programme.

Selling and distribution costs during the quarter were £10,000.

What is the value of the inventories held at 31 December 20X7?

Solution

	£
Material cost	16,000
Labour cost	2,500
Variable overhead	700
Fixed overhead $\dfrac{£200,000}{20}$ x 1,000 hrs	2,000
	21,200

Fixed overheads are absorbed on the basis of the labour hours worked, 1,000 hours, as a proportion of normal working hours for the period, 20,000 hours.

The industrial dispute will not increase the value of the inventories even though it reduced the number of hours actually worked in the quarter.

Selling and distribution overheads have been ignored as the inventories have not been sold or distributed.

2 Methods of costing inventories

2.1 Acceptable inventory accounting methods

When a number of identical items of inventories have been purchased or made at different times, the actual cost of the items in inventories at the year-end may not be known, so assumptions have to be made of the way in which the inventory items flowed through the business. Only methods that give the fairest practicable approximation to actual cost are acceptable.

2.2 Acceptable methods

IAS 2 accepts the use of any one of the following methods, consistently applied:

(i) **Unit cost** – The actual cost of purchasing or manufacturing identifiable units of inventory.

(ii) **Weighted average cost** – The calculation of the cost of inventories and work in progress on the basis of the application to the units of inventories on hand of an average price computed by dividing the total cost of units by the total number of such units (this average price may be arrived at by means of a continuous calculation, a periodic calculation or a moving periodic calculation).

(iii) **FIFO (first in, first out)** – The calculation of the cost of inventories and work in progress on the basis that the quantities in hand represent the latest purchases or production.

○ EXAMPLE   ○○○○

RJ plc made the following purchases and sales of grommets in May 20X1:

1 May	Opening stock	Nil
8 May	Bought 200 units	@ £5 each
13 May	Bought 400 units	@ £5.60 each
20 May	Sold 300 units	@ £8 each

Determine the closing inventories valuation at 31 May and the gross profit for the month using:

(a) FIFO
(b) Weighted average cost.

Solution

(a) There are 300 units in inventory and the FIFO method assumes that these consist of the purchases on 13 May as the earlier purchase has all been sold.

Closing inventories = 300 units @ £5.60 = £1,680
Gross profit:

Sales (300 x £8)	£2,400
Less cost of sales (200 x £5 + 100 x £5.60)	£1,560
Gross profit	£840

(b) The WAC method calculates an average price for the inventory purchases.

$$\text{Average price} = \frac{200 \times £5 + 400 \times £5.60}{600 \text{ units}} = £5.40$$

∴ Closing inventories = 300 x £5.40 = £1,620

Sales (300 x £8)	£2,400
Less cost of sales (300 x £5.40)	£1,620
Gross profit	£780

▷ ACTIVITY 1 ▷▷▷▷

S Ltd

S Ltd is a manufacturing company. It held its annual inventory count on 31 March 20X2, the company's year-end. The accounts department is currently working its way through the inventory sheets placing a value on the physical inventories. The company has had a difficult year and profits are likely to be lower than in the previous year.

Raw materials

Inventories of raw materials are valued at cost. The finance director has suggested that the cost has been understated in previous years because the company has not taken the costs of delivery or insurance into account. These can be substantial in the case of imported goods. It has been proposed that these costs be taken into account in the valuation of closing inventories of raw materials.

Finished goods

Finished goods have already been valued at £400,000. This figure includes some obsolete goods which cost £70,000 to produce, but which are likely to be sold at a scrap value of £500. There are also several batches of a new product which will be launched early in the new financial year. These cost £90,000 to manufacture. Independent market research suggests that it is very likely that the new product will be sold for considerably more than this. If, however, the launch is unsuccessful, the new product will have to be sold as scrap for £1,000. The finance director has said that the aggregate net realisable value of all closing inventories of finished goods is at least £500,000 and so there is no need to worry about the obsolete and new inventory products.

Required:

(a) Explain whether the costs of delivery and insurance should be included in the valuation of raw materials.

(b) (i) Explain whether the valuation of closing inventories at the lower of cost and net realisable value should be done on an item–by–item basis or on the basis of the aggregate cost of all items as compared with their aggregate net realisable value.

   (ii) State how you would value the obsolete items and the new product line, giving reasons for your valuation in each case.

[Answer on p. 231]

▷ ACTIVITY 2   ▷ ▷ ▷ ▷

(a) Why is an adjustment made for closing inventories in the financial state-
     ments?

(b) How should inventories be valued in the financial statements?

[Answer on p. 231]

3   Test your knowledge ▷ ▷ ▷

1   A company has closing inventories of 100 items of Unit X. Each unit cost
     £4 but can only be sold for £3.50. What is the total closing inventories val-
     uation?

2   State two circumstances when NRV is likely to be lower than cost.

3   What methods of valuation can be used per IAS 2?

4   Give two examples of items excluded from the cost of inventories.

[Answers on p. 232]

4   Summary

IAS 2 requires that inventories should be stated in the balance sheet at the
lower of cost and net realisable value.

Cost comprises all expenditure which has been incurred in the normal course
of business in bringing the product or service to its present location and condition.

NRV is the expected selling price less further costs to completion and costs to
be incurred in selling the item.

If the actual costs of the items in closing inventories are not known (since the
items are interchangeable), an assumption has to be made of how the items
physically flow through the business. The usual assumption is FIFO (First In
First Out).

Answers to chapter activities & 'test your knowledge' questions

△ ACTIVITY 1   △ △ △ △

S Ltd

(a)   Raw materials should be valued at the lower of cost and net realisable value where cost includes all costs in bringing the items to their balance sheet location and conditions.

Both delivery and insurance costs could be included in this definition and so legitimately be added to the valuation, as long as they have been incurred in bringing the inventory items to their present location and condition.

(b) (i)   Valuation at cost or net realisable value should be carried out on a product line-by-line basis. The value of assets and liabilities should be determined for individual items not in aggregate. The finance director's statement is therefore incorrect.

(ii)   Obsolete items must be valued at £500, their net realisable value since this is lower than cost.

New product line. It seems likely from the initial market research that net realisable value will be considerably greater than the cost of £90,000. These items should thus be included at £90,000. If in a later period the launch proves unsuccessful the inventories will need to be written down to £1,000 and, if material, may be shown as an exceptional item.

△ ACTIVITY 2   △ △ △ △

(a)   We must match costs with related revenues. The cost of unsold inventories is therefore carried forward to be matched with revenue when it arises. So the cost of inventories is not shown in the year in which the cost is incurred but rather in the year the sale is made.

(b)   Inventories should be valued at the lower of cost and net realisable value.

Test your knowledge

1   100 x £3.50 = £350.

2   Physical deterioration, obsolescence.

3   Cost, FIFO, Weighted average.

4   Select from:
·   abnormal amounts of wasted materials, labour and other production costs
·   storage costs, unless necessary in the production process before a further production stage
·   administrative overheads that do not contribute to bringing inventories to their present location and condition
·   selling costs.

KAPLAN PUBLISHING

TAX IN COMPANY ACCOUNTS

INTRODUCTION

In order to prepare a set of limited company accounts you need to know how to deal with corporation tax in the income statement and the balance sheet. This is covered by IAS 12 *Income Taxes*. You also need to know the definition of deferred tax , and the circumstances in which it should be accounted for and where disclosed. No computations for current tax or deferred tax will be assessed.

KNOWLEDGE & UNDERSTANDING

· The presentation of Corporation Tax in financial statements (Element 11.1)
· The UK regulatory framework for financial reporting and the main requirements of relevant International Financial Reporting Standards (Element 11.1)

CONTENTS

1 IAS 12 *Income Taxes*
2 Deferred tax
3 Disclosure

1   IAS 12 *Income Taxes*

1.1 Introduction

The current tax for a company is the amount of corporation tax estimated to be payable in respect of the taxable profit for the year, along with adjustments to estimates in respect of previous periods.

1.2 Corporation tax

Companies pay corporation tax on their profits. In principle, the amount of current corporation tax should be calculated using the tax rates that the legislation has laid down for the company's financial year. In assessment tasks you will normally be told the rate, and often the amount, of corporation tax.

It is obvious that corporation tax cannot be calculated until after the profit figure has been found. When preparing a balance sheet, current tax for current and prior periods recognised as a liability. If the amount already paid in respect of current and prior periods exceeds the amount due for those periods, the excess shall be recognised as an asset.

○ EXAMPLE   ○○○○

A company makes an operating profit before taxation of £300,000. Corporation tax is estimated at £105,000. (The corporation tax charge is not 30% of the accounting profit before tax, since accounting profits are adjusted to calculate the taxable profit before tax.)

Solution

Income statement (extract) for the year end 31 December 20X1

	£
Profit on before taxation	300,000
Tax on profit	
Corporation tax based on the profit of the year @ 30%	(105,000)
Profit after taxation	195,000

Corporation tax liability account

	£		£
Balance c/f 31 Dec X1	105,000	Income statement charge	105,000
	105,000		105,000
		Balance b/f 1 Jan X2	105,000

The balance on the corporation tax account is carried forward and will appear on the balance sheet under the 'current liabilities' heading.

1.3 Adjustments relating to prior years

When the provision for corporation tax is made in the accounts, it is only an estimate of the actual liability which will eventually be agreed with the Inland Revenue. Any difference between the original estimate and the actual figure will be adjusted in the next year's provision. If material this figure will be shown separately.

○ EXAMPLE   ○○○○

Continuing with the previous example, suppose that in 20X2 the company pays £99,000 corporation tax on the 20X1 profit, not the £105,000 as estimated. The profit for the year 20X2 is £400,000 and corporation tax is estimated at £132,000.

Income statement (extract) 20X2

	£	£
Profit before taxation		400,000
Tax		
Corporation tax based on the profit of the year @ 30%	132,000	
Adjustment for over provision in previous year	(6,000)	
		(126,000)
Profit after taxation		274,000

Corporation tax account

	£		£
01.10.X2 Bank	99,000	01.01.X2 Balance b/f	105,000
31.12.X2 Over provision	6,000	31.12.X2 Income statement	132,000
31.12.X2 Balance c/f	132,000		
	237,000		237,000
		01.01.X3 Balance b/f	132,000

The double entry for the over provision is:
Debit   Corporation tax liability £6,000
Credit Corporation tax charge

This reduces both the liability and the charge.

▷ ACTIVITY 1   ▷▷▷▷

Rubislaw plc

Rubislaw was formed in 20X0. It has a 31 December year-end.

The balance on its corporation tax account at 1 January 20X3 was £74,000. During 20X3 this liability was settled for £69,000. The taxable profits for 20X3 are estimated to be £150,000, and the tax rate is 30%.

Required:

Disclose how the above should be presented in the income statement for the year ended 31 December 20X3 and in the balance sheet as at that date

 [Answer on p. 238]

2   Deferred tax

□ **DEFINITION**   □□□□

A deferred tax liability shall be recognised for all taxable temporary differences.

A temporary difference is the difference between the carrying amount of an asset in the balance sheet and its tax base.

A taxable temporary difference is a difference that will result in taxable amounts in determining taxable profit of future periods when the carrying amount of the asset or liability is recovered or settled.

2.1 An example of a taxable temporary difference

An example of a temporary difference is that depreciation charges appear in the financial accounts, but are not allowed as an expense for tax purposes. Instead, capital allowances reduce taxable profits. Over the lifetime of a non-current asset total depreciation charges will equal (roughly) total capital allowances. However, in any particular accounting period the two amounts will differ - a taxable difference.

The common feature of taxable differences, is simply this: timing differences originate in one period and are capable of reversal in later periods.

○ **EXAMPLE**   ○○○○

XY Ltd expects the tax liability for the current year to be £46,000. There was an under provision of £3,000 in the previous year. The deferred tax balance at the beginning of the year was £20,000 and this is to increase to £26,000 at the year end.

Calculate the tax charge for the current year.

Solution

The tax charge in the income statement consists of three things:

Tax on profits	X
Under /(Over) provision from prior year	X
Movement on deferred tax provision	X
Tax charge	X

To calculate the movement on the deferred tax provision, we just take the difference between the opening and closing provision. This will be a £6,000 increase (£26,000 - £20,000). This is an increase in the liability so the double entry will be:

| DR | Tax expense | £6,000 |
| CR | Deferred tax liability | £6,000 |

The tax charge will be as follows:

Tax on profits	46,000
Under /(Over) provision from prior year	3,000
Movement on deferred tax provision	6,000
Tax charge	55,000

3 Disclosure

The tax charge related to profit or loss for the period shall be presented on the face of the income statement.

The aggregate current and deferred tax relating to items that are charged or credited to equity must be disclosed separately.

4 Test your knowledge ▷ ▷ ▷

1 A company has a profit for the period of £100,000. The tax rate is 30%. Last year there was an over provision of £2,000. How much should be charged in this period's income statement?

2 Give an example of a taxable temporary difference.

[Answers on p. 238]

5 Summary

This chapter has summarised all the information regarding tax that you need for the preparation of a set of limited company financial statements. The current corporation tax provision appears as an expense in the income statement and as a current liability in the balance sheet. If there is a balance on the corporation tax account already this will represent an under or over provision from the previous year. This is also included as part of the current year tax charge.

Deferred tax, is a tax adjustment to reflect taxable temporary differences.

Answers to chapter activities & 'test your knowledge' questions

△ ACTIVITY 1 △ △ △

Rubislaw plc

Income statement (extract) for the year ended 31 December 20X3

	£
Tax on profit (W1)	(40,000)

Balance sheet (extract) at 31 December 20X3

	£
Current liabilities	
Tax liabilities	45,000

Workings

(1) *CT for accounting period ended 31.12.X3*	£
Profits	150,000
Corporation tax at 30%	45,000

Tax charge for the year	£
CT for year ended 31.12.X3	45,000
Overprovision for 31.12.X2 (£74,000 – £69,000)	(5,000)
	40,000

Test your knowledge △ △ △

1 £28,000 (£30,000 - £2,000).

2 Capital allowances versus depreciation.

KAPLAN PUBLISHING

14

LEASES

INTRODUCTION

Leases are covered by IAS 17 *Leases*. For Unit 11 you need an appreciation of the difference between finance and operating leases and an overview of the differences in accounting treatment but no detailed computations will be assessed.

KNOWLEDGE & UNDERSTANDING

· The UK regulatory framework for financial reporting and the main requirements of relevant International Financial Reporting Standards (Element 11.1)

CONTENTS

1 Types of extended credit agreement
2 Accounting for finance leases
3 Operating leases

1 Types of extended credit agreement

1.1 Introduction

A business may acquire the use of a fixed asset by outright purchase (cash or credit) or by some form of 'extended credit' agreement – credit sale, hire purchase, a finance lease or operating lease.

If these transactions were to be recorded according to their strict legal form, the picture presented by the balance sheet and income statement of the business using the asset could be quite misleading. This is because neither the asset used nor the liability for future payments would be recognised in the balance sheet.

IAS 17 ensures that transactions that are in substance loans to acquire an asset, even if not in legal form, are treated as any other loan agreement or asset purchase.

1.2 Leases

Lease – involves a contract to hire out an asset between the lessor (who owns the asset and will continue to own the asset) and the lessee (who gains the right to use the asset for an agreed period of time). Normally, the asset is never actually sold to the lessee and remains the property of the lessor.

IAS 17 distinguishes between two types of lease, finance and operating:

A finance lease is a lease that effectively is the sale of the asset to the lessee. The terms of the lease transfers substantially all the risks and rewards of ownership of an asset to the lessee.

If an asset meets any of the following situations it would be considered a finance lease:

(a) lease transfers ownership of the asset to the lessee by the end of the lease term
(b) lessee has the option to purchase the asset at a price that is expected to be sufficiently lower than the fair value at the date the option becomes exercisable for it to be reasonably certain, at the inception of the lease, that the option will be exercised
(c) the lease term is for the major part of the economic life of the asset
(d) at inception the present value of the minimum lease payments amounts to at least substantially all of the fair value of the leased asset
(e) the leased assets are of such a specialised nature that only the lessee can use them without major modifications.
(f) the lessee can cancel the lease and the lessors loss associated with the cancellation are borne by the lessee
(g) gains or losses from the fluctuation in the fair value of the residual accrue to the lessee
(h) lessee has the ability to continue the lease for a secondary period at a rent that is substantially lower than market rent.

For a lease to be considered as a finance lease, the term of the lease would be close to the life of the asset and the present value of total rentals paid would be close to the value of the asset.

An *operating lease* is a lease other than a finance lease.

1.3 Land and buildings

Land

A characteristic of land is that it normally has an indefinite economic life and if title is not expected to pass to the lessee by the end of the lease term, the lessee normally does not receive substantially all the risks and rewards of ownership. Therefore leases of land are classified as operating leases.

Buildings

Buildings can be treated separately to land even if the contract entered into is a joint one to lease land and buildings. Therefore if the lease covers the life of the building, then it can be classified as a finance lease even if the land element is classified as an operating lease.

2 Accounting for finance leases

2.1 Capitalisation of finance leases in the lessee accounts

The two critical questions to be answered are:

(a) At what value should the asset be capitalised?
(b) What finance charge should be made in the income statement?

2.2 The capitalised value in the balance sheet

At the start of the lease, the sum to be recorded both as an asset and as a liability should be the fair value of the leased asset or, if lower, the present value of the minimum lease payments, derived by discounting them at the interest rate implicit in the lease.

Minimum lease payments - the payments over the lease term that the lessee is required to make.

Interest rate implicit in the lease – this will approximate to the rate of interest on a loan to purchase the asset.

The asset that is capitalised must also be depreciated as per in accordance with similar types of assets held by the entity. The depreciation should be calculated in accordance with either IAS 16 *Property, plant and equipment* or IAS 38 *Intangible Assets.*

2.3 The finance charge

The excess of the minimum lease payments over the initial capitalised value represents the finance charge. The total finance charge should be allocated to accounting periods during the lease term so as to produce a constant periodic rate of charge on the remaining balance of the obligation for each accounting period (i.e. the actuarial method), or a reasonable approximation.

○ **EXAMPLE**   ○○○○

A lessee enters into a lease on 1 January 20X1 for an item of plant with a life of five years. The following details are relevant:

Fair value of asset	£10,000
Residual value	Nil after five years
Lease terms	£2,500 pa in advance for five years, the first rental payable on 1.1.X1

The interest rate implicit in the lease is 12.6%.

Required:

Show how this transaction would be recorded in the ledger accounts of the lessee for the first two years, and show also how the transaction would be reflected in the income statement and balance sheet over the five years.

Solution

The total amount payable for the lease is £12,500 (5 x £2,500). Included in these payments will be the interest element. When the lease starts, the fair value of the asset (£10,000) is capitalised into non current assets and shown as the lease creditor. As the payments are made at the beginning of the year, the first payment of £2,500 will reduce the creditor to the £7,500 shown below.

The finance charge will be calculated as follows for each year:

Year	Amount outstanding £	Interest @ 12.6% £	Repayment on 1 January following £
1	7,500	945	2,500
2	5,945	749	2,500
3	4,194	528	2,500
4	2,222	278	2,500
5	–	–	–
			————
			2,500
			————

The annual depreciation charge will be:

$$\frac{£100,000}{5} = £2,000 \text{ pa}$$

The ledger entry at the beginning of the lease will be:

	£	£
Dr Leased assets	10,000	
Cr Obligation under finance leases		10,000

being the recording of the 'purchase' of an asset under a finance lease at its fair value and the assumption of a liability.

Thereafter the entries in the leased asset account and the depreciation account will be exactly the same as for a purchased asset. The entries in the leasing obligation account will be as follows:

Obligation under finance leases account

	£		£
1.1.X1 Cash	2,500	1.1.X1 Leased asset	10,000
31.12.X1 Balance c/f	8,445	31.12.X1 Interest expense	945
	10,945		10,945
1.1.X2 Cash	2,500	1.1.X2 Balance b/f	8,445
31.12.X2 Balance c/f	6,694	31.12.X2 Interest expense	749
		(8,445 – 2,500) x 12.6%	
	9,194		9,194
		1.1.X3 Balance b/f	6,694

The charges to the income statement over the period of the lease are:

Year	1	2	3	4	5	Total
	£	£	£	£	£	£
Depreciation	2,000	2,000	2,000	2,000	2,000	10,000
Interest	945	749	528	278	–	2,500
	2,945	2,749	2,528	2,278	2,000	12,500

The balance sheets would reflect the net book value of the asset and the outstanding principal of the loan together with the accrued interest for the year which will be paid on the first day of the next period.

Balance sheets

Year	1	2	3	4	5
	£	£	£	£	£
Fixed assets					
Leased plant					
Cost	10,000	10,000	10,000	10,000	10,000
Accumulated dep'n	2,000	4,000	6,000	8,000	10,000
Net book value	8,000	6,000	4,000	2,000	–

Year	1	2	3	4	5
	£	£	£	£	£
Current liabilities					
Obligations under finance leases:					
Principal	1,555	1,751	1,972	2,222	–
Accrued interest	945	749	528	278	–
	2,500	2,500	2,500	2,500	–
Non-current liabilities					
Obligations under finance leases (principal only)	5,945	4,194	2,222	–	–
	8,445	6,694	4,722	2,500	–

Obligations under finance leases have been split between the current portion (payable within 12 months of the balance sheet date) and the long-term portion.

▷ ACTIVITY 1

Finch

Finch Ltd entered into a leasing agreement with Tyrrell plc on 1 October 20X5. This involves a specialised piece of manufacturing machinery which was purchased by Tyrrell plc to Finch Ltd's specifications.

The contract involves an annual payment in arrears of £1,200,000 for five years.

At the start of the lease with Tyrrell plc the present value of the minimum lease payments was calculated in accordance with the rules contained in IAS 17 and found to be £4,100,000. The fair value of the machinery at the commencement of the contract was £4,680,000.

Finch Ltd is responsible for the maintenance of the machinery and is required to insure it against accidental damage.

The machinery would normally be expected to have a useful life of approximately seven years. Finch Ltd depreciates its property, plant and equipment on the straight line basis.

The implied rate of interest is 14.2% per annum.

Required:
(a) Discuss how you would classify this lease with reference to the rules in IAS 17.
(b) Describe the impact in the accounts of Finch Ltd on the assumption you decide to classify the lease as a finance lease.

[Answer on p.246]

3 Operating leases

An operating lease is a lease other than a finance lease, under which there is no suggestion that the risks and rewards of ownership are transferred from the lessor to the lessee. A business may lease a photocopier or fax machine under this type of shorter-term lease.

Thus the asset is treated as a fixed asset in the books of the lessor and the rental is treated as income for the lessor and as expense for the lessee. The treatment of operating leases in the lessee's books is that the rental should be charged on a straight-line basis over the lease term.

4 Test your knowledge

1 A lessor hires out an asset with a five-year life to a lessee for a period of five years. Is this a finance lease or an operating lease?

2 Are assets which are the subject of operating leases shown on the lessee's balance sheet?

3 Explain briefly how IAS 17 requires finance leases to be shown on the balance sheet.

[Answers on p. 247]

5 Summary

The important matters which you must appreciate are:
(a) the distinction between a finance lease and an operating lease
(b) looking at the substance of the transaction rather than the form of the contract
(c) the capitalisation of finance leases in the lessee's books and the recognition of the obligation
(d) the treatment of operating lease rentals in the lessee's books.

Answers to chapter activities & 'test your knowledge' questions

△ ACTIVITY 1   △ △ △ △

Finch

(a) IAS 17 explains that a finance lease is a lease that transfers substantially all the risks and rewards of ownership to the lessee. It should be presumed that such a transfer of risks and rewards occurs if, at the inception of a lease, the present value of the minimum lease payments, including any initial payment, amounts to substantially all of the fair value of the leased asset.

In this case the present value of the minimum lease payments is £4,100,000 and the fair value of the machinery was £4,680,000. This amounts to:

$$\frac{4,100,000}{4,680,000} \times 100 = 88\% \text{ of the fair value of the machinery}$$

Additionally, the machinery was purchased by Tyrrell plc to Finch Ltd's specifications and it is therefore unlikely that Tyrrell plc would be able to lease it to any other organisation. Secondly, the lease period covers five years of the seven-year useful life of the machinery, which provides further evidence that it would be difficult to lease the asset to another organisation as it will effectively be obsolete at the end of the current lease. Thirdly, Finch Ltd is responsible for the maintenance and insurance of the machinery.

The lease should therefore be classified as a finance lease.

(b) If we treat the lease as a finance lease we capitalise it at fair value, or at the present value of the minimum lease payments if this is lower. This means we will include it in the balance sheet as an asset and as an obligation to pay future rentals, i.e. a liability. The asset will then be depreciated over the shorter of the lease term and its useful life.

The income statement will be charged with a finance charge.

The accounting treatment required for the balance sheet is to debit fixed assets and credit creditors with £4,100,000.

Test your knowledge △ △ △

1 Finance lease. The term of the lease is for the entire useful life of the leased asset.

2 No.

3 IAS 17 requires lessees to show assets acquired under finance leases, and the related obligation, on the balance sheet.

EVENTS AFTER THE BALANCE SHEET DATE AND CONTINGENCIES

INTRODUCTION

For Unit 11 you need to know all aspects of IAS 10 *Events After the Balance Sheet Date* and almost all aspects of IAS 37 *Provisions, Contingent Liabilities and Contingent Assets*.

KNOWLEDGE & UNDERSTANDING

· The UK regulatory framework for financial reporting and the main requirements of relevant International Financial Reporting Standards (Element 11.1)

CONTENTS

1 IAS 10 *Events After the Balance Sheet Date*

1.1 Introduction

Events after the balance sheet date are those events, both favourable and unfavourable, which occur between the balance sheet date and the date on which the financial statements are authorised for issue. There are two types of event:

(a) adjusting events, which require the accounts to be adjusted to reflect their impact; and

(b) non-adjusting events, which are merely noted in the accounts if material.

1.2 Adjusting events

These are events which provide additional evidence of conditions existing at the balance sheet date. Such events are relevant because they relate to items appearing in the accounts or transactions reported in them. Examples of adjusting events are:

(a) The settlement post year end of a court case that confirms that the entity had a present obligation at the balance sheet date. The entity must adjust any previously recognised provisions related to the court case in accordance with IAS 37 *Provisions, Contingent Liabilities and Contingent Assets* or recognise a new provision.

(b) The receipt of information post year end indicating an asset was impaired at the balance sheet date, or the amount of a previously recognised impairment loss for that asset needs to be adjusted. For example:

    (i) bankruptcy of a customer usually confirms that a loss existed at the balance sheet date on a trade receivable and the entity needs to adjust the carrying amount of the trade receivable;

    (ii) sale of inventories after the balance sheet date may give evidence about their net realisable value at the balance sheet date.

(c) The subsequent determination of the purchase price or of the proceeds of sale of assets purchased or sold before the year-end.

(d) The determination after the balance sheet date of the amount of profit-sharing or bonus payments, if the entity had a present legal or constructive obligation at the balance sheet date to make such payments as a result of events before that date.

(e) The discovery of errors or frauds which show that the financial statements were incorrect.

1.3 Non-adjusting events

These events which concern conditions which did not exist at the balance sheet date. These events therefore shall not be adjusted for in the financial statements. Some examples of non-adjusting events are:

(a) mergers and acquisitions;

(b) reconstructions;

(c) issues of shares and debentures;

(d) purchases and sales of non-current assets and investments;

(e) losses of non-current assets or inventories as a result of a catastrophe, such as a fire or flood;

(f) decline in the value of property and investments held as non-current assets, if it can be demonstrated that the decline occurred after the year end

1.4 Dividends

If an entity declares dividends after the balance sheet date, the entity shall not recognise those dividends as a liability at the balance sheet date.

1.5 Going concern

The financial statements should not be prepared on a going concern basis if management determines after the balance sheet date that it intends to liquidate or cease trading.

1.6 Disclosure

·   The date the financial statements were authorised for issue and who gave that authorisation.

·   Material non-adjusting events
    (i)   the nature of the event; and
    (ii) an estimate of the financial effect, or a statement that it is not practicable to make such an estimate.

○ EXAMPLE   ○ ○ ○ ○

How would the following events be accounted for in the financial statements for the year to 31 December 20X2? Assume that each event is material in size in the context of the accounts as a whole.

(a) On 5 January 20X3 a large debtor went into liquidation owing £100,000 as at the balance sheet date. It is likely that this debtor balance will realise nothing.

(b) On 10 January 20X3 all the stocks in the Dudley warehouse were destroyed by fire. They had a cost at that date of £50,000 and a net realisable value of £70,000. Although this loss is serious, it is not so serious that the company is no longer able to continue as a going concern.

Solution

(a) This is an adjusting event giving additional information on the receivables figure at the year end. The £100,000 bad debt must be written off in the 20X2 accounts.

(b) This is a non-adjusting event as the fire occurred after the balance sheet date. The damage to the stock occurred post year end so the year end position is not affected. This should be described in a note to the accounts.

▷ ACTIVITY 1

Jam Limited

As the company accountant to Jam Limited you have started to finalise your company's accounts for the year ended 31 October 20X1. This follows a very hectic month during which, in addition to normal business, the events recorded below occurred:

October	10	Paid for a press advertising campaign due to take place during the last two weeks in October.
	14	A company warehouse was flooded during storms. Much of the company's inventories were lost and a considerable quantity of returnable containers, on loan from a supplier, were severely damaged.
	25	The second week of the advertising campaign was deferred because of a strike by printers.
November	7	Letter received from company's insurers agreeing the full claim in respect of the flood on 14 October, except for the returnable containers which, they say, are not covered by the company's insurance policy.
	9	The government announced a ban on one of the company's major activities.

Required:

State how the events listed above would affect the financial statements for the year ended 31 October 20X1.

[Answer on p. 257]

2   IAS 37 *Provisions, Contingent Liabilities and Contingent Assets*

2.1 Introduction

The objective of the IAS 37 is to ensure that:
· provisions and contingencies are recognised and measured consistently
· sufficient information is disclosed to enable a user of the accounts to

understand the nature, timing and amount of any provisions and contingencies included in the accounts.

□ DEFINITION

Provision - liability of uncertain timing or amount

Liability - present obligation of the entity arising from past events, the settlement of which is expected to result in an outflow from the entity of resources embodying economic benefits.

Obligating event-an event that creates a legal or constructive obligation that results in the entity having no realistic alternative to settling the obligation

Constructive obligation - A constructive obligation arises from the entity's past actions, where there is a pattern of past practice that indicates that an entity will behave in a certain way, for example:

· A retail store that habitually refunds purchases for dissatisfied customers and could not change its policy without damaging its reputation.

· An entity that has caused environmental damage and is obliged to rectify this because of its published policies and previous actions, even though there may be no legal obligation for it to do so.

Contingent liability - a possible obligation from a past event whose existence will be confirmed only by the occurrence or non-occurrence of one or more uncertain future events not wholly within the control of the entity; or a present obligation that arises from past events that is not recognised because the outflow required to settle the obligation is not probable or the amount of the obligation cannot be measured with sufficient reliability.

Contingent asset - a possible asset that arises from past events and whose existence will be confirmed only by the occurrence or non-occurrence of one or more uncertain future events not wholly within the control

2.2 Provisions versus other liabilities versus contingent liabilities

A provision is a liability of uncertain timing or amount. This means that a provision can only be recognised if it meets the definition and recognition criteria of a liability. These are as follows:

(1) A present obligation must exist at the balance sheet date as a result of a past transaction or event, and

(2) It is probable that an outflow of economic resources will be required to settle the obligation; and

(3) A reliable estimate can be made of the amount of the obligation.

Other liabilities such as trade payables, are liabilities to pay for goods that have been received and invoiced, therefore there is no uncertainty over their timing or amount. This makes them different.

Contingent liabilities are never recognised in the financial statements because there existence will be confirmed only by the occurrence or non-occurrence of one or more uncertain future events not wholly within the control of the entity.

2.3 Recognition

The amount recognised as a provision shall be the best estimate of the expenditure required to settle the present obligation at the balance sheet date.

Where the time value of money is material, the amount of the provision shall be the present value of the expenditures expected to be required to settle the obligation.

The provisions must be reviewed at each balance sheet date and adjusted to reflect the current best estimate. If it is no longer probable an outflow of resources will be required to settle the obligation then the provision shall be reversed.

The provision must only be used for expenditures for which the provision was originally recognised.
· Contingent assets are never recognised
· Contingent liabilities are never recognised

2.4 Restructuring provisions

A restructuring is a programme that is planned and controlled by management and materially changes either:
(a) the scope of a business undertaken by an entity: or
(b) the manner in which the business is conducted.

The following are examples of events that may fall under the definition of restructuring:
· Sale or termination of a line of business
· Closure of business locations in a country or region or relocation from one country/region to another
· Changes in management structure
· Fundamental reorganisations

A constructive obligation to restructure arises when an entity:
(a) has a detailed formal plan for the restructuring and
(b) has raised a valid expectation to those affected that it will carry out the restructuring by starting to implement the plan or announcing its main features to those affected.

In the above case therefore a restructuring provision may be recognised as there is:

(i)   an obligation (detailed plan and people know about it)

(ii)   probable outflow of resources (cost of relocation or redundancy etc.)

(iii)   reliable estimate of the expenditure can be made

The restructuring provision shall include only the direct expenditures arising from the restructuring, which are those that are both:

(a)   necessarily entailed by the restructuring: and

(b)   not associated with the ongoing activities of the entity.

2.5 Disclosure of contingent liabilities and contingent assets

The accounts should give the following disclosures for each material class of contingent liability and asset that are not recognised in the balance sheet, unless the possibility of transfer of economic benefits is remote:

·   The nature of the contingency

·   The uncertainties expected to affect the ultimate outcome

·   An estimate of the potential financial effect.

▷ ACTIVITY 2 ▷▷▷▷

Hill plc

The year end of Hill plc is 31 March 20X0. Hill plc is a very diverse group. One of its consistent features is that it has a reputation as an ethical organisation. Much is made of the company's policies with regard to recycling, controls over emission of noxious substances and making use only of renewable resources.

Many of its goods in its beauty and cosmetic range (Sophie Beauty Products) use ingredients that are sourced overseas and the company publishes full details of its environmental policies as part of its annual report.

You are the chief accountant of the group and your assistant has prepared draft accounts for the year ended 31 March 20X0. Your assistant, however, is uncertain as to the application of IAS 37 *Provisions, Contingent Liabilities and Contingent Assets* to three material items described below and has requested your advice.

Required:

(a)   Explain the circumstances under which a provision should be recognised in the financial statements according to IAS 37.

(b)   Explain how each of the following issues should be treated in the consolidated financial statements for the year ended 31 March 20X0.

(i)   On 12 February 20X0 the board of Hill plc decided to close down a large factory in Aylesbury. The board expects that production will be transferred to other factories. No formal plan has yet been drawn up but it is expected the closure will occur on 31 August 20X0. As at the balance sheet date this decision has not been announced to the employees or to any other interested parties. The overall costs of this closure are foreseen as £79 million.

(ii) During the year to 31 March 20X0, a customer started legal proceedings claiming one of the products from the 'Sophie Beauty' range had caused a skin complaint. The group's lawyers have advised that the chances of this action succeeding are remote.

(iii) The group has an overseas subsidiary 'Melinat' that is involved in mining certain minerals. These activities cause significant damage to the environment, including deforestation. The company expects to abandon the mine in eight years time. The country where the subsidiary is based has no environmental legislation obligating companies to rectify environmental damage and it is unlikely that such legislation will be enacted within the next eight years. It has been estimated that the cost of putting right the site will be £10 million if the tree re-planting were successful at the first attempt, but it will probably be necessary to have a further attempt costing an additional £5 million.

[Answer on p. 258]

3 Test your knowledge

1   A debtor goes into liquidation on 12 January 20X8, owing £300,000 to the company on its balance sheet date of 31 December 20X7. Is this an adjusting or a non-adjusting event?

2   A company issues new shares soon after its balance sheet date. Is this an adjusting or a non-adjusting event?

3   Should contingent assets be shown on the balance sheet?

[Answers on p. 259]

4 Summary

You need to be able to recognise both adjusting and non-adjusting events. You should also ensure that you understand what is meant by a provision and when provisions should be shown as a liability in the balance sheet. You should be able to distinguish a provision from a contingent liability and understand the different treatment of contingent liabilities and contingent assets.

The key in deciding whether a provision should be recognised is to ask whether:

1   A present **obligation** must exist at the balance sheet date as a result of a past transaction or event, and

2   It is **probable** that an outflow of economic resources will be required to settle the obligation; and

3   A **reliable estimate** can be made of the amount of the obligation.

If these factors can be satisfied then a provision should be made in the financial statements otherwise it is a contingent liability which should just be disclosed.

Anwers to chapter activities & 'test your knowledge' questions

△ **ACTIVITY 1**   △ △ △ △

Jam Limited

Events after the balance sheet date are those events, both favourable and unfavourable, which occur between the date of the balance sheet and the date on which the financial statements are approved by the board of directors. There are two types of event: an adjusting event provides additional evidence of conditions existing at the balance sheet date which thus need to be reflected in the financial statements, whereas a non-adjusting event concerns conditions which did not exist at the balance sheet date but which need to be disclosed by way of notes in the financial statements to ensure a true and fair view is shown.

(i) **Inventory loss by flood:** the loss occurred before the year end. The agreement of the company's insurers to the full claim is an adjusting event within the meaning of IAS 10 and thus the amount of the full claim should be accrued in current assets. The financial consequences of the flood (e.g. non-availability of inventories) is a non-adjusting event and thus (in the accounts) full disclosure should be made of:
·   details of the flood; and
·   an estimate of the financial effect, or a statement that an estimate cannot be made.

(ii) **Returnable containers:** the company should enquire about the supplier's insurance and review the conditions on which the containers were received on loan. If liability is admitted then this is an adjusting event and a suitable accrual should be made. If liability is not admitted then the company should consider disclosure as a contingent liability after taking appropriate legal advice (i.e. where the ultimate outcome will be confirmed only on the occurrence or non-occurrence of one or more uncertain future events (e.g. a pending or possible lawsuit)).

(iii) **Payment for advertising:** advertising expenses are charged against the income of the period in which the advertising or clearly definable services took place (accruals concept). Thus the first week's advertising will be charged to the year ended 31 October 20X1. The amount of prepayment of the second week carried forward depends on the value of the work already done. For instance if printing has been completed before the year end then this cost should be charged in 20X1, but any subsequent distribution and advertising costs not incurred until after the year end should be charged in the 20X2 accounts.

(iv) **Ban on company's activities:** the ban may involve both adjusting and non-adjusting events. Since the ban will probably result in the closing of a significant part of the company's trading activities and is thus a non-adjusting event, a note to the accounts stating a description and estimate of the financial effect will be required.

The ban may also affect estimates of amounts in the financial statements for the year ended 20X1, e.g. realisable value of inventories, value of patents, and is thus an adjusting event.

Additionally, a review of the application of the going concern principle may be necessary, depending on the effect of the ban, eg are adequate alternative markets available? Is adequate finance available to enable the company to expand into these alternative markets?

△ ACTIVITY 2 △△△△

Hill plc

(a) A provision should be recognised when, and only when:
  (1) A present **obligation** must exist at the balance sheet date as a result of a past transaction or event, and
  (2) It is **probable** that an outflow of economic resources will be required to settle the obligation; and
  (3) A **reliable estimate** can be made of the amount of the obligation.

An obligation exists when the entity has no realistic alternative to making a transfer of economic benefits. This is the case only where the obligation can be enforced by law or in the case of constructive obligation (see below).

(b) (i) *Factory closure*
  The key issue is whether or not a provision should be made for the £79 million cost of restructuring. This will depend on whether the group has an obligation to incur this expenditure.

  There is clearly no legal obligation to close this factory but there may be a constructive obligation. A constructive obligation only exists if the group has created valid expectations in other parties such as customers, employees and suppliers, that the restructuring will be carried out.

  As no formal plan exists and no announcements have been made to any of the affected parties, no constructive obligation exists. A board decision alone is not sufficient – no provision should be made.

  (ii) *Legal proceedings*
  It is unlikely the group has a present obligation to compensate the customer and therefore no provision should be recognised.

  There may be a contingent liability but as the possibility of a transfer of economic benefit is remote we can ignore this in the accounts.

(iii) *Environmental damage*

The company has no legal obligation to rectify this damage, but through its published policies it has created expectation on the part of those affected that it will take action to do so. There is therefore a constructive obligation to rectify the damage. It is probable that a transfer of economic benefits will take place and an estimate of the amount involved can be made.

A provision should be made of the best estimate of the cost involved, ie the full amount of ?15 million should be provided for.

Test your knowledge

1   Adjusting event.

2   Non-adjusting event.

3   No. Contingent assets should be disclosed in a note to the accounts.

OTHER ACCOUNTING STANDARDS

INTRODUCTION

In this chapter we will briefly consider the few remaining accounting standards that have not been covered earlier in this text. In each case the knowledge that will be assessed for each of these standards is very limited and we will only cover what is required for the assessment.

KNOWLEDGE & UNDERSTANDING

· The UK regulatory framework for financial reporting and the main requirements of relevant International Financial Reporting Standards (Element 11.1)

CONTENTS

1 IFRS 5 *Non-current Assets Held for Sale and Discontinued Operations*
2 IAS 14 *Segment Reporting*
3 IAS 18 *Revenue*
4 IAS 33 *Earnings per Share*

1 IFRS 5 *Non-current Assets Held for Sale and Discontinued Operations*

1.1 Introduction

This IFRS specifies accounting for assets held for sale and the presentation of discontinued operations.

1.2 Non-current assets as held for sale

An entity should classify a non-current asset as held for sale if its carrying amount will be recovered principally through a sale transaction rather than continuing use.

The asset held for sale should be valued at the lower of its carrying amount and fair value less costs to sell.

An entity shall present a non-current asset held for sale separately on the balance sheet. The major classes of assets held for resale should be separately disclosed either on the face of the balance sheet or in the notes.

1.3 Discontinued operations

A discontinued operation is a component of an entity that either has been disposed of or is classified as held for sale and:

(a) represents a separate major line of business or geographical area of operations

(b) is part of a single co-ordinated plan to dispose of a separate major line of business or geographical area of operations or

(c) is a subsidiary acquired exclusively with a view to resale

The entity must disclose a single amount on the face of the income statement showing the post tax profit or loss of discontinued operations. (see chapter 4 pro-forma income statement)

2 IAS 14 *Segment Reporting*

2.1 Introduction

This standard deals with reporting information about the different types of products and services an entity produces and the different geographical areas in which it operates.

2.2 Scope and definitions

This standard applies only to entities whose equity or debt is publicly traded or those who voluntarily wish to disclose segmental information.

Business segment - a distinguishable component of an entity that is engaged in providing an individual product or service or a group of related products or services and that is subject to risks and returns that are different from those of other business segments.

Geographical segment - a distinguishable component of an entity that is engaged in providing products or services within a particular economic environment and that is subject to risks and returns that are different from those of components operating in other economic environments.

The dominant source and nature of an entity's risks and returns shall govern whether its primary segment reporting format will be its business segment or its geographical segment.

Segment information shall be prepared in conformity with the accounting policies adopted for preparing and presenting the financial statements of the entity.

3   IAS 18 *Revenue*

3.1 Introduction

Revenue is recognised when it is probable that future economic benefits will flow to the entity and these benefits can be measured reliably. This standard identifies the circumstances in which these criteria will be met and therefore revenue recognised.

3.2 Scope and definitions

This standard applies when accounting for revenue from sales of goods, the rendering of services and the use by others of the entities assets yielding dividends.

Revenue-gross inflow of economic benefits during the period arising in the course of the ordinary activities of an entity when those inflows result in increases in equity, other than increases relating to contributions from equity participants.

3.3 Recognition and measurement

Revenue shall be measured at the fair value of the consideration received or receivable.

Revenue from the sale of goods shall be recognised when all the following conditions have been satisfied:
(a)   entity has transferred to the buyer the significant risks and rewards of ownership of the goods;

(b) entity retains neither continuing managerial involvement to the degree usually associated with ownership nor effective control over the goods sold;

(c) amount of revenue can be measured reliably;

(d) probable that the economic benefits associated with the transaction will flow to the entity

(e) costs incurred or to be incurred in respect of the transaction can be measured reliably.

Revenue from the rendering of services should only be recognised when it can be estimated reliably. Revenue associated with the transaction shall be recognised by reference to the stage of completion of the transaction at the balance sheet date. The outcome can be estimated reliably when all the following are satisfied:

(a) amount of revenue can be measured reliably;

(b) it is probable that the economic benefits associated with the transaction will flow to the entity;

(c) the stage of completion of the transaction at the balance sheet can be measured reliably; and

(d) costs incurred for the transaction and the costs to complete the transaction can be measured reliably.

Revenue arising from the use by others of entity assets yielding dividends shall be recognised when the shareholder's rights to receive payment is established and

(a) it is probable that the economic benefits associated with the transaction will flow to the entity;

(b) the amount of the revenue can be measured reliably.

4 IAS 33 *Earnings per Share*

4.1 Introduction

This standard prescribes principles for the determination and presentation of earnings per share so at to improve performance comparisons between different entities in the same reporting period and between different reporting periods for the same entity.

4.2 Scope

This standard applies to all entities whose shares are publicly traded.

4.3 Measurement

The basic earnings per share (EPS) calculation is simply:

$$\frac{\text{Earnings for the year}}{\text{Number of shares in issue}}$$

Here 'earnings' means the profit attributable to ordinary equity holders; and 'shares' means the weighted average number of ordinary shares outstanding during the period.

Profit attributable to ordinary equity holders is after tax and must be adjusted for preference dividends.

Using the weighted average number of ordinary shares outstanding during the period reflects the possibility that the amount of shareholders' capital varied during the period as a result of issuing or redeeming shares.

○ EXAMPLE   ○○○○

Gerard plc
    Draft income statement for the year ended 31 December 20X4

	£000	£000
Profit before tax		5,060
Taxation		(2,300)
		———
Profit after tax		2,760
		———
Dividends		
Paid – preference dividend	276	
Paid – ordinary dividend	368	

On 1 January 20X4 the issued share capital of Gerard plc was 9,200,000 3% preference shares of £1 each and 8,280,000 ordinary shares of £1 each.

Required:

Calculate the earnings per share (EPS) in respect of the year ended 31 December 20X4 on the basis that there was no change in the issued share capital of the company during the year.

Solution

The amount of earnings available to the ordinary shares (ie excluding the preference dividend) is divided by the number of ordinary shares.

$$\frac{£2,760,000 - £276,000}{8,280,000} = 30p$$

The EPS of 30p would be disclosed at the bottom of the income statement for the year 20X4.

4.4 Issue of shares during the year (to show weighted average number of shares)

In the example of Gerard plc, suppose that the company had issued 3,312,000 new ordinary shares at their full market value on 30 June 20X4. The money raised would have had an impact on the earnings. We would need to reflect this in the earnings per share working by recognising the impact on the earnings using a weighted average number of shares.

Date	Actual number of shares	Fraction of year	Total
1 January 20X4	8,280,000	$\frac{6}{12}$	4,140,000
30 June 20X4	11,592,000 (W1)	$\frac{6}{12}$	5,796,000
Number of shares in EPS calculation			9,936,000

(W1) New number of shares

Original number	8,280,000
New issue	3,312,000
New number	11,592,000

The earnings per share for 20X4 would now be calculated as:

$$\frac{£2,760 - £276,000}{11,592,000} = 21p$$

5 Test your knowledge

1   How should assets held for sale be valued?

2   What is the definition of revenue?

3   An entity has earnings of £19,200 and share capital of £120,000 comprising 240,000 shares at 50p each. What is the EPS?

[Answers on p. 267]

6   Summary

IFRS 5 states that assets held for re-sale must be classified separately on the balance sheet and post tax profit from discontinued operations must be disclosed separately on the face of the income statement.

IAS 14 states that PLC's must disclose segmental information relating to the business or geographical segments of the entity.

IAS 18 states that revenues should be recognised at fair value and only when they are probable and can be measured reliably.

IAS 33 states that PLC's must disclose their EPS at the bottom of the income statement.

Anwers to 'test your knowledge' questions

> **Test your knowledge** △ △ △
>
> 1 The asset held for sale should be valued at the lower of its carrying amount and fair value less costs to sell.
>
> 2 Revenue-gross inflow of economic benefits during the period arising in the course of the ordinary activities of an entity when those inflows result in increases in equity, other than increases relating to contributions from equity participants.
>
> 3 0.08p.

INTERPRETATION OF ACCOUNTS

INTRODUCTION

Element 2 of this Unit is entitled 'Interpret Limited Company Financial Statements' therefore it is likely that every assessment will include some task which asks you to apply ratio analysis to company financial statements and analyse and interpret the results.

KNOWLEDGE & UNDERSTANDING

- Analysing and interpreting the information contained in financial statements (Element 11.2)
- Computing and interpreting accounting ratios (Element 11.2)
- Identify the relationships between the elements within financial statements of limited companies (Element 11.2)
- Interpret the relationship between elements of limited company financial statements using ratio analysis (Element 11.2)
- Identify unusual features or significant issues within financial statements of limited companies (Element 11.2)
- Draw valid conclusions from the information contained within financial statements of limited companies (Element 11.2)
- Present issues, interpretations and conclusions clearly to the appropriate people (Element 11.2)

CONTENTS

1 Profitability ratios
2 Liquidity ratios and asset utilisation
3 Investor ratios
4 Risk
5 Answering an exam question
6 General points about financial ratios
7 The working capital cycle

1 Profitability ratios

1.1 Introduction

Ratios calculated from financial statements help to interpret the information they present. Various users may use these ratios to analyse financial statements.

We can break down the ratios into categories to make our discussion more structured. To begin with we look at ratios relating to profitability.

1.2 Return on capital employed (ROCE)

Capital employed is normally measured as non-current assets plus current assets less current liabilities and represents the long-term investment in the business, or owners' capital plus long-term liabilities. Return on capital employed is frequently regarded as the best measure of profitability, indicating how successful a business is in utilising its assets. The ratio is only meaningful when the true values of assets are known and used in the formula.

$$\text{Return on capital employed} = \frac{\text{Profit before interest and taxation (PBIT)}}{\text{Average capital employed}} \times 100\%$$

Note that the profit *before* interest is used, because the loan capital rewarded by that interest is included in capital employed.

A low return on capital employed (assets used) is caused by either a low profit margin or a low asset turnover or both. This can be seen by breaking down the primary ROCE ratio into its two components: profit margin and asset turnover.

$$\text{ROCE} = \frac{\text{PBIT}}{\text{Capital employed}}$$

$$= \frac{\text{PBIT}}{\text{Revenue}} \times \frac{\text{Revenue}}{\text{Capital employment}}$$

$$= \text{Profit margin} \times \text{Asset turnover}$$

1.3 Profit margin (on revenue)

Operating profit margin = x 100%

A low margin indicates low selling prices or high costs or both. Comparative analysis will reveal the level of prices and costs in relation to competitors.

1.4 Asset turnover

This will show how fully a company is utilising its assets.

$$\text{Asset turnover} = \frac{\text{Revenue}}{\text{Capital employed}}$$

A low turnover shows that a company is not generating a sufficient volume of business for the size of the asset base. This may be remedied by increasing sales or by disposing of some of the assets or both.

1.5 Gross profit margin

$$\text{Gross profit margin} = \frac{\text{Gross profit}}{\text{Revenue}} \times 100\%$$

The gross profit margin focuses on the trading account. A low margin could indicate selling prices too low or cost of sales too high.

1.6 Return on owners' equity

$$\text{Return on owners' equity} = \frac{\text{Profit after interest and preference dividends but before tax}}{\text{Ordinary share capital and reserves}} \times 100\%$$

This looks at the return earned for ordinary shareholders. We use the profit after preference dividends and interest (i.e. the amounts that have to be paid before ordinary shareholders can be rewarded).

2 Liquidity ratios and asset utilisation

2.1 Current ratio

This is a common method of analysing working capital (net current assets) and is generally accepted as a good measure of short-term solvency. It indicates the extent to which the claims of short-term creditors are covered by assets that are expected to be converted to cash in a period roughly corresponding to the maturity of the claims.

$$\text{Current ratio} = \frac{\text{Current assets}}{\text{Current liabilities}}$$

The current ratio should ideally fall between 1:1 and 2:1.

2.2 Acid test ratio (quick ratio)

This is calculated in the same way as the current ratio except that inventories are excluded from current assets.

$$\text{Acid test ratio} = \frac{\text{Current assets} - \text{Inventories}}{\text{Current liabilities}}$$

This ratio is a much better test of the immediate solvency of a business because of the length of time necessary to convert inventories into cash (via revenue and debtors).

Contrary to what might be expected, this ratio may fall in a time of prosperity since increased activity may lead to larger inventories but less cash; conversely, when trade slows down inventories may be disposed of without renewal and the ratio will rise.

Although increased liquid resources more usually indicate favourable trading, it could be that funds are not being used to their best advantage (e.g. a large cash balance).

2.3 Receivables ratio

This is computed by dividing the trade receivables by the average daily sales to determine the number of days sales held in debtors.

$$\text{Average collection period} = \frac{\text{Trade receivables}}{\text{Credit sales}} \times 365 \text{ days}$$

A long average collection period probably indicates poor credit control, but it may be due to other factors such as overseas sales where the collection period will be much longer, or a deliberate decision to extend the credit period to attract new customers

2.4 Payables ratio

This is computed by dividing the trade payables by the average daily purchases to determine the number of days purchases held in creditors.

$$\text{Average payment period} = \frac{\text{Trade payable}}{\text{Credit purchase}} \times 365 \text{ days}$$

If only cost of sales rather than purchases is available in the information given this can be used as an approximation to purchases. If the payables period is very low, then the business might not be making the best use of its cash by paying suppliers early. If the period is very long then this is a free source of credit but the business must be careful not to harm relations with suppliers.

2.5 Inventory turnover

This ratio indicates whether inventory levels are justified in relation to cost of sales. The higher the ratio, the healthier the cash flow position, but with the qualification that the profit margin must also be acceptable.

$$\text{Inventory turnover} = \frac{\text{Cost of sales}}{\text{Inventories}}$$

It is usual to calculate this ratio using the closing inventories. A limitation on this ratio is that in a seasonal business inventories may fluctuate considerably during the year. The level of inventory turnover will vary between businesses. A retailer will have a fairly fast inventory turnover as goods are bought and sold fairly quickly. A manufacturing company will have a much slower inventory turnover as inventory is held in the business much longer as it goes through the production process.

2.6 Inventory turnover in days

Inventory turnover can also be calculated in days like debtors and creditors.

$$\text{Inventory turnover period} = \frac{\text{Inventories}}{\text{Cost of sales}} \times 365 \text{ days}$$

3 Investor ratios

3.1 Earnings per share

This ratio has no connection with the other profitability ratios and is used primarily by potential investors. It is, however, a very important ratio and it is required that listed companies actually disclose the figure for earnings per share at the foot of the income statement

$$\text{Earnings per share} = \frac{\text{Earnings available for ordinary shareholders}}{\text{Number of ordinary}}$$

The calculation can be complicated in some instances but, for the purposes of this chapter, it is enough to be aware that 'earnings available for ordinary shareholders' means profits after interest, taxation and preference dividends.

3.2 Price earnings ratio

Earnings per share is used by investors in calculating the price–earnings ratio or PE ratio. This is simply calculated as follows.

$$\text{PE ratio} = \frac{\text{Market price of share}}{\text{Earnings per share}}$$

A high PE ratio means that the shares are seen as an attractive investment. For example, if the PE ratio is 20, it means that investors are prepared to pay 20 times the annual level of earnings in order to acquire the shares.

3.3 Dividend cover

$$\text{Dividend cover} = \frac{\text{Earnings available to ordinary shareholders}}{\text{Dividend paid}}$$

This gives an indication of the security of future dividends. A high dividend cover ratio means that available profits comfortably cover the amount being paid out in dividends.

4 Risk

4.1 Gearing

Gearing measures the extent to which a business is dependent on non-equity funds, as opposed to equity funding. A high gearing ratio means that the business has a high proportion of borrowed funds in its total capital.

Gearing gives an indication of long-term liquidity and the financial risk inherent within the business. Highly geared companies have to meet large interest commitments before paying dividends and may have problems raising further finance if expansion is necessary.

$$\text{Gearing} = \frac{\text{Long} - \text{term debt and preference share capital}}{\text{Shareholder funds and long} - \text{term debt and preference share capital}} \times 100\%$$

4.2 Interest cover

$$\text{Interest cover} = \frac{\text{Profit before interest}}{\text{Interest paid}}$$

Interest on debt has to be paid before shareholders can receive dividends. Therefore a good measure of risk is to compare available profit with the amount of interest to be paid.

○ EXAMPLE ○○○○

Fieldsomer Ltd

Data

Maurice Sun plans to invest in Fieldsomer Ltd. This is a chain of shops. He is to meet his consultants to discuss the profitability of the company. To prepare for the meeting he has asked you to comment on the change in profitability and the return on capital of the company. He also has some questions about the company's balance sheet. He has given you Fieldsomer's income statements and the summarised balance sheets for the past two years prepared for internal purposes. These are set out below.

Fieldsomer Ltd
Summary Income Statements for the year ended 31 March

	20X4 £000	20X3 £000
Revenue	8,420	7,595
Cost of sales	(3,536)	(3,418)
Gross profit	4,884	4,177
Distribution costs	(1,471)	(1,016)
Administrative expenses	(1,224)	(731)
Profit from operations	2,189	2,430
Interest payable and similar charges	(400)	(480)
Profit before taxation	1,789	1,950
Tax	(465)	(569)
Profit for the financial year	1,324	1,381

Fieldsomer Ltd
Summary Balance Sheets as at 31 March

	20X4 £000	20X4 £000	20X3 £000	20X3 £000
Property, plant and equipment		15,132		13,880
Current assets	4,624		3,912	
Current liabilities	(2,215)		(1,855)	
Net current assets		2,409		2,057
Capital employed		17,541		15,937
Long term loan		(5,000)		(6,000)
		12,541		9,937

Called up share capital:

ordinary shares of £1 each	6,000	5,000
Share premium	2,000	2,000
Retained earnings	4,541	3,937
	12,541	9,937

Prepare a report for Maurice Sun that includes the following:

(a) a calculation of the following ratios of Fieldsomer Ltd for each of the two years:
  (i) return on capital employed
  (ii) net profit percentage
  (iii)gross profit percentage
  (iv)asset turnover (based on net assets).

(b) an explanation of the meaning of each ratio and a comment on the performance of Fieldsomer Ltd as shown by each of the ratios

(c) a conclusion on how the overall performance has changed over the two years.

Solution

REPORT

To: Maurice Sun **Subject:** Interpretation of financial statements
From: A Student **Date:** June 20X4

This report has been prepared to assist in the interpretation of the financial statements of Fieldsomer Ltd. It considers the profitability and return on capital of the business over 20X3 and 20X4.

(a) Calculation of the ratios

	20X4	20X3
Return on capital employed	$\dfrac{2,189}{17,541} = 12.5\%$	$\dfrac{2,430}{15,937} = 15.2\%$
Net profit percentage	$\dfrac{2,189}{8,420} = 26\%$	$\dfrac{2,430}{7,595} = 32\%$
Gross profit percentage	$\dfrac{4,884}{8,420} = 58\%$	$\dfrac{4,177}{7,595} = 55\%$
Asset turnover	$\dfrac{8,420}{17,541} = 0.48$	$\dfrac{7,595}{15,937} = 0.48$

(b) Explanation and comment

Return on capital employed
- This ratio shows in percentage terms how much profit is being generated by the capital employed in the company.
- The company is showing a lower return on capital employed in 20X4 compared to 20X3 and hence is generating less profit per £ of capital employed in the business.

Net profit percentage
- This ratio shows in percentage terms how much net profit is being generated from revenues.
- The ratio has decreased over the two years.
- This could be explained either by a decrease in the gross profit margin or by an increase in expenses, or both.
- In fact, the percentage of expenses to revenues has increased from 23% in 20X3 to 32% in 20X4.

Gross profit ratio
- This ratio shows in percentage terms how much gross profit is being generated from the company's revenues and thus indicates the gross profit margin on sales.
- The ratio has improved over the two years with an increase in the percentage from 55% to 58%.
- The company is increasing its revenue without significantly cutting its margins.
- This may be due to increasing its sales price or reducing the cost of sales or both.

Asset turnover
- This ratio shows how efficient the company is in generating revenue from the available capital employed/net assets.
- The ratio has stayed the same between the two years and so a similar level of revenue has been generated from the available capital employed/net assets in 20X4 than in 20X3.
- The new investment that has been made in property, plant and equipment and current assets in 20X4 has generated a proportional increase in sales

(c) Overall

The ratios show that the return on capital employed has deteriorated in 20X4 and that the company is thus generating less profit from the capital employed/net assets. Although there are increased margins there is less control over expenses and this has contributed to the deteriorating position. Control of expenses needs to be addressed by management. The efficiency in the use of assts has remained the same in 20X4 and the increased investment in assets that has taken place in 20X4 has yielded benefits in terms of increased sales.

Regards

AAT Student

5 Answering an exam question

5.1 Introduction

The first stage of answering questions on interpretation is to calculate the ratios; the second is to draw conclusions about the company based on those ratios. It is important to remember that there are limitations to the use of ratios, not the least of which is that a study of the trend of ratios for several years is desirable before drawing firm conclusions about many aspects of a company's position.

The usual question format is to be given two years of income statements and balance sheets from a company or to compare two different companies. You are then usually asked to:
(i)   calculate the ratios
(ii)   comment on your calculations
(iii) reach a conclusion.

When calculating the ratios you should produce a table (similar to the one above showing the formulae and the calculation for each year/company

You must then comment on each ratio in turn giving one sentence on what the ratio shows, one sentence relating the ratio to the user and one sentence that links the ratio to other ratios or absolute figures.

When looking for comments review the balance sheet and the income statement and look for significant movements. For example, if revenue has increased, check that gross profit has increased in line with the increase in revenue. Then you can check receivables, inventories and payables to see what effect the increased trade has had. Often with ratio questions the company has poor working capital management so look for significant increases in the working capital and liquidity ratios.

Finally if the question asks for a conclusion you must make a sensible assessment based on the points you have made.

▷ ACTIVITY 1

Falcon Ltd

The draft accounts of Falcon Ltd for the years ended 30 June 20X8 and 30 June 20X7 are as follows.

Summary balance sheets

	20X8 £	20X8 £	20X7 £	20X7 £
Freehold premises at cost		125,000		75,000
Plant at cost	210,000		125,000	
Less: Depreciation	80,000		55,000	
		130,000		70,000
Trade receivables		80,000		60,000
Inventories		120,000		100,000
		455,000		305,000
?1 ordinary shares		100,000		50,000
Retained earnings		135,000		120,000
Share premium account		90,000		35,000
7% debentures		50,000		50,000
Trade payables		45,000		30,000
Bank overdraft		15,000		5,000
Current taxation		20,000		15,000
		455,000		305,000

Income statements

	20X8 £	20X8 £	20X7 £	20X7 £
Revenue		525,000		425,000
Trading profit		78,500		61,000
Depreciation	25,000		20,000	
Debenture interest	3,500		3,500	
Corporation tax	20,000		15,000	
		(48,500)		(38,500)
Retained earnings for year		30,000		22,500

Note:

Dividends paid (shown in SOCE)	15,000	10,000

Required:

Draw as many conclusions as you can from these accounts using ratio analysis.

[Answer on p. 287]

6   General points about financial ratios

There are some more points on ratio analysis which should be particularly noted.

6.1 Caution in interpretation

Dogmatic conclusions should be avoided. For example, a reduction in the inventory holding period may be a good thing, but if it is likely to cause loss of customer goodwill or production dislocations due to inventory shortages, it may not be such an advantage. Ratios rarely answer questions but they can highlight areas where questions might usefully be asked.

6.2 Balance sheet figures

Many of the ratios considered in this chapter involve the use of balance sheet figures. These ratios should be interpreted with caution since the balance sheet shows the position at a specific moment only and this may not be typical of the general position.

This point is particularly important where the ratio is derived from a balance sheet figure in conjunction with a figure from the income statement. This is because the first figure relates to a moment in time whereas the second is a total for a period. A sensible way to try to avoid possible distortions here is to use the average figure for the balance sheet figure. So, for example, the debtor collection period would relate credit sales to the average of the trade receivables figures at the beginning and at the end of the year.

However in many industries the existence of recurrent seasonal factors may mean that averaging beginning and end of year figures will not solve the problem. It may, for example, be that the date up to which a business draws up its final accounts has been selected because it is a time when inventory levels are always low, so that inventory is relatively easy to value. In such cases, averaging the inventory figures for two consecutive year end dates would simply be averaging two figures which were totally untypical of inventory levels throughout the rest of the year. Averaging monthly figures would usually be the solution to this problem. However, outsiders would not typically have access to such information.

6.3 Other financial ratios

There are an almost infinite number of ratios which can be calculated from a set of final accounts. The ones shown above are those most commonly used in practice and include those which have been specifically asked about in examination questions. It should be noted, however, that there are many other ratios which could be useful in particular contexts.

6.4 Partial sightedness of ratios

It is usually unwise to limit analysis and interpretation only to information revealed by ratios. For example, revenue for a business could double from one year to the next. This would be a dramatic and important development, yet none of the ratios whose use is advocated in most textbooks would reveal this, at least not directly. However, this significant increase in turnover would be fairly obvious from even a superficial glance at the final accounts. There is the danger that excessive reliance on ratios in interpretation and analysis can lead to a 'blinkered' approach.

7 The working capital cycle

7.1 Introduction

The working capital cycle can be illustrated by the following set of activities which underpin the process of manufacture and trade:

· a company acquires inventories on credit;
· inventories are held until sold (or used in production);
· the sale is usually made on credit;
· trade payables need to be paid and cash needs to be collected from trade receivables;
· more inventories are then acquired and the cycle starts again.

The working capital cycle

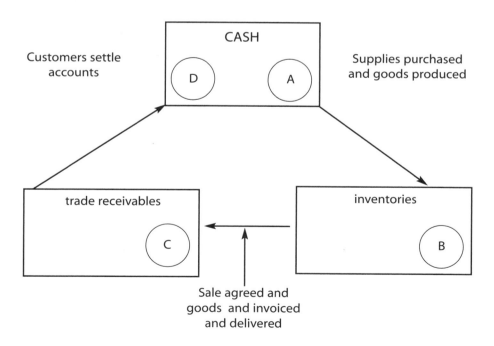

7.2 Effect on cash flows

All of these activities affect cash flows:
· acquisition of inventories on credit helps cash flow temporarily;
· when trade payables are paid cash flows out;
· while inventories are held, and until customers settle, cash is 'tied up', i.e. cash inflow is deferred;
· when customers settle, cash flows in.

The longer the period over which cash is tied up, the greater is the exposure of the firm to exceptional demands for cash. In terms of cash management:
· a working cash balance must be retained at the bank to avoid the bank imposing bank interest and charges;
· any surplus cash in excess of the working balance could be invested in higher interest earning accounts.

The longer the period of time that cash is tied up in working capital the more cost that is incurred by companies either directly, by virtue of bank interest, or indirectly, as a result of the inability to invest cash surpluses into higher interest yielding accounts.

7.3 Working capital management

The company must therefore ensure that inventory levels are watched very carefully and that trade receivables are collected on a timely basis whilst simultaneously monitoring the cash balance to ensure that sufficient funds are held for short-term requirements. Any genuinely surplus funds in excess of a working cash balance should be reinvested in higher interest accounts.

▷ ACTIVITY 2   ▷ ▷ ▷ ▷

C plc

You are the accountant of C plc. F plc is a competitor in the same industry and it has been operating for many years. You have the following information relating to F plc.

(1) *Summarised income statements for the year ended 31 December*

	20X6		20X7		20X8	
	£m	£m	£m	£m	£m	£m
Revenue		3,120		2,700		3,000
Materials	630		480		600	
Labour	480		480		600	
Overhead	390		420		450	
		(1,500)		(1,380)		(1,650)
Gross profit		1,620		1,320		1,350
Administrative expenses	780		690		720	
Distribution costs	750		570		690	
		(1,530)		(1,260)		(1,410)
Profit before taxation		90		60		(60)

(2) *Extracts from the balance sheets at 31 December*

	20X6		20X7		20X8	
	£m	£m	£m	£m	£m	£m
Non-current assets at net book value		1,170		1,110		1,050
Raw material	300		300		300	
Work in progress and finished goods	480		450		480	
Trade receivables	390		420		450	
		1,170		1,170		1,230
		2,340		2,280		2,280
Current liabilities (including bank overdraft)		(810)		(810)		(870)
Capital employed		1,530		1,470		1,410

(3) Ignore inflation.

(4) No non-current assets were purchased or sold by F plc between 20X6 and 20X8.

Required:

Write a report for the board of directors of C plc:

(a) analysing the profitability and liquidity of F plc and showing any calculations in an appendix to this report

(b) explaining the limitations of your analysis of the performance of F plc.

[Answer on p. 288]

▷ ACTIVITY 3　　　　　　　　　　　　　　▷ ▷ ▷ ▷
Big Brother plc

Big Brother plc serves the growing market for electronic security systems and equipment. The accounts for the year ended 31 December 20X8 are summarised below.

Income statements	20X8	20X7
	£000	£000
Revenue	51,882	43,217
Cost of sales	(21,705)	(18,221)
Gross profit	30,177	24,996
Expenses	(17,020)	(14,235)
Profit from operations	13,157	10,761
Finance costs	(4,695)	(3,574)
Profit before tax	8,462	7,187
Taxation	(3,071)	(2,694)
Profit after tax	5,391	4,493

Balance sheets	20X8		20X7	
	£000	£000	£000	£000
Non-current assets		62,247		51,457
Current assets				
Inventories	8,159		7,181	
Trade receivables	10,021		8,715	
Cash	3,609		1,924	
	21,789		17,820	
Current liabilities	(15,215)		(12,615)	
Net current assets		6,574		5,205
Total assets less current liabilities		68,821		56,662
Non-current liabilities				
Loans		(30,105)		(27,419)
Rentals in advance		(8,261)		(4,357)
		30,455		24,886
Equity				
Called up share capital (see note)		10,000		10,000
Share premium account		11,095		10,217
Retained earnings		9,360		4,669
		30,455		24,886

Note 1 Called up share capital

Authorised	£000
40,000,000 Ordinary shares of 50p each	20,000
10,000,000 6% Preference shares of £1 each	10,000
	30,000
Issued (all fully paid)	
10,000,000 Ordinary shares of 50p each	5,000
5,000,000 6% Preference shares of £1 each	5,000
	10,000

Note 2 The directors have paid a dividend of £700,000 in 20X8 (£600,000 in 20X7)

The directors have asked for your comments about the profitability, liquidity and solvency of the group and have provided you with the following typical industry statistics which have been independently assimilated from the statutory accounts of companies in the security systems and equipment sector. The industry statistics have been calculated on the basis that accruals and deferred income are included within 'current liabilities and that preference shares are treated as debt.

Gross profit margin	50%
Net profit margin (based on operating profit)	25%
Current ratio	1.20
Quick ratio	0.90
Gearing (debt divided by total capital employed)	50%
Inventory turnover (based on year end inventories and cost of sales)	3.5
trade receivables turnover (based on year end trade receivables and net sales)	5.0
Return on capital employed (profit before interest and tax divided by total capital employed)	17%

Required:

In your capacity as a financial advisor write a report for submission to the directors of Big Brother plc.

[Answer on p. 291]

8 Test your knowledge ▷ ▷ ▷

1   What is the numerator of the formula for return on capital employed?

2   What is the numerator for return on owners' equity?

3   What is the difference between the current ratio and the acid test ratio?

4   What does the PE ratio measure?

5   What does interest cover measure?

[Answers on p. 293]

9   Summary

Many ratios can be calculated from a set of financial statements. By comparison with the ratios of other businesses, or of the same business in previous years, it is possible to interpret the messages conveyed by the accounts.

To give structure to your solutions in an assessment it is helpful to analyse ratios under a number of categories. In this chapter we have used the following categories:
·   profitability
·   liquidity and asset utilisation
·   investor ratios
·   ratios relating to risk.

Answers to chapter activities & 'test your knowledge' questions

△ **ACTIVITY 1** △△△△

Falcon Ltd

As a first step, produce a table which shows your ratio calculations.

	20X8	*20X7*
Return on capital employed	$\dfrac{53,500}{375,000} \times 100 = 14.27\%$	$\dfrac{41,000}{255,000} \times 100 = 16.08\%$
Profit margin	$\dfrac{53,500}{525,000} \times 100 = 10.19\%$	$\dfrac{41,000}{425,000} \times 100 = 9.65\%$
Asset turnover rate	$\dfrac{525,000}{375,000} = 1.4$	$\dfrac{425,000}{255,000} = 1.67$
Inventory turnover rate	$\dfrac{525,000}{120,000} = 4.37$	$\dfrac{425,000}{100,000} = 4.25$
Current ratio	$\dfrac{200,000}{80,000} = 2.5$	$\dfrac{160,000}{50,000} = 3.2$
Acid test ratio	$\dfrac{80,000}{80,000} = 1.0$	$\dfrac{60,000}{50,000} = 1.2$
Profit margin	$\dfrac{80,000}{525,000} \times 365 = 56 \text{ days}$	$\dfrac{60,000}{425,000} \times 365 = 52 \text{ days}$

Comments

Profitability
The return on capital employed has worsened and this is as a result of less efficient use of assets. (The asset turnover has deteriorated whereas the profit margin has improved.)

If we look at the assets individually the inventory turnover and the trade receivables turnover should not have caused any substantial reduction of the asset turnover.

The major change appears to have occurred in the non-current assets where at some point during the year, extra capital has been raised for a major investment in non-current assets.

If these assets were purchased towards the end of the year then this would have made the figure for assets at the year end unrepresentative of the assets used throughout the year. If we take the average of the beginning and year end assets, the return on capital employed is 16.98%. Therefore, before we can draw any firm conclusions about the performance of the company, we need further information about the purchase of the non-current assets.

Liquidity
The ratios used to measure liquidity have also worsened during the year.

This is mostly due to a large increase in the overdraft, perhaps to part-finance the purchase of the fixed assets.

Once again, it is necessary to establish whether the year end picture is really representative of the year as a whole before coming to any firm conclusions.

Inventory turnover has remained fairly stable which is good. The receivables collection period has worsened slightly so this is an area the company need to keep under control. This is likely to lead to a further increase in the overdraft if the collection period is allowed to get longer.

Finance
The gearing ratio has been reduced over the year owing entirely to the large amount of share capital raised to finance the purchase of the fixed assets. There has been no change in the level of the debenture loan so the company have managed to finance the new assets wholly from equity.

△ ACTIVITY 2   △ △ △ △

C plc

(a)   **REPORT**

To	The Board of Directors of C plc
From	The Accountant
Subject	Analysis of F plc
Date	X.X.20XX

This report analyses the profitability and liquidity of our competitor F plc over the period 20X6 to 20X8. I draw attention to the Appendix to the report which gives a statistical analysis of key ratios.

Profitability
In absolute terms, the net profit of the company has fallen in recent years, from £90 million in 20X6, through £60 million in 20X7, to a net loss of £60 million in 20X8. This deterioration in performance has arisen for a number of reasons.

Revenue slumped in 20X7, falling 13% from the 20X6 level, and only partially recovered in 20X8.

While material costs and overheads have been reasonably constant as a proportion of revenue, labour costs have increased. The direct costs have reached a point, therefore, such that in 20X8 the indirect expenses exceeded the gross profit.

The levels of both administrative expenses and distribution costs are high, each consuming 20 to 25% of revenue. Though the proportions of revenue that these represent have remained reasonably level over the period under review, the absolute levels nevertheless are high.

Liquidity

The current ratio is constant at a level of about 1.4 to 1, which may be satisfactory for companies in certain sectors, but the low quick ratio of around 0.5 is almost certainly a cause for significant concern.

The difference between the two arises from the high inventory levels held: for example, around 200 days' supply of raw materials. A lack of control over inventories is indicated

There is also a lack of control over trade receivables. This is indicated by the high debtor days figure. If the company is offering the traditional one month's credit for goods supplied, the debtor days figure should be able to be substantially below the current 50 days.

No non-current assets were purchased or sold in the period, so the net book value has fallen only through the effects of depreciation of £60 million per year. Such a low depreciation charge suggests that the non-current assets have a long average remaining life of around 20 years.

In each of 20X7 and 20X8, the absolute level of capital employed fell by £60 million during the year. This has arisen due to a combination of tax and dividend payments and losses incurred. Unless a net increase in capital employed is forecast in the future, new funds will have to be raised to support the net operating assets of the business.

Conclusion

The profitability of the company has fallen over the period 20X6 to 20X8, due to falling revenue, high labour costs and high indirect costs.

The liquidity of the company is low but seems stable. There appears to be poor control over working capital, with high inventory levels, high debtors and no cash in hand.

APPENDIX TO THE REPORT

Profitability ratios

	20X6	20X7	20X8
Percentage of revenue			
Materials	20.2	17.8	20.0
Labour	15.4	17.8	20.0
Overhead	12.5	15.5	15.0
Administrative expenses	25.0	25.6	24.0
Distribution costs	24.0	21.1	23.0
Net profit	2.9	2.2	(2.0)
	100.0	100.0	100.0
Gross profit	51.9%	48.9%	45.0%
ROCE	5.9%	4.1%	(4.3%)

Liquidity ratios

	20X6	20X7	20X8
Current ratio	1.44	1.44	1.41
Quick ratio	0.48	0.52	0.52
Receivables days	46 days	57 days	55 days
Non-current asset turnover	2.67	2.43	2.86
Working capital turnover	8.67	7.5	8.33
Raw materials purchases	174 days	228 days	182 days

(b) The limitations of my analysis above of the performance of F plc are as follows.

The accounts have presumably been drawn up using historic cost. Many accountants would argue that a current value for non-monetary assets such as plant property and equipment would give more meaningful information for ratio analysis.

We are not told the split between cash sales and credit sales, but even assuming that all sales are on credit, the receivables collection period (receivables days) looks unhealthy.

A breakdown of the current liabilities would be useful, to determine for example just how big the bank overdraft is.

The most recent figures given are for 20X8; by now it might be possible to include figures for later years.

It would be useful to know the sector in which F plc operates so that the ratios we have calculated could be compared with sector norms. Only then would it be possible to draw firmer conclusions about the performance of the company.

△ ACTIVITY 3   △△△△

Big Brother plc

REPORT

To	The Directors, Big Brother plc
From	AN Accountant
Date	20 July 20X9
Subject	Big Brother plc — Profitability, liquidity and solvency of the group

(a) **Terms of reference**

This report examines the profitability, liquidity and solvency of Big Brother in 20X7 and 20X8, and recommends necessary action. It is based on financial statements and industry statistics provided. Ratios calculated from the statutory accounts are included in Appendix 1.

(b) **Executive summary**

The group is under capitalised, highly geared, and approaching a liquidity crisis. It is, however, profitable and the ordinary dividend was covered 12 times in 20X8 (20X7 14 times).

(c) **Profitability**

The gross margin has exceeded the industry norm at the same time as the net margin remained at industry levels. This discrepancy is probably due to non-standard cost allocations between cost of sales and other categories. This would also explain the low inventory turnover ratio.

It is possible that the gross margins are genuinely high, in which case overheads are also high, and savings may be available. A comparison of Big Brother's and the industry's usual cost allocation methods would allow more conclusive analysis.

Return on capital has improved in the year, and is well above industry levels. The apparent improvement is due mainly to the lack of extra long-term finance referred to below, and is not an underlying strength.

(d) **Liquidity**

Liquidity has deteriorated in the period, and the company is exhibiting signs of overtrading, its expansion not being financed by long-term methods.

The company is financing its increased working capital requirements out of rentals in advance. The low industry quick ratio indicates that some reliance on short-term finance is usual, but Big Brother's is excessive.

Unless further long-term finance (e.g. by a rights issue) is raised soon, the company will have liquidity problems.

(e) **Solvency**

The company is highly geared compared to the industry average, although a slight improvement occurred in the year. The gearing ratios referred to in the Appendix exclude any overdrafts and loans included within current liabilities, and it is likely that underlying gearing is substantially higher.

The high level of gearing, allied to poor liquidity, casts doubt over the company's continued stability.

Appendix 1: Ratios

	Big Brother plc 20X8	Big Brother plc 20X7	Industry average
Gross profit margin	58.2%	57.8%	50%
Net profit margin 25.4%	24.9%	25%	
Current ratio (including rentals in advance)	0.93	1.05	1.20
Quick ratio (including rentals in advance)	0.58	0.63	0.90

Gearing

$$\frac{5,000 + 30,105}{30,455 + 30,105} = 58\% \qquad \frac{5,000 + 27,419}{24,886 + 27,419} = 62\% \qquad 50\%$$

Inventory turnover

$$\frac{21,705}{8,159} = 2.66 \qquad \frac{18,221}{7,181} = 2.54 \qquad 3.5$$

Debtors turnover

$$\frac{51,882}{10,021} = 5.2 \qquad \frac{43,217}{8,715} = 5.0 \qquad 5.0$$

ROCE

$$\frac{13,157}{30,455 + 30,105} = 21.7\% \qquad \frac{10,761}{24,886 + 27,419} = 20.6\% \qquad 17\%$$

Dividend cover

$$\frac{5,391 - 300}{400} = 12.73 \qquad \frac{4,493 - 300}{300} = 13.98$$

Appendix 2

A rights issue could bring in fresh long-term funds and bring the company's gearing down to the industry average level.

Assuming that £10 million is raised from a rights issue

Gearing $\qquad \dfrac{5,000 + 30,105}{30,455 + 30,105 + 10,000} = 49.8\%$

Quick ratio $\qquad \dfrac{10,021 + 3,609 + 10,000}{15,215 + 8,261} = 1.01$

(including rentals in advance)

Test your knowledge

1 Profit before interest and tax.

2 Profit after interest and preference dividends but (usually) before tax.

3 The current ratio includes inventories in the numerator, while the acid test ratio excludes inventories.

4 The market's expectations for future growth in earnings.

5 The risk that profits might be insufficient to pay the interest payments due.

KEY TECHNIQUES
QUESTIONS

Chapters 1 and 2
The regulatory and conceptual framework of accounting

▷ **ACTIVITY 1**   ▷ ▷ ▷ ▷

The International Accounting Standards Board's Framework for the Preparation and Presentation of Financial Statements identifies a number of user groups to which financial statements should be appropriate.

(a)   List the groups referred to in the Framework.
(b)   Choose any three of the user groups and, with reference to the accounts of a limited company, consider the type of decisions that they are likely to wish to make in using the published accounting information.

▷ **ACTIVITY 2**   ▷ ▷ ▷ ▷

A major objective of published financial statements is 'to provide information about the financial position, performance and financial adaptability of an enterprise that is useful to a wide range of users for assessing the stewardship of management and for making economic decisions'.

What characteristics contribute to making financial information useful in terms of both content and presentation, and how do these characteristics fulfil their objective?

▷ **ACTIVITY 3**   ▷ ▷ ▷ ▷

The elements of financial statements comprise:
·   Assets
·   Liabilities
·   Equity interest
·   Income
·   Expenses

Define these terms and state which of these terms comprise the 'accounting equation'.

▷ **ACTIVITY 4** (December 2000)   ▷ ▷ ▷ ▷

Data
The accounting equation of a business is as follows:
Assets £1,200 - Liabilities £800 = Equity interest £400
The business subsequently makes two transactions:
(1)   it purchases on credit inventories costing £120; and
(2)   it sells inventories purchased in (1) for £180 cash.

Task
(a)   Explain what is meant by 'assets', 'liabilities' and 'equity interest'.
(b)   Explain the effect of each transaction on the elements in the balance sheet.
(c)   State the accounting equation for the business after the two transactions have taken place.

(d) Draft a simple income statement for the two transactions.

(e) Give an example of a user who might be interested in an income state-
     ment. Explain how the user you have chosen might find the statement
     useful.

▷ ACTIVITY 5 (December 1999)

The International Accounting Standards Board's Framework for the
Preparation and Presentation of Financial Statements states that:

'The objective of financial statements is to provide information about the
financial position, performance and changes in financial position of an
entity that is useful to a wide range of users in making economic decisions. Financial statements also show the results of the stewardship management or the accountability of management for the resources entrusted
to it.' Illustrate this objective by:

(a) Selecting one external user of financial statements from profit-making
     organisations and showing how it uses financial statements to assess
     the stewardship of management.

(b) Selecting one external user of financial statements from profit-making
     organisations and showing how it uses financial statements to make
     economic decisions.

▷ ACTIVITY 6 (June 2002, amended)

Data

The Framework for the Preparation and Presentation of Financial
Statements says that:
'The elements of the financial statements are:

(a) Assets

(b) Liabilities

(c) Equity interest

(d) Income

(e) Expenses

Task

(a) (i)   In which primary financial statement are 'assets', 'liabilities' and
           'equity interest' shown?

     (ii) How are they related to each other in that statement?

(b) What is meant by income' and 'expenses' and in which primary financial
     statements are they shown?

▷ ACTIVITY 7 (December 2002)

(a) What sort of information in the financial statements does the IASB's
     Framework for the Preparation and Presentation of Financial
     Statements say that potential investors are interested in and for what
     purpose?

(b) How does inventories meet the definition of an asset in the IASB's
     Framework?

Chapter 3
Drafting financial statements

▷ **ACTIVITY 8**   ▷ ▷ ▷ ▷

G Hick is a retailer of sports equipment.

The following is the trial balance as at 31 December 20X3.

	Dr £	Cr £
Motor vehicle at cost	12,500	
Depreciation provision 1/1/X3		5,000
Fixtures and fittings at cost	7,500	
Depreciation provision 1/1/X3		2,500
Premises at cost	40,000	
Depreciation provision 1/1/X3		8,000
Capital account		43,450
Inventories 1/1/X3	17,500	
Trade receivables	12,500	
Doubtful debts allowance		1,000
Cash in hand	1,250	
Cash at bank	1,700	
Trade payables		21,000
Drawings	13,100	
Purchases	120,000	
Revenue		170,000
Wages	14,100	
Advertising	2,100	
Insurance	1,400	
Heat and light	2,300	
Business rates	3,200	
Maintenance	150	
Motor vehicle running costs	1,650	
	250,950	250,950

The following additional information is available.

(1) Depreciation is to be provided as follows:
   Premises   4% on cost
   Fixtures   20% on cost
   Motor vehicle   20% on cost
(2) A debt of £500 is irrecoverable and is to be written off, and the bad debts allowance is to be revised to £1,500.
(3) Advertising includes £350 which was incurred on a private advert for sale of Hick's wife's car.
(4) £650 of the motor vehicle running costs are for private motoring.
(5) Wages are accrued due £270.
(6) Inventories at 31 December 20X3 had been valued at £19,500.
(7) The business rates include a pre-payment of £800 to 31 March 20X4.

Task

Prepare an income statement for the year ended 31 December 20X3 and a balance sheet at that date.

▷ **ACTIVITY 9** ▷ ▷ ▷ ▷

Michael Jay is a retailer of antiques. He also supplies goods to trade customers. The trial balance of the business at 31 December 20X3 was:

	Dr £	Cr £
Capital account		50,405
Freehold premises	50,000	
Fixtures and fittings at cost	13,100	
Motor vehicle	14,350	
Accumulated depreciation		
- Premises		5,000
- Fittings		7,860
- Motor vehicle		5,740
Inventories 1/1/X3	23,150	
Drawings	11,000	
Trade receivables	15,200	
Trade payables		19,100
Allowance for doubtful debts		500
Purchases	131,100	
Revenue		193,000
Wages	13,150	
Rates	3,250	
Insurances	1,850	
Heat and light	1,260	
Motor vehicle running costs	1,050	
Maintenance	780	
Cash in hand	970	
Cash at bank	1,395	
	281,605	281,605

The following information is also available.

(1) Inventories at 31 December 20X3 are valued at £25,600.
(2) Depreciation is to be provided as:
 · Premises 5% on cost.
 · Fixtures 20% on cost.
 · Motor vehicles 20% on cost.
(3) The allowance for doubtful debts is to be revised to 6% of trade receivables, after making any further adjustments and after writing off irrecoverable amounts.
(4) Rates are prepaid by £250.

(5) Wages are accrued due £720.

(6) An amount of £260 for insurance has been wrongly analysed as heat and light.

(7) Some fixtures and fittings which had cost £2,100, with a net book value of £840 had been sold for £1,000 on credit terms to a dealer, but no entries had been made in the books. No depreciation is charged in the year of disposal of an asset.

(8) An amount of £280 analysed as maintenance was for some private decorating at Michael's home.

(9) An irrecoverable debt of £200 is to be written off.

Task

Prepare an income statement for the year ended 31 December 20X3 and a balance sheet at that date.

▷ ACTIVITY 10

You work as an accounting technician for a firm of chartered accountants. Karl Hayes, a self-employed builder, is one of your clients and the following issues relate to his year end accounts.

(1) The trade receivables balance is £19,100, a debt of £400 is considered to be irrecoverable and is to be written off. The balance on the allowance for doubtful debts account is currently £735 and the allowance is to be revised to 5% of trade receivables.

The amount to be charged to the income statement for the change in the bad debts allowance is:
(A) £935
(B) £735
(C) £200
(D) £220

(2) During the year a non-current asset had been disposed of, the profit on sale was £750. The cost of the asset had been £3,400 and the proceeds on sale were £2,150.

The accumulated depreciation to date was:
(A) £2,150
(B) £2,650
(C) £2,000
(D) £1,250

(3) The balance on the rent and rates account as shown on the trial balance was £2,850 Dr.

At the year end, rates had been prepaid by £720 and the rent was accrued due £500.

The amount to be charged to the income statement for the year was:
(A) £2,630
(B) £3,070
(C) £1,630
(D) £4,070

(4) The following information relates to items in the purchase ledger account:

Opening balance	£15,100 Cr
Payments to suppliers	£83,200
Returns to suppliers	£1,100
Discounts received	£4,100
Amounts offset against items in the sales ledger	£1,560
Purchases on credit from suppliers	£96,000

(NB: A supplier was also a customer.)

The closing balance on the purchase ledger account would be:
(A) £34,660
(B) £23,340
(C) £21,140
(D) None of these

(5) The trial balance included the following information:
Revenue £131,700, returns outward £1,100, returns inward £1,700, purchases £96,000, opening inventory valuation £16,200 and a note to the information showed that the closing inventory valuation was £17,220 and that goods which had cost £1,500 had been used by Karl for his own use.
(a) The cost of goods sold for the period was:
    (A)   £91,780
    (B)   £94,420
    (C)   £95,380
    (D)   £92,380
(b) The gross profit for the period was:
    (A)   £32,080
    (B)   £37,620
    (C)   £38,220
    (D)   None of these

▷ ACTIVITY 11 (December 2002)   ▷ ▷ ▷ ▷

Data

Elizabeth Ogier has asked you to assist in the preparation of the year end financial statements of her business. She operates a wholesale perfume business. The trial balance as at 30 September 20X9 is set out below:

Elizabeth Ogier - Trial balance as at 30 September 20X9

	Debit £	Credit £
Purchases	113,565	
Rent, rates and insurance	8,291	
Motor expenses	5,813	
Bad debts	1,420	
Drawings	24,000	
Trade receivables	38,410	
Trade payables		18,928
Capital as at 1 October 20X8		83,707
Revenue		230,461
Returns outwards		2,911
Carriage inwards	1,256	
Returns inwards	3,053	
Carriage outwards	1,571	
Salesperson's commission	2,561	
Bank charges	710	
Depreciation - office equipment	2,312	
Depreciation - fixtures and fittings	602	
Inventories as at 1 October 20X8	46,092	
Motor vehicles at cost	36,000	
Office equipment at cost	11,560	
Fixtures and fittings at cost	6,019	
Accumulated depreciation - motor vehicles		18,360
Accumulated depreciation - office equipment		3,825
Accumulated depreciation - fixtures and fittings		1,352
Wages, salaries and National Insurance contributions	47,564	
Lighting and heating	3,056	
Postage and stationery	1,037	
Telephone	3,571	
Cash at bank	2,131	
Cash in hand	102	
Accruals		1,562
Discounts allowed	410	
	361,106	361,106

Further information:

· The inventories at the close of business on 30 September 20X9 were valued at cost at £49,477. However, included in this balance were some goods which had cost £8,200 but it is estimated that they could not be sold for any more than £4,800.

· Included in the rent, rates and insurance balance is a payment of £1,200 which relates to rent for the period from 1 October 20X9 to 31 December 20X9.

· The purchases figure includes goods to the value of £2,000 which Elizabeth took from the business for personal use and for gifts to friends.

· Although depreciation for office equipment and fixtures and fittings has been calculated and charged for the year, no depreciation has been calculated or charged for motor vehicles. Motor vehicles are depreciated using the reducing balance method at a rate of 30% per annum.

Task 11.1

Make any additional adjustments you feel necessary to the balances in the trial balance as a result of the matters set out in the further information above. Set out your adjustments in the form of journal entries.

Note: Narratives are not required.

Task 11.2

Draft an income statement for the year ended 30 September 20X9.

Task 11.3

Draft a letter to Elizabeth justifying any adjustment you have made to:
· the inventory valuation on 30 September 20X9.
· the balances in the trial balance as a result of Elizabeth taking goods out of the business for her personal use or for gifts to friends.

Your explanations should make reference, where relevant, to accounting concepts, accounting standards or generally accepted accounting principles.

Chapter 4
Preparing limited company accounts

▷ ACTIVITY 12 (June 1999)

Data

You have been assigned to assist in the preparation of the financial statements of Typeset Ltd for the year ended 31 March 20X9. The company is a wholesale distributor of desktop publishing equipment. You have been provided with the extended trial balance of Typeset Ltd as at 31 March 20X9 which is set out below.

Typeset Ltd - Extended trial balance as at 31 March 20X9								
	Trial balance		Adjustments		Income statement		Balance sheet	
Description	Debit £000	Credit £000	Debit £000	Credit £000	Debit £000	Credit £000	Debit £000	Credit £000
Trade receivables	3,136						3,136	
Cash at bank	466						466	
Interest	125				125			
Retained earnings		3,533						3,533
Allowance for doubtful debts		37						37
Distribution costs	3,549			59	36	3,572		
Administration expenses	3,061			63	613,063			
Revaluation reserve		500						500
Revenue		18,757				18,757		

Land – cost	2,075						2,075	
Buildings – cost	2,077						2,077	
Fixtures and fittings –cost	1,058						1,058	
Motor vehicles – cost	2,344						2,344	
Office equipment –cost	533						533	
Inventories	3,921		4,187	4,187	3,921	4,187	4,187	
Purchases	10,582				10,582			
Trade payables		1,763						1,763
Buildings – accumulated depreciation		383						383
Fixtures and fittings – accumulated depreciation		495						495
Motor vehicles – accumulated depreciation		1,237						1,237
Office equipment – accumulated depreciation		152						152
Pre-payments			97				97	
Ordinary share capital		5,000						5,000
Share premium		1,200						1,200
Accruals				122				122
Investments	1,580						1,580	
Long-term loan		1,450						1,450
Profit						1681		1681
TOTAL	34,507	34,507	4,406	4,406	22,944	22,944	17,553	17,553

You have been given the following further information:
- The authorised share capital of the business, all of which has been issued, consists of ordinary shares with a nominal value of £1.
- Depreciation has been calculated on a monthly basis on all of the non current assets of the business and has already been entered into the distribution costs and administration expenses ledger balances as shown on the extended trial balance.
- The corporation tax charge for the year has been calculated as £493,000.
- The final dividend has not yet been proposed.
- One of the customers who owed the company £36,000 at the end of the year is in financial difficulties. The directors have estimated that only half of this amount is likely to be paid. No adjustment for the required allowance has been made for this matter in the extended trial balance. The general allowance for doubtful debts is to be maintained at 2% of the remaining trade receivables excluding the £36,000 balance.

Task

Using the proforma which follows, and making any adjustments required as a result of the further information provided, draft a balance sheet for Typeset Ltd as at 31 March 20X9.

Note:

· You are not required to produce notes to the accounts.

· You must show any workings relevant to understanding your calculation of figures appearing in the balance sheet.

· You are not required to produce journal entries for any adjustments to the figures in the extended trial balance that are required.

· You should ignore any effect of these adjustments on the tax charge for the year as given above.

Proforma balance sheet

	£000
Non-current assets	
Intangible assets	
Property, plant and equipment	
Investments	
	————
	————
Current assets	
Inventories	
Trade receivables	
Cash and cash equivalents	
	————
	————
Total assets	————
Current liabilities	
Trade payables	
Tax liabilities	
	————
Net current assets (liabilities)	————
Non-current liabilities	
Long-term loans	
Total liabilities	
	————
Net assets	————
	————
Equity	
Called-up share capital	
Share premium account	
Revaluation reserve	
Retained earnings	
	————
	————

Chapter 5
Preparing limited company accounts: additional information

▷ **ACTIVITY 13** (June 2002)   ▷ ▷ ▷ ▷

Data

You have been asked to help prepare the financial statements of Hightink Ltd for the year ended 31 March 20X2. The trial balance of the company as at 31 March 20X2 is set out below.

Hightink Ltd Trial balance as at 31 March 20X2		
	Debit £000	*Credit* £000
Interest	240	
Distribution costs	6,852	
Administrative expenses	3,378	
Trade receivables	5,455	
Trade payables		2,363
Interim dividend	400	
Ordinary share capital		4,000
Revenue		31,710
Long term loan		6,000
Land - cost	5,000	
Buildings - cost	3,832	
Fixtures and fittings - cost	2,057	
Motor vehicles - cost	3,524	
Office equipment - cost	2,228	
Purchases	15,525	
Cash at bank	304	
Retained earnings		6,217
Inventories as at 1 April 20X1	6,531	
Share premium		2,000
Buildings - accumulated depreciation		564
Fixtures and fittings - accumulated depreciation		726
Motor vehicles - accumulated depreciation		1,283
Office equipment - accumulated depreciation		463
	55,326	55,326

Further information:

· The authorised share capital of the company, all of which has been issued, consists of ordinary shares with a nominal value of £1.

· The company paid an interim dividend of 10p per share during the year. No final dividend has been proposed.

· Inventories at the close of business on 31 March 20X2 were valued at cost at £7,878,000.

· The corporation tax charge for the year has been calculated as £1,920,000.

· Credit sales relating to April 20X2 amounting to £204,000 had been entered incorrectly into the accounts in March 20X2.
· Interest on the long term loan has been paid for six months of the year. No adjustment has been made for the interest due for the final six months of the year. Interest is charged on the loan at a rate of 8% per annum.
· The land has been revalued by professional valuers at £5,500,000. The revaluation is to be included in the financial statements for the year ended 31 March 20X2.
· On 21 April 20X2 there was a fire at the company's premises that destroyed non current assets and inventory. The losses from the fire amounted to £487,000 and they were not covered by the company's insurance. This amount is considered by the directors to constitute a material loss to the company.
· All of the operations are continuing operations.

Task 13.1
Using the proforma provided, make the journal entries required as a result of the further information given above. Dates and narratives are not required.

Note:
(1)   You must show any workings relevant to these adjustments.
(2)   Ignore any effect of these adjustments on the tax charge for the year given above.

JOURNAL			
Date	Narration	Debit £	Credit £

Task 13.2

Using the proforma provided, and making any adjustments required as a result of the further information given above, draft an income statement for the year ended 31 March 20X2, a statement of changes in equity and a balance sheet for Hightink as at that date.

Note: You are NOT required to produce notes to the accounts.

Hightink Ltd
Income statement for the year ended 31 March 20X2

	£000
Revenue	
Cost of sales	
Gross profit (or loss)	_____
Distribution costs	
Administrative expenses	_____
	_____
Profit from operations	
Finance costs	_____
Profit (or loss) before tax	
Tax	_____
Profit (or loss) for the period from continuing operations	_____

Statement of changes in Equity for the year ended 31 March 20X2

	Share capital	Revaluation reserve	Retained earnings	Total
At 31 March 20X1				
Revaluation				
Profit for year				
Dividends				
At 31 March 20X2				

Hightink Ltd
Balance sheet as at 31 March 20X2

	£000
Non-current assets	
Intangible assets	
Property, plant and equipment	
Investments	_____
	_____
Current assets	
Inventories	
Trade and other receivables	
Cash and cash equivalents	_____
	_____
Total assets	_____
Current liabilities	
Trade and other payables	
Tax liabilities	

Bank overdraft and loans _____
_____
Net current assets (liabilities) _____
Non-current liabilities
Bank loans _____
Long-term provisions _____
Total liabilities _____
Net assets _____
Equity
Called-up share capital
Share premium
Revaluation reserve
Retained earnings _____
_____

Task 13.3

(a) Explain what is meant by 'events after the balance sheet date'.
(b) Explain the difference between an event that is an 'adjusting event' and one that is a 'non-adjusting event'.
(c) Explain the appropriate treatment in the financial statements for the year ended 31 March 20X2 of the losses that arose from the fire on the company's premises on 21 April 20X2.

▷ ACTIVITY 14 (December 2002) ▷ ▷ ▷ ▷

Data

The Chief Accountant of Quine Ltd has asked you to help prepare the financial statements for the year ended 30 September 20X2. The trial balance of the company as at 30 September 20X2 is set out below.

Quine Ltd
Trial balance as at 30 September 20X2

	Debit	Credit
	£000	£000
Ordinary share capital		3,000
Interest	200	
Trade receivables	1,802	
Interim dividend	600	
Long term loan		2,500
Distribution costs	980	
Administrative expenses	461	
Revenue		10,884
Retained earnings		1,457
Cash at bank	103	
Accruals		105
Prepayments	84	
Share premium		500
Land - cost	2,800	
Buildings - cost	1,480	
Fixtures and fittings - cost	645	

Motor vehicles - cost	1,632	
Office equipment - cost	447	
Buildings - accumulated depreciation		702
Fixtures and fittings - accumulated depreciation		317
Motor vehicles - accumulated depreciation		903
Office equipment - accumulated depreciation		182
Inventories as at 1 October 20X1	2,003	
Trade payables		1,309
Purchases	7,854	
Allowance for doubtful debts		72
Capitalised development phase expenditure	840	
	21,931	21,931

Further information:
· The authorised share capital of the company, all of which has been issued, consists of ordinary shares with a nominal value of £1.
· The company paid an interim dividend of 20p per share during the year. A final dividend has not yet been proposed.
· Inventories at the close of business on 30 September 20X2 were valued at cost at £2,382,000.
· The corporation tax charge for the year has been calculated as £548,000.
· The land has been revalued by professional valuers at £3,200,000. The revaluation is to be included in the financial statements for the year ended 30 September 20X2.

Task
Using the proforma provided, make any adjustments required as a result of the further information provided, and draft a balance sheet for Quine Ltd as at 30 September 20X2.

Note
(1) You are not required to produce notes to the accounts.
(2) You must show any workings relevant to understanding your calculation of figures appearing in the balance sheet.
(3) You are not required to produce journal entries for any adjustments required to the figures in the trial balance.

<table>
<tr><td colspan="3" align="center">Quine Ltd
Balance sheet as at 30 September 20X2</td></tr>
<tr><td></td><td>£000</td><td>£000</td></tr>
<tr><td>Non-current assets</td><td></td><td></td></tr>
<tr><td>Other intangible assets</td><td></td><td></td></tr>
<tr><td>Property, plant and equipment</td><td></td><td></td></tr>
<tr><td>Investments</td><td></td><td></td></tr>
<tr><td></td><td></td><td></td></tr>
<tr><td>Current assets</td><td></td><td></td></tr>
<tr><td>Inventories</td><td></td><td></td></tr>
<tr><td>Trade and other receivables</td><td></td><td></td></tr>
<tr><td>Cash and cash equivalents</td><td></td><td></td></tr>
<tr><td></td><td></td><td></td></tr>
<tr><td>Total assets</td><td></td><td></td></tr>
</table>

Current liabilities
Trade and other payables
Tax liabilities
Bank loans and overdrafts

Net current assets (liabilities)

Non-current liabilities
Bank loans
Long term provisions

Total liabilities
Net assets

Equity
Called-up share capital
Share premium
Revaluation reserve
Retained earnings

▷ ACTIVITY 15   ▷▷▷▷

An extract from the accounts of Bay Ltd for the year ended 31 March 20X1 showed:

	£000
Revenue	9,320
Cost of sales	5,120
Gross profit	4,200
Distribution costs	1,230
Admin expenses	940
Profit from operations	2,030
Finance costs	230
Profit before taxation	1,800
Tax	480
Profit for the financial year	1,320

Extract from the balance sheet

	£000
Equity:	
Share capital	3,500
Share premium	1,400
Revaluation reserve	600
Retained earnings	1,850
	7,350

Dividends paid in the year were £420,000

The revaluation reserve arose in the year ended 31 March 20X1 as a result of land being revalued by a professional valuer. The revaluation is also reflected in the value of the tangible assets.

Task

Prepare a statement of changes in equity for the year ended 31 March 20X1.

▷ ACTIVITY 16 (Dec 2003)   ▷ ▷ ▷ ▷

Senander Plc

Data

The directors of Senander plc have asked you to draft an income statement for the year ended 30 September 20X3. They have given you the trial balance of the company which is set out below.

	Debit £000	Credit £000
Senander Plc **Trial balance as at 30 September 20X3**		
Property, plant and equipment at cost	27,214	
Accumulated depreciation on property, plant and equipment		8,449
Trade receivables	4,611	
Long term loan		4,200
Distribution costs	6,851	
Administration expenses	3,763	
Ordinary share capital		6,000
Share premium		2,000
Loss on disposal of discontinued operation	264	
Revenue		36,892
Inventories as at 1 October 20X2	9,523	
Cash at bank	285	
Accruals		108
Interest	310	
Trade payables		2,706
Purchases	21,645	
Retained earnings		14,111
	74,466	74,466

Further information:

· The share capital of the business consists of ordinary shares with a nominal value of £1.

· Depreciation has been calculated on all the non-current assets of the business and has already been entered into the ledger balances in the trial balance.

- Inventories at the close of business on 30 September 20X3 were valued at cost at £11,402,000.
- The corporation tax charge for the year has been estimated at £1,481,000.

During the year the company discontinued part of its operations. The results of the discontinued operation for the year have already been analysed by the company accountant. All of these results are included in the figures in the trial balance. The analysed results are set out below.

	Discontinued operation £000
Revenues	831
Cost of sales	(457)
	———
Gross profit	374
Distribution costs	(184)
Administration expenses	(162)
	———
Net profit	28
	———

Task 16.1

Draft the necessary journal entries as a result of the further information given above. Dates and narratives are not required.

Note: You must show any workings relevant to these adjustments.

Task 16.2

Using the pro-forma income statement, draft an income statement for Senander plc for the year ended 30 September 20X3.

Senander plc
Income Statement for the year ended 30 September 20X3

	£000
Continuing operations	
Revenue	
Cost of sales	
Gross profit	
Distribution costs	
Administrative expenses	
Profit from operations	
Finance costs	
Profit before tax	
Tax	
Profit for the period from continuing operations	
Discontinued operations	
Profit/(loss) for the period from discontinued operations	
	———
Profit for the period	
	———

▷ ACTIVITY 17

Burysane Ltd
Data

You have been asked to help prepare the financial statements of Burysane Ltd for the year ended 31 March 20X4. The extended trial balance of the company as at 31 March 20X4 is shown as follows.

	Burysane Ltd Extended trial balance as at 31 March 20X4							
	Trial balance		Adjustments		Income statement		Balance sheet	
Description	Debit £000	Credit £000	Debit £000	Credit £000	Debit £000	Credit £000	Debit £000	Credit £000
Trade payables		2,409						2,409
Prepayments			207				207	
Ordinary share capital		18,000						18,000
Inventories	8,912		9,432	9,432	8,912	9,432	9,432	
Share premium		6,000						6,000
Administration expenses	6,143		185	115	6,213			
Distribution costs	9,459		177	92	9,544			
Retained earnings		15,411						15,411
Land – cost	14,000						14,000	
Buildings – cost	12,068						12,068	
Fixtures and fittings – cost	10,217						10,217	
Motor vehicles – cost	18,548						18,548	
Office equipment – cost	3,004						3,004	
Revenue		39,773				39,773		
Trade receivables	1,359						1,359	
Accruals				362				362
Cash at bank	463						463	
Interest	400				400			
Long-term loan		10,000						10,000
Buildings – accumulated depreciation		2,603						2,603
Fixtures and fittings – accumulated depreciation		2,754						2,754
Motor vehicles – accumulated depreciation		5,621						5,621
Office equipment – accumulated depreciation		835						835
Purchases	16,858				16,858			
Interim dividend	2,160				2,160			
Allowance for doubtful debts		185						185
Profit					5,118			5,118
Total	103,591	103,591	10,001	10,001	49,205	49,205	69,298	69,298

Further information:
- All of the operations are continuing operations
- The authorised share capital of the company, all of which has been issued, consists of ordinary shares with a nominal value of £1.
- The company paid an interim dividend of 12p per share during the year. No final dividend has been proposed.
- The corporation tax charge for the year has been calculated as £2,822,000.
- Credit sales relating to March 20X4 amounting to £3,200,000 had not been entered into the accounts at the year end.
- Interest on the long-term loan has been paid for the first six months of the year. No adjustment has been made for the interest due for the last six months of the year. Interest is charged on the loan at a rate of 8% per annum.
- The land has been revalued by professional valuers at £15,000,000. The revaluation is to be included in the financial statements for the year ended 31 March 20X4.

Task 17.1
Draft the necessary journal entries as a result of the further information given above. Dates and narratives are not required.

Notes:
1 You must show any workings relevant to these adjustments.
2 Ignore any effect of these adjustments on the tax charge for the year given above.

Task 17.2
(a) Draft and income statement for Burysane Ltd for the year ended 31 March 20X4.
(b) Draft a balance sheet for Burysane Ltd as at 31 March 20X4.

Note: No notes are required.

▷ ACTIVITY 18 (December 2004)   ▷ ▷ ▷ ▷

Leakingman Ltd

Data
You have been asked to help prepare the financial statements of Leakingman Ltd for the year ended 30 September 20X4 and to advise the directors on the accounting treatment of certain items. The trial balance of the company as at 30 September 20X4 is shown below.

<table>
<tr><td colspan="3" align="center">**Leakingman Ltd**
Trial balance as at 30 September 20X3</td></tr>
<tr><td></td><td>Debit
£000</td><td>Credit
£000</td></tr>
<tr><td>Inventories as at 1 October 20X3</td><td>4,219</td><td></td></tr>
</table>

Purchases	22,324	
Interim dividend	300	
Share premium		2,000
Accruals		46
8% debentures		6,000
Distribution costs	5,211	
Administrative expenses	3,107	
Non-current assets - cost	37,524	
Retained earnings		9,236
Ordinary share capital		6,000
Revaluation reserve		2,000
Trade payables		2,045
Revenue		37,299
Trade receivables	4,175	
Cash at bank	146	
Interest	240	
Non-current assets - accumulated depreciation		12,683
Carriage inwards	63	
	77,309	77,309

Further information:

· The authorised share capital of the company, all of which has been issued, consists of ordinary shares with a nominal value of £1.

· Credit sales of £557,000 were made in September 20X4, but were recorded in the accounts in October 20X4.

· Inventories at the close of business on 30 September 20X4 was valued at cost at £5,384,000. However, items that had cost £480,000 will only be sold for £200,000 in the coming year.

· Distribution costs amounting to £242,000 were incurred before the year end, but have not yet been invoiced to the company.

· Interest on the debentures has not been paid or charged in the accounts for the last six months of the year.

· The corporation tax charge for the year has been calculated as £2,048,000.

· The company paid an interim dividend of 5p per share during the year. A final dividend has not been proposed.

· Land and buildings included in non-current assets at a net book value of £8,000,000 are to be revalued at the end of the year at £9,000,000.

· All of the operations of the business are continuing operations. There were no acquisitions in the year.

Task 18.1

Using the pro-forma in your answer booklet, make the necessary journal entries as a result of the further information given above.

Notes:

1 You do not need to give any dates or narratives.
2 You must show any workings relevant to these adjustments.
3 Ignore any effect of these adjustments on the tax charge for the year given above.

Task 18.2
Draft an income statement for Leakingman Ltd for the year ended 30 September 20X4.

Note: You do not need to prepare any of the notes to the financial statements.

Task 18.3
Answer the following questions that have been asked by the directors of Leakingham Ltd. Where appropriate, make reference to relevant accounting standards.

(a) (i) Why is an adjustment made for closing inventories in the financial statements?

(ii) How should inventories be valued in the financial statements?

(iii) How did you apply the requirements of relevant accounting standards in your treatment of inventories when you prepared the company's financial statements?

(b) (i) When would an impairment review of non current assets be necessary?

(ii) What would you do in an impairment review?

▷ ACTIVITY 19 (December 2005) ▷▷▷▷

Leakingman Ltd

Data
The financial accountant of Moatsart Ltd is away from work due to ill health. You have been asked to take over the preparation of the financial statements of Moatsart Ltd for the year ended 30 September 20X5. An extended trial balance of the company as at 30 September has been produced by the accountant, but some of the balances need to be adjusted. The extended trial balance is below.

MOATSART LTD
EXTENDED TRIAL BALANCE AS AT 30 SEPTEMBER 20X5

Description	Trial balance Debit £000	Trial balance Credit £000	Adjustments Debit £000	Adjustments Credit £000	Income statement Debit £000	Income statement Credit £000	Balance sheet Debit £000	Balance sheet Credit £000
Purchases	37,543				37,543			
Sales		70,613				70,613		
Returns inwards	2,372				2,372			
Returns outwards		1,463				1,463		
Ordinary share capital		8,000						8,000
Share premium		3,000						3,000
Revaluation reserve		2,500						2,500
Interim dividend paid	2,400				2,400			
Long-term loan		15,000						15,000
Inventories	7,454				7,454			

Non current asset investments	4,000				4,000	
Administration expenses	7,115		7,115			
Distribution costs	12,386		12,386			
Prepayments	403				403	
Non current assets – cost	84,856				84,856	
Non current assets – accumulated		26,422				26,422
Allowance fo r receivables		682				682
Trade receivables	8,754				8,754	
Trade payables		8,939				8,939
Accruals		642				642
Cash at bank	1,535				1,535	
Interest	600		600			
Retained earnings		32,157				32,157
Profit				2,206		2,206
Total	169,418	169,418	72,076	72,076	99,548	99,548

Further information is as follows.

All of the operations are continuing operations.

· The authorised share capital of the company consists of 20,000,000 ordinary shares with a nominal value of £1.
· At the beginning of the year the issued share capital was 8,000,000 ordinary shares. At the end of the year another 2,000,000 ordinary shares were issued at a price of £1.50 per share. This issue of shares has not been accounted for in the ledger accounts in the extended trial balance.
· The closing inventories at 30 September 20X5 were £8,731,000.
· Non current assets that had cost £2,300,000 and had accumulated depreciation of £1,250,000 were sold at the end of the year for £1,500,000 cash. The sale has not been accounted for in the ledger accounts in the extended trial balance.
· The tax charge for the year has been calculated as £3,948,000.
· Interest on the long-term loan has been paid for six months of the year. No adjustment has been made for the interest due for the final six months of the year. Interest is charged on the loan at a rate of 8% per annum.
· No final dividend has been paid.

Task 19.1
Using the pro-forma in your answer booklet, make the necessary journal entries as a result of the further information given above.

Notes:
1   You do not need to give any dates or narratives, but must show account names.
2   You must show any workings relevant to these adjustments.
3   Ignore any effect of these adjustments on the tax charge for the year given above.

Task 19.2

(a) Draft an income statement for Moatsart Ltd for the year ended 30 September 20X5.

(b) Draft a balance sheet for Moatsart Ltd as at 30 September 20X05.

DATA

The directors of Moatsart Ltd are interested in the principles to be followed in selecting accounting policies for the company.

Task 19.3

(a) (i) According to IAS 8, how should an entity decide what accounting policies should be adopted?

    (ii) What are the objectives against which an entity should judge the appropriateness of accounting policies to its particular circumstances? Explain two of the objectives.

Chapter 6
Cash flow statements

▷ ACTIVITY 20

IAS 7 *Cash Flow Statements* requires organisations to report their cash flows under standard headings.

Task

Outline these standard headings and explain briefly what each category aims to show.

▷ ACTIVITY 21

The financial statements of Fylingdales Ltd for the year ended 31 March 20X1 include:

Income statement	
	£000
Revenue	205,000
Cost of sales	(191,250)
Profit from operations	13,750
Finance costs	(2,150)
Profit before taxation	11,600
Taxation	(2,850)
Profit after tax	8,750

Note: The depreciation charge for the year was £6.5m. There had been no disposals of non current assets in the year.

Balance sheet as at 31 March 20X1		
	20X1	20X0
	£000	£000
Property, plant and equipment	73,000	70,500
Current assets		
Inventories	27,500	25,500
Trade receivables	37,500	33,000
Cash and cash equivalents	4,250	1,250
	69,250	59,750
Current liabilities		
Trade payables	31,500	31,950
Taxation	2,850	2,260
	34350	34210
Net current assets	34900	25540
Non-current liabilities		
10% debenture	21,500	20,000
Net assets	86,400	76,040
Equity:		
Share capital	11,610	10,000
Retained earnings	74,790	66,040
	86,400	76,040

Task

Prepare a cash flow statement for Fylingdales Ltd for the year ended 31 March 20X1 in accordance with IAS 7.

▷ **ACTIVITY 22** (December 2000)   ▷ ▷ ▷ ▷

Data

You have been asked to assist in the preparation of financial statements for Paton Ltd for the year ended 30 September 20X1. The draft income statement and balance sheets of Paton Ltd are set out below.

Paton Ltd - Income statement for the year ended 30 September 20X1

	£000
Revenue	24,732
Cost of sales	(11,129)
Gross profit	13,603
Profit on the sale of non current assets	131
Distribution costs	(4,921)
Administrative expenses	(2,875)
Profit from operations	5,938
Finance costs	(392)
Profit before taxation	5,546
Tax	(1,821)
Profit for the financial year	3,725

Paton Ltd - Balance sheet as at 30 September

	20X1	20X1	20X0	20X0
	£000	£000	£000	£000
Property, plant and equipment		13,383		9,923
Investment in MacNeal Ltd		5,000		
Current assets				
Inventories	7,420		6,823	
Trade receivables	4,122		3,902	
Cash and cash equivalents	1,402		1,037	
	12,944		11,762	
Current liabilities				
Trade payables	1,855		1,432	
Taxation	1,821		1,327	
	3,676		2,759	
Net current assets		9,268		9,003
Long-term loan		(5,000)		(1,500)
		2,2651		17,426
Equity				
Called up share capital		10,000		9,000

Share premium	3,500	3,000
Retained earnings	9,151	5,426
	22,651	17,426

You have been given the following further information:

· A fixed asset costing £895,000 with accumulated depreciation of £372,000 was sold in the year. The total depreciation charge for the year · All sales and purchases were on credit. Other expenses were paid for in cash.

Task

Produce a cash flow statement for Paton Ltd for the year ended 30 September 20X1.

▷ ACTIVITY 23 (June 2000)   ▷ ▷ ▷ ▷

Data

You have been asked to assist in the preparation of financial statements for Angle Ltd for the year ended 31 March 20X1. The income statements and balance sheets of the company are set out below:

Angle Ltd – Income statement for the year ended 31 March 20X1

	£000
Revenue	8,975
Cost of sales	(5,013)
Gross profit	3,962
Distribution costs	(1,172)
Administration expenses	(953)
Profit from operations	1,837
finance costs	(202)
Profit before taxation	1,635
Tax	(490)
Profit for the financial year	1,145

Angle Ltd – Balance sheet as at 31 March 20X1

	20X1		20X0	
	£000	£000	£000	£000
Property, plant and equipment		7,287		4,009
Current assets				
Inventories	1,982		1,346	
Trade receivables	812		1,086	
Cash and cash equivalents	833		82	
	3,627		2,514	
Current liabilities				
Trade payables	423		397	
Taxation	490		370	
	913		767	
Net current assets		2,714		1,747
Long-term loan		(2,500)		(1,500)
		7,501		4,256
Equity				
Called up share capital		3,000		2,200
Share premium		1,200		400
Revaluation reserve		500		-
Retained earnings		2,801		1,656
		7,501		4,256

Further information:

· Land included in property, plant and equipment was valued at market value at the end of the year by a professional valuer. The valuation has been incorporated into the financial statements of the company as at 31 March 20X1.

· No property, plant and equipment was sold during the year to 31 March 20X1. Depreciation has been calculated on the property, plant and equipment of the business and has already been entered in the income statement. The charge for the year was £875,000.

· All sales and purchases were on credit. Other expenses were paid for in cash.

· Net cash inflow from operating activities for the year was £1,804,000.

· There was no over/under-provision of corporation tax for 20X0.

Task

Using the proforma provided, prepare a cash flow statement for Angle Ltd for the year ended 31 March 20X1.

<table>
<tr><td colspan="2" align="center">**Proforma cash flow statement**</td></tr>
<tr><td></td><td align="right">*£000*</td></tr>
<tr><td>Net cash from operating activities</td><td></td></tr>
<tr><td>Investing activities</td><td></td></tr>
<tr><td></td><td align="right">_____</td></tr>
<tr><td>Net cash used in investing activities</td><td></td></tr>
<tr><td>Financing activities</td><td></td></tr>
<tr><td></td><td align="right">_____</td></tr>
<tr><td>Net cash from financing activities</td><td></td></tr>
<tr><td></td><td align="right">_____</td></tr>
<tr><td>Increase/(decrease) in cash and cash equivalents</td><td></td></tr>
<tr><td>Cash and cash equivalents at beginning of year</td><td></td></tr>
<tr><td>Cash and cash equivalents at end of year.</td><td></td></tr>
<tr><td></td><td align="right">_____</td></tr>
</table>

▷ ACTIVITY 24 (June 1999)   ▷ ▷ ▷ ▷

Data

The directors of Machier Ltd have asked you to assist them in producing a cash flow statement for the year ended 31 March 20X9 using the information in the balance sheet and income statement which follows.

The following further information is provided:

· Property, plant and equipment costing £28,000 with accumulated depreciation of £19,000 were sold in the year.
· All sales and purchases were on credit. Other expenses were paid for in cash.

Machier Ltd - Income statement for the year ended 31 March 20X9		
	20X9	*20X8*
	£000	*£000*
Revenue	2,636	1,687
Cost of sales	(923)	(590)
	———	———
Gross profit	1,713	1,097
Depreciation	(856)	(475)
Other expenses	(126)	(101)
Profit on the sale of property, plant and equipment	7	2
	———	———
Profit from operations	738	523
Finance costs	(252)	(120)

Profit before tax	486	403
Tax	(165)	(137)
Profit for the period	321	266

Machier Ltd - Balance sheet as at 31 March 20X9

	20X9	20X8
	£000	£000
Property, plant and equipment	4,282	2,376
Current assets		
Inventories	448	287
Trade receivables	527	337
Cash and cash equivalents	-	86
	975	710
Current liabilities		
Trade payables	381	212
Taxation	165	137
Bank overdraft	153	-
	699	349
Net current assets	276	361
Long-term loan	2,800	1,500
	1,758	1,237
Equity		
Called up share capital	200	100
Share premium	100	-
Retained earnings	1,458	1,137
	1,758	1237

Task

Using the proforma which follows, prepare a cash flow statement for Machier Ltd for the year ended 31 March 20X9

Proforma cash flow statement

	£000
Net cash from operating activities	
Investing activities	
	————
Net cash used in investing activities	
Financing activities	
	————
Net cash from financing activities	
	————
Increase/(decrease) in cash and cash equivalents	
Cash and cash equivalents at beginning of year	
Cash and cash equivalents at end of year	

▷ ACTIVITY 25 (December 2002)) ▷▷▷▷

Data

The Financial Controller of Duhem Ltd has asked you to take over the drafting of a cash flow statement for the year ended 30 September 20X2. The financial statements of the company - drafted for internal purposes are set out below, along with some further information relating to the reporting year.

Duhem Ltd
Income statement for the year ended 30 September 20X2

	£000
Revenue	8,742
Cost of sales	(4,458)
	————
Gross profit	4,284
Profit on the sale of property, plant and equipment	106
Distribution costs	(931)
Administrative expenses	(615)
	————
Profit from operations	2,844
Finance costs	(513)
	————
Profit before taxation	2,331

Tax		(720)
Profit for the financial year		1,611

Duhem Ltd
Balance sheets as at 30 September

	20X2		20X1	
	£000	£000	£000	£000
Property, plant and equipment		17,144		12,710
Current assets				
Inventories	1,115		1,002	
Trade receivables	1,457		1,213	
Cash and cash equivalents	817		324	
	3,389		2,539	
Current liabilities				
Trade payables	1,042		671	
Taxation	720		618	
	1,762		1,289	
Net current assets		1,627		1,250
Long term loan		(6,400)		(4,800)
		1,2371		9,160
Capital and reserves				
Called up share capital		4,000		2,500
Share premium		200		100
Retained earnings		8,171		6,560
		1,2371		9,160

Further information:
· Property, plant and equipment costing £980,000 with accumulated depreciation of £420,000 was sold during the year.
· The depreciation expense for the year amounted to £1,906,000.
· All sales and purchases were on credit. Other expenses were paid for in cash.

Task
Using the proforma provided, prepare a cash flow statement for Duhem Ltd for the year ended 30 September 20X2.

Duhem Ltd
Cash flow statement for the year ended 30 September 20X2

	£000	£000
Proforma cash flow statement		
Net cash from operating activities		
Investing activities		
	———	
Net cash used in investing activities		
Financing activities		
	———	
Net cash from financing activities		
Increase/(decrease) in cash and cash equivalents	———	
Cash and cash equivalents at beginning of year		
Cash and cash equivalents at end of year.	———	
	———	

▷ ACTIVITY 26 (December 2003) ▷ ▷ ▷ ▷

Kaypiemgee Ltd
Data

You have been asked to prepare a cash flow statement for Kaypiemgee Ltd for the year ended 30 September 20X3. The income statement and balance sheets of Kaypiemgee Ltd are set out below.

Kaypiemgee Ltd
Income statement for the year ended 30 September 20X3

	£000
Revenue	12,372
Cost of sales	(4,948)
Gross profit	7,424

Profit on the sale of non current assets	107
Distribution costs	(3,029)
Administrative expenses	(1,395)
Profit from operations	3,107
Finance costs	(226)
Profit before taxation	2,881
Tax	(721)
Profit for the financial year	2,160

Kaypiemgee Ltd
Balance sheet as at 30 September 20X3

	20X4		20X3	
	£000	£000	£000	£000
Property, plant and equipment		17,904		15,657
Current assets				
Inventories	2,013		1,843	
Trade receivables	1,546		1,321	
Cash and cash equivalents	1,468		-	
	5,027		3,164	
Current liabilities				
Trade payables	(873)		(744)	
Taxation	(840)		(635)	
Bank overdraft	-		(384)	
	(1,713)		(1,763)	
Net current assets		3,314		1,401
Long term loan		(4,000)		(4,000)
		17,218		13,058
Equity				
Called up share capital		5,000		4,000
Share premium		1,000		-
Retained earnings		11,218		9,058
		17,218		13,058

Further information:
· Property, plant and equipment costing £1,252,000 with accumulated depreciation of £648,000 was sold in the year. The total depreciation charge for the year was £1,995,000.
· All sales and purchases were on credit. Other expenses were paid for in cash.

Task

Prepare a cash flow statement for Kaypiemgee Ltd for the year ended 30 September 20X3 in accordance with the requirements IAS 7.

▷ ACTIVITY 27 (June 2004)

Scote Ltd

Data

You have been asked to prepare a cash flow statement for Scote Ltd for the year ended 31 March 20X4. The income statement and balance sheets of Scote Ltd are set out below.

Scote Ltd Income statement for the year ended 31 March 20X4	£000
Revenue	18,953
Cost of sales	(9,841)
Gross profit	9,112
Profit on the sale of non current assets	365
Distribution costs	(3,133)
Administrative expenses	(1,772)
Profit from operations	4,572
Finance costs	(1,000)
Profit before taxation	3,572
Tax	(893)
Profit for the financial year	2,679

Scote Ltd
Balance sheet as at 31 March 20X4

	20X4 £000	20X4 £000	20X3 £000	20X3 £000
Property, plant and equipment		22,561		16,143
Current assets				
Inventories	4,017		3,860	
Trade receivables	1,492		1,321	
Cash	1,314		-	
	6,823		5,181	
Current liabilities				
Trade payables	(1,003)		(827)	
Taxation	(893)		(643)	

Bank overdraft	-	(1,045)
	(1,896)	(2,515)
Net current assets	4,927	2,666
Long-term loan	(10,000)	(8,000)
	17,488	10,809
Equity		
Called-up share capital	9,000	6,000
Share premium	2,000	1,000
Retained earnings	6,488	3,809
	17,488	10,809

Further information:

· Plant costing £2,037,000 with accumulated depreciation of £1,432,000 was sold during the year. The total depreciation charge for the year was £4,120,000.

· All sales and purchases were on credit. Other expenses were paid for in cash.

Task

Prepare a cash flow statement for Scote Ltd for the year ended 31 March 20X4.

▷ ACTIVITY 28 (June 2005) ▷▷▷▷

Data

You have been asked to prepare a cash flow statement for Canes Ltd for the year ended 31 March 20X5. The income statement and balance sheet of Canes Ltd are set out below.

Canes Ltd	
Income statement for the year ended 31 March 20X5	

	£000
Revenue	18,871
Cost of sales	(9,475)
Gross profit	9,396
Profit on the sale of non current assets	402
Distribution costs	(3,205)
Administrative expenses	(1,923)

Profit before taxation	4,670
Tax	(1,027)
Profit for the financial year	3,643

Canes Ltd
Balance sheet as at 31 March 20X5

	20X5		20X4	
	£000	£000	£000	£000
Non current assets				
Property, plant and equipment		13,552		11,192
Current assets				
Inventories	4,342		3,851	
Trade receivables	1,781		1,404	
Cash	214		87	
	6,337		5,342	
Current liabilities				
Trade payables	(1,497)		(1,358)	
Taxation	(1,027)		(854)	
	(2,524)		(2,212)	
Net current assets		3,813		3,130
		17,365		14,322
Capital and reserves				
Share capital		4,000		4,000
Retained earnings		13,365		10,322
		17,365		14,322

Further information:
· The total depreciation charge for the year was £1,678,000.
· A non current asset costing £1,450,000 with accumulated depreciation of £870,000 was sold in the year.
· During the year, a dividend of £600,000 was paid to the ordinary share-holders.
· All sales and purchases were on credit. Other expenses were paid for in cash.

Task
Prepare the cash flow statement for Canes Ltd for the year ended 31 March 20X5 in accordance with the requirements of IAS 7.

▷ ACTIVITY 29 (December 2005)   ▷ ▷ ▷ ▷

Data

You have been asked to prepare a reconciliation between profit from operations and cash flows from operating activities and to interpret the cash flow statement for Bateoven Ltd for the year ended 30 September 20X5. The balance sheet and cash flow statement of Bateoven Ltd are set out below.

Bateoven Ltd
Balance sheet as at 30 September 20X5

	20X5		20X4	
	£000	£000	£000	£000
Non current assets		23,814		18,507
Current assets				
Inventories	3,670		3,162	
Trade receivables	1,777		1,306	
Cash	93		1,401	
	5,540		5,869	
Current liabilities				
Trade payables	(646)		(975)	
Taxation	(1,923)		(1,284)	
	(2,569)		(2,259)	
Net current assets		2,971		3,610
Long-term loan		(9,100)		(5,000)
		17,685		17,117
Capital and reserves				
Called up share capital		8,000		5,000
Share premium		4,000		2,000
Retained earnings		5,685		10,117
		17,685		17,117

Bateoven Ltd
Cash Flow Statement for the year ended 30 September 20X5

	£000	£000
Net cash inflow from operating activities		1,290
Investing activities		
Interest paid	(560)	
Purchase of property, plant and equipment	(9,138)	
Net cash used in investing activities		(9,698)

Financing activities		
Equity dividends paid	(2,000)	
Issue of ordinary share capital	5,000	
Increase in loan	4,100	
Net cash used in financing activities		7,100
Decrease in cash		(1,308)

Further information is as follows.

· The profit from operations for the year ended 30 September 20X5 was £312,000. This was after depreciation of £3,570,000 was charged. The tax expense in the income statement was £1,923,000.

· All sales and purchases were on credit. Other expenses were paid for in cash.

Task 29.1

Provide a reconciliation of profit from operations to net cash flows from operating activities for Bateoven Ltd for the year ended 30 September 20X5.

Task 29.2

Draft a letter to the directors of Bateoven Ltd commenting on the sources and uses of cash during the year ended 30 September 20X5 as indicated by the cash flow statement.

Chapters 7, 8 and 9
Consolidated accounts

▷ ACTIVITY 30

The following are the balance sheets of Dunsley Ltd and its subsidiary undertaking Ravenscar Ltd as at 31 December 20X1.

	Dunsley Ltd		Ravenscar Ltd	
	£000	£000	£000	£000
Non-current assets		5,210		1,250
Investment in Ravenscar Ltd		1,800		
Current assets				
Inventories	1,520		610	
Trade receivables	1,120		520	
Cash	120		85	
	2,760		1,215	
Current liabilities	(1,610)		(710)	

Net current assets	1,150	505
	8,160	1,755
Equity		
Share capital	3,000	500
Share premium	1,000	100
Retained earnings	4,160	1,155
	8,160	1,755

Additional information

· The share capital of both companies consists of ordinary shares of £1 each.

· Dunsley Ltd acquired 300,000 shares in Ravenscar Ltd on 31 December 20X1.

· The fair value of the property, plant and equipment of Ravenscar Ltd at 31 December 20X1 was £1,750,000.

Task

Prepare a consolidated balance sheet for Dunsley Ltd and its subsidiary undertaking as at 31 December 20X1.

▷ ACTIVITY 31

Shireoaks Ltd acquired a 60% holding in Harkhill Ltd on 1 January 20X1.

The balance sheets as at 31 December 20X1 showed the following:

	Shireoaks Ltd		Harkhill Ltd	
	£000	£000	£000	£000
Property, plant and equipment		17,500		5,750
Investment in Harkhill		5,100		
Current assets	4,750		1,520	
Current liabilities	(2,250)		(940)	
Net current assets		2,500		580
Total assets less current liabilities		25,100		6,330
Non-current liabilities				
Debentures		(4,100)		(1,000)
		21,000		5,330
Equity				
Share capital		8,000		1,000
Share premium		1,500		500
Retained earnings		11,500		3,830
		21,000		5,330

Additional information
- The share capital of both companies comprises ordinary shares of £1 each and there have been no changes during the year.
- Shireoaks acquired 600,000 shares in Harkhill Ltd.
- At 1 January 20X1 the balance of retained earnings of Harkhill Ltd was £3m.
- The fair value of freehold land at Harkhill Ltd as at 1 January 20X1 was £3.5m as compared with a book value of £3.1m. This revaluation has not been reflected in the books.

Task
Prepare a consolidated balance sheet as at 31 December 20X1.

▷ ACTIVITY 32 (December 2000)

Data

Paton Ltd, the company, has one subsidiary undertaking, MacNeal Ltd, which it acquired on 30 September 20X0. The balance sheet of MacNeal Ltd as at 30 September 20X0 is set out below.

MacNeal Ltd - Balance sheet as at 30 September 20X0		
	£000	£000
Non-current assets		4,844
Current assets	3,562	
Current liabilites	(1,706)	
	———	
Net current assets		1,856
Long-term loan		(1,900)
		———
		4,800
		———
Equity		
Called up share capital		1,200
Share premium		800
Retained earnings		2,800
		———
		4,800
		———

You have been given the following further information:
(i) The share capital of MacNeal Ltd consists of ordinary shares of £1 each.
(ii) Paton Ltd acquired 900,000 shares in MacNeal Ltd on 30 September 20X0 at a cost of £5,000,000.
(iii) The fair value of the non-current assets of MacNeal Ltd at 30 September 20X0 was £5,844,000. The revaluation has not been reflected in the books of MacNeal Ltd.

Task

Calculate the goodwill on consolidation that arose on the acquisition of MacNeal Ltd on 30 September 20X0.

▷ ACTIVITY 33 (June 2000)   ▷ ▷ ▷ ▷

Data

You have been asked to assist in the preparation of the consolidated accounts of the Norman Group. Set out below are the balance sheets of Norman Ltd and Saxon Ltd for the year ended 31 March 20X1.

Balance sheets as at 31 March 20X1				
	Norman Ltd		Saxon Ltd	
	£000	£000	£000	£000
Property, plant and equipment		12,995		1,755
Investment in Saxon Ltd		1,978		-
		_____		_____
		14,973		1,755
		_____		_____
Current assets				
Inventories	3,586		512	
Trade receivables	2,193		382	
Cash	84		104	
	_____		_____	
	5,863		998	
	_____		_____	
Total assets		20,836		2,753
		_____		_____
Current liabilities				
Tradepayables	2,080		273	
Taxation	667		196	
	_____		_____	
	2,747		469	
	_____		_____	
Net current assets		3,116		529
		_____		_____
Long-term loan		-		400
		_____		_____
Total liabilities		2,747		869
		_____		_____
Net assets		18,089		1,884
		_____		_____
Share capital		2,000		1,000
Share premium		-		200
Retained earnings		16,089		684
		_____		_____
		18,089		1,884
		_____		_____

Further information:

- The share capital of both Norman Ltd and Saxon Ltd consists of ordinary shares of £1 each. There have been no changes to the balances of share capital and share premium during the year. No dividends were paid by Saxon Ltd during the year.
- Norman Ltd acquired 750,000 shares in Saxon Ltd on 31 March 20X0.
- At 31 March 20X0 the balance of retained earnings of Saxon Ltd was £424,000.
- The fair value of the property, plant and equipment of Saxon Ltd at 31 March 20X0 was £2,047,000 as compared with a book value of £1,647,000. The revaluation has not been reflected in the books of Saxon Ltd. (Ignore any depreciation implications.)

Task

Using the proforma which follows, prepare the consolidated balance sheet of Norman Ltd and its subsidiary undertaking as at 31 March 20X1

Proforma consolidated balance sheet

	£000
Non-current assets	
Goodwill	
Property, plant and equipment	
Investments	___
	___
Current assets	
Inventories	
Trade receivables	
Cash	___
	___
Total assets	
Current liabilities	___
Net current assets (liabilities)	___
Non-current liabilities	___
Total liabilities	___
	___
Net assets	
	___
Equity	
Equity attributable to holders of the parent	
Minority interest	
	___

▷ ACTIVITY 34 (December 1999)　　　　▷▷▷▷

Data

You have been asked to assist in the preparation of the consolidated accounts of the Shopan Group. Set out below are the balance sheets of Shopan Ltd and its subsidiary undertaking, Hower Ltd, as at *30 September 20X9*.

Balance sheets as at 30 March 20X9				
	Shopan Ltd		Hower Ltd	
	£000	£000	£000	£000
Non-current assets		6,273		1,633
Investments in Hower Ltd		2,100		-
		_____		_____
Current assets		8,373		1,633
		_____		_____
Inventories		1,901		865
Trade receivables		1,555		547
Cash		184		104
		_____		_____
		3,640		1,516
		_____		_____
Total assets		12,013		3,149
		_____		_____
Current liabilities				
Trade payables		1,516		457
Taxation		431		188
		_____		_____
		1,947		645
		_____		_____
Net current assets		1,693		871
		_____		_____
Long-term loan		2,870		400
		_____		_____
Total liabilities		4,817		1,045
		_____		_____
Net assets		7,196		2,104
		_____		_____
Equity				
Called up share capital		2,000		500
Share premium		950		120
Retained earnings		4,246		1,484
		_____		_____
		7,196		2,104
		_____		_____

Further information:

· The share capital of both Shopan Ltd and Hower Ltd consists of ordinary shares of £1 each.

· Shopan Ltd acquired 375,000 shares in Hower Ltd on 30 September 20X9.

· The fair value of the non-current assets of Hower Ltd at 30 September 20X9 was £2,033,000.

Task 34.1

Using the proforma which follows, prepare a consolidated balance sheet for Shopan Ltd and its subsidiary undertaking as at 30 September 20X9.

Task 34.2

A parent undertaking should prepare consolidated financial statements for its group. Give two criteria that determine whether an undertaking is the parent undertaking of another undertaking.

Proforma consolidated balance sheet

	£000
Non-current assets	
Goodwill	
Property, plant and equipment	
Investments	_____
	_____
Current assets	
Inventories	
Trade receivables	
Cash	
	_____
Total assets	_____
Current liabilities	_____
	_____
Net current assets (liabilities)	
Non-current liabilities	
Total liabilities	_____
Net assets	_____
Equity	
Equity attributable to holders of the parent	_____
Minority interest	
	_____

▷ **ACTIVITY 35** (December 1998)   ▷ ▷ ▷ ▷

Data

The directors of Fun Ltd have a number of questions relating to the financial statements of their recently acquired subsidiary undertaking, Games Ltd. Fun Ltd acquired 75% of the ordinary share capital of Games Ltd on 30 September 20X8 for £2,244,000. The fair value of the non-current assets in Games Ltd as at 30 September 20X8 was £2,045,000. The directors have provided you with the balance sheet of Games Ltd as at 30 September 20X8 along with some further information.

Games Ltd - Balance sheet as at 30 September 20X8

	20X8 £000	20X7 £000
Non-current assets	1,845	1,615
Current assets		
Inventories	918	873
Trade receivables	751	607
Cash	23	87
	1,692	1,567
Total assets	3,537	3,182
Current liabilities		
Trade payables	635	560
Taxation	62	54
	697	614
Net current assets	995	953
Non-current liabilities	560	420
Total liabilities	1,257	1,034
Net assets	2,280	2,148
Equity		
Called up share capital	1,000	1,000
Share premium	100	100
Retained earnings	1,180	1,048
	2,280	2,148

Further information:

· No non-current assets were sold during the year. The depreciation charge for the year amounted to £277,000.

· All sales and purchases were on credit. Other expenses were paid for in cash.

· The profit before taxation was £246,000. Interest of £56,000 was charged in the year.

Task

Prepare notes to take to the Board meeting to answer the following questions of the directors:

· What figure for minority interest would appear in the consolidated balance sheet of Fun Ltd as at 30 September 20X8?

· Where in the consolidated balance sheet would minority interest be disclosed?

· What is a minority interest?

▷ ACTIVITY 36 (June 1998) ▷▷▷▷

Data

The directors of Machier Ltd have been in negotiation with the directors of another company, Papier Ltd, regarding the possibility of Papier Ltd buying 75% of the share capital of Machier Ltd.

The Equity of Machier Ltd showed:

	£
Share capital 200,000 ordinary shares £1 each	200,000
Share premium 100,000	
Retained earnings	1,408,000
	1,708,000

If the acquisition goes ahead Papier Ltd will pay £1,716,000 for the shares based on the value of the company on 31 March 20X9. The fair value of the non-current assets in Machier Ltd at 31 March 20X9, the agreed date of acquisition, is £4,682,000. The NBV of the non-current assets is £4,282,000 on that date. All the other assets and liabilities are stated at fair value.

The directors of Machier ask you to attend a meeting to explain some of the accounting issues involved in the acquisition of Machier Ltd by Papier Ltd.

Task 36.1
Calculate the goodwill on consolidation that would arise on acquisition if Papier Ltd had purchased 75% of the shares in Machier Ltd on 31 March 20X9.

Note: You are not required to produce a consolidated balance sheet for the group.

Task 36.2
In a note to the directors, explain the accounting treatment of goodwill arising on acquisition in group accounts.

▷ ACTIVITY 37 (June 2002) ▷▷▷▷

Data

Fertwrangler Ltd has one subsidiary undertaking, Voncarryon Ltd, which it acquired on 1 April 20X1. The balance sheet of Voncarryon Ltd as at 31 March 20X2 is set out below.

Voncarryon Ltd
Balance sheet as at 31 March 20X2

	£000	£000
Non-current assets		3,855
Current assets	4,961	
Current liabilities	(2,546)	
Net current assets		2,415
Non-current liabilities		(1,500)
		4,770
Equity		
Called up share capital		2,000
Share premium		1,000
Retained earnings		1,770
		4,770

Further information:
- The share capital of Voncarryon Ltd consists of ordinary shares of £1 each. There have been no changes to the balances of share capital and share premium during the year. No dividends were paid by Voncarryon Ltd during the year.
- Fertwrangler Ltd acquired 1,200,000 shares in Voncarryon Ltd on 1 April 20X1 at a cost of £3,510,000.
- At 1 April 20X1 the balance of retained earnings of Voncarryon Ltd was £1,350,000.
- The fair value of the non-current assets of Voncarryon Ltd at 1 April 20X1 was £4,455,000. The book value of the non-current assets at 1 April 20X1 was £4,055,000. The revaluation has not been reflected in the books of Voncarryon Ltd.

Task

Calculate the goodwill figure relating to the acquisition of Voncarryon Ltd that will appear in the consolidated balance sheet of Fertwrangler Ltd as at 31 March 20X2.

▷ ACTIVITY 38   ▷ ▷ ▷ ▷

You work as an accounting technician for Malton Ltd which has a single subsidiary, Whitby Ltd.

The income statements for the two companies for the year ended 31 December 20X1 were:

	Malton Ltd	Whitby Ltd
	£000	£000
Revenue	14,100	5,100
Cost of sales	(7,150)	(2,750)
Gross profit	6,950	2,350
Distribution costs	(1,600)	(450)
Admin costs	(1,450)	(375)
Dividends received from Whitby Ltd	360	
Profit from operations	4,260	1,525
Finance costs	(760)	(125)
Profit before tax	3,500	1,400
Taxation	(1,200)	(400)
Profit for the year	2,300	1,000

Additional information

· Malton Ltd acquired 80% of the ordinary share capital of Whitby Ltd on 1 January 20X1.

· During the year Whitby Ltd sold goods which had cost £500,000 to Malton Ltd for £800,000. All the goods had been sold outside the group by the end of the year.

Task

Draft a consolidated income statement for Malton Ltd and its subsidiary for the year ended 31 December 20X1. Ignore goodwill.

▷ ACTIVITY 39 (December 2002)

Data

The Managing Director of Skuhn plc has asked you to prepare the draft consolidated income statement for the group. The company has one subsidiary undertaking, e-Lakatos Ltd. The income statements for the two companies prepared for internal purposes for the year ended 30 September 20X2 are set out below.

Income statements for the year ended 30 September 20X2		
	Skuhn plc	e-Lakatos Ltd
	£000	£000
Revenue	25,300	8,600
Cost of sales	(11,385)	(3,870)
Gross profit	13,915	4,730
Distribution costs	(3,655)	(985)
Administrative expenses	(2,730)	(320)

Profit from operations	7,530	3,425
Dividends received from e-Lakatos Ltd	600	-
Finance costs	(2,100)	(400)
Profit before taxation	6,030	3,025
Tax	(1,870)	(695)
Profit for the year	4,160	2,330

Additional information:
· Skuhn plc acquired 60% of the ordinary share capital of e-Lakatos Ltd on 1 October 20X1.
· During the year e-Lakatos Ltd sold goods which had cost £800,000 to Skuhn plc for £1,200,000. All of the goods had been sold by Skuhn plc by the end of the year.

Task

Using the proforma provided, draft a consolidated income statement for Skuhn plc and its subsidiary undertaking for the year ended 30 September 20X2.

Skuhn plc
Consolidated income statement for the year ended 30 September 20X2

	£000
Revenue	
Cost of sales	
Gross profit	_____
Distribution costs	
Administrative expenses	
Profit from operations	_____
Finance costs	
Profit before taxation	_____
Tax	
Profit for the year	
	_____
Attributable to:	
Equity holders of the parent	
Minority interests	_____
	_____

▷ **ACTIVITY 40** (June 2005) ▷ ▷ ▷ ▷

Data

Bell plc owns 60% of its subsidiary undertaking, Clive Ltd, and 25% of its associate company, Grant Ltd. The balance sheet of Bell plc as at 31 March 20X5 is set out below.

Bell plc Balance sheets as at 31 March 20X5		
	£000	£000
Non current assets		
Property, plant and equipment		85,386
Investment in Clive Ltd		25,160
Investment in Grant Ltd		5,000
Current assets	24,052	
Current liabilities	(11,981)	
Net current assets		12,071
		127,617
Equity		
Share capital		35,000
Share premium		25,000
Retained earnings		67,617
		127,617

The balance sheets of Clive Ltd and Grant Ltd as at 31 March 20X5 are set out below.

Balance sheets as at 31 March 20X5				
	Clive Ltd		Grant Ltd	
	£000	£000	£000	£000
Non current assets				
Property, plant and equipment		32,504		18,465
Current assets	11,585)		4,852	
Current liabilities	(6,159)		(4,317)	
Net current assets		5,426		535
		37,930		19,000
Equity				
Share capital		20,000		10,000
Share premium		5,000		-

Retained earnings	12,930	9,000
	37,930	19,000

You also have the following information.
· The share capital of Clive Ltd consists of ordinary shares of £1 each. There have been no changes to the balances of share capital and share premium during the year. No dividends were paid by Clive Ltd during the year.
· Bell plc acquired 12,000,000 shares in Clive Ltd on 1 April 20X4 at a cost of £25,160,000.
· At 1 April 20X4 the balance on the retained earnings of Clive Ltd was £10,600,000.
· The fair value of the non current assets of Clive Ltd at 1 April 20X4 was £33,520,000. The book value of the non current assets at 1 April 20X4 was £30,520,000. The revaluation has not been reflected in the books of Clive Ltd. There were no other differences between fair values and book values as at 1 April 20X4.
· The share capital of Grant Ltd consists of ordinary shares of £1 each. There have been no changes to the balance of share capital during the year. No dividends were paid by Grant Ltd during the year.
· Bell plc acquired 2,500,000 shares in Grant Ltd on 1 April 20X4 at a cost of £5,000,000.
· At 1 April 20X4 the balance on the retained earnings of Grant Ltd was £8,000,000.
· The fair value of the net assets of Grant Ltd at 1 April 20X4 was £18,000,000, the same as the book value as at this date.
· Goodwill on both acquisitions has been impaired by 10% at the balance sheet date.

Task 40.1
Calculate the goodwill figure relating to the acquisition of Clive Ltd that will appear in the consolidated balance sheet of Bell plc as at 31 March 20X5.

Task 40.2
(a) Calculate the amount of the investment in the associate, Grant Ltd, that will appear in the consolidated balance sheet of Bell plc as at 31 March 20X5.
(b) Define an 'associate' making reference to relevant accounting standards.

▷ ACTIVITY 41 (December 2005)   ▷ ▷ ▷ ▷

Data

Haydn plc has one subsidiary undertaking, Seek Ltd, which was acquired on 1 October 20X4. The balance sheets of Haydn plc and Seek Ltd as at 30 September 20X5 are set out below.

	Haydn plc		Seek Ltd	
	£000	£000	£000	£000
Tangible non current assets		88,301		45,523
Investment in Seek Ltd		39,500		
Current assets:				
Inventories	25,205		6,861	
Receivables	9,147		4,725	
Cash	401		1,028	
	34,753		12,614	
Current liabilities				
Trade payables	(11,669)		(5,002)	
Accruals	(2,984)		(991)	
Taxation	(1,832)		(714)	
	(16,485)		(6,707)	
Net current assets		18,268		5,907
Non current liabilities:				
Long-term loan		(50,000)		(7,000)
		96,069		44,430
Equity				
Share capital		30,000		5,000
Share premium		20,000		2,000
Retained earnings		46,069		37,430
		96,069		44,430

You have been given the following further information.

- The share capital of Seek Ltd consists of ordinary shares of £1 each. There have been no changes to the balances of share capital and share premium during the year. No dividends were paid or proposed by Seek Ltd during the year.
- Haydn plc acquired 3,000,000 shares in Seek Ltd on 1 October 20X4.
- At 1 October 20X4 the balance on the retained earnings of Seek Ltd was £32,550,000.
- The fair value of the non current assets of Seek Ltd at 1 October 20X4 was £42,500,000. The book value of the non current assets at 1 October 20X4 was £38,500,000. The revaluation has not been recorded in the books of Seek Ltd (ignore any effect on the depreciation for the year).
- The directors of Haydn plc consider that the goodwill in the consolidated financial statements has an indefinite economic life and that this can be demonstrated. They also believe that the goodwill is capable of continued measurement.

Task 41.1

Prepare the consolidated balance sheet of Haydn plc and its subsidiary undertaking as at 30 September 20X5.

> **Task 41.2**
> Advise the directors of Haydn plc on the accounting treatment of the good-will in the consolidated financial statements.
>
> **Note:** Your answer should make reference to relevant accounting standards.

Chapters 10 to 16
Reporting financial performance

▷ ACTIVITY 42 (December 2000)

Data

The directors of Mattesich Limited are to hold a board meeting next week to consider the performance of the company in the past year. They will also discuss the accounting policy for valuing non-current assets. The company accountant, who would normally prepare the documents for the meeting, is ill. He has completed the extended trial balance for the year ended 30 September 20X0 which is set out below.

Mattesich Limited – Extended trial balance as at 30 September 20X0								
	Trial balance		Adjustments		Income statement		Balance sheet	
Description	Debit £000	Credit £000	Debit £000	Credit £000	Debit £000	Credit £000	Debit £000	Credit £000
Buildings – accumulated depreciation		2,731						2,731
Office equipment – accumulated depreciation		2,456						2,456
Motor vehicles – accumulated depreciation		5,502						5,502
Fixtures and fittings – accumulated depreciation		2,698						2,698
Loss on disposal of discontinued operation	473				473			
Trade payables		2,727						2,727
Trade receivables	6,654						6,654	
Distribution costs	5,695		206	38	5,863			
Administrative expenses	3,337		181	49	3,469			
Land – cost	8,721						8,721	
Buildings – cost	12,873						12,873	
Office equipment – cost	6,182						6,182	
Motor vehicles – cost	11,522						11,522	
Fixtures and fittings – cost	6,913						6,913	
Interest	544				544			
Revenue		40,448				40,448		
Loan		6,800						6,800
Ordinary share capital		14,000						14,000

Inventories	12,973		13,482	13,482	12,973	13,482	13,482	
Retained earnings		12,214						12,214
Accruals				387				387
Share premium		7,200						7,200
Interim dividend	2,100				2,100			
Prepayments			87				87	
Cash at bank and in hand	107						107	
Purchases	18,682				18,682			
Profit					9,826			9,826
	96,776	96,776	13,956	13,956	53,930	53,930	66,541	66,541

You have been given the following further information:
- The share capital of the business consists of ordinary shares with a nominal value of ?1.
- The company paid an interim dividend of 15 pence per share this year. No final dividend has been proposed
- Depreciation has been calculated on all the non-current assets of the business and has already been entered into the distribution expenses and administrative expenses ledger balances as shown on the extended trial balance.
- The corporation tax charge for the year has been estimated at ?3,813,000, all of which relates to continuing activities.

During the year the company discontinued part of its operations. The results for the discontinued operation for the year have already been analysed by the company accountant. All of these results are included in the figures in the extended trial balance. The analysed results are set out below:

	Discontinued operations £000
Revenue	1,213
Cost of sales	788
Gross profit	425
Distribution costs	234
Administration expenses	178
Net profit	13

Task 42.1
Using the proforma income statement which follows, draft an income statement for the year ended 30 September 20X0

Note:
You do NOT need to prepare any of the notes to the financial statements You do NOT need to prepare journal entries for any additional adjustments that may be necessary as a result of the further information given above.

You do NOT need to do an analysis of distribution costs and administrative expenses.

Mattesich Limited Income statement for year ended 30 September 20X0

	£000
Revenue	
Cost of sales	
	————
Gross profit	
Distribution costs	
Administrative expenses	
	————
Profit from operations	
Finance costs	
	————
Profit before taxation	
Tax	————
Profit for the year from continuing operations	————
Profit for the year from discontinued operations	————
Profit for the year	————

Task 42.2

Prepare brief notes to take to the board meeting covering the following questions of the directors:

(a) If we decide to adopt a policy of revaluation of land and buildings, do we need to revalue all the land and buildings that we own or can some continue to be shown at historical cost?

(b) If we do revalue land and buildings:
   (i) what should be the carrying value at the balance sheet date?
   (ii) what valuation basis should we adopt for our land and buildings given that they are non-specialised properties?
   (iii) where should we recognise any gain that is made on revaluation?

Explain your answers by reference to relevant accounting standards.

▷ ACTIVITY 43 (December 1998)   ▷ ▷ ▷ ▷

Data

You have been asked to assist in the preparation of the financial statements of Fun Ltd for the year ended 30 September 20X8. The company is a distributor of children's games. You have been provided with the extended trial balance of Fun Ltd as at 30 September 20X8 which follows.

Fun Ltd – Extended trial balance as at 30 September 20X8

Description	Trial balance Debit £000	Trial balance Credit £000	Adjustments statement Debit £000	Adjustments statement Credit £000	Income Debit £000	Income Credit £000	Balance sheet Debit £000	Balance sheet Credit £000
Trade receivables	2,863						2,863	
Bank overdraft		316						316
Interest	300				300			
Retained earnings		3,811						3,811
Allowance for doubtful debts		114						114
Distribution costs	2,055		614		2,669			
Administration expenses	1,684		358		2,042			
Returns inwards	232				232			
Revenue		14,595				14,595		
Land – cost	2,293						2,293	
Buildings – cost	2,857						2,857	
Fixtures and fittings – cost	1,245						1,245	
Motor vehicles – cost	2,524						2,524	
Office equipment – cost	872						872	
Inventories	1,893		2,041	2,041	1,893	2,041	2,041	
Purchases	6,671				6,671			
Interim dividend	480				480			
Trade payables		804						804
Buildings – accumulated depreciation		261		51				312
Fixtures and fittings – accumulated depreciation		309		124				433
Motor vehicles – accumulated depreciation		573		603				1,176
Office equipment – accumulated depreciation		184		81				265
Pre-payments	63						63	
Carriage inwards	87				87			
Returns outwards		146				146		
Accruals				113				113
Investments	2,244						2,244	
Loan		3,600						3,600
Ordinary share capital		2,000						2,000
Share premium		1,300						1,300
Revaluation reserve		350						350
Profit						2,408		2,408
TOTAL	28,363	28,363	3,013	3,013	16,782	16,782	17,002	17,002

You have been given the following further information:

· The share capital of the business consists of ordinary shares with a nominal value of 25 pence.
· The company has paid an interim dividend of 6 pence per share this year. A final dividend has not yet been proposed
· Depreciation has been calculated on all of the non-current assets of the business and has already been entered into the distribution costs and administrative expenses ledger balances as shown on the extended trial balance.
· The corporation tax charge for the year has been calculated as ?972,000.
· Interest on the loan has been paid for the first eleven months of the year only, but no interest has been paid or charged for the final month of the year. The loan carries a rate of interest of 8% per annum of the balance outstanding on the loan.

Task 43.1
Make any additional adjustments you feel to be necessary to the balances in the extended trial balance as a result of the matters set out in the further information above. Set out your adjustments in the form of journal entries.

Note:
· Narratives and dates are not required.
· Ignore any effect of these adjustments on the tax charge for the year as given above.

Task 43.2
Using the proforma income statement provided below, and taking account of any adjustments made in Task 37.1, draft an income statement for the year ended 30 September 20X8.

Note: You are NOT required to produce notes to the accounts.

Data

The directors are interested in expanding operations next year. They wish to be clear about the constituents of the equity on the balance sheet and on the impact that leasing equipment, rather than purchasing equipment, might have on the company's balance sheet. They would like you to attend the next meeting of the Board.

Task 43.3
Prepare notes to bring to the Board meeting dealing with the following matters.

(a) How the balances on the share premium and the revaluation reserve arose.
(b) The recommendation of one of the directors is to lease the assets as he says that this means that the asset can be kept off the balance sheet. Comment on this recommendation.

Proforma Income Statement

	£000
Revenue	
Cost of sales	
	_____
Gross profit (or loss)	
Distribution costs	
Administrative expenses	
	_____
Profit from operations	
Finance costs	
	_____
Profit (or loss) before taxation	
Tax	
	_____
Profit for the year	_____

▷ ACTIVITY 44

Data

The Chief Accountant of Quine Ltd has heard that IAS 8 requires that an entity should adopt accounting policies that enable its financial statements to give a true and fair view. However, he is not sure how this will affect the year end financial statements and has asked you to clarify certain aspects. He has arranged a meeting with you to discuss these matters.

Task

Prepare notes for the meeting covering the following matters:
(a) What accounting requirements should Quine Ltd have in selecting accounting policies according to IAS 8?
(b) What four objectives should be used to assess the appropriateness of any particular accounting policies?
(c) What two concepts are the most important in the preparation of financial statements and hence in the selection of accounting policies?

▷ ACTIVITY 45 (June 2005)

Data

Otto Line is the managing director of More Ales Ltd. He wishes you to advise him on the accounting treatment of some matters that have arisen during the financial year as follows:

During the year the board of More Ales Ltd decided to close down a division of the company and developed a detailed plan for implementing the decision. More Ales wrote to customers warning them to seek an alternative source of supply. Redundancy notices were sent to the staff of the division. The board has a reliable estimate that the cost of closing the division would be £1,854,000.

During the year three people were seriously injured as a result of food poisoning. It was claimed that the food poisoning came from beer sold by More Ales Ltd. Legal proceedings have started seeking damages from the company of £2,000,000. Lawyers working for More Ales Ltd have advised that it is probable that the company will not be found liable.

Task

Prepare notes for a meeting with the directors covering the following:

(a) Explain what is meant by a 'provision'.

(b) When should a provision be recognised?

(c) Describe and justify the accounting treatment of the matters set out in the data above.

Note: You should make reference, where appropriate, to relevant accounting standards.

Chapter 17
Interpretation of accounts

▷ ACTIVITY 46   ▷ ▷ ▷ ▷

Fylingdales Quarries Ltd is a medium sized business which supplies a variety of products to the civil engineering sector of industry.

The following is an extract from its accounts for the year ended 31 December 20X1. The company contributes to an inter-firm comparison scheme through the Quarrying Trade Association and a summary of performance indicators are also shown below.

Income statement	£m	
Revenue		6.90
Cost of sales		(6.08)
Operating profit before tax		0.82
Taxation		(0.24)
Profit after tax		0.58
Balance sheet		
	£m	£m
Property, plant and equipment		2.90
Current assets		
Inventories	0.60	
Trade receivables	1.84	
Bank	0.05	
	2.49	
Less current liabilities	(1.90)	
Net current assets		0.59
Total assets less current liabilities		3.49
Financed by:		
Equity		3.49

Note: The finished goods valuation included in inventories was £0.40m.

Distribution and administration costs included in cost of sales were

Quarrying Trade Association performance indicators - year ended 31 December 20X1

Return on capital employed	25.60%
Asset turnover	1.80
Net profit before tax to sales	14.22%
Current ratio	1.50 : 1
Liquidity ratio (acid test)	1.02 : 1
Receivables collection period	82 days
Cost of sales to finished goods	8.10
Labour cost % of sales	18.10%
Operating costs % of sales	72.1%
Distribution and admin costs as % of sales	14.12%

NB: Operating costs are defined as cost of sales less distribution and administration costs.

Task

(a) Calculate for Fylingdales Quarries Ltd the ratios listed in the Trade Association data based on the accounts for the year ended 31 December 20X1.

(b) Compare the performance of Fylingdales Quarries with the performance for the sector as a whole based on the data from the Trade Association.

▷ ACTIVITY 47

Wodehouse

Your firm has been asked by Wodehouse plc, a company owning a chain of hardware shops, to carry out a preliminary investigation with a view to the possible acquisition of two smaller companies in the same trade, Pelham Ltd and Grenville Ltd.

You are not yet able to visit either of the companies' premises, but have obtained copies of their latest accounts, both for the year ended 31 March 20X8. The income statements and balance sheets are set out below.

Income statements

	Pelham Ltd		Grenville Ltd	
	£000	£000	£000	£000
Revenue		840		762
Cost of sales		(610)		(505)
Gross profit		230		257
Distribution costs	115		56	
Administrative expenses	30		57	
		(145)		(113)
Profit from operations		85		144
Finance costs		(10)		(6)
Net profit before taxation		75		138
Taxation		(30)		(40)
Profit for the financial year		45		98

Balance sheets

	Pelham Ltd		Grenville Ltd	
	£000	£000	£000	£000
Non-current assets		216		268
Current assets				
Inventories	104		80	
Trade receivables	38		86	
Cash at bank	205		3	
	347		169	
Current liabilities				
Trade and other payables	101		92	
Taxation payable	30		40	
	131		132	
Net current assets		216		37
Total assets less current liabilities		432		305
Non-current liabilities				
10% debentures		150		-
Bank loan (secured)		-		56
		282		249
Capital and reserves				
Share capital - £1 ordinary shares		100		100
Retained earnings		182		149
		282		249

Task

Write notes for a meeting with the directors of Wodehouse plc to discuss your findings.

Include in your notes the following:

(a) Appropriate accounting ratios indicating the profitability and liquidity of the two companies.

(b) Brief comments on these ratios.

(c) An indication of the reasons for which one company might be preferable to the other as an investment.

▷ ACTIVITY 48 (December 2000) ▷ ▷ ▷ ▷

Data

Duncan Tweedy wishes to invest some money in one of two private companies. He has obtained the latest financial statements for Byrne Ltd and May Ltd prepared for internal purposes. As part of his decision making process he has asked you to assess the relative profitability of the two companies. The financial statements of the companies are set out below.

Summary income statement for the year ended 30 September 20X0

	Byrne Ltd £000	May Ltd £000
Revenue	5,761	2,927
Cost of sales	(2,362)	(966)
Gross profit	3,399	1,961
Distribution costs	(922)	(468)
Administrative expenses	(1,037)	(439)
Profit from operations	1,440	1,054
Finance costs	(152)	(40)
Profit before taxation	1,288	1,014
Tax	(309)	(243)
Profit for the financial year	979	771

Balance sheets as at 30 September 20X0

	Byrne Ltd		May Ltd	
	£000	£000	£000	£000
Non-current assets		6,188		2,725
Current assets	1,522		1,102	
Current liabilities	(1,015)		(545)	
Net current assets		507		557
Long-term loan		(1,900)		(500)
		4,795		2,782
Equity				
Called up share capital:				
ordinary shares of ?1 each		2,083		939
Retained earnings		2,712		1,843
		4,795		2,782

You have also been given the following ratios:

	Byrne Ltd	May Ltd
Return on capital employed	21.5%	32.1%
Gross profit percentage	59.0%	67.0%
Net profit percentage	25.0%	36.0%
Earnings per share	47p	82p

Task

Prepare a report for Duncan Tweedy that:

(a)   explains the meaning of each ratio.

(b)   uses each ratio to comment on the relative profitability of the companies.

(c)   concludes, with reasons, which company is the more profitable.

▷ ACTIVITY 49 (June 2000)   ▷▷▷▷

Data

Magnus Carter has recently inherited a majority shareholding in a company, Baron Ltd. The company supplies camping equipment to retail outlets. Magnus wishes to get involved in the management of the business, but until now he has only worked in not-for-profit organisations.

He would like to understand how the company has performed over the past two years and how efficient it is in using its resources. He has asked you to help him to interpret the financial statements of the company which are set out below.

Baron Ltd – Summary income statement for the year ended 31 March

	20X1 £000	20X0 £000
Revenue	1,852	1,691
Cost of sales	(648)	(575)
Gross profit	1,204	1,116
Expenses	(685)	(524)
Profit before tax	519	592
Tax	(125)	(147)
Profit after tax	394	445

Baron Ltd – Summary balance sheets as at 31 March

	20X1 £000	20X1 £000	20X0 £000	20X0 £000
Non-current assets		1,431		1,393
Current assets				
Inventories	217		159	
Trade receivables	319		236	
Cash	36		147	
	572		542	
Current liabilities				
Trade payables	48		44	
Taxation	125		130	
	173		174	
Net current assets		399		368
		1,830		1,761
Share capital		500		500
Retained earnings		1,330		1,261
		1,830		1,761

Task 49.1

Prepare a report for Magnus Carter that includes:
(a) A calculation of the following ratios for the two years:
   (i) gross profit percentage.

(ii)   net profit percentage.
(iii) debtor turnover in days (trade receivables collection period).
(iv)   creditor turnover in days (trade payables payment period based on cost of sales).
(v)   inventory turnover in days (inventory turnover period based on cost of sales).

(b)   For each ratio calculated:
(i)   a brief explanation in general terms of the meaning of the ratio.
(ii)   comments on how the performance or efficiency in the use of resources has changed over the two years.

Task 49.2
Prepare brief notes to answer the following questions asked by Magnus:
(a)   How can the accounting equation in a company balance, when, unlike a not-for-profit organisation, there are no funds to balance with net assets on its balance sheet?
(b)   Can you give me two examples of users outside of the company, other than myself and the other shareholders, who may be interested in the financial statements of Baron Ltd. For each user can you tell me for what purpose they would use them?
(c)   A statement, with reasons, identifying the areas that could be improved over the next year as indicated by the ratios and analysis performed.

▷ ACTIVITY 50 (December 1999)   ▷ ▷ ▷ ▷

Data

Jonathan Fisher is intending to invest a substantial sum of money in a company. A colleague has suggested to him that he might want to invest in a private company called Carp Ltd which supplies pond equipment to retail outlets. You have been asked to assist him in interpreting the financial statements of the company which are set out below.

Carp Ltd – Summary income statement for the year ended 30 September 20X9

	20X9	20X8
	£000	£000
Revenue	3,183	2,756
Cost of sales	(1,337)	(1,020)
Gross profit	1,846	1,736
Expenses	(1,178)	(1,047)
Profit from operations	668	689
Finance costs	(225)	(92)
Profit before tax	443	597
Taxation	(87)	(126)
Profit for the year	356	471

Carp Ltd - Summary balance sheets as at 30 September 20X9

| | 20X9 | | 20X8 | |
	£000	£000	£000	£000
Non-current assets		4,214		2,030
Current assets				
Inventories	795		689	
Trade receivables	531		459	
Cash	15		136	
	1,341		1,284	
Current liabilities				
Trade payables	751		485	
Taxation	87		126	
	838		611	
Net current assets		503		673
Long-term loan		(2,500)		(1,000)
		2,217		1,703
Share capital		700		500
Retained earnings		1,517		1,203
		2,217		1,703

Task

Prepare notes for Jonathan Fisher covering the following points:

(a) Explain what a 'balance sheet' is and what an 'income statement' is and identify the elements that appear in each statement.

(b) Explain the 'accounting equation' and demonstrate that the balance sheet of Carp Ltd as at 30 September 20X9 confirms to it.

(c) Calculate the following ratios for the two years:
  (i) gearing.
  (ii) net profit percentage.
  (iii) current ratio.
  (iv) return on equity (after tax).

(d) Using the ratios calculated, comment on the company's profitability, liquidity and financial position and consider how these have changed over the two years.

(e) Using only the calculation of the ratios and the analysis of the changes over the two years, state whether the company is a better prospect for investment in 20X9 than it was in 20X8. Give reasons for your answer.

Data

Machier Ltd is a company that supplies stationery for business and domestic purposes. You have been asked to assist the directors in the interpretation of the financial statements of the company. They are intending to apply to the bank for a substantial loan. The bank has asked them for their financial statements for the last two years. The directors wish to know how the bank will view their profitability, liquidity and financial position on the evidence of these financial statements.

The directors are also concerned that they do not fully understand the financial statements of customers to whom they supply stationery. The customers include public sector and other not-for-profit organisations.

You have been supplied with the income statement and the balance sheet of Machier Ltd for two years, prepared for internal purposes. These are set out below.

Machier Ltd - Income statement for the year ended 31 March 20X9		
	20X9	20X8
	£000	£000
Revenue	2,636	1,687
Cost of sales	(923)	(590)
Gross profit	1,713	1,097
Depreciation	(856)	(475)
Other expenses	(126)	(101)
Profit on the sale of non current assets	7	2
Profit from operations	738	523
Finance costs	(252)	(120)
Profit before tax	486	403
Taxation on profit	(165)	(137)
Profit for the year	321	266

Machier Ltd - Balance sheet as at 31 March 20X9		
	20X9	20X8
	£000	£000
Non-current assets	4,282	2,376
Current assets		
Inventories	448	287
Trade receivables	527	337
Cash	-	86
	975	710

Current liabilities		
Trade payables	401	222
Taxation	165	137
Bank overdraft	183	-
	749	359
Net current assets	226	351
Long-term loan	2,800	1,500
	1,708	1,227
Equity		
Called up share capital	200	100
Share premium	100	-
Retained earnings	1,408	1,127
	1,708	1,227

Task 51.1

Prepare a report for the directors which includes the following:

(a) A calculation of the following ratios of Machier Ltd for the two years:
   (i) return on equity (after tax).
   (ii) net profit percentage.
   (iii) quick ratio/acid test.
   (iv) gearing ratio.
   (v) interest cover.
(b) Comments on the profitability, liquidity and the financial position of the company as revealed by the ratios and a statement of how this has changed over the two years covered by the financial statements.
(c) An opinion as to whether the bank would be likely to give the company a substantial loan based solely on the information in the financial statements.

Task 51.2

Prepare notes for the directors answering the following questions:

(a) What are the elements in a balance sheet of a company? State which of the balances in the balance sheet of Machier Ltd fall under each element.
(b) How are the elements related in the accounting equation? Show numerically that the accounting equation is maintained in the balance sheet of Machier Ltd.

▷ **ACTIVITY 52** (December 1998)　　　　　　▷ ▷ ▷ ▷

Data

Bimbridge Hospitals Trust has just lost its supplier of bandages. The company that has been supplying it for the last five years has gone into liquidation. The Trust is concerned to select a new supplier which it can rely on to supply it with its needs for the foreseeable future. You have been asked by the Trust managers to analyse the financial statements of a potential supplier of bandages. You have obtained the latest financial statements of the company, in summary form, which are set out below.

Patch Ltd - Summary income statement for the year ended 30 September 20X8

	20X8 £000	20X7 £000
Revenue	2,300	2,100
Cost of sales	(1,035)	(945)
Gross profit	1,265	1,155
Expenses	(713)	(693)
Net profit before interest and tax	552	462

Patch Ltd - Summary balance sheet as at 30 September 20X8

	20X8 £000	20X8 £000	20X7 £000	20X7 £000
Non-current assets		4,764		5,418
Current assets				
Inventories	522		419	
Trade receivables	406		356	
Cash	117		62	
	1,045		837	
Current liabilities				
Trade payables	305		254	
Taxation	170		211	
	475		465	
Net current assets		570		372
Long-term loan		(1,654)		(2,490)
		3,680		3,300
Share capital		1,100		1,000
Share premium		282		227
Retained earnings		2,298		2,073
		3,680		3,300

You have also obtained the relevant industry average ratios which are as follows:

	20X8	20X7
Return on capital employed	9.6%	9.4%
Net profit percentage	21.4%	21.3%
Quick ratio/acid test	1.0 : 1	0.9 : 1
Gearing (debt/capital employed)	36%	37%

Task

Prepare a report for the managers of Bimbridge Hospitals Trust recommending whether or not to use Patch Ltd as a supplier of bandages. Use the information contained in the financial statements of Patch Ltd and the industry averages supplied.

Your answer should:
- Comment on the company's profitability, liquidity and financial position.
- Consider how the company has changed over the two years.
- Include a comparison with the industry as a whole.

The report should include calculation of the following ratios for the two years:
(i)   Return on capital employed.
(ii) Net profit percentage.
(iii) Quick ratio/acid test.
(iv) Gearing.

▷ ACTIVITY 53 (June 2002)   ▷ ▷ ▷ ▷

Data

Michael Beacham has been asked to lend money to Goodall Ltd for a period of three years. He employed a financial adviser to advise him whether to make a loan to the company. The financial adviser has obtained the financial statements of the company for the past two years, calculated some ratios and found the industry averages. However, she was unable to complete her report. Michael has asked you to analyse the ratios and to advise him on whether he should make a loan to Goodall Ltd. The ratios are set out below.

	20X2	20X1	Industry average
Gearing ratio	67%	58%	41%
Interest cover	1.2	2.3	4.6
Quick ratio/acid test	0.5	0.8	1.1
Return on equity	9%	13%	19%

Task

Write a report for Michael Beacham that includes the following:
(a) an explanation of the meaning of each ratio.
(b) a comment on Goodall Ltd's financial position and the performance of the company as shown by the ratios.
(c) a statement of how the financial position and performance have changed over the two years, and how they compare with the industry average.
(d) a conclusion on whether Michael should lend money to Goodall Ltd. Base your conclusion only on the ratios calculated and the analysis performed.

▷ ACTIVITY 54 (December 2002)   ▷ ▷ ▷ ▷

Data

Karel Popper is the Managing Director of Zipps Ltd, a company that distributes clothing accessories. The company wishes to raise a loan to finance the expansion of activities. The bank has asked for information about the company including a copy of the financial statements for the past two years. Karel wants to know how likely it is that the bank would be willing to lend the company money on the basis of the financial position revealed in the financial statements alone. He has asked you to advise him on this matter. He also has some questions about financial accounting and reporting. He has given you the income statements of Zipps Ltd and the summarised balance sheets for the past two years. These are set out below.

Zipps Ltd
Income statement for the year ended 30 September

	20X2 £000	20X1 £000
Revenue	2,412	2,496
Cost of sales	(1,158)	(1,123)
Gross profit	1,254	1,373
Distribution costs	(814)	(651)
Administrative expenses	(486)	(452)
(Loss) profit from operations	(46)	270
Finance costs	(104)	(77)
Profit/(loss) before taxation	(150)	193
Tax	-	(42)
(Loss)/Profit for the financial year	(150)	151

Zipps Ltd
Balance sheet as at 30 September

	20X8 £000	20X8 £000	20X7 £000	20X7 £000
Non-current assets		1,220		1,118
Current assets				
Inventories	845		620	
Trade receivables	402		416	
Cash	183		266	
	1,430		1,302	
Current liabilities				
Trade payables	(650)		(620)	
Net current assets		780		682
		2,000		1,800
Called up share capital:				
Ordinary shares of £1 each		200		200
Retained earnings		500		700
Long term loan		1,300		900
		2,000		1,800

Task

Prepare a letter for Karel Popper that includes the following:

(a)   A calculation of the following ratios of Zipps Ltd for each of the two years:
   ·   Current ratio
   ·   Quick ratio/acid test
   ·   Gearing ratio
   ·   Interest cover
(b)   An explanation of the meaning of each ratio.
(c)   A comment on how each ratio has changed over the two years and how this has affected the liquidity and the financial position of Zipps Ltd.
(d)   A brief indication of other ratios that the bank may wish to calculate and why (you do not need to calculate them or comment on them in any way).
(e)   A conclusion, with reasons, as to whether it is likely that the bank will lend the company money based solely on the ratios calculated and their analysis.

▷ ACTIVITY 55 (December 2003)   ▷▷▷▷

Youngernst Ltd

Data

A colleague has asked you to take over an assignment. He has been helping a shareholder of Youngernst Ltd to understand the financial statements of the company for the past two years. The shareholder is interested in finding out how well the company has managed working capital. Your colleague has obtained the financial statements of Youngernst Ltd for the past two years and has calculated the following ratios:

Ratio	20X3	20X2
Current ratio	2.8 : 1	2.3 : 1
Quick ratio	0.6 : 1	1.1 : 1
Receivables turnover in days	48 days	32 days
Payables turnover in days	27 days	30 days
Inventory turnover in days (inventory turnover period based on cost of sales)	84 days	67 days

Task

Prepare notes for a meeting with the shareholder that includes the following:
(a)   the formulas used to calculate each of the ratios
(b)   an explanation of the meaning of each of the ratios

(c) your comments on the change in the ratios of Youngernst Ltd over the two years, including an analysis of whether the change in each of the ratios shows that the management of the components of working capital has improved or deteriorated.

▷ ACTIVITY 56 (June 2004)

Data

Maurice Sun plans to invest in Fieldsomer Ltd. This is a chain of shops. He is to meet his consultants to discuss the profitability of the company. To prepare for the meeting he has asked you to comment on the change in profitability and the return on capital of the company. He also has some questions about the company's balance sheet. He has given you Fieldsomer's income statements and the summarised balance sheets for the past two years prepared for internal purposes. These are set out below.

Fieldsomer Ltd
Summary Income statements for year ended 31 March

	20X4	20X3
	£000	£000
Revenue	8,420	7,595
Cost of sales	(3,536)	(3,418)
Gross profit	4,884	4,177
Distribution costs	(1,471)	(1,016)
Administrative expenses	(1,224)	(731)
Profit from operations	2,189	2,430
Finance cost	(400)	(480)
Profit before taxation	1,789	1,950
Tax	(465)	(569)
Profit for the year	1,324	1,381
Note		
Dividends paid were:	720	600

Fieldsomer Ltd
Balance sheets as at 31 March

	20X4		20X3	
	£000	£000	£000	£000
Non current assets				
Property, plant and equipment		15,132		13,880

Current assets	4,624		3,912
Current liabilities	(2,215)		(1,855)
Net current assets		2,409	2,057
Total assets less current liabilities		17,541	15,937
Long-term loan		(5,000)	(6,000)
		12,541	9,937
Equity			
Share capital	6,000		5,000
Share premium	2,000		1,000
Retained earnings	4,541		3,937
		12,541	9,937

Task 56.1

Prepare a report for Maurice Sun that includes the following:

(a) a calculation of the following ratios of Fieldsomer Ltd for each of the two years:
   (i)   Return on capital employed
   (ii) Net profit percentage
   (iii) Gross profit percentage
   (iv) Asset turnover (based on net assets)

(b) an explanation of the meaning of each ratio and a comment on the performance of Fieldsomer Ltd as shown by each of the ratios

(c) a conclusion on how the overall performance has changed over the two years.

Task 56.2

Prepare notes for a meeting with Maurice that answers the following questions relating to the balance sheet of Fieldsomer Ltd.

(a) What are the monetary values of the ownership interest, the assets and the liabilities in Fieldsomer Ltd as at 31 March 20X4 and how are they related in the accounting equation?

(b) What does the retained earnings balance in the balance sheet at 31 March 20X4 represent? What is the connection between the profit shown in the income statement and the balance of retained earnings in the balance sheet?

▷ ACTIVITY 57 (June 2005)   ▷ ▷ ▷ ▷

Data

Leopard Scratchy plans to invest in shares in a private company. He has identified two companies that might be suitable, Partridge Ltd and Carington Ltd. He has obtained the latest financial statements of the companies in order to learn more about the risk inherent in, and return provided by, a potential investment in these companies. The income statements and the summarised balance sheets for the two companies are set out below:

Summary Income Statements for year ended 31 March 20X5

	Partridge Ltd £000	Carington Ltd £000
Revenue	16,241	11,147
Cost of sales	(6,659)	(4,570)
Gross profit	9,582	6,577
Distribution costs	(2,204)	(1,513)
Administrative expenses	(1,820)	(1,250)
Profit from operations	(5,558)	3,814
Finance cost	(640)	(30)
Profit before taxation	4,918	3,784
Tax	(1,230)	(946)
Profit for the period from continuing operations	3,688	2,838
Note Dividends paid were:	3,150	450

Balance sheets as at 31 March 20X5

	Partridge Ltd £000	Partridge Ltd £000	Carington Ltd £000	Carington Ltd £000
Non current assets				
Property, plant and equipment		16,835		9,714
Current assets	2,030		1,393	
Current liabilities	(1,109)		(761)	
Net current assets		921		632
Non current liabilities				
Long term loan		(8,000)		(500)
		9,756		9,846
Equity				
Share capital	7,000		7,000	
Share premium	1,000		-	
Retained earnings	1,756		2,846	
		9,756		9,846

Task 57.1

Prepare a report for Leopold Scratchy that includes:

(a) the formulas that are used to calculate each of the following ratios:

     (i)   Return on equity (Return on shareholders' capital)

     (ii)   Earnings per share

     (iii)   Gearing (Debt/equity)

     (iv)   Gross profit percentage

(b) a calculation of the above ratios for Partridge Ltd and Carington Ltd

(c) an explanation of the meaning of each ratio, and a comment on the relative return and risk of the two companies based on the ratios calculated.

Task 57.2

In note form:

(a) State the objective of financial statements according to the Framework for the Preparation and Presentation of Financial Statements

(b) Identify the type of user of financial statements in Task 57.1 and explain how financial statements are being used to meet the objective of financial statements in these circumstances.

▷ ACTIVITY 58 (December 2005)   ▷ ▷ ▷ ▷

Data

John Brams is a shareholder of Ma Leer Ltd. He has obtained some ratios that are based on the financial statements of the company for the last two years. He is interested in how the directors have managed the business in the past year and in the company's financial performance. You have been asked to explain how the ratios were calculated and to analyse the financial performance of the company using the ratios computed. The ratios John has obtained are set out below.

Ratio	20X5	20X4
Return on capital employed	15%	19%
Net profit ratio	20%	22%
Gross profit ratio	46%	42%
Expenses ratio	26%	24%
Asset turnover (based on net assets)	0.75	0.86
Inventory turnover in days (inventory turnover period based on cost of sales)	93 days	71 days

Receivables turnover in days (receivables payment period)	54 days	47 days
Payables turnover in days (Payables payment period based on cost of sales)	25 days	29 days

Task 58.1

Prepare a report for John Brams that includes the following:

(a) the formulas used to calculate each of the ratios

(b) a statement of whether the ratios have, in your opinion, improved or deteriorated in 20X5 when compared with 20X4, along with your reasons for thinking so

(c) your comments on the overall change in financial performance of Ma Leer Ltd over the two years based on your analysis of the ratios and the relationship between them.

Task 58.2

(a) Explain how the use of financial information in Task 58.1 illustrates the objective of financial statements.

(b) Give TWO examples of other classes of user who might be interested in the information in financial statements. Explain what they might use this information for.

MOCK EXAMINATION QUESTIONS

Data and tasks

Instructions
This exam paper is in two sections.

You must show competence in **both** sections, so attempt and aim to complete **every** task in **each** section.

Please use the answer booklet provided. All workings should be shown in the answer booklet.

The answer booklet includes the following pro-formas:
· Journal entries
· Company income statement
· Company balance sheet
· Consolidated balance sheet
· Cash flow statement

You should spend about 125 minutes on Section 1 and about 55 minutes on Section 2.

SECTION 1

You should spend about 125 minutes on this section.

This section is in three parts.

PART A

You should spend about 50 minutes on this part.

DATA

You have been asked to help prepare the financial statements of Wolf Ltd for the year ended 31 March 2006. The trial balance of the company as at 31 March 2006 is shown below:

Wolf Ltd Trial Balance as at 31 March 2006	Debit £000	Credit £000
Sales		72,813
Purchases	35,108	
Inventories as at 1 April 2005	12,572	
Final dividend paid for year end 31 March 2005	1,000	
Interim dividend paid for year end 31 March 2006	600	
Interest	700	
Distribution costs	12,533	
Administrative expenses	9,311	
Trade receivables	9,122	
Cash at bank	473	
7% debentures		20,000
Ordinary share capital		10,000
Share premium		8,000
Retained earnings		17,349
Trade payables		2,927
Accruals		412
Property, plant and equipment – cost	71,338	
Property, plant and equipment – accumulated depreciation		21,256
	152,757	152,757

Further information:

· The authorised share capital of the company consists of ordinary shares with a nominal value of 25p. All of this has been issued.
· The inventories at the close of business on 31 March 2006 cost £14,186,000.
· The corporation tax charge for the year has been calculated as £3,537,000.
· Interest on the debentures for the last six months of the year has not been included in the accounts in the trial balance.
· Land included in Property, plant and equipment at a net book value of £24,000,000 is to be revalued at the end of the year at £29,000,000.
· All of the operations of the business are continuing operations.

· On 21 April 2006 there was a fire at the company's premises that destroyed property, plant and equipment and inventories. The losses from the fire amounted to £487,000 and they were not covered by the company's insurance. This amount is considered by the directors to constitute a material loss to the company.

· On 3 May 2006 the company declared a final dividend for the year ended 31 March 2006 of 6p per share.

Task 1.1

Using the pro-forma in your answer booklet, make the necessary journal entries as a result of the further information given above.

Task 1.2

(a) Using the pro-forma in your answer booklet, draft the income statement for Wolf Ltd for the year ended 31 March 2006.

(b) Using the pro-forma in your answer booklet, draft the balance sheet for Wolf Ltd as at 31 March 2006.

Task 1.3

(a) Explain what is meant by 'events after the balance sheet date'.

(b) Distinguish between events after the balance sheet date that are 'adjusting events' and ones that are 'non-adjusting events'.

(c) Explain your treatment of:

  i) the losses that arose from the fire on the company's premises on 21 April 2006

  ii) the final dividend declared on 3 May 2006.

PART B

You are advised to spend 35 minutes on this part.

DATA

Alasmith plc has one subsidiary undertaking, Jones Ltd, acquired on 1 April 2005. The balance sheets of Alasmith plc and Jones Ltd as at 31 March 2006 are set out below:

Balance sheets as at 31 March 2006		
	Alasmith plc £000	Jones Ltd £000
Non-current assets		
Property, plant and equipment	56,320	39,320
Investment in Jones Ltd	26,680	
	83,000	39,320
Current assets	13,638	5,470
Inventories	7,839	3,218
Trade and other receivables	1,013	1,184
Cash and cash equivalents	22,490	9,872
Total assets	105,490	49,192
Current liabilities		
Trade and other payables	(9,183)	(4,831)
Tax liabilities	(1,059)	(311)
	(10,242)	(5,142)
Net current assets	12,248	4,730)
Non-current liabilities		
Long term loan	(20,000)	(8,850)
Total liabilities	(30,242)	(13,992)
Net assets	75,248	35,200
EQUITY		
Share capital	25,000	6,000
Share premium account	10,000	4,000
Retained earnings	40,248	25,200
Total equity	75,248	35,200

You have been given the following further information:

· The share capital of Jones Ltd consists of ordinary shares of £1 each. There have been no changes to the balances of share capital and share premium during the year. No dividends were paid or proposed by Jones Ltd during the year.

· Alasmith plc acquired 3,600,000 shares in Jones Ltd on 1 April 2005.

- At 1 April 2005 the balance of retained earnings of Jones Ltd was £19,800,000.
- The fair value of the non-current assets of Jones Ltd at 1 April 2005 was £43,470,000. The book value of the non-current assets at 1 April 2005 was £35,470,000. The revaluation has not been recorded in the books of Jones Ltd (ignore any effect on the depreciation for the year). There were no other differences between the book value and fair value of the other assets and liabilities of Jones Ltd at the date of acquisition.
- The directors have concluded that goodwill on the acquisition of Jones Ltd has been impaired during the year. They estimate that the impairment loss amounts to 10% of the goodwill.

Task 1.4

Using the pro-forma in the answer booklet, prepare the consolidated balance sheet of Alasmith plc and its subsidiary undertaking as at 31 March 2006.

PART C

You should spend about 30 minutes on this part.

DATA

You have been asked to prepare a reconciliation between profit from operations and net cash from operating activities and to prepare a cash flow statement for Unwittington Ltd for the year ended 31 March 2006. The income statement and balance sheet of Unwittington Ltd are set out below.

Unwittington Ltd
Income Statement for the year ended 31 March 2006

	£000
Continuing Operations	
Revenue	14,734
Cost of sales	(8,104)
Gross profit	6,630
Profit on disposal of property, plant and equipment	217
Distribution costs	(2,641)
Administrative expenses	(1,993)
Profit from operations	2,213
Finance costs	(210)
Profit before tax	2,003
Tax	(501)
Profit for the period from continuing operations attributable to equity holders	1,502

Unwittington Ltd
Balance sheet as at 31 March

	2006 £000	2005 £000
Non-current assets		
Property, plant and equipment	22,708	16,797
Current assets		
Inventories	2,701	2,019
Trade and other receivables	2,456	1,009

Cash and cash equivalents	-	392
	5,157	3,420
Total assets	27,865	20,217
Current liabilities		
Trade and other payables	(1,140)	(1,113)
Tax liabilities	(501)	(466)
Bank overdraft	(684)	-
	(2,325)	(1,579)
Net current assets	2,832	1,841
Non-current liabilities		
Bank loans	(3,000)	(2,000)
Total liabilities	(5,325)	(3,579)
Net assets	22,540	16,638
EQUITY		
Share capital	6,000	4,000
Share premium account	4,000	1,000
Retained earnings	12,540	11,638
Total equity	22,540	16,638

Note to the accounts: Retained earnings

	£000
Balance at 1 April 2005	11,638
Dividends paid	(600)
Profit for the year	1,502
Balance at 31 March 2006	12,540

Further information:

- The total depreciation charge for the year was £2,952,000.
- Property, plant and equipment costing £2,048,000 with accumulated depreciation of £1,011,000 was sold in the year.
- All sales and purchases were on credit. Other expenses were paid for in cash.

Task 1.5

Provide a note to the accounts showing the reconciliation of profit from operations to net cash from operating activities for Unwittington Ltd for the year ended 31 March 2006.

Task 1.6

Using the pro-forma in the answer booklet, prepare the cash flow statement for Unwittington Ltd for the year ended 31 March 2006.

SECTION 2

You are advised to spend approximately 55 minutes on this section.

DATA

Madge Keygone is the managing director of Asbeen Ltd.

She has just returned from a meeting with one of the major shareholders of the company.

The shareholder was concerned about the current ratio, quick ratio, inventories turnover and trade receivables turnover and how they compare with the industry averages.

Madge did not understand the shareholder's concern and has asked you to help her.

She has given you the summarised financial statements of Asbeen Ltd and has obtained the industry averages for these ratios from computerised databases.

These are set out below.

Asbeen Ltd Summary Income Statement for the year ended 31 March 2006	
	£000
Continuing Operations	
Revenue	14,994
Cost of sales	(8,716)
Gross profit	6,278
Distribution costs	(2,037)
Administrative expenses	(1,541)
Profit from operations	2,700
Finance costs	(274)
Profit before tax	2,426
Tax	(631)
Profit for the period from continuing operations attributable to equity holders	1,795

Note: All sales are on credit.

Asbeen Ltd	
Balance sheet as at 31 March 2006	
	£000
Non-current assets	
Property,plant and equipment	11,432
Current assets	
Inventories	4,200
Trade and other receivables	2,095
Cash and cash equivalents	145
	6,440
Total assets	17,872
Current liabilities	
Trade and other payables	(2,169)
Tax liabilities	(631)
	(2,800)
Net curren tassets	3,640
Non-current liabilities	
Bank loans	(4,500)
Total liabilities	(7,300)
Net assets	10,572
Equity	
Share capital	5,000
Retained earnings	5,572
Total equity	10,572

Industry averages:

Current ratio	1.9:1
Quick ratio (acid test)	0.9:1
Inventories turnover in days (inventories turnover period based on cost of sales)	98 days
Trade receivables turnover in days (trade receivables payment period)	47 days

Task 2.1

Prepare a letter for Madge Keygone that includes the following:

(a)   the formulas used to calculate the following ratios:
   (i)   current ratio
   (ii)   quick ratio (acid test)
   (iii)   inventories turnover (inventories turnover period based on cost of sales)
   (iv)   trade receivables turnover in days (trade receivables payment period);

(b)   an explanation of what the ratios in (a) above tell you about a company;

(c)   a calculation of the ratios in (a) above for Asbeen Ltd;

(d)   a statement of how the ratios for Asbeen Ltd calculated in (c) above compare withthe industry averages and whether they are a cause for concern.

DATA

The accounting equation is:

Assets – Liabilities = Equity

Task 2.2

(a)   Define the following elements of financial statements:
   (i)   assets
   (ii)   liabilities
   (iii)   equity

(b)   Explain why inventories are an asset of a company.

MOCK EXAMINATION
ANSWER BOOKLET

SECTION 1

PART A

Task 1

JOURNAL		
	Dr £000	Cr £000

Task 1.2

Wolf Ltd **Income statement for the year ended 31 March 2006**
£000
Continuing operations
Revenue
Cost of sales
Gross profit
Distribution costs
Administrative expenses
Profit from operations
Finance costs
Profit before tax
Tax
Profit for the period from continuing operations attributable to equity holders

Wolf Ltd
Balance sheet as at 31 March 2006

£000

Non-current assets

Current assets

Total assets

Current liabilities

Net current assets
Non-current liabilities

Total liabilities

Net assets
Equity

Total equity

WORKINGS

PART B

Task 1.4

Alasmith plc
Consolidated balance sheet as at 31 March 2006

	£000
Non-current assets	
Current assets	
Total assets	
Current liabilities	
Net current assets	
Non-current liabilities	
Total liabilities	
Net assets	———
Equity	———
Equity attributable to equity holders of the parent	———
Minority interest	
Total equity	———
	———

WORKINGS

PART C

Task 1.5 and 1.6

Unwittington Ltd
Cash Flow Statement for the year ended 31 March 2006

	£000
Net cash from operating activities before tax	
Tax	
	————
Net cash from operating activities	
	————
Investing activities	
Net cash used in investing activities	————
Financing activities	————
Net cash (used in)/from financing activities	————
Net increase/(decrease) in cash and cash equivalents	————
Cash and cash equivalents at beginning of year	
	————
Cash and cash equivalents at end of year	
	————

WORKINGS

SECTION 2

Task 2.1

LETTER

Task 2.2

(a)

   (i)

   (ii)

   (iii)

(b)

KEY TECHNIQUES QUESTION BANK ANSWERS

Chapters 1 and 2
The regulatory and conceptual framework of accounting

△ ACTIVITY 1   △△△△

(a) The user groups identified in the Framework are:
· Present and potential investors
· Lenders
· Suppliers and other trade creditors
· Employees
· Customers
· Government
· The public

(b) **Present and potential investors**
This group would consider whether to invest or disinvest in the entity. Equity investors consider two elements to their investment, income and capital gain. Income is received in the form of dividends, and capital gain in the upward move- ment of share price.

If the investor takes a short-term view then current dividends are the focus, where- as a longer term view would concern future earnings.

A guide to the future can to some extent be seen in a company report with the chairman's statement. Although it is largely based on current performance, the company's forward strategy is often reviewed.

The investor group would also be interested in profitability and its trend over a peri- od of time, with particular emphasis on its effect on earnings per share.

Employees
Some companies produce a separate employees' report together with their annual report. Employees and their representatives require information on business per- formance for two principal reasons:
· Wage and salary negotiation.
· Assessment of current and forward opportunity in terms of employment.

They would be interested in both the current financial stability and the longer term financial viability of the business.

They need information in a clear, simple and understandable form.

Lenders
This group is often referred to as the loan creditor group. It would include the long, medium and short-term lenders of money. The principal concern of the existing and/or potential loan creditor is 'will we get our money back?'.

A short-term loan creditor will immediately focus on cash flow and the cash flow statement based on IAS 7 will be of particular interest here. The banks make up much of this group and they would have an interest in the net realisable value of the assets.

Medium and long-term loan creditor groups will be concerned with the future and long-term cash flow potential of the business.

The priority of claims on the business' resources would also be of concern to this group. They would be interested in the current and future profitability and growth prospects of the entity.

△ ACTIVITY 2   △ △ △ △

The Framework identified four key characteristics which make financial information useful:
· Relevance
· Reliability
· Comparability
· Understandability

Relevance and reliability relate to the content of information, whereas comparability and understandability concern the presentation of information.

Relevance   Information is relevant when it influences the economic decision of users by helping them evaluate past, present or future events.

Reliability   Information is reliable when it is free from material error and bias and can be depended upon to represent faithfully what it claims to represent. Accounting standards and the audit are all means of ensuring that accounting information is reliable.

Comparability   Information is comparable when it can be compared over time to identify trends in financial performance and position. It is also useful to be able to compare the performance of different entities. To achieve comparability an entity needs to apply accounting policies consistently over a period of time and also disclose those accounting policies so that users can see on what basis the accounts have been prepared. Comparative figures must also be shown in the financial statements to assist with comparability.

Understandability Information provided in the financial statements should be readily understandable by users. The users are assumed to have a reasonable knowledge of business and economic activities and accounting and a willingness to study the information with reasonable diligence. Therefore the focus of financial statements is the informed user. Information in the financial statements should not be excluded because it may be too difficult for certain users to understand.

△ ACTIVITY 3   △ △ △ △

· The Framework defines an asset as:
  'A resource controlled by the entity as a result of past events and from which future economic benefits are expected to flow to the entity'.
· The Framework defines a liability as:
  'A present obligation of the entity arising from past events, the settlement of which is expected to result in an outflow from the entity of resources embodying economic benefits'.

· The Framework defines equity as:
'The residual interest in the assets of the entity after deducting all its liabilities'.
In other word, equity is what is left when all liabilities have been settled. This is essentially the net assets of a business.

· Income consists of both revenue and gains. Revenue arises from a business's ordinary activities such as the sale of goods. Gains represent increases in economic benefits such as a gain on disposal of a non current asset.

· Expenses are losses as well as expenses that arise in the normal course of business such as cost of sales, wages and depreciation. Losses represent a decrease in economic benefits such as losses on disposal of non current assets or disasters such as fire or flood.

Accounting equation
Assets less liabilities = equity interest

△ ACTIVITY 4   △△△△

(a) 'Assets' are resources controlled by the entity as a result of past events and from which future economic benefits are expected to flow to the entity.

'Liabilities' are present obligations of the entity arising from past events, the settlement of which is expected to result in an outflow from the entity of resources embodying economic benefits

'Equity interest' is the residual amount found by deducting all of the entity's liabilities from all of the entity's assets.

(b) The first transaction would increase the assets (inventories) by £120 and increase the liabilities (trade payables) by £120.

The second transaction would decrease the asset (inventories), i.e. inventories at cost, by £120, but increase the asset cash by £180. This would increase net assets by £60 and equity interest, i.e. capital, by £60 (the profit on the transaction).

(c) The accounting equation would then appear as:
          Assets £1,380 - Liabilities £920 = equity interest £460

(d) A simple income statement would show:

	£
Revenue	180
Cost of sales	(120)
Profit	60

(e) Users identified in the Framework would include shareholders, customers, suppliers, loan creditor group, employees, public, government. For example, existing or potential shareholders would be interested in the business' profitability and its earning

potential. They may compare current performance with the previous year's performance. Using such information they may decide to invest or disinvest in the
business.

△ ACTIVITY 5   △ △ △ △

(a) Assessing the stewardship of management
Examples may include:

Organisation	User	Use
Limited company	Shareholders both potential and existing	Assess return on capital, return on equity and EPS
Limited company	Employees	Trade unions could campaign for failing managers to be replaced, in order to secure their members' employment.

(b) Economic decisions

Organisation	User	Use
Limited company	Potential investor	Decision whether or not to invest
Partnership/sole trader	Loan creditor group	Whether to grant additional loan funding

△ ACTIVITY 6   △ △ △ △

(a) The elements of assets, liabilities and equity interest are shown in the balance sheet.
The relationship between these elements is shown by the accounting equation as:
Assets - liabilities = equity interest

(b) 'Income' encompasses revenue and gains. Income increases the equity interest.
· Expenses' leads to a decrease in equity interest.
· Both are shown either in the income statement or in the statement of changes in equity

△ ACTIVITY 7   △ △ △ △

(a) Potential investors are interested in information that is useful to them in taking decisions about potential investment in the company. They need information about the
entity's potential return to investors and the risk inherent in those returns.
Information about the entity's past financial performance helps them to assess its
anticipated performance and cash-generation abilities. Information about its financial position and structure can be useful in assessing how future cash flows will be
distributed and whether the company can meets its commitments as they fall due
and raise finance in the future. Information about its financial adaptability is useful
in assessing risk or benefit from unexpected changes.

(b) Assets are defined by the Framework as 'resources controlled by the entity as a result of past events and from which future economic benefits are expected to flow to the entity'. Inventories are an asset because they give rise to future economic benefits controlled by the company in the form of cash that will be received from the sale of the goods. The benefits came about as a result of the past transaction of purchasing the inventories for resale.

Chapter 3
Drafting financial statements for a sole trader

△ ACTIVITY 8   △ △ △ △

G Hick - Income statement for the year ended 31 December 20X3

	£	£
Revenue		170,000
Inventories 1/1/X3	17,500	
Purchases	120,000	
	137,500	
Less inventories 31/12/X3	(19,500)	
Cost of goods sold		(118,000)
Gross profit		52,000
Expenses		
Wages (14,100 + 270)	14,370	
Advertising (2,100 - 350)	1,750	
Insurance	1,400	
Heat and light	2,300	
Business rates (3,200 - 800)	2,400	
Maintenance	150	
Motor vehicle running costs (1,650 - 650)	1,000	
Receivables written off	500	
Allowance for doubtful debts (1,500 - 1,000)	500	
Depreciation: (see working)		
Fixtures	1,500	
Premises	1,600	
Motor vehicles	2,500	
		(29,970)
Net profit for the year		22,030

Balance sheet as at 31 December 20X3

	Cost £	Depreciation £	NBV £
Non-current assets			
Premises	40,000	9,600	30,400
Fixtures and fittings	7,500	4,000	3,500
Motor vehicle	12,500	7,500	5,000
	60,000	21,100	38,900
Current assets			
Inventories		19,500	
Trade receivables (12,500 - 500)	12,000		
Less allowance for bad debts	(1,500)		
		10,500	
Prepayments - business rates		800	
Cash in hand		1,250	
Cash at bank		1,700	
		33,750	
Less current liabilities			
Trade payables		21,000	
Accruals - wages		270	
		21,270	
Net current assets			12,480
Net assets			51,380
Financed by			
Capital		43,450	
Add profit for the year		22,030	
		65,480	
Less drawings (13,100 + 350 +650)		(14,100)	
			51,380

Workings

Depreciation:

Premises: 40,000 x 4% = £1,600
Accumulated depreciation: 8,000 + 1,600 = £9,600

Fixtures: 7,500 x 20% = £1,500
Accumulated depreciation: 2,500 + 1,500 = £4,000

Vehicles: 12,500 x 20% = £2,500
Accumulated depreciation: 5,000 + 2,500 = £7,500

△ ACTIVITY 9

△△△△

Michael Jay - Income statement for the year ended 31 December 20X3

	£	£
Revenue		193,000
Inventories 1/1/X3	23,150	
Purchases	131,100	
	154,250	
Less inventories 31/12/X3	(25,600)	
Cost of goods sold		(128,650)
Gross profit		64,350
Expenses		
Wages (13,150 + 720)	13,870	
Rates (3,250 - 250)	3,000	
Insurances (1,850 + 260)	2,110	
Heat and light (1,260 - 260)	1,000	
Motor vehicle running costs	1,050	
Maintenance (780 - 280)	500	
Receivables written off	200	
Allowance for doubtful debts (W1)	460	
Profit on disposal of asset (W2)	(160)	
Depreciation: (W2)		
Premises	2,500	
Fixtures	2,200	
Motor vehicle	2,870	
		(29,600)
Net profit for the year		34,750

Balance sheet as at 31 December 20X3

	Cost £	Depreciation £	NBV £
Non-current assets			
Premises	50,000	7,500	42,500
Fixtures	11,000	8,800	2,200
Motor vehicles	14,350	8,610	5,740
	75,350	24,910	50,440
Current assets			
Inventories		25,600	
Trade receivables (W1)	16,000		
Less allowance for bad debts (W1)	(960)	15,040	
Prepayments - rates		250	

Cash in hand	970	
Cash at bank	1,395	
	43,255	
Less current liabilities		
Trade payables	19,100	
Accruals - wages	720	
	(19,820)	
Net current assets		23,435
		73,875
Financed by		
Capital	50,405	
Add profit for the year	34,750	
	85,155	
Less drawings (11,000 + 280)	(11,280)	
		73,875

Workings

W1 Trade receivables
The allowance for bad debts is calculated as follows:

	£
Receivables per trial balance	15,200
Add non current asset receivable	1,000
Less receivable written off	(200)
Trade receivables	16,000
Allowance for receivables (6%)	960
Opening allowance per TB	500
Increase in allowance	460

W2 Depreciation

Premises:	50,000 x 5% = £2,500
	Accumulated depreciation: 5,000 + 2,500 = £7,500
Vehicles:	14,350 x 20% = £2,870
	Accumulated depreciation: 5,740 + 2,870 = £8,610

Fixtures:
Profit on sale of asset: 1,000 - 840 = £160

Accumulated depreciation relating to disposal of £1,260 (2,100 - 840) must be removed from the accumulated depreciation.

The asset is not depreciated in the year of disposal so the cost to be depreciated is £11,000 (13,100 - 2,100).

Depreciation charge: 11,000 x 20% = £2,200

Accumulated depreciation: 2,200 + 7,860 - 1,260 = £8,800

△ ACTIVITY 10   △ △ △ △

(1) (C)

	£
Trade receivables	19,100
Less bad debt	(400)
	18,700
5% allowance	935
Existing allowance	(735)
Increase in allowance	200

(2) (C)

Disposal of asset

	£		£
Asset at cost	3,400	Proceeds	2,150
Profit on sale	750	Accumulated depreciation (bal)	2,000
	4,150		4,150

(3) (A)

Rent and rates account

	£		£
Balance b/d	2,850	Pre-payment balance c/d	720
Accrual balance c/d	500	Income statement (bal)	2,630
	3,350		3,350
Balance b/d	720	Balance b/d	500

(4) (C)

Purchase ledger account

	£		£
Returns	1,100	Balance b/d	15,100
Discounts	4,100	Purchases	96,000
Payments to suppliers	83,200		
Contra offset against sales			
ledger	1,560		
Balance c/d	21,140		
	_____		_____
	111,100		111,100
	_____		_____
		Balance b/d	21,140

(5) (a) (D)

Cost of goods sold:

	£	
Inventories at start	16,200	
Add purchases	94,500	(net of drawings £1,500)
Less returns	(1,100)	
Less closing inventories	(17,220)	
	_____	
	92,380	
	_____	

(b) (B)

	£	
Net sales	130,000	i.e. sales less returns inward
Cost of goods sold	92,380	
	_____	
	37,620	
	_____	

△ ACTIVITY 11   △△△△

Task 11.1

			£	£
1	DR	Inventories (balance sheet) (see working)	46,077	
	CR	Inventories (income statement)		46,077
2	DR	Prepayments	1,200	
	CR	Rent, rates and insurance		1,200
3	DR	Drawings	2,000	
	CR	Purchases		2,000
4	DR	Depreciation - motor vehicles	5,292	
	CR	Motor vehicles - accumulated depreciation		5,292

Workings

Inventories:	£49,477 - £3,400	=	£46,077
Depreciation:	30% x (£36,000 - £18,360)	=	£5,292

Task 11.2

Elizabeth Ogier
Income statement for the year ended 30 September 20X9

	£	£
Revenue		230,461
Less Returns inwards		(3,053)
		───────
		227,408
Less Cost of sales		
Opening inventories	46,092	
Purchases (113,565 - 2,000)	111,565	
Carriage inwards	1,256	
Less Returns outwards	(2,911)	
	───────	
	156,002	
Less Closing inventories	(46,077)	(109,925)
	───────	───────
Gross profit		117,483
Less Expenses		
Rent, rates and insurance (8,291 - 1,200)	7,091	
Motor expenses	5,813	
Bad debts	1,420	
Carriage outwards	1,571	
Salesperson's commission	2,561	
Bank charges	710	
Depreciation - Motor vehicles	5,292	
- Office equipment	2,312	
- Fixtures and fittings	602	
Wages, salaries and NIC	47,564	
Lighting and heating	3,056	
Postage and stationery	1,037	

Telephone	3,571
Discounts allowed	410
	————
	(83,010)
	————
Net profit	34,473
	————

Task 11.3

LETTER TO MS OGIER

AAT Student
Address
Date

Dear Ms Ogier

I write to explain the purpose of a number of adjustments I have made to your accounts at 30 September 20X9.

The inventory valuation has been adjusted to account for goods which had previously cost £8,200, which now have a net realisable value, i.e. can only realise on sale £4,800. This is required to comply with IAS 2 which states that inventories should be valued at the lower of cost or net realisable value. The final inventory valuation is therefore £46,077.

A second adjustment is one regarding the purchases figure. The affairs of the business need to be separate from the affairs of the owner and, because some of the purchases were for personal use, they need to be deducted from the cost of purchases and charged to your drawings account.

If you have any questions relating to these adjustments, please do not hesitate to contact me.

Yours sincerely

AAT Student

AAT Student

Chapter 4
Preparing limited company accounts

△ **ACTIVITY 12**   △△△△

Typeset Ltd
Balance sheet as at 31 March 20X9

	£000
Non-current assets	
Property, plant and equipment (W1)	5,820
Investments	1,580
	7,400
Current assets	
Inventories	4,187
Trade receivables(W2)	3,153
Cash and cash equivalents	466
	7,806
Total assets	15,206
Current liabilities	
Trade and other payables (1,763 + 122)	1,885
Tax liabilities	493
	2,378
Net current assets	5,428
Non-current liabilities	
Long term loan	1,450
Total liabilities	3,828
	11,378
Equity	
Called up share capital	5,000
Share premium account	1,200
Revaluation reserve	500
Retained earnings (W3)	4,678
	11,378

Workings (all figures £000)

W1   *Non current assets*

	Cost	Acc Dep'n	NBV
Land	2,075	-	2,075
Buildings	2,077	383	1,694
Fixtures and fittings	1,058	495	563
Motor vehicles	2,344	1,237	1,107
Office equipment	533	152	381
	8,087	2,267	5,820

W2   *Trade receivables*

Trade receivables	3,136	
Less allowance for doubtful debts (see below)	(80)	
		3,056
Prepayments		97
		3,153

Allowance for doubtful debts

(x 36) + 2% x (3,136 - 36) = 80

W3   *Retained earnings*

At 1/4/X8	3,533
Retained profit for the year	1,145
At 31/3/X9	4,678

Retained profit: 1,681 - 493 - 43 = 1,145
i.e. (retained profit- corporation tax - increase in provision for doubtful debts)

Chapter 5
Preparing limited company accounts: additional information

△ **ACTIVITY 13**   △ △ △ △

Task 13.1

			£000	£000
1	DR	Inventories (balance sheet)	7,878	
	CR	Inventories (trading account)		7,878
2	DR	Taxation expense	1,920	
	CR	Taxation payable		1,920
3	DR	Revenue	204	
	CR	Trade receivables		204

4	DR	Interest expense	240	
	CR	Interest payable		240
5	DR	Land	500	
	CR	Revaluation reserve		500

Workings

| Interest accrual: | £6,000,000 x 8% x $\frac{1}{2}$ | = | £240,000 |
| Revaluation surplus: | £5,500,000 - £5,000,000 | = | £500,000 |

Task 13.2

Hightink Ltd
Income statement for the year ended 31 March 20X2

	£000	£000
Revenue (W1)		31,506
Cost of sales (W2)		(14,178)
		———
Gross profit		17,328
Distribution costs		(6,852)
Administrative expenses		(3,378)
		———
Profit from operations		7,098
Finance costs (W3)		(480)
		———
Profit before tax		6,618
Tax		(1,920)
		———
Profit from continuing operations		4,698
		———

Workings
All figures in £000

W1	**Revenue**	
	Revenue per TB	31,710
	Less: Credit sales recorded in wrong period	(204)
		———
		31,506
		———

W2	**Cost of sales**	
	Opening inventories	6,531
	Purchases	15,525
	Closing inventories	(7,878)
		———
		14,178
		———

W3	**Interest paid**	
	Interest per TB	240

Accrued interest   240
                                               ─────
                                                480
                                               ─────

Statement of changes in Equity for the year ended 31 March 20X2

	Share capital	Share premium	Revaluation reserve	Retained earnings	Total
At 31 March 20X1	4,000	2,000	-	6,217	12,217
Revaluation			500		500
Profit for year				4,698	4,698
Dividends paid				(400)	(400)
At 31 March 20X2	4,000	2,000	500	10,515	17,015

Hightink Ltd
Balance sheet as at 31 March 20X2

	£000	£000
Property, plant and equipment (W1)		14,105
Current assets		
Inventories		7,878
Trade receivables (5,455 - 204)		5,251
Cash and cash equivalents		304
		─────
		13,433
Total assets		27,538
		─────
Current liabilities		
Trade and other payables (2,363 + 240)		2,603
Taxation		1,920
		─────
		4,523
Net current assets		8,910
Non-current liabilities		
Long term loan		6,000
Total liabilities		10,523
Net assets		17,015
		─────
Equity		
Called up share capital		4,000
Share premium		2,000
Revaluation reserve		500
Retained Earnings (see SOCE)		10,515
		─────
		17,015
		─────

Workings
All figures in £000

W1   Property, plant and equipment

	Cost	Accumulated depreciation	NBV
Land	5,500	-	5,500*
Buildings	3,832	564	3,268
Fixtures and fittings	2,057	726	1,331
Motor vehicles	3,524	1,283	2,241
Office equipment	2,228	463	1,765
	17,141	3,036	14,105

*Land: 5,000 + 500 = £5,500

Task 13.3

(a) An 'event after the balance sheet date' is an event, either favourable or unfavourable, that occurs between the balance sheet date and the date on which the financial statements are authorised for issue.

(b) An 'adjusting event' is an event that provides additional evidence of conditions existing at the date of the balance sheet. A 'non-adjusting event' is an event that arises after the balance sheet date that relates to conditions that did not exist at the date of the balance sheet.

(c) The losses that arose from the fire on the company's premises on 21 April 20X2 constitute a 'non-adjusting' event after the balance sheet date. The condition did not exist at the balance sheet date, but came into existence after that date. No adjustment is required for the event as the conditions did not exist at the balance sheet date and thus do not constitute an adjusting event. However, the event is so material that failure to disclose may render the financial statements misleading. Hence, this non-adjusting event is to be disclosed by way of notes to the accounts.

△ ACTIVITY 14   △ △ △ △

Quine Ltd
Balance sheet as at 30 September 20X2

	£000	£000
Non-current assets		
Other Intangible assets		840
Property, plant and equipment (W1)		5,300
		6,140
Current assets		
Inventories		2,382
Trade and other receivables (W2)		1,814
Cash and cash equivalents		103
		4,299

Total assets	10,439
Current liabilities	
Trade and other payables (1,309 + 105)	1,414
Tax liabilities	548
	1,962
Net current assets	2,337
Non-current liabilities	
Bank loans	2,500
Total liabilities	4,462
	5,977
Equity	
Called up share capital	3,000
Share premium	500
Revaluation reserve (3,200 - 2,800)	400
Retained earnings (bal fig)	2,077
	5,977

Workings (all figures £000)

(W1) **Property, plant and equipment**

	Cost	Accumulated depreciation	NBV
Land (at valuation)	3,200	–	3,200
Buildings	1,480	702	778
Fixtures and fittings	645	317	328
Motor vehicles	1,632	903	729
Office equipment	447	182	265
	7,404	2,104	5,300

(W2) **Trade and other receivables**

Trade receivables	1,802
Less allowance for doubtful debts	(72)
Prepayments	84
	1,814

△ ACTIVITY 15 △△△△

Bay Ltd - Statement of changes in Equity for the year ended 31 March 20X2

all figures in £000

	Share capital	Share premium	Revaluation reserve	Retained earnings	Total
Balance at 31 March 20X0	3,500	1,400	-	950	5,850
Gain on property revaluation			600		600
Profit for the financial year				1,320	1,320
Dividends				(420)	(420)
Balance at 31 March 20X1	3,500	1,400	600	1,850	7,350

△ ACTIVITY 16 △△△△

Senander plc

Task 16.1

			£000	£000
1.	Dr	Inventories (balance sheet)	11,402	
	Cr	Inventories (income statement)		11,402
2.	Dr	Taxation expense	1,481	
	Cr	Taxation payable		1,481

Task 16.2

Income statement
for the year ended 30 September 20X3

	£000
Continuing operations	
Revenue (36,892 - 831)	36,061
Cost of sales (9,523 + 21,645 - 11,402 - 457)	(19,309)
Gross profit	16,752
Distribution costs (6,851 - 184)	(6,667)
Administrative expenses (3,763- 162)	(3,601)
Profit from operations	6,484
Finance costs	(310)
Profit before tax	6,174
Tax	(1,481)
Profit for the period from continuing operations	4,693
Discontinued operations	
Loss for the period from discontinued operations (264 - 28)	(236)
Profit for the period	4,457

Note: The figure for discontinued operations is the sum of the profit for the period relating to discontinued operations and the gain or loss on sale of discontinued operations.

△ ACTIVITY 17   △△△△

Task 17.1

Burysane Ltd

			£000	£000
1.	Dr	Taxation expense	2,822	
	Cr	Taxation payable		2,822
2.	Dr	Trade receivables	3,200	
	Cr	Revenue		3,200
3.	Dr	Interest expense	400	
	Cr	Interest payable		400
4.	Dr	Land	1,000	
	Cr	Revaluation reserve		1,000

Workings

Interest:	£10,000,000 x 8% x ½	=	£400,000
Revaluation:	£15,000,000 - £14,000,000	=	£1,000,000

Task 17.2 (a)

Burysane Ltd
Income statement for the year ended 31 March 20X4

	£000
Revenue (W1)	42,973
Cost of sales (W2)	(16,338)
Gross profit	26,635
Distribution costs	(9,544)
Administrative expenses	(6,213)
Profit from operations	10,878
Finance costs (W3)	(800)
Profit before taxation	10,078
Tax	(2,822)
Profit for the period	7,256

Workings

(W1) Revenue

	£000
Sales per TB	39,773
Plus credit sales omitted	3,200
	42,973

(W2) Cost of sales

	£000
Opening inventories	8,912

Purchases	16,858
Closing inventories	(9,432)
	16,338

(W3) Finance costs

	£000
Interest per TB	400
Accrued interest	400
	800

Task 17.2 (b)

Burysane Ltd
Balance sheet as at 31 March 20X4

	£000
Non-current assets	
Property, plant and equipment (W1)	47,024
Current assets	
Inventories	9,432
Trade receivables (W2)	4,581
Cash and cash equivalents	463
Total assets	14,476
Current liabilities	
Trade and other payables (2,409 + 400 + 362)	3,171
Corporation tax payable	2,822
	5,993
Net current assets	8,483
Non-current liabilities	10,000
Total liabilities	15,993
Net assets	45,507
Equity	
Called-up share capital	18,000
Share premium	6,000
Revaluation reserve	1,000
Retained earnings (15,411 + 7,256 - 2,160)	20,507
	45,507

Workings (all £000)

1   **Property, plant and equipment**

	Cost	Acc. Depn.	NBV
Land	15,000	-	15,000
Buildings	12,068	2,603	9,465
Fixtures and fittings	10,217	2,754	7,463
Motor vehicles	18,548	5,621	12,927
Office equipment	3,004	835	2,169
	58,837	11,813	47,024

2   **Trade and other receivables**

Trade receivables per TB	1,359
Adjustment for omitted credit sales	3,200
Less allowance for doubtful debts	(185)
Prepayments	207
	4,581

△ ACTIVITY 18   △△△△

Task 18.1

Journal entries:

		£000	£000
1	DR Trade receivables	557	
	CR Revenue		557
2	DR Inventories (balance sheet) (5,384 - 280)	5,104	
	CR Inventories (income statement)		5,104
3	DR Distribution costs	242	
	CR Accruals		242
4	DR Interest	240	
	CR Accruals		240
5	DR Taxation	2,048	
	CR Taxation payable		2,048
6	DR Non-current assets	1,000	
	CR Revaluation reserve		1,000

Task 18.2

> **Leakingham Ltd**
> **Income statement for the year ended 30 September 20X4**
>
> | | £000 |
> | --- | ---: |
> | Revenue (37,299 + 557) | 37,856 |
> | Cost of sales (W1) | (21,502) |
> | | ——— |
> | Gross profit | 16,354 |
> | Distribution costs (5,2100 + 242) | (5,453) |
> | Administrative expenses | (3,107) |
> | | ——— |
> | Profit from operations | 7,794 |
> | Finance costs (W2) | (480) |
> | | ——— |
> | Profit before taxation | 7,314 |
> | Tax | (2,048) |
> | | ——— |
> | Profit for the financial year | 5,266 |
> | | ——— |

Workings

(W1) Cost of sales

	£000
Opening inventories	4,219
Purchases	22,324
Carriage inwards	63
Closing inventories	(5,104)
	———
	21,502
	———

(W2) Interest

£6,000,000 x 8% x $^1/_2$ = £240,000 + (per TB) £240,000 = £480,000

Task 18.3

(a) (i) Determining profit for the financial year requires the matching of costs with related revenues. The cost of unsold inventories is thus carried forward to be matched with revenue when it arises. So the cost is not shown in the year in which the cost is incurred.

(ii) The inventories should be valued at the lower of cost and net realisable value.

(iii) The cost of the closing inventories of £5,104,000 was credited against purchases in the calculation of the cost of sales, as the majority of this cost is to be matched against future revenues and hence carried forward as an asset in the balance sheet. Where some items of inventory will realise less than their cost, the irrecoverable cost of £280,000 was charged to revenue by reducing the cost of inventories carried forward of £480,000 to its net realisable value of £200,000.

(b) (i) According to IAS 36 an impairment review should be carried out if events or changes in circumstances indicate that the carrying amount of the property, plant and equipment may not be recoverable. An impairment review must also be carried out if the useful economic life is thought to be infinite.

(ii) An impairment review comprises a comparison of the carrying value of the asset with its recoverable amount, which is the higher of its net realisable value and its value in use.

△ ACTIVITY 19   △ △ △ △

Task 19.1

		£000	£000
1	DR Cash	3,000	
	CR Ordinary share capital		2,000
	CR Share premium		1,000
2	DR Inventories (Balance sheet)	8,731	
	CR Inventories (Income statement)		8,731
3	DR Cash	1,500	
	DR Non-current asset - accumulated depreciation	1,250	
	CR Non-current asset - cost		2,300
	CR Profit on sale of non current assets		450
4	DR Tax expense	3,948	
	CR Tax payable		3,948
5	DR Interest	600	
	CR Interest payable		600

Workings

Interest: £15,000,000 x 8% x ½ = £600,000

Task 19.2

(a)

Moatsart Ltd	
Income statement for the year ended 30 September 20X5	
	£000
Revenue (W1)	68,241
Cost of sales (W2)	(34,803)
Gross profit	33,438
Distribution costs	(12,386)
Administration expenses	(7,115)
Profit from operations	13,937
Profit on sale of non current assets	450
Profit before finance costs	14,387
Finance costs (600 + 600)	(1,200)
Profit before tax	13,187
Tax	3,948
Profit for the period	9,239

Workings

(W1) **Revenue**	£000
Sales revenue per TB	70,613
less returns inwards	(2,372)
	68,241

(W2) **Cost of sales**	£000
Opening inventories	7,454
Purchases	37,543
less Returns outwards	(1,463)
	43,534
Closing inventories	(8,731)
	34,803

(b)

> **Moatsart Ltd**
> **Balance sheet as at 30 September 20X5**
>
> | | £000 | £000 |
> |---|---|---|
> | Non-current assets (W1) | | |
> | Property, plant and equipment | | 57,384 |
> | Investment | | 4,000 |
> | Current assets | | |
> | Inventories | 8,731 | |
> | Trade receivables (W2) | 8,475 | |
> | Cash (1,535 + 3,000 + 1,500) | 6,035 | 23,241 |
> | | | |
> | Total assets | | 84,625 |
> | | | |
> | Current liabilities (W3) | | 14,129 |
> | Non-current liabilities | | 15,000 |
> | | | |
> | Total liabilities | | 29,129 |
> | | | |
> | Net assets | | 55,496 |
> | | | |
> | Equity | | |
> | Share capital | | 10,000 |
> | Share premium | | 4,000 |
> | Revaluation | | 2,500 |
> | Retained earnings (W4) | | 38,996 |
> | | | |
> | | | 55,496 |

Workings (all £000)

(W1) Non-current assets

	Cost	Acc.Depn.	NBV
Per ETB	84,856	26,422	58,434
Disposal	(2,300)	(1,250)	(1,050)
	82,556	25,172	57,384

(W2) Trade receivables

Trade receivables	8,754
less allowance for receivables	(682)
Prepayments	403
	8,475

(W3) Current liabilities

Trade payables	8,939
Corporation tax payable	3,948
Accruals	642
Interest payable	600
	_____
	14,129
	_____

Task 19.3

(a) (i) An entity should adopt accounting policies that enable the financial statements to give a fair presentation or a true and fair view. An entity should follow the guidance in a particular accounting standard if one exists for the transaction being dealt with.

(ii) In the absence of an accounting standard for a particular transaction, the objectives against which an entity should judge the appropriateness of accounting policies to its particular circumstances are relevance, reliability, comparability and understandability.

These are explained by the framework as follows:

Relevance	Financial information is relevant if it has the ability to influence the economic decisions of users and in time to influence those decisions.
Reliability	Financial information is reliable if it represents faithfully and reflects the substance of transactions and other events, if it is free from bias and error, is complete within the bounds of materiality and under conditions of uncertainty, it has been prudently prepared.
Comparability	Information is comparable if it can be compared with similar information about the entity for some other period and with similar information about other entities.
Understandability	Information provided by financial statements needs to be capable of being understood by users having a reasonable knowledge of business and economic activities and accounting and a willingness to study with reasonable diligence the information provided.

Chapter 6
Cash flow statements

△ ACTIVITY 20   △△△△

IAS 7 requires organisations to report their cash flows under standard headings which include:

· Cash flows from operating activities
· Cash flows from investing activities
· Cash flows from financing activities
· Net increase/decrease in cash and cash equivalents
· Cash and cash equivalents at beginning of period
· Cash and cash equivalents at end of the period

Operating activities

This comprises the cash flows generated from the principal revenue-producing activities of the entity and other activities that are not investing or financing activities.

Investing activities

This shows the cash flows from the acquisition and disposal of long term assets and other investments not included in cash equivalents.

Financing activities

This shows the cash flows from the changes in the size and composition of the contributed equity and borrowings of the entity.

Cash and cash equivalents

This includes cash in hand, bank deposits and short term investments (usually to be sold within 3 months), less any overdrafts repayable on demand. Hence the cash flow statement will show cash and cash equivalents at the beginning and end of the period and the movement within the year will be explained via the above activities e.g. operating, investing and financing activities.

△ **ACTIVITY 21**   △△△△

Cash flow statement for the year ended 31 March 20X1

	£000	£000
Cash flows from operating activities		
Profit before tax	11,600	
Adjustments for:		
Depreciation charges	6,500	
	18,100	
Increase in trade and other receivables (37,500 - 33,000)	(4,500)	
Increase in inventories (27,500 - 25,500)	(2,000)	
Decrease in trade payables (31,500 - 31,950)	(450)	
Cash generated from operations	11,150	
Tax paid	(2,260)	
Net cash from operating activities		8,890
Cash flows from investing activities		
Purchase of property plant and equipment (W1)	(9,000)	
Net cash used in investing activities		(9,000)
Cash flows from financing activities		
Proceeds from issue of shares (11,610 - 10,000)	1,610	
Proceeds from long-term borrowing (21,500 - 20,000)	1,500	
Net cash used in financing activities		3,110
Net increase in cash and cash equivalents (4,250 - 1,250)		3,000
Cash and cash equivalents at beginning of period		1,250
Cash and cash equivalents at end of period		4,250

Workings

(W1) **Purchase of property, plant and equipment:**

	£000
NBV 20X0	70,500
Less depreciation 20X1	(6,500)
	64,000
NBV 20X1	73,000
Purchases	9,000

△ ACTIVITY 22   △ △ △ △

Paton Ltd
Cash flow statement for the year ended 30 September 20X1

	£000	£000
Cash flows from operating activities		
Profit before tax	5,546	
Adjustments for:		
Depreciation charges	2,007	
Profit on sale of fixed asset	(131)	
	7,422	
Increase in trade and other receivables	(220)	
(4,122 - 3,902)		
Increase in inventories (7,420 - 6,823)	(597)	
Increase in trade payables (1,855 - 1,432)	423	
Cash generated from operations	7,028	
Tax paid	(1,327)	
Net cash from operating activities		5,701
Cash flows from investing activities		
Purchase of property, plant and equipment (W1)	(5,990)	
Purchase of investment	(5,000)	
Proceeds from sale of equipment	654	
(895 - 372 + 131)		
Net cash used in investing activities		(10,336)
Cash flows from financing activities		
Proceeds from issue of shares	1,500	
(10,000 + 3,500) - (9,000 + 3,000)		
Proceeds from long-term borrowing	3,500	
(5,000 - 1,500)		
		5,000
Net increase in cash and cash equivalents		365
(1,402 - 1,037)		
Cash and cash equivalents at beginning of period		1,037
Cash and cash equivalents at end of period		1,402

(W1)

NBV Property, plant and equipment

	£		£
Balance b/f	9,923	Disposals	523
Additions (bal)	5,990	Charge	2,007
		Balance c/f	13,383
	15,913		15,913

△ ACTIVITY 23   △ △ △ △

Angle Ltd
Cash flow statement for the year ended 31 March 20X1

	£000	£000
Net cash from operating activities		1,804
Investing activities		
Payments to acquire property, plant and equipment (W)		(3,653)
Financing activities		
Proceeds from long term borrowing (2,500 - 1,500)	1,000	
Issue of ordinary share capital (3,000+1,200)-(2,200-1,600)	1,600	
		2,600
Increase in cash and cash equivalents (833 - 82)		751
Cash and cash equivalents at the beginning of the year		82
Cash and cash equivalents at end of year		833

Working

Tangible non current assets

	£000		£000
Balance b/f	4,009	Depreciation charge	875
Revaluation	500	Balance c/f	7,287
Additions (bal fig)	3,653		
	8,162		8,162

△ ACTIVITY 24   △ △ △ △

Cash flow statement of Machier Ltd for the year ended 31 March 20X9

	£000
Net cash from operating activities	
Profit before tax	486
Depreciation	856
Profit on sale of non current assets	(7)
Increase in inventories (448 - 287)	(161)
Increase in trade receivables (527 - 337)	(190)
Increase in trade payables (381 - 212)	169
Cash generated from operations	1,153
Tax paid	(137)
Net cash from operating activities	1,016
Investing activities	
Payments to acquire property, plant and equipment (W1)	(2,771)
Proceeds on sale of asset (9 + 7)	16
Net cash used in investing activities	(2,755)
Proceeds from long term borrowing (2,800 -1,500)	1,300
Issue of ordinary share capital (200 + 100) - 100	200
Net cash from financing activities	1,500
Increase/(decrease) in cash and cash equivalents (-153 - 86)	(239)
Cash and cash equivalents at beginning of year	86
Cash and cash equivalents at end of year	(153)

Workings

(W1) **Property, plant and equipment additions:**

Property, plant and equipment

	£000		£000
Balance b/f	2,376	Depreciation charge	856
Additions (bal fig)	2,771	Disposal (28 - 19)	9
		Balance c/f	4,282
	─────		─────
	5,147		5,147
	─────		─────

△ ACTIVITY 25 △ △ △ △

Duhem Ltd
Cash flow statement for the year ended 30 September 20X2

	£000	£000
Net cash inflow from operating activities		
Profit before tax	2,331	
Depreciation	1,906	
Profit on sale of property, plant and equipment	(106)	
Increase in inventories(1,115 - 1,002)	(113)	
Increase in trade receivables (1,457 - 1,213)	(244)	
Increase in trade payables (1,042 - 671)	371	
	4,145	
Tax paid	(618)	
Net cash from operating activities		3,527
Investing activities		
Payments to acquire property, plant and equipment (W1)	(6,900)	
Proceeds from sale of property,) plant and equipment (W2)	666	
		(6,234)
Financing activities		
Proceeds from long term borrowing (6,400 - 4,800)	1,600	
Issue of ordinary share capital (4,000 + 200) - (2,500 + 100)	1,600	
		3,200
Increase in cash and cash equivalents (817 -324)		493
Cash and cash equivalents at the beginning of the period		324
Cash and cash equivalents at the end of the period		817

Workings
(All figures £000)

(W1)

Property, plant and equipment at NBV

Balance b/f	12,710	Depreciation	1,906
Additions (bal fig)	6,900	Disposal (980 - 420)	560
		Balance c/f	17,144
	19,610		19,610

(W2)

Disposal of property, plant and equipment

Cost	980	Accumulated depreciation	420
Profit on disposal	106	Proceeds (bal)	666
	1,086		1,086

△ ACTIVITY 26 △ △ △ △

Kaypiemgee Ltd

**Cash flow statement for the year ended
30 September 20X3**

	£000	£000
Cash flows from operating activities		
Profit before tax	2,881	
Adjustments for:		
Depreciation charges	1,995	
Profit on sale of property, plant and equipment	(107)	
	4,769	
Increase in trade receivables (1,546 - 1,321)	(225)	
Increase in inventories (2,013 - 1,843)	(170)	
Increase in trade payables (873 - 744)	129	
	⎯⎯	
Cash generated from operations	4,503	
Tax paid (W3)	(516)	
	⎯⎯	
Net cash from operating activities		3,987
Cash flows from investing activities		
Purchase of property, plant and equipment (W2)	(4,846)	
Proceeds from sale of equipment (W1)	711	
	⎯⎯	
Net cash used in investing activities		(4,135)
Cash flows from financing activities		
Proceeds from issue of shares	2,000	
(5,000 + 1,000) - 4,000)		
	⎯⎯	
Net cash used in financing activities		2,000
Net increase in cash and cash equivalents (1,468 + 384)		1,852
Cash and cash equivalents at beginning of period		(384)
		⎯⎯
Cash and cash equivalents at end of period		1,468

Workings

(1) Proceeds from sale
       NBV of asset sold £604
       Add Profit   £107
       Proceeds   £711

(2) Non-current asset additions

Non current assets NBV

Bal b/f	15,657	Depreciation	1,995
Additions (bal fig)	4,846	Disposal	604
		Bal c/f	17,904
	20,503		20,503

(3) Taxation paid:

Taxation

Cash	516	Bal b/f	635
Bal c/f	840	Charge	721
	1,356		1,356

△ ACTIVITY 27 △ △ △ △

Scote Ltd

Cash flow statement for the year ended 31 March 20X4

	£000	£000
Cash flows from operating activities		
Profit before tax	3,572	
Adjustments for:		
Depreciation charges	4,120	
Profit from sale of property, plant and equipment	(365)	
	7,327	
Increase in trade and other receivables (1,492 - 1,321)	(171)	
Increase in inventories (4,017 - 3,860)	(157)	
Increase in trade payables (1,003 - 827)	176	
Cash generated from operations	7,175	
Tax paid	(643)	
Net cash from operating activities		6,532
Cash flows from investing activities		
Purchase of property, plant and equipment (W2)	(11,143)	
Proceeds from sale of equipment (W1)	970	
Net cash used in investing activities		(10,173)
Cash flows from financing activities		
Proceeds from issue of shares (9,000 + 2,000) - (6,000 + 1,000)	4,000	
Proceeds from long-term borrowing (10,000 - 8,000)	2,000	
Net cash used in financing activities		6,000
Net increase in cash and cash equivalents (1,314 + 1,045)		2,359
Cash and cash equivalents at beginning of period		(1,045)
Cash and cash equivalents at end of period		1,314

Workings (all figures £000)

(W1) Proceeds from sale

NBV of asset sold	605
Add Profit	365
Proceeds	970

(W2) Non-current asset additions

Non current assets NBV

Bal b/f	16,143	Depreciation		4,120
Additions (bal fig)	11,143	Disposal		605
		Bal c/f		22,561
	27,286			27,286

△ ACTIVITY 28   △ △ △ △

Task

Canes Ltd
Cash Flow Statement for the year ended 31 March 20X5

	£000	£000
Profit from operations	4,670	
Adjustments for:		
Depreciation	1,678	
Profit on disposal of non current asset	(402)	
	———	
Operating cash flows before movements in working capital	5,946	
Increase in inventories	(491)	
Increase in trade receivables	(377)	
Increase in trade payables	139	
	———	
Cash generated by operations	5,217	
Tax paid	(854)	
	———	
Net cash from operating activities		4,363
Investing activities		
Proceeds on disposal of property, plant and equipment	982	
Purchase of property, plant and equipment	(4,618)	
Net cash used in investing activities		(3,636)
Financing activities		
Equity dividends paid	(600)	
Net cash used in financing activities		(600)
		———
Increase in cash (214 - 87)		127
		———

Workings (all figures in £000)

(W1) Fixed asset additions:

Opening balance	11,192
Less disposal	(580)
Less depreciation	(1,678)
	9,514
Additions (bal fig)	4,618
Closing balance	13,552

(W2) Proceeds from sale = NBV of asset sold £580 +Profit £402
     Therefore, Proceeds from sale = £982

△ ACTIVITY 29

Task 29.1

Bateoven Ltd
Reconciliation of profit from operations to net cash flows
from operating activities

	£000
Profit from operations	312
Adjustments for:	
Depreciation	3,570
	3,882
Operating cash flows before movements in working capital	3,882
Increase in inventories	(508)
Increase in trade receivables	(471)
Decrease in trade payables	(329)
Cash generated by operations	2,574
Interest paid	(560)
Tax paid	(1,284)
Net cash from operating activities	730

Task 29.2

AAT Student
Address
7 December 20X5

Dear Directors,

I am writing to you to comment upon the sources and uses of cash in Bateoven Ltd during the past year.

The largest source of cash in the year was from an issue of share capital of £5,000,000. Shares were issued at a nominal value of £5,000,000. In addition, a further loan of £4,100,000 was taken out during the year. This long-term financing amounting to £9,100,000 was used to fund the purchase of non-current assets of £9,138,000 that are to be used in the business - also over the long term.

The other source of cash in the year was from operating activities. This amounted to £2,574,000 and was used to fund the interest paid of £560,000, taxation paid of £1,284,000 and equity dividends paid of £2,000,000. These total outflows of cash amounted to £3,844,000. As only £2,574,000 flowed from operations, this left a shortfall of £1,270,000. This was met by cash balances from last year and was mainly responsible for the decrease in cash balances of £1,308,000 during the year. The decrease in cash could have been avoided if the inventories, trade receivables and trade payables had been kept at levels similar to last year. The increase in inventories, trade receivables and trade payables resulted in a reduction of cash inflow from operating activities of £1,308,000, an amount equal to the shortfall in cash from operating activities.

I hope that this helps you to understand the sources and uses of cash in Bateoven Ltd during the past year. If you have any further questions relating to this, do not hesitate to contact me.

Yours sincerely,

AAT Student

AAT Student

Chapters 7, 8 and 9
Consolidated accounts

△ **ACTIVITY 30**   △△△△

Consolidated balance sheet
Dunsley Ltd and its subsidiary undertaking, Ravenscar Ltd, as at 31 December 20X1

	£000	£000
Non-current assets		
Goodwill (W3)		447
Property, plant and equipment (5,210 + 1,750)		6,960
Current assets		
Inventories (1,520 + 610)	2,130	
Trade receivables (1,120 + 520)	1,640	
Cash and cash equivalents (120 + 85)	205	
	3,975	
Less current liabilities (1,610 + 710)	(2,320)	
Net current assets		1,655
		9,062
Equity		
Share capital		3,000
Share premium		1,000
Retained earnings		4,160
Equity attributable to equity holders of the parent		8,160
Minority interest (W4)		902
Total equity		9,062

Workings

(W1) **Group structure:**

D

| 60% | $\dfrac{300,000}{500,000}$ =60% holding |

R

(W2) **Net assets of Ravenscar Ltd:**

	At acquisition date = balance sheet date £000
Per balance sheet	1,755
Fair value adjustment	500
	2,255

(W3) **Goodwill:**

	£000
Price paid	1,800
Less: Net assets acquired (60%x 2,255 (W2))	(1,353)
	447

(W4) **Minority interest:**

	£000
40% x 2,255 (W2)	902

△ ACTIVITY 31 △△△△

Consolidated balance sheet as at 31 December 20X1		
	£000	*£000*
Non-current assets		
Goodwill (W3)		2,160
Property, plant and equipment (17,500 + 5,750 + 400)		23,650
Current assets (4,750 + 1,520)	6,270	
Less current liabilities (2,250 + 940)	(3,190)	
Net current assets		3,080
Total assets less current liabilities		28,890
Non-current liabilities		
Debentures (4,100 + 1,000)		(5,100)

	23,790
Equity	
Share capital	8,000
Share premium	1,500
Retained earnings (W4)	11,998
Equity attributable to equity holders of the parent	21,498
Minority interest (W5)	2,292
	23,790

Workings

(W1) **Group structure:**

S

| 60%

H

(W2) **Net assets of Harkhill Ltd:**

	At date of acquisition £000	At balance sheet date £000
Share capital	1,000	1,000
Share premium	500	500
Retained earnings	3,000	3,830
	4,500	5,330
Fair value adjustment (3,500 - 3,100)	400	400
	4,900	5,730

(W3) **Goodwill:**

	£000
Price paid	5,100
Less: Net assets acquired (60% x 4,900 (W2))	(2,940)
	2,160

(W4) **Consolidated retained earnings:**

	£000
Shireoaks Ltd	11,500
Harkhill Ltd 60% x (3,830 - 3,000)	498
	11,998

(W5) Minority interest:

	£000
40% x 5,730 (W2)	2,292

△ ACTIVITY 32 △△△△

	£000
Price paid	5,000
Less: Net assets acquired 75% x	(4,350)
(4,800 + 1,000 fair value adjustment)	
Goodwill arising	
	650

△ ACTIVITY 33 △△△△

Norman Ltd
Consolidated balance sheet as at 31 March 20X1

	£000	£000
Non-current assets		
Goodwill (W3)		460
Property, plant and equipment		15,150
(12,995 + 1,755 + 400)		
		15,610
Current assets		
Inventories (3,586 + 512)	4,098	
Trade receivables (2,193 + 382)	2,575	
Cash (84 + 104)	188	
	6,861	
Total assets		22,471
Current liabilities		
Trade payables (2,080 + 273)	2,353	
Taxation (667 + 196)	863	
	3,216	
Net current assets		3,645
Non-current liabilities		
Long-term loan		400
Total liabilities		3,616
Net assets		18,855
Equity		
Called-up share capital		2,000

Retained earnings (W4)	16,284
Equity attributable to holders of the patent	18,284
Minority interest (W5)	571
	18,855

Workings

(W1) Group structure:

N

75% $\dfrac{750,000}{1,000,000}$ =75% holding

S

(W2) Net assets of Saxon Ltd:

	At date of acquisition £000	At balance sheet date £000
Share capital	1,000	1,000
Share premium	200	200
Retained earnings	424	684
	1,624	1,884
Fair value adjustment	400	400
	2,024	2,284

(W3) Goodwill:

	£000
Price paid	1,978
Less: Net assets acquired (75% x 2,024 (W2))	(1,518)
Goodwill	460

(W4) Consolidated retained earnings:

	£000
Norman Ltd	16,089
Saxon Ltd (75% x (684 - 424))	195
	16,284

(W5) Minority interest:

	£000
25% x 2,284 (W2)	571

△ ACTIVITY 34

Task 34.1

Shopan Ltd
Consolidated balance sheet as at 30 September 20X9

	£000
Non-current assets	
Goodwill (W3)	222
Property, plant and equipment (6,273 + 1,633 + 400)	8,306
	8,528
Current assets	
Inventories (1,901 + 865)	2,766
Trade receivables (1,555 + 547)	2,102
Cash (184 + 104)	288
	5,156
Total assets	13,684
Current liabilities	
Trade payables (1,516 + 457)	1,973
Taxation (431 + 188)	619
	2,592
Net current assets	2,564
Non-current liabilities (2,870 + 400)	3,270
Total liabilities	5,862
Net assets	7,822
Equity	
Called-up share capital	2,000
Share premium	950
Retained earnings	4,246
Equity attributable to holders of the parent	7,196
Minority interest (W4)	626
	7,822

Workings

(W1) Shopan Ltd holding in Hower Ltd:

$$\frac{375,000}{500,000} = 75\%$$

Minority interest:

$$\frac{125,000}{500,000} = 25\%$$

Shopan

| 75%

Hower

(W2) **Net assets of Hower Ltd:**

	At acquisition date = balance sheet date £000
Per balance sheet	2,104
Fair value adjustment (2,033 - 1,633)	400
	2,504

(W3) **Goodwill:**

	£000
Price paid	2,100
Less: Net assets acquired (75% ? 2,504)	(1,878)
Goodwill	222

(W4) **Minority interest:**

	£000
25% x 2,504 (W2)	626

Task 34.2

An undertaking is the parent undertaking of another undertaking (a subsidiary undertaking) if any of the following apply:

· It holds a majority of voting rights.
· Power over majority of voting rights through agreement with other investors
· Power to govern the financial or operating policies of the entity under statute or an agreement
· Power to appoint/remove majority of members of the board of directors or equivalent governing body.
· Power to cast the majority of votes at meetings of the board of directors or equivalent.

△ ACTIVITY 35   △△△△

As Fun Ltd own 75% of Games Ltd, the minority interest is 25%.

The minority interest in the balance sheet is the minority share of the net assets of the subsidiary at the balance sheet date. At 30 September 20X8, the minority interest would be 25% x (2,280 + 200 fair value adjustment) = £620,000.

The minority interest on the consolidated balance sheet of Fun Ltd would be shown after equity attributable to the equity holders of the parent.

Minority interest is that proportion of the subsidiary undertaking's net assets which are not held by the parent company, Fun Ltd. It is shown on the consolidated balance sheet to reflect the ownership of the subsidiary. Fun Ltd may control the assets and liabilities of Games Ltd, but it does not own all of those net assets.

△ ACTIVITY 36 △△△△

Task 36.1

Goodwill on acquisition:

	£000
Price paid	1,716
Less: Net assets acquired (75% x (1,708 + 400 fair value adjustment))	(1,581)
Goodwill arising	135

Task 36.2

Under IFRS 3 *Business combinations*, goodwill is capitalised at cost and classified as a non-current asset on the balance sheet.

It must be reviewed for impairment on an annual basis.

△ ACTIVITY 37 △△△△

Workings

(W1) Fertwrangler Ltd holding in Voncarryon Ltd:

$$\frac{1,200,000}{2,000,000} = 60\%$$

(W2) **Net assets of Voncarryon Ltd:**

	At acquisition £000
Share capital	2,000
Share premium	1,000
Retained earnings	1,350
Fair value adjustment (4,455 - 4,055)	400
	4,750

(W3) **Goodwill:**

	£000
Price paid	3,510
Less: Net assets acquired (60% x 4,750)	(2,850)
Goodwill	660

△ ACTIVITY 38 △△△△

Consolidated income statement for the year ended 31 December 20X1	
	£000
Revenue (W1)	18,400
Cost of sales (W2)	(9,100)

Gross profit	9,300
Distribution costs (1,600 + 450)	(2,050)
Admin costs (1,450 + 375)	(1,825)
Profit from operations	5,425
Finance costs (760 + 125)	(885)
Profit before tax	4,540
Tax (1,200 + 400)	(1,600)
Profit for the year	2,940
Attributable to:	
Equity holders of the parent	2,740
Minority interest (W3)	200
	2940

Workings

		£000
(W1)	**Revenue:**	
	Malton Ltd	14,100
	Whitby Ltd	5,100
	Less inter-company sales	(800)
		18,400
(W2)	**Cost of sales:**	
	Malton Ltd	7,150
	Whitby Ltd	2,750
	Less inter-company purchase	(800)
		9,100
(W3)	**Minority interest:**	
	20% of £1,000	200

△ ACTIVITY 39 △ △ △ △

Skuhn plc
Consolidated income statement for the year ended 30 September 20X2

	£000
Revenue (W1)	32,700
Cost of sales (W2)	(14,055)
Gross profit	18,645

Distribution costs (3,655 + 985)	(4,640)
Administrative expenses (2,730 + 320)	(3,050)
Profit from operations	10,955
Finance costs (2,100 + 400)	(2,500)
Profit before tax	8,455
Tax (1,870 + 695)	(2,565)
Profit for the year	5,890
Attributable to:	
Equity holders of the parent	4,958
Minority interests (W3)	932

Workings

All figures £000

(W1) **Revenue**

Skuhn sales	25,300
e-Lakatos sales	8,600
Less intercompany sale	(1,200)
	32,700

(W2) **Cost of sales**

Skuhn cost of sales	11,385
e-Lakatos cost of sales	3,870
Less intercompany purchase	(1,200)
	14,055

(W3) **Minority interests**: 40% x 2,330 =   932

△ ACTIVITY 40   △△△△

Task 40.1

Calculation of goodwill on acquisition of Clive Ltd as at 31 March 20X5:

	£000	£000
Cost of investment		25,160
Less group share of net assets at acquisition:		
Share capital	20,000	

Share premium	5,000	
Retained earnings	10,600	
Fair value adjustment (33,520 - 30,520)	3,000	
	_____	
	38,600	
Group share 60 % x 38,600		(23,160)
		_____
Goodwill arising on consolidation		2,000
Less impairment of goodwill (10% x 2,000)		(200)
		_____
Goodwill as at 31 March 20X5		1,800
		_____

Task 40.2

(a) Investment in associate

Goodwill on acquisition of Grant Ltd

	£000
Cost of investment	5,000
Less group share of net assets at acquisition:	
£18,000 x 25%	(4,500)
	_____
Goodwill on acquisition	500
Less impairment (500 x 10%)	(50)
	_____
	450
	_____
Investment in associate	
Group share of net assets at balance sheet date:	
25% x 19,000	4,750
Add goodwill	450
	_____
Investment in associate	5,200
	_____

(b) IAS 28 defines an associate as an entity over which the group exerts significant influence but not control. This would usually be a shareholding of between 20% and 50%.

△ ACTIVITY 41   △△△△

Task 41.1 Haydn plc

Consolidated Balance Sheet as at 30 September 20X5

	£000	£000
Non-current assets		
Property, plant and equipment		137,824

Goodwill (W3)		13,370
Current assets:		
Inventories	32,066	
Trade receivables	13,872	
Cash	1,429	47,367
Total assets		198,561
Current liabilities:		
Trade payables	16,671	
Accruals	3,975	
Tax	2,546	23,192
Non-current liabilities		57,000
Total liabilities		80,192
Net assets		118,369
Equity		
Share capital		30,000
Share premium		20,000
Retained earnings (W5)		48,997
Equity attributable to equity holders of the parent		98,997
Minority interest (W4)		19,372
		118,369

Workings

(W1) **Group structure:**

H

60% $\dfrac{3,000,000}{5,000,000} = 60\%$

S

(W2) **Net assets of Saxon Ltd:**

	At date of acquisition £000	At balance sheet date £000
Share capital	5,000	5,000
Share premium	2,000	2,000
Retained earnings	32,550	37,430
	39,550	44,430
Fair value adjustment (42,500 - 38,500)	4,000	4,000
	43,550	48,430

(W3) **Goodwill**:

	£000
Cost of investment	39,500
Less: Net assets acquired (60% x 43,550 (W2))	(26,130)
	———
Goodwill	13,370
	———

(W4) **Consolidated retained earnings**:

	£000
Haydn Ltd	46,069
Seek Ltd (60% x (37,430 - 32,550))	2,929
	———
	48,997
	———

(W5) **Minority interest**:

	£000
40% x 48,430 (W2)	19,372
	———

Task 41.2
Goodwill must be recognised in the balance sheet at cost less any impairment losses. Even if the goodwill is regarded as having an indefinite useful economic life, it must be reviewed for impairment at the end of each reporting period. Impairment reviews should be performed in accordance with the requirements of IAS 36.

Chapters 10 to 16
Reporting financial performance

△ ACTIVITY 42 △△△△

Task 42.1

Mattesich Ltd
Income statement for the year ended 30 September 20X0

	£000
Continuing operations	
Revenues (W1)	39,235
Cost of sales (W2)	(17,385)
	———
Gross profit	21,850
Distribution costs (5,863 - 234)	(5,629)
Administrative expenses (3,469- 178)	(3,291)
	———
Profit from operations	12,930
Finance costs	(544)
	———
Profit before taxation	12,386
Tax	(3,813)
	———
Profit for the period from continuing operations	8,573

Discontinued operations	
Loss for the period from discontinued operations (13 - 473)	(460)
Profit for the year	8,113

Workings

(W1) Revenue

	£000
Revenue per ETB	40,448
Less discontinued operations	(1,213)
Revenue from continuing operations	39,235

(W2) Cost of sales

	£000
Opening inventory	12,973
Purchases	18,682
Closing inventory	(13,482)
Less discontinued operations	(788)
	17,385

Task 42.2

NOTES FOR THE BOARD MEETING

(a) IAS 16 *Property, plant and equipment* requires that where a policy of revaluation is adopted, it should be applied to individual classes of property, plant and equipment.

   If a policy is adopted to revalue land and buildings, then all the assets included in land and buildings would have to be the subject of revaluation. It is not possible under the standard to show some at cost and others at valuation.

(b) IAS 16:

   (i) states that where property, plant and equipment is subject to revaluation, the carrying amount should not differ materially from that which would be determined using fair value at the balance sheet date.

   (ii) states the basis of valuation for non-specialised properties should be market-based evidence by appraisal, that is normally undertaken by professionally qualified valuers.

   (iii) states that any gain on revaluation should be recognised in equity (in a revaluation reserve) and shown in the statement of total changes in equity. Any loss should go through the income statement assuming it does not relate to a previous revaluation gain on that asset in which case it can be offset against any remaining revaluation surplus relating to that asset.

△ ACTIVITY 43   △ △ △ △

Task 43.1

			£000	£000
(1)	DR	Tax charge	972	
	CR	Corporation tax payable		972
(2)	DR	Interest charges (3,600 x 8% x ¹/₁₂)	24	
	CR	Interest charges		24

Task 43.2

> **Fun Ltd**
> **Income statement for the year ended 30 September 20X8**
>
> | | £000 |
> |---|---:|
> | Revenue (14,595 - 232) | 14,363 |
> | Cost of sales (W1) | (6,464) |
> | | |
> | Gross profit | 7,899 |
> | Distribution costs | (2,669) |
> | Administrative expenses | (2,042) |
> | | |
> | Profit from operations | 3,188 |
> | Finance costs | (324) |
> | | |
> | Profit before taxation | 2,864 |
> | Tax | (972) |
> | | |
> | Profit for the financial year | 1,892 |
>
> *Workings (all figures £000)*
>
> | 1 | Calculation of cost of sales: | |
> |---|---|---:|
> | | Opening inventories | 1,893 |
> | | Purchases | 6,671 |
> | | *Plus* carriage inwards | 87 |
> | | *Less* returns outwards | (146) |
> | | | |
> | | | 8,505 |
> | | *Less* closing inventories | (2,041) |
> | | | |
> | | Cost of sales | 6,464 |

Task 43.3

(a) Share premium arises when shares are issued at a price more than their nominal value.

For example, if 50,000 ordinary shares of £1 each were issued at £1.50 then the accounting procedure would be:

Dr Cash/bank	£75,000	
Cr Share capital		£50,000
Cr Share premium		£25,000

The revaluation reserve represents the excess of the valuation of an asset over its book value.

For example, an asset with a NBV of £250,000 might have its market value to be considered to be £400,000 established by valuation.

The accounting procedure would be:

Dr Property, plant and equipment	£150,000	
Cr Revaluation reserve		£150,000

(b) IAS 17 deals with the way in which leased assets are accounted for.
The accounting treatment depends on whether the lease is a finance lease or operating lease.

The standard defines a finance lease as one which transfers substantially all the risks and rewards of ownership to the lessee.

An operating lease is a lease other than a finance lease.

An asset acquired under a finance lease should be recorded in the lessee's balance sheet as a non-current asset and also as an obligation to pay future rentals. If the asset was leased on an operating lease it would not be shown as an asset on the lessee's balance sheet.

△ ACTIVITY 44   △△△△

Notes for meeting with the Chief Accountant
(a) Accounting policies are the specific principles, bases, conventions, rules and practices applied by an entity in preparing and presenting financial statements.

Management should select and apply appropriate accounting policies so that the financial statements comply with all international standards (IFRSs and IASs) and interpretations.

If there is no specific standard for a particular item then management should choose policies that are relevant and reliable. Management should refer to IFRSs, IASs and Interpretations dealing with similar issues and to the Framework.

All material accounting policies should be disclosed and explained in the notes to the financial statements.

An entity should select and apply accounting policies consistently for similar transactions.

(b) The objectives are:
- Relevance
- Reliability
- Comparability
- Understandability

These objectives are noted in the Framework as being the four characteristics of useful financial information.

(c) The two concepts are:
- Going concern
- Accruals

△ ACTIVITY 45   △ △ △ △

Task

(a) According to IAS 37, a provision is a liability that is of uncertain timing or amount, which will be settled by an outflow of resources from the entity.

(b) A provision should be recognised when:
(i) an entity has a present obligation as a result of a past event
(ii) it is probable that a transfer of economic benefits will be required to settle the obligation
(iii) a reliable estimate can be made of the amount of the obligation.

(c) The accounting treatment of the matters arising in the year is as follows:
(i) A restructuring provision can be recognised when there is an obligation to close the division. This will occur when there is a detailed formal plan for the restructuring and the business has raised a valid expectation to those affected that the restructuring will be carried out. In this example, customers and employees have been notified of the closure and therefore there is a valid expectation that the division will be closed. Therefore, a provision of £1,854,000 is recognised at the year-end for the costs of closing the division.
(ii) On the basis of the evidence that has arisen during the year there is no obligation to transfer economic benefits as a result of past events. No provision is required. The matter may be disclosed in a note to the accounts as a contingent liability unless the probability of any transfer is regarded as remote.

Chapter 17
Interpretation of accounts

△ ACTIVITY 46   △ △ △ △

(a) **Return on capital employed**

$$\frac{\text{Profit before interest and tax}}{\text{Total assets less current liabilities}} \times 100\%$$

(If the balance sheet had included long-term debt then this figure of total assets less current liabilities would comprise 'capital and reserves' plus 'long-term debt'.)

$$\frac{0.82}{3.49} \times 100\% \qquad = \qquad 23.50\%$$

Asset turnover

$$\frac{\text{Revenues}}{\text{Total assets less current liabilities}}$$

$$\frac{6.90}{3.49} \qquad = \qquad 1.98 \text{ times}$$

% net profit before tax to revenue

$$\frac{0.82}{6.90} \times 100\% \qquad = \qquad 11.88\%$$

Current ratio

Current assets : current liabilities

$$2.49 : 1.90 \qquad = \qquad 1.31 : 1$$

Liquidity ratio/acid test

Current assets less inventories : current liabilities

$$1.89 : 1.90 \qquad = \qquad 0.99 : 1$$

Receivables collection period

$$\frac{\text{Receivables}}{\text{Revenues}} \times 365$$

$$\frac{1.84}{6.90} \times 365 \qquad = \qquad 97 \text{ days}$$

Cost of sales to finished goods

$$6.08 : 0.40 \qquad = \qquad 15.2$$

Labour cost % of revenue

$$\frac{1.26}{6.90} \times 100\% \qquad = \qquad 18.26\%$$

Operating costs as % of revenue

$$\frac{6.08-0.88}{6.90} \times 100\% \qquad = \qquad 75.36\%$$

Distribution and admin costs % of revenue

$$\frac{0.88}{6.90} \times 100\% \qquad = \qquad 12.75\%$$

(b) **Comparison of Fylingdales Quarries Ltd with sector as a whole**

Ratio	Fylingdales	Sector	Comment
Return on capital employed	23.50%	25.60%	Marginally less than sector as a whole but still giving a more than adequate return on investment.
Asset turnover	1.98	1.80	The company is generating more volume of output per '?' worth of investment than its competitors.
% net profit to revenue	11.88%	14.22%	The company is less profitable than the sector as a whole. It seems to be achieving volume at the expense of profitability.
Current ratio	1.31 : 1	1.50 : 1	The company has a sound level of liquidity, but marginally less than the sector.
Acid test	0.99 : 1	1.02 : 1	An ideal ratio here would be 1 : 1, the company has almost achieved this desired level of liquidity; again marginally less than the sector.
Trade receivables collection period	97 days	82 days	Tighter controls are required here.
			The collection period is typically high for the sector but the company needs to review its position. There is always the danger of the incidence of bad debts.

Cost of sales to finished goods	15.2	8.10	The company is turning over its finished goods inventories faster than the industry as a whole. It is holding approx 0.8 months compared with 1.48 month for the sector.
Labour costs as % of revenue	18.26%	18.10%	Almost in line with the industry average.
Operating costs % of revenue	75.36%	72.10%	The lack of profitability is highlighted here. Costs may need review and control or selling prices may need revising.
Distribution and admin cost % of revenue	12.75%	14.12%	More favourable than the sector as a whole.

Overall the company performance is marginally worse than the average performance for the sector.

The lack of profitability as highlighted in the % of operating costs to revenue is the significant factor which affects the return on capital. The company is achieving a good level of activity but is marginally less profitable.

△ ACTIVITY 47   △△△△

Wodehouse

(a) Accounting ratios

Profitability

Ratios			Pelham Ltd		Grenville Ltd
(i)	Gross profit margin	$\dfrac{GP}{Revenues}$	$\dfrac{230}{840} = 27.4\%$		$\dfrac{257}{762} = 33.7\%$
(ii)	Net profit margin	$\dfrac{Op\ profit}{Revenues}$	$\dfrac{85}{840} = 10.1\%$		$\dfrac{144}{762} = 18.9\%$
(iii)	ROCE	$\dfrac{Op\ profit}{Cap\ employed}$	$\dfrac{85}{432} = 19.7\%$		$\dfrac{144}{305} = 47.2\%$
(iv)	Asset turnover	$\dfrac{Revenue}{Cap\ employed}$	$\dfrac{840}{432} = 1.9$		$\dfrac{762}{305} = 2.5$
(v)	Inventory turnover	$\dfrac{Cost\ of\ sales}{Inventory}$	$\dfrac{610}{104} = 5.9$		$\dfrac{505}{80} = 6.3$

Liquidity

(i)	Current ratio	$\dfrac{CA}{CL}$	$\dfrac{347}{131} = 2.65$		$\dfrac{169}{132} = 1.28$
(ii)	Quick ratio	$\dfrac{CA - Inventory}{CL}$	$\dfrac{243}{131} = 1.85$		$\dfrac{89}{132} = 0.67$
(iii)	Receivables collection period	$\dfrac{Receivables}{Revenues} \times 365$ days		$\times 365 = 16\,\tfrac{1}{2}$	

days $\quad \dfrac{86}{762} \times 365 = 41.2$ days

(b) Comments
Profitability
(1) Fairly large difference in both GP and NP margins between two companies in same retailing sector. Grenville is much better than Pelham.
Possible reasons:
· Grenville may have shops in better positions than Pelham.
· Pelham may have a higher proportion of cash sales or prompt payment discounts.
· Grenville may simply be more effective in its control of costs.
· Pelham's comparatively low NBV of non-current assets could indicate a need for high maintenance costs.
(2) ROCE much lower for Pelham: high cash balance may point to under-use of resources. With a lower gross margin, Pelham's asset turnover should be considerably higher than Grenville's to compensate. This is not the case so more revenue volume is needed by Pelham.

Liquidity
(1) Pelham's large cash balance makes its current ratio unnecessarily high: it could afford an increase in capital expenditure, leading potentially to increased production and revenue.
(2) Grenville's liquidity looks alarming but may not be if the amount of the bank loan can be increased and if trade receivables will pay promptly. Its credit period of 41 days is somewhat high, and there could be a problem here. Further information needed as to the ageing of receivables and the terms of the bank loan.

(c) Comparison of two companies as investments
Pelham: could be said to be ripe for a takeover as it appears to be under-using its assets. A safe but unexciting performance which could be improved with more dynamic management.

Grenville: more of a risk. Needs an injection of cash for security, but given a state of continued solvency it has the potential to make high profits and a good return on investment.

△ ACTIVITY 48   △ △ △ △

REPORT

To:	Duncan Tweedy
From:	A Student
Subject:	Assessment of relative profitability of Byrne Ltd and May Ltd
Date:	X - X - XX

Introduction

This report has been prepared to assist in determining the relative profitability and performance of Byrne Ltd and May Ltd and is based on the information you supplied on both companies.

Ratios

	Byrne Ltd	May Ltd
Return on capital employed	21.5%	32.1%
Gross profit percentage	59.0%	67.0%
Net profit percentage	25.0%	36.0%
Earnings per share	47p	82p

Explanation and comment

· *Return on capital employed*

This measure shows the percentage of operating profit to capital employed in the business. It is a prime measure of profitability. It is expressed as:

$$\frac{\text{Operating profit before interest and tax}}{\text{*Capital employed}} \times 100\%$$

*Capital employed is defined here as equity plus long-term debt.

May Ltd shows the higher return than Byrne Ltd and is thus generating more profit per '£' of capital employed than Byrne.

· *Gross profit percentage*

This measure is often referred to as the gross margin and represents the percentage of gross profit in relation to revenue. It is expressed as:

$$\frac{\text{Gross profit}}{\text{Revenue}} \times 100\%$$

May Ltd shows a higher gross profit to revenue ratio and is therefore generating more gross profit per '£' of revenue than Byrne Ltd which indicates they are achieving higher margins.

· *Net profit percentage*

This measure of profitability shows the percentage of net profit in relation to revenue and is directly affected by the gross margin and levels of other expenses in the accounting period. It is expressed as:

$$\frac{\text{Net profit}}{\text{Revenue}} \times 100\%$$

May Ltd also has a higher net profit ratio to revenue than Byrne Ltd as it is generating more net profit per '£' of revenue than Byrne which is influenced by both the gross margin and the level of other costs in relation to revenue.

· *Earnings per share (EPS)*

This measure considers the earnings attributable to ordinary shareholders in relation to the number of shares issued. It is expressed as:

$$\frac{\text{Net profit after tax and preference dividend}}{\text{Number of ordinary shares in issue}}$$

May Ltd's earnings per share is approximately double that of Byrne Ltd. However, the EPS of two different companies are not directly comparable since they may have different numbers of shares in issue.

Conclusion

In terms of profitability, May Ltd has a much higher level of performance than Byrne Ltd as indicated by both the profitability measures calculated.

△ ACTIVITY 49

Task 49.1

REPORT

To:	Magnus Carter
From:	A Student
Subject:	Interpretation of financial statements
Date:	23 June 20X1

This report has been prepared to support the interpretation of the financial statements of Baron Ltd and to compare and contrast the company performance over the two year period.

(a) **Calculation of the ratios**

	20X1		20X0	
Gross profit percentage	$\frac{1,204}{1,852}$	= 65%	$\frac{1,116}{1,691}$	= 66%
Net profit percentage	$\frac{519}{1,852}$	= 28%	$\frac{592}{1,691}$	= 35%
Receivables collection period in days	$\frac{319}{1,852} \times 365$	= 63 days	$\frac{236}{1,691} \times 365$	= 51 days
Payables payment period in days	$\frac{48}{648} \times 365$	= 27 days	$\frac{44}{575} \times 365$	= 28 days
Inventory turnover in days	$\frac{217}{648} \times 365$	= 122 days	$\frac{159}{575} \times 365$	= 101 days

(b) **Explanation and comment**
   · *Gross profit percentage*
     This measure of profitability shows the percentage of gross profit in relation to revenue, it is often termed the gross margin.

The ratio has remained fairly constant over the two year period with only a marginal decrease from 66% to 65%. It is expressed as:

$$\frac{\text{Gross profit}}{\text{Revenues}} \quad \text{x } 100\%$$

The company has achieved a greater volume of business without having to reduce its margins.

· *Net profit percentage*

This measure of profitability shows the percentage of net profit in relation to revenue. It is influenced by the gross margin and the level of other costs in relation to revenue. There has been a significant fall in the net return over the period. The gross margin has only fallen marginally, however the expenses in relation to revenue have increased from 31% to 37% over the period and this has had an adverse effect on the performance.

This indicates that the company is generating less net profit per '£' of revenue than previously achieved.

· *Receivables collection period*

This is a measure of management control as it relates to the effectiveness of the credit control policy.

The ratio shows the average number of days it takes to collect debts. It is expressed as:

$$\frac{\text{Debtors}}{\text{Revenues}} \quad \text{x } 365 \text{ days}$$

The collection period has increased over the two year period and it is taking 12 days longer to collect debts than previously experienced. This may be due to either customer cash flow problems or poor and less effective credit control.

· *Payables payment period*

This ratio shows the average days it takes for the company to pay its suppliers. This period has remained similar over the two years.

It indicates that the company can meet its demands from trade payables on a timely and regular basis.

· *Inventory turnover*

This is a measure of the effectiveness of the inventory control policy. It shows the average number of days it takes to turn over inventories.

There has been a deterioration in this control over the two years as it is taking a further 21 days to turn over inventories than previously experienced.

Task 49.2

(a) The accounting equation is:

Assets - Liabilities = Equity interest

In a not-for-profit entity, funds given to the organisation by donors and those generated from within are utilised to meet the entity's objective. Such funds are equivalent to the equity interest element of the accounting equation.

In a company's balance sheet the equity interest of the shareholders is represented by the share capital and reserves of the company.

(b)   Examples of outside users and uses:

User	Uses
Potential investors	To decide whether to invest in the company.
Bank	To decide whether to grant a loan to the company.
Creditors	To decide whether to supply goods or services to the company.

Other reasonable examples of outside users are also acceptable.

(c)   **Areas for improvement**

The measures of performance and other ratios indicate that Baron Ltd should focus on the control of expenses, trade receivables and inventories.

The gross margin and payables payment periods have remained similar to the previous year, but there has been a decline in the net profit percentage due to a more than proportional increase in the level of expenses to revenue, which suggests controls are needed.

The credit control policy and procedures need review and there is also the danger of bad debts occurring. The inventory holding policy needs considering with a full analysis of both moving and slow moving inventories.

△ ACTIVITY 50   △ △ △ △

Notes to Jonathan Fisher

(a)   A balance sheet shows the financial position of an entity at a point in time. It lists the assets, liabilities and equity interest at the balance sheet date.

An income statement shows the financial performance of an entity over a specific period of time. It shows income and expenditure, the difference between these elements being profit over the accounting period.

(b)   The accounting equation is:

Assets - Liabilities = Equity interest

Figures in £000 at 30 September 20X9

Assets	£4,214 + £1,341	= £5,555
Liabilities	£838 + £2,500	= £3,338
Equity interest		= £2,217

The accounting equation is: £5,555 - £3,338   = £2,217

(c)   **Calculation of ratios**

The following ratios for the company have been computed:

		20X9		20X8	
(i)	*Gearing*				
	Debt/capital employed	$\frac{2,500}{4,717}$	= 53%	$\frac{1,000}{2,703}$	= 37%

or

Debt/equity	$\dfrac{2,500}{2,217} = 113\%$	$\dfrac{1,000}{1,703} = 59\%$

(ii) *Net profit percentage* $\quad\dfrac{668}{3,183} = 21\%$ $\qquad\dfrac{689}{2,756} = 25\%$

(iii) *Current ratio* $\qquad\quad\dfrac{1,341}{838} = 1.6:1$ $\qquad\dfrac{1,284}{611} = 2.1:1$

(iv) *Return on equity* $\qquad\dfrac{356}{2,217} = 16\%$ $\qquad\dfrac{471}{1,703} = 28\%$

(d) · *Gearing ratio*
This measure represents the company's reliance on debt in relation to total equity. The gearing has increased over the two years and the company is now a 'high geared' organisation. There is a greater reliance on borrowed funds in the second year. This increases shareholder risk as when profits reduce, interest payments must still be met.

· *Net profit percentage*
The net return to revenue has fallen over the period. This is a result of a fall in the gross margin from 63% to 58%, the level of expenses to revenue remaining fairly constant.

· *Current ratio*
There has been a reduction in this measure of liquidity over the period, there has been a deterioration in the cash position and the acid test ratio has fallen significantly from 0.97 to 0.65. The business now has less current assets per '?' of current liabilities than previously.

· *Return on equity*
The return has fallen over the two year period which has been influenced by the overall reduction in profitability as shown in the net profit percentage to revenue.

The company is not generating as much profit for each '£' worth of equity investment as it did in the previous year.

(e) The decrease in both profitability and liquidity indicates that the company is a worse prospect for investment than it was in the previous year.

△ ACTIVITY 51 △△△△

Task 51.1

REPORT

To:	Directors of Machier Ltd
From:	AAT Student
Date:	17 June 20X9
Re:	Analysis of Machier Ltd financial statements

Introduction

The purpose of this report is to analyse the company financial statements for 20X8 and 20X9 and comment on its profitability, liquidity and financial position and assess the likelihood of the bank providing a substantial loan to fund future business strategy.

(a) Calculation of ratios
   The following ratios for the company have been computed:

	20X9		20X8	
Return on equity	$\dfrac{321}{1,708}$ =	18.8%	$\dfrac{266}{1,227}$ =	21.7%
Net profit percentage	$\dfrac{738}{2,636}$ =	28%	$\dfrac{523}{1,687}$ =	31%
Quick ratio/acid test	$\dfrac{527}{719}$ =	0.7 : 1	$\dfrac{423}{359}$ =	1.2 : 1
Gearing ratio: Debt/capital employed	$\dfrac{2,800}{4,508}$ =	62%	$\dfrac{1,500}{2,727}$ =	55%
Interest cover	$\dfrac{738}{252}$ =	2.9 times	$\dfrac{523}{120}$ =	4.4 times

(b) *Comment and analysis*

   The company profitability has fallen over the two year period.

   The return on equity has decreased from 21.7% to 18.8%. This indicates that the company is generating less profit per '?' of equity investment than before.

   The percentage of net profit to revenue has also fallen; the gross margin remained fairly constant but the relationship of expenses to revenue increased from 34% to 37%, the influencing factor being the additional depreciation incurred on the extra investment in non-current assets.

   The company liquidity also deteriorated in the year with the acid test showing that the business has only 70p worth of liquid assets for each '?' worth of current liabilities. The business may be entering a period of cash flow difficulty.

   The business has a high level of gearing, 62% in the current year compared with 55% previously.

   High gearing is a risk to shareholders as, in periods of reduced profit, interest charges still have to be met and the company may struggle to pay this obligation.

   This increase in gearing also reflects in the fall in the interest cover.

(c) *Conclusion*

   The additional investment in non-current assets, funded mainly by the increased debt, has not resulted in a proportional increase in revenue but may achieve a higher volume in future years.

   Based on this information and assessment it is unlikely that the bank will agree to further funding in the form of a substantial loan. The company is already highly geared and profitability has fallen.

   I hope that this assessment and review is meaningful and useful to you.

Task 51.2

Notes for the directors

(a) The elements in a balance sheet and those in Machier Ltd comprise:

Elements	Balances
Assets	Non current assets and current assets
Liabilities	Current liabilities
	Long-term loan
Equity interest	Capital and reserves

(b) The accounting equation shows (figures in £000 at 31 March 20X9):

Assets	$(4,282 + 975) = 5,257$
Liabilities	$(749 + 2,800) = 3,549$
Equity interest	$= 1,708$

The accounting equation is: $5,257 - 3,549 = 1,708$

△ ACTIVITY 52   △ △ △ △

REPORT

To:	Managers of Bimbridge Hospitals Trust
From:	AAT Student
Date:	3 December 20X8
Re:	Analysis of Patch Ltd's financial statements

Introduction

The purpose of this report is to analyse the financial performance of Patch Ltd for 20X8 and 20X7 to consider it as a major supplier of bandages and dressings to the Trust.

The following are key financial ratios together with industry benchmarks.

	Patch Ltd 20X8	Industry average 20X8	Patch Ltd 20X7	Industry average 20X7
Return on capital employed	$\frac{552}{5,334} = 10.3\%$	9.6%	$\frac{462}{5,790} = 8.0\%$	9.4%
Net profit percentage	$\frac{552}{2,300} = 24\%$	21.4%	$\frac{462}{2,100} = 22\%$	21.3%
Quick ratio/acid test	$\frac{523}{475} = 1.1:1$	1.0 : 1	$\frac{418}{465} = 0.9:1$	0.9 : 1
Gearing: Debt/capital employed	$\frac{1,654}{5,334} = 31\%$	36%	$\frac{2,490}{5,790} = 43\%$	37%

Comment and analysis

Overall company profitability has improved over the two years with return on capital employed strengthening from 8% to 10.3%.

The company is generating more net profit per '£' of investment in 20X8 than in the previous year.

Compared with the sector average their performance was adverse in 20X7 but more favourable in 20X8.

The percentage of net profit to revenue also increased over the period increasing from 22% to 24%.

The company is therefore more profitable in the current year and is performing more favourably than the sector as a whole and a good indicator for the future.

Company liquidity has shown an improvement with a slightly stronger acid test ratio than the sector as a whole.

The company currently has £1.10 worth of liquid assets for each '£' worth of current liabilities. This appears to be a sound liquidity position.

There has been a reduction in gearing over the two year period, with a much less reliance on debt than previously experienced.

High geared companies increase shareholder risk in times of profit decline. The company is moving to a 'lower' geared structure and to a position less than the industry average.

The company is considered to be a lower risk than previously.

Conclusion
Based on this assessment of the financial statements provided, it is recommended that Patch Ltd can be used as a supplier to the Trust.

Its profitability, liquidity and gearing suggest that the company is financially sound.

△ ACTIVITY 53 △ △ △ △

	REPORT		
To:	Michael Beacham	**From:**	Accounting Technician
Subject:	Interpretation of ratios	**Date:**	21 June 20X2

Introduction
This report has been prepared to assist in the interpretation of the accounting ratios of Goodall Ltd, the company that you are considering making a loan to. It analyses the financial position and performance of the company over the years 20X1 and 20X2 and compares the results with the industry averages.

Explanation and comment
Gearing ratio. The gearing ratio measures the percentage of debt finance and preference share finance to total capital employed. The ratio is higher in 20X2 than 20X1, which suggests that the company is becoming riskier than in the previous year. Lending money to this company will increase the risk of failure to meet interest payments unless increased profits earned by the use of the loan are generated. In comparison with the industry average, the company is highly geared. This means that there is a higher than average risk in lending money to the company.

Interest cover. This ratio shows how many times the company could meet its interest payments out of operating profit. The interest cover has decreased from last year. This means that it is more difficult for the company to meet interest payments out of profits than last year. The ratio is very low in comparison with the industry average, which means that the company is earning considerably less profit in relation to the interest payments than other companies. This, again, makes it a riskier company to lend to.

Quick ratio/acid test. This ratio measures the extent to which the company has sufficient current assets that are quickly convertible into cash to meet its current liabilities. This ratio has decreased between the two years. In neither year did it have sufficient quick current assets to meet its current liabilities. The ratio is significantly worse than the industry average. This suggests that it has more of a liquidity problem when compared with other companies within the industry and hence that it is a riskier prospect.

Return on equity. This ratio measures the percentage of profit available for equity shareholders that is generated by the use of equity finance. The return on equity has fallen during the year. This means that there is less profit available for equity shareholders and makes it less likely that additional investment will be made in the company to enable additional profits to be made or to cover liquidity shortfalls. The return on equity is substantially less than the industry average, which makes it a less attractive prospect for investment than other companies within the sector.

Conclusion

The fact that Goodall Ltd is already highly geared and has deteriorating interest cover suggests that it is a risky prospect for a loan. It is riskier than other companies in its sector. The liquidity problems it is experiencing suggest that it may be unable to meet its interest payments in the future and it is unlikely, given the poor performance in profitability for equity investors, that they would be willing to meet any shortfall. It would not be advisable to lend money to Goodall Ltd.

△ ACTIVITY 53   △ △ △ △

AAT Student
Address
X December 20X2

Dear Mr Popper

As requested, I am writing to you about the liquidity and financial position of Zipps Ltd. In this letter, I analyse the financial statements and conclude as to whether it is likely that the bank will lend the company money. My analysis is based solely on the financial statements of the business for the two years 20X1 and 20X2.

I have calculated the following ratios of the company for each of the years ending 30 September 20X1 and 20X2:

	Ratios	20X2	20X1
Current ratio	$= \dfrac{\text{Current assets}}{\text{Current liabilities}}$	$\dfrac{1{,}430}{630} = 2.2 : 1$	$\dfrac{1{,}302}{620} = 2.1 : 1$
Quick ratio (acid test)	$= \dfrac{\text{Current assets less inventory}}{\text{Current liabilities}}$	$\dfrac{585}{650} = 0.9 : 1$	$\dfrac{682}{620} = 1.1 : 1$
Gearing ratio	$= \dfrac{\text{Long term debt}}{\text{Long term debt} + \text{equity}}$	$\dfrac{1{,}300}{2{,}000} = 65\%$	$\dfrac{900}{1{,}800} = 50\%$

[Alternative ratio]				
Debt/equity ratio	$=$	$\dfrac{\text{Long term debt}}{\text{Equity}}$	$\dfrac{1,300}{700} = 186\%$	$\dfrac{900}{620} = 100\%$
Interest cover	$=$	$\dfrac{\text{Profit/(loss) before interest and tax}}{\text{Interest charges}}$	$\dfrac{(46)}{104} = -0.4$ times	$\dfrac{270}{77} = 3.5$ times

My comments on the ratios are set out below:

Current ratio

The current ratio measures the extent to which the company has sufficient current assets to meet its current liabilities. It gives an indication of the liquidity of the company. Companies with low ratios may have difficulty in meeting creditor payments next year without a further injection of finance, and if this is not forthcoming it might be difficult to continue to trade. The ratio has increased during the year, which should mean that the company has better liquidity. However, if the increase in the ratio is due to increases in current assets that are not easily convertible to cash, the company may have poorer liquidity despite the increase in the ratio. A better test of liquidity in such a situation is given by a quick ratio or acid test.

Quick ratio/acid test

This ratio measures the extent to which the company has sufficient current assets that are quickly convertible into cash to meet its current liabilities. This ratio has decreased in the year from a position where it had more than enough quick current assets to meet its current liabilities to a position where there is a shortfall. The improvement in the current ratio seems to have come about due to an increase in inventories and not an increase in quick assets. This means that the company has worse liquidity than last year. However, it still has almost enough quick assets to meet current liabilities and so may be able to continue trading.

Gearing ratio

The gearing ratio measures the percentage of debt finance and preference share finance to total capital employed (the debt/ capital employed ratio) or to total equity (the debt/equity ratio). A high ratio increases the risk that if profits reduce, the company may not be able to meet its interest payments or borrow further funds to overcome any liquidity problems. The ratio is higher in 20X2 than in 20X1. The company is highly geared and hence would be considered a risk by a lender.

Interest cover

This ratio shows how many times the company could meet its interest payments out of operating profit. Low levels of cover may make it difficult for the company to borrow more funds. Ordinary shareholders are unlikely to invest further funds in a company whose profits are reduced by interest costs leaving no return for them. The interest cover has significantly decreased from last year to the point where there are no available profits to cover the interest payments.

Given the difficulty in covering interest out of profits, the bank may well look at the profitability ratios of the company. These might include the net profit and gross profit ratios. It is clear that profits are substantially down on last year and the bank is likely to want to know why this is the case. Calculating those ratios might assist them in understanding why this is the case. They will want to know whether this is likely to continue in the future and hence whether the company is likely to be able to cover interest out of profits and eventually have enough funds to pay back the loan.

In conclusion, the company has poorer liquidity this year than last. The increase in the current ratio seems attributable to an increase in inventory rather than an increase in cash or near cash current assets. The quick ratio shows relatively less quick assets to meet current liabilities. This is already a highly geared company and it is not making sufficient profits to cover its interest payments. Its financial position has deteriorated and looks insecure. A loan to the company would be risky and the bank is unlikely to lend money to the company on the basis of the ratios and analysis alone.

Yours sincerely

AAT Student

AAT Student

△ ACTIVITY 55 △△△△

Task 55
Youngernst Ltd
Notes for a meeting
(a) **Formulas used in calculating the ratios:**

$$\text{Current ratio} = \frac{\text{Current Assets}}{\text{Current Liabilities}}$$

$$\text{Quick ratio} = \frac{\text{Current Assets less Inventories}}{\text{Current Liabilities}}$$

$$\text{Receivables turnover} = \frac{\text{Trade receivables}}{\text{Revenue}} \times 365$$

$$\text{Payables turnover} = \frac{\text{Trade payables}}{\text{Cost of sales}} \times 365$$

$$\text{Inventories turnover} = \frac{\text{Inventories}}{\text{Cost of sales}} \times 365$$

(b) Explanation of the meaning of the ratios
Current ratio:
· this ratio measures the extent to which the company has sufficient current assets to meet its current liabilities
· it gives an indication of the liquidity of the company, but can also show that too much is invested in current assets such as inventories and trade receivables and cash in relation to current liabilities

Quick ratio/Acid test:
· this ratio measures the extent to which the company has sufficient current assets that are quickly convertible into cash to meet its current liabilities
· it also gives an indication of the liquidity of the company, but can also indicate whether too much is invested in trade receivables and cash in relation to current liabilities

Debtor turnover (trade receivables collection period):
·   this ratio shows the average number of days it takes to collect trade receivables

Creditor turnover (trade payables payment period):
·   this ratio shows the average number of days it takes for the company to pay its trade payables

Inventory turnover
·   this ratio shows the average number of days that it takes to sell the inventories of the company

(c)   **Comment on change in ratios**
Current ratio:
·   this ratio has increased during the year suggesting that the company has more current assets to meet its current liabilities than in previous years and hence better liquidity
·   however, this might be because inventories or trade receivable balances have increased rather than cash balances and these may not be readily convertible to cash to pay off trade payables and so does not necessarily mean more liquidity and may indicate problems in selling inventories or collecting trade receivables

Quick ratio/Acid test:
·   this ratio has deteriorated during the year which means that there are less current assets that are quickly convertible into cash to meet its current liabilities which suggests decreased liquidity
·   the fact that this ratio has decreased even though the current ratio has increased suggests that the reason why the current ratio has increased is due to increases in the amount of inventories held in relation to current liabilities rather than any genuine improvement in liquidity
·   because the quick assets include trade receivables, this ratio might conceal further liquidity problems since a failure to collect trade receivable balances may also result in a higher ratio

Receivables turnover:
·   the ratio has deteriorated over the two years as it now takes, on average, 16 more days to collect debts than last year
·   the fact that it takes longer this year to collect debts than last year may be due to liquidity problems of customers, an increase in bad debts or a failure to chase up overdue debts which might point to failures of management of working capital

Payables turnover:
·   the number of days taken to pay trade payables has fallen a little over the two years
·   this does not suggest that the company has had difficulty in finding funds to pay trade payables and, therefore, does not appear to have liquidity problems that have forced the business to pay trade payables more slowly
·   the decrease may be due to inefficiencies in management and the failure to make full use of credit terms, but it is possible that trade payables have tightened up on the period of credit allowed which might indicate suspicions about the liquidity of the company

Inventory turnover:
·   this ratio has deteriorated over the two years as it now takes 17 days longer to sell inventories than it did last year
·   this shows that there may be problems with inventory control which may point to overstocking or to increasing amounts of old inventories being included against which provisions may be required to be made

△ ACTIVITY 56   △ △ △ △

Task 56.1

REPORT

To:	Maurice Sun
From:	A Student
Date:	June 20X4
Subject:	Interpretation of financial statements

This report has been prepared to assist in the interpretation of the financial statements of Fieldsomer Ltd. It considers the profitability and return on capital of the business over 20X3 and 20X4.

(a) Calculation of the ratios

	20X4		20X3	
Return on capital employed	$\dfrac{2,189}{17,541}$	= 12.5%	$\dfrac{2,430}{15,937}$	= 15.2%
Net profit percentage	$\dfrac{2,189}{8,420}$	= 26%	$\dfrac{2,430}{7,595}$	= 32%
Gross profit percentage	$\dfrac{4,884}{8,420}$	= 58%	$\dfrac{4,177}{7,595}$	= 55%
Asset turnover	$\dfrac{8,420}{17}$	= 0.48	$\dfrac{7,595}{15,937}$	= 0.48

(b) Explanation and comment

Return on capital employed
- This ratio shows in percentage terms how much profit is being generated by the capital employed in the company.
- The company is showing a lower return on capital employed in 20X4 compared to 20X3 and hence is generating less profit per £ of capital employed in the business.

Net profit percentage
- This ratio shows in percentage terms how much net profit is being generated from sales revenue.
- The ratio has decreased over the two years.
- This could be explained either by a decrease in the sales margins or by an increase in expenses, or both.
- In fact, the percentage of expenses to sales revenue has increased from 23% in 20X3 to 32% in 20X4.

Gross profit ratio
- This ratio shows in percentage terms how much gross profit is being generated by the sales revenue of the company and thus indicates the gross profit margin on sales revenue

---

· The ratio has improved over the two years with an increase in the percentage from 55% to 58%.
· The company is increasing its sales revenue without significantly cutting its margins.
· This may be due to increasing its sales price or reducing the cost of sales or both.

Asset Turnover
· This ratio shows how efficient the company is in generating sales from the available capital employed/net assets.
· The ratio has stayed the same between the two years and so a similar level of sales has been generated from the available capital employed/net assets in 20X4 than in 20X3.
· The new investment that has been made in non current assets and current assets in 20X4 has generated a proportional increase in sales.

(c) **Overall**

The ratios show that the return on capital employed has deteriorated in 20X4 and that the company is thus generating less profit from the capital employed/net assets. Although there are increased margins there is less control over expenses and this has contributed to the deteriorating position. Control of expenses needs to be addressed by management. The efficiency in the use of assets has remained the same in 20X4 and the increased investment in assets that has taken place in 20X4 has yielded benefits in terms of increased sales.

Regards

AAT Student

AAT Student

Task 56.2

(a) The monetary values are as follows:

	£
Ownership interest	12,541
Assets	19,756
Liabilities	7,215

These figures are related in the accounting equation as follows:

Assets - Liabilities	=	Ownership interest
£19,756 - £7,215	=	£12,541

(b) The balance for the retained earnings on the balance sheet of £4,541,000 represents the accumulated undistributed retained profit of the company since its inception. The profit for the year in the income statement of £1,324,000 less the dividends of £720,000 is added to the retained profits brought forward from previous years of £3,937,000 in order to get the retained profits carried forward of £4,541,000 which is shown in the balance sheet of the company.

△ ACTIVITY 57 △△△△

Task 57.1

REPORT

To: Leopold Scratchy
From: AAT student
Date: June 20X5
Subject: Interpretation of financial statements

This report has been prepared to assist in the decision as to whether to invest in Partridge Ltd or Carington Ltd. It considers the risk and return associated with an investment in these companies based solely on an analysis and interpretation of the financial statements of these companies for the year ended 31 March 20X5.

(a) Formulae used in calculating the ratios

(i) Return on equity = $\dfrac{\text{Profit after tax}}{\text{Ordinary share capital and reserves}}$

or

$\dfrac{\text{Profit before tax}}{\text{Ordinary share capital and reserves}}$

(ii) Earnings per share = $\dfrac{\text{Profit attributable to ordinary shareholders}}{\text{Weighted average number of ordinary shares outstanding during the period}}$

(iii) Gearing (Debt/equity) = $\dfrac{\text{Long term debt (prior change capital)}}{\text{Ordinary share capital and reserves}}$

(iv) Gross profit = $\dfrac{\text{Gross profit}}{\text{Revenue}}$

(b) Calculation of ratios

Ratio	Partridge Ltd	Carington Ltd
Return on equity	$\dfrac{3,688}{9,756} = 38\%$	$\dfrac{2,838}{9,846} = 29\%$
or	$\dfrac{4,918}{9,756} = 50\%$	$\dfrac{3,784}{9,846} = 38\%$
Earnings per share	$\dfrac{3,688}{7,000} = 53\text{p}$	$\dfrac{2,838}{7,000} = 41\text{p}$
Gearing (Debt/equity)	$\dfrac{8,000}{9,756} = 82\%$	$\dfrac{500}{9,846} = 5\%$
Gross profit	$\dfrac{9,582}{16,241} = 59\%$	$\dfrac{6,577}{11,147} = 59\%$

(c) **Explanation of the meaning of the ratios and comment on the two companies**

Return on equity: This ratio measures the percentage of profit available for equity shareholders that is generated by the use of equity finance. Partridge Ltd gives a higher return on equity than Carington Ltd. This means that more profits for equity shareholders are generated from an investment in Partridge Ltd than from one in Carington Ltd. The higher return makes an investment in Partridge Ltd initially more attractive than an investment in Carington Ltd.

Earnings per share: This ratio measures the earnings attributable to each ordinary share. Partridge Ltd gives a higher earnings per share than Carington Ltd. This means that more earnings are attributable to each share in Partridge Ltd than in Carington Ltd. Again, this makes an investment in Partridge Ltd initially more attractive than an investment in Carington Ltd.

Gearing ratio: The gearing ratio based on debt/equity measures the percentage of debt finance to equity finance. The ratio in Partridge Ltd is much higher than that in Carington Ltd. This indicates that Partridge Ltd is more reliant on debt finance than Carington Ltd. This makes Partridge Ltd a riskier company to invest in than Carington Ltd. There is a higher risk that Partridge Ltd may not generate sufficient profits to maintain the dividend to ordinary shareholders and may result in returns to shareholders being more volatile. The company may also fail to meet interest or loan repayments payments from profits if there is a downturn in profitability. The greater risk to ordinary shareholders makes Partridge Ltd a relatively less attractive investment.

Gross profit ratio: This ratio shows in percentage terms how much gross profit is being generated by the sales revenue of the company. It indicates the gross profit margin on sales. The gross profit ratio in the two companies is virtually the same. This indicates that the trade in the two companies is equally profitable.

AAT Student

AAT Student

Task 57.2

(a) According to the Framework for the preparation and presentation of financial statements, the objective of financial statements is to provide information about the reporting entity's financial performance and financial position to the users of those financial statements. The users of the financial statements are shareholders, potential investors, customers, suppliers, employees and any other interested party.

(b) In the circumstances in Task 57.1 the user is Leopold Scratchy, a potential investor in one of the companies (or an analyst giving investment advice to a potential investor). The financial statements are being used to make an economic decision as to whether to invest in one of the companies. The potential investor is concerned with the risk inherent in, and return provided by, an investment in the companies. They need information about the companies' financial performance and financial position which helps them to assess the cash-generation abilities and financial adaptability of the companies. The financial statements provide this information

△ ACTIVITY 58 △△△△

Task 58.1

REPORT

To: John Brams   **Subject:**   Analysis of financial performance of Ma Leer Ltd
From: A Student

This report has been prepared in order to analyse the financial performance of Ma Leer Ltd for 20X5 and 20X4.

(a) Formulas for the calculation of the ratios

Ratio	Formula
Return on capital employed	$\dfrac{\text{Profit before interest and tax}}{\text{Capital employed}}$
Net profit ratio	$\dfrac{\text{Profit before interest and tax}}{\text{Revenue}}$
Gross profit ratio	$\dfrac{\text{Gross profit}}{\text{Revenue}}$
Expenses ratio	$\dfrac{\text{Expenses}}{\text{Revenue}}$
Asset turnover (based on net assets)	$\dfrac{\text{Revenue}}{\text{Capital employed (net assets)}}$
Inventories turnover in days	
(Inventories turnover period based on cost of sales)	$\dfrac{\text{Inventories}}{\text{Cost of sales}} \times 365$
Trade receivables turnover in days	
(Trade receivables payment period)	$\dfrac{\text{Trade receivables}}{\text{Revenue}} \times 365$
Trade payables turnover in days	
(Trade payables payment period based on cost of sales)	$\dfrac{\text{Trade payables}}{\text{Cost of sales}} \times 365$

(b) **Changes in the ratios**

Ratio	Improved/ Deteriorated	Reason
Return on capital employed	Deteriorated	There is less profit generated from the capital employed, meaning that the capital is not so efficient in generating profits.
Net profit ratio	Deteriorated	The percentage of net profit generated by the sale has decreased, which means that the company is generating less net profit from its sales.
Gross profit ratio	Improved	The percentage of gross profit generated by sales revenue has increased due to increases in margins. This may be due to increases in sales prices or a reduction in cost of sales or both.
Expenses ratio	Deteriorated	The percentage of expenses in relation to sales has increased. This means that it costs more in operating expenses to make sales.
Asset turnover	Deteriorated	Fewer sales are generated from the capital employed (net assets) than last year.
Inventories turnover in days	Deteriorated	The company is keeping inventory for a longer period of time. This means that additional costs are incurred from holding inventory.
Trade receivables turnover in days	Deteriorated	It is taking longer to get customers to pay than last year. This may indicate that some customers have liquidity problems or that the company is not chasing the debts as effectively as last year.
Trade payables turnover in days	Deteriorated	The company is paying its debts more quickly. This suggests that the company is not taking full advantage of credit terms.

(c) **Overall change in financial performance**

Overall, the financial performance of the company has deteriorated in the year, as shown by the decline in the return on capital employed. Both the profitability of the sales revenue, as shown by the net profit ratio, and the efficiency in generating sales from capital employed, as shown by the asset turnover ratio, have deteriorated. The deterioration of the net profit ratio is not due to the underlying profitability of the sales in trading, given an improvement in the gross profit ratio. The decline is due to the increasing proportion of profits on sales revenue being used to cover operating expenses, as shown by the deterioration of the expenses ratio. It may be that part of the inefficiency revealed by the asset turnover ratio is due to inefficiencies in control of working capital as shown by the inventory, receivables and payables turnover.

Task 58.2

(a) The IASB Framework states that 'the objective of financial statements is to provide information about the financial position, performance and changes in financial position of an entity that is useful to a wide range of users in making economic decisions.'

In the circumstances of Task 58.1, you were a user of financial information. You were acting as an analyst to assist John Brams who is an existing shareholder of Ma Leer Ltd. Both of you were using information about the financial performance of the business to determine how well the directors had managed the business in the past year. In effect, you were using the financial statements for stewardship purposes.

(b) Two examples of other classes of user who might be interested in the information in financial statements would be:

User	Purpose
Lenders	To assess whether loans will be repaid and related interest will be repaid when due, and to help potential investors decide whether to lend and on what terms
Suppliers and other creditors	To decide whether to sell to the entity and to assess the likelihood that amounts owing will be paid when due
Employees	To enable them to assess their employer's ability to provide remuneration, employment opportunities and retirement and other benefits
Customers	To find out about the continued existence of the entity where they may have long-term involvement or are dependent on the entity
Governments and their agencies	To assist them in regulating the activities of the entity, assessing taxation and providing a basis for national statistics
The public	To assess trends and recent developments in the entity's prosperity and range of activities
Present and potential investors	To assist them in making stewardship decisions and in taking decisions about their investment or potential investment.

MOCK EXAMINATION ANSWERS

SECTION 1

PART A

Task 1.1

		£000	£000
1	DR Inventories (Balance sheet)	14,186	
	CR Inventories (P & L)		14,186
2.	DR Taxation	3,537	
	CR Taxation payable		3,537
3	DR Interest payable	700	
	CR Interest		700
4.	DR Property, plant and equipment	5,000	
	CR Revaluation reserve		5,000

Task 1.2
(a)

Wolf Ltd
Income Statement for the year ended 31 March 2006

	£000
Continuing Operations	
Revenue	72,813
Cost of sales	(33,494)
Gross profit	39,319
Distribution costs	(12,533)
Administrative expenses	(9,311)
Profit from operations	17,475
Finance costs	(1,400)
Profit before tax	16,075
Tax	(3,537)
Profit for the period from continuing operations attributable to equity holders	12,538

Workings (all £000)

W1 Cost of sales

Opening inventories	12,572
Purchases	35,108
Closing inventories	(14,186)
	33,494

W2 Finance costs

Interest per TB	700
Interest payable	700
	1,400

(b)

Wolf Ltd
Balance sheet as at 31 March 2006

	£000
Non-current assets	
Property, plant and equipment	55,082
Current assets	
Inventories	14,186
Trade receivables	9,122
Cash and cash equivalents	473
	23,781
Total assets	78,863
Current liabilities	
Trade and other payables	(4,039)
Tax liabilities	(3,537)
	(7,576)
Net current assets	16,205
Non-current liabilities	
7% debentures	(20,000)
Total liabilities	(27,576)
Net assets	51,287
EQUITY	
Share capital	10,000
Share premium account	8,000
Revaluation reserve	5,000
Retained earnings	28,287
Total equity	51,287

Workings (all £000)

W1 Property, plant and equipment

Cost per TB	71,338
Accumulated depreciation per TB	(21,256)
Revaluation of land	5,000
	55,082

W2 Trade and other payables

Trade payables per TB	(2,927)
Interest	(700)
Accruals	(412)
	(4,039)

W3 Retained earnings

Balance at 1 April 2005	17,349
Profit for the year	12,538
	29,887
Final dividend for 2005	(1,000)
Interim dividend for 2006	(600)
Balance at 30 September 2006	28,287

Task 1.3

(a) IAS 10 states that events after the balance sheet date are 'those events, favourable and unfavourable, that occur between the balance sheet date and the date when the financial statements are authorised for issue'.

(b) 'Adjusting events' are those events that provide additional evidence of conditions that existed at the balance sheet date'. "Non-adjusting events" are those events that are indicative of conditions that arose after the balance sheet date.

(c) (i) The losses that arose from the fire on the company's premises on 21 April 2006 constitute a 'non-adjusting' event. The condition did not exist at the balance sheet date, but came into existence after that date. No adjustment is required for the event as the conditions did not exist at the balance sheet date and hence none was made in the financial statements of Wolf Ltd. However, if the event is so material that nondisclosure could influence the economic decisions of users taken on the basis of the financial statements then the entity should disclose the nature of the event and an estimate of its financial effect, or a statement that such an estimate cannot be made, by way of a note to the accounts.

(ii) IAS 10 states that if an entity declares a dividend after the balance sheet date then the entity shall not recognise those dividends as a liability at the balance sheet date. For this reason no adjustment for the dividends declared by Wolf Ltd on 2 May 2006, after the balance sheet date, was made in the financial statements.

Part B

Task 1.4

Alasmith plc
Consolidated balance sheet as at 31 March 2006

	£000
Non-current assets	
Goodwill	3,600
Property, plant and equipment	103,640
	107,240
Current assets	
Inventories	19,108
Trade and other receivables	11,057
Cash and cash equivalents	2,197
	32,362

Total assets	139,602

Current liabilities

Trade and other payables	(14,014)
Tax liabilities	(1,370)
	(15,384)

Net current assets	16,978

Non-current liabilities

Bank loans	(28,850)

Total liabilities	(44,234)

Net assets	95,368

EQUITY

Share capital	25,000
Share premium account	10,000
Retained earnings	43,088
Equity attributable to equity holders of the parent	78,088

Minority interest	17,280

Total equity	95,368

Workings

(i) Alasmith plc holding in Jones Ltd:

$$\frac{4,000,000}{6,000,000} = 60\%$$

(ii) Revaluation of assets in Jones Ltd to fair value at date of acquisition:

DR Fixed assets	£8,000,000
CR Revaluation reserve	£8,000,000

(iii)   Calculation of goodwill arising on consolidation and minority interest:

	Attributable to Alasmith plc			(all £000)
	Total Equity 100%	At Acquisition 60%	Since Acquisition 60%	Minority Interest 40%
Share capital	6,000	3,600		2,400
Share premium	4,000	2,400		1,600
Revaluation reserve	8,000	4,800		3,200
Retained earnings:				
- at acquisition	19,800	11,880		7,920
- earnings since acquisition	5,400		3,240	2,160
		22,680		17,280
Consideration		26,680		
Goodwill arising on consolidation		4,000		
Retained earnings Alasmith plc			40,248	

Consolidated retained earnings of Alasmith plc		43,488
Impairment loss	(400)	(400)
	3,600	43,088

Part C

Unwittington Ltd
Reconciliation of operating profit to net cash inflow from operating activities

	£000
Profit from operations	2,213
Adjustments for:	
Depreciation	2,952
Gain on disposal of property, plant and equipment	(217)
Operating cash flows before movements in working capital	4,948
Increase in inventories	(682)
Increase in trade receivables	(1,447)
Increase in trade payables	27
Cash generated by operations	2,846
Income taxes paid	(466)
Interest paid	(210)
Net cash from operating activities	2,170

Task 1.6

Unwittington Ltd
Cash Flow Statement for the year ended 31 March 2006

	£000
Net cash from operating activities	2,170
Investing activities	
Proceeds on disposal of property, plant and equipment	1,254
Purchases of property, plant and equipment	(9,900)
Net cash used in investing activities	(8,646)
Financing activities	
New bank loans raised	1,000
Proceeds of share issue	5,000
Dividends paid	(600)
Net cash from financing activities	5,400
Net increase/(decrease) in cash and	(1,076)

cash equivalents	
Cash and cash equivalents at beginning of year	392
Cash and cash equivalents at end of year	(684)

Workings (all figures £000)

W1 Proceeds from sale – NBV of asset sold £1,037 = Profit £217
therefore, Proceeds from sale = NBV of asset sold £1,037 + Profit £217 = £1,254

W2 Fixed asset additions:
Opening balance £16,797 - depreciation £2,952 - Net book value of asset sold £1,037 + additions ? = Closing balance £22,708
therefore ? = £9,900

Section 2

Task 2.1

> AAT Student
> Address
> June 2006
>
> Dear Ms Keygone,
> Following our meeting about the ratios of Asbeen Ltd, I am writing to assist you in understanding of the significance of the ratios mentioned by the shareholder and to appreciate their concerns as to how they compare with the industry averages.
>
> (a) The formulas used in calculating the ratios are as follows:
>
> Current ratio $= \dfrac{\text{Current Assets}}{\text{Current Liabilities}}$
>
> Quick ratio $= \dfrac{\text{Current Assets less inventories}}{\text{Current Liabilities}}$
>
> Inventories turnover $= \dfrac{\text{Inventories}}{\text{Cost of sales}} \times 365$
>
> Trade receivables turnover $= \dfrac{\text{Trade receivables}}{\text{Sales}} \times 365$
>
> (b) The ratios tell you the following about a company
>
> (i)   The Current ratio measures the extent to which the company has sufficient current assets to meet its current liabilities. It gives an indication of the liquidity of the company, but can also show that too much is invested in current assets like inventories and trade receivables and cash in relation to current liabilities.

(ii) The quick ratio (Acid test) measures the extent to which the company has sufficient current assets that are quickly convertible into cash to meet its current liabilities. It also gives an indication of the liquidity of the company, but can also indicate whether too much is invested in trade receivables and cash in relation to current liabilities.

(iii) The inventories turnover ratio shows the average number of days that it takes to sell the inventories of the company.

(iv) The trade receivables turnover ratio shows the average number of days it takes to collect debts.

(c) The ratios are calculated as follows:

Ratio	
Current ratio	$\frac{6,440}{2,800} = 2.3 : 1$
Quick ratio/acid test	$\frac{2,240}{2,800} = 0.8 : 1$
Inventories turnover	$\frac{4,200}{8,716} \times 365 = 176$ days
Trade receivables turnover	$\frac{2,095}{14,994} \times 365 = 51$ days

(d) In comparison with the industry averages:

(i) The current ratio is higher than the industry average. This suggests that the company has more current assets to meet its current liabilities than is normally the case in the industry. This might indicate that Asbeen Ltd has better liquidity than other companies in the industry. This would not be a cause for concern as it suggests that the company is in a better position to meet current liabilities than other companies in the industry. However, it may be that inventories or trade receivables balances have increased rather than cash balances and these may not be readily convertible to cash to pay off current liabilities. This does not necessarily mean more liquidity and may indicate problems in selling inventories or collecting trade receivables. This would be a cause for concern as it might indicate that Asbeen Ltd has poor liquidity and may not be able to meet current liabilities as they fall due as well as other companies in the industry.

(ii) The quick ratio (acid test) ratio for Asbeen Ltd is lower than the industry average. This might mean that there are fewer current assets that are quickly convertible into cash to meet current liabilities than is normally the case in the industry. This suggests that it has lower liquidity than the rest of the industry. This is a cause for concern as it suggests that the company may not be as capable of paying current liabilities as they fall due than other companies in the industry. Because the quick assets include trade receivables this ratio might conceal further liquidity problems since a failure to collect trade receivables balances may also result in a higher ratio. This might indicate that the company is in an even worse liquidity position.

(iii) The inventories turnover in days is much greater than the average in the industry. This means that it takes longer to sell the inventories than it does in other companies. This may be responsible for the fact that the current ratio is higher than in other companies in the industry. Instead of suggesting greater liquidity the higher current ratio in conjunction with the inventories turnover ratio may indicate there are problems with inventories control which may point to overstocking or to increasing amounts of old inventories being included against which provisions may be required to be made. This is a cause for concern as it may point to inventories losses that need to be recognised in the financial statements or it might point to failures in the management of inventories.

iv) The trade receivables turnover is worse than the industry average. This shows that it takes longer to collect trade receivables than in other companies. This may be due to liquidity problems of customers, an increase in bad debts or a failure to chase up overdue debts that might point to failures of management of working capital. This suggests that the liquidity problem indicated by the quick ratio may be worse than the quick ratio indicates as it takes a long time to convert the trade receivables into cash than in the rest of the industry. This is a cause for concern as it suggests that the company may have greater liquidity problems than other companies in the industry.

I hope that this explains the meaning and significance of the ratios and indicates why the shareholder may have concerns about the company when the ratios are compared to those of other companies in the industry. If any further clarification is required do not hesitate to contact me.

Yours sincerely,

AAT Student

AAT Student

Task 2.2

(a) The elements of financial statements are defined by the IASB's Framework for the Preparation and Presentation of Financial Statements as follows:

(i) An asset is a resource controlled by the entity as a result of past events or transactions from which future economic benefits are expected to flow to the entity.

(ii) A liability is a present obligation of the entity arising from past events, the settlement of which is expected to result in an outflow from the entity of resources embodying economic benefits.

(iii) Equity is the residual interest in the assets of the entity after deducting all its liabilities.

(b) Inventories fits the definition of an asset in that:

- the purchase of inventories for resale gives rise to a resource controlled by the entity
- this is which is the result of a past transaction
- future economic benefits are expected flow to the entity because it can sell the inventories or to use the inventories to manufacture products with a view to generating cash.

GLOSSARY

Term	Description
Abbreviated accounts	Simplified set of statements that small and medium-sized companies can choose to file at Companies House rather than a full set of accounts.
Accounting concepts	Also called accounting principles, these are the broad basic assumptions underlying the preparation of financial statements that give a true and fair view.
Accounting standards	Official statements describing how accounts should be prepared if they are to give a true and fair view The accounting standards in this text are International Accounting Standards (IASs) and International Financial Reporting Standards (IFRSs) which have been issued by the International Accounting Standards Boards (IASB).
Acquisition	The normal type of business combination.
Associate	Entity over which the group exerts significant influence but not control.
Balance sheet	Accounting statement showing an entity's financial position at a particular date.
Books of prime entry	Accounting records in which entries are made individually, before being totalled to be entered in the ledgers. Examples are the sales day book and the purchases day book.
Carrying amount	Amount at which an asset is recognised after deducting any accumulated depreciation (amortisation) and accumulated impairment losses.
Cash	Cash on hand and demand deposits.
Cash equivalents	Short term, highly liquid investments that are readily convertible to known amounts of cash.
Cash flow statement	Accounting statement showing an entity's receipts and payments of cash over a particular period of time.
Cash flows	Inflows and outflows of cash and cash equivalents.
Cash generating unit	The smallest identifiable group of assets that generates cash inflows that are largely independent of the cash inflows from other assets or group of assets.
Consolidated accounts	The usual form of group accounts, presenting a consolidated balance sheet and consolidated income statement as though the group were a single economic entity.
Consolidated balance sheet	Balance sheet prepared for a group as though the group were a single economic entity.
Consolidated income statement	Income statement prepared for a group as though the group were a single economic entity.
Cost of inventories	That expenditure which has been incurred in the normal course of business in bringing the product or service to its present location and condition.
Debenture	Borrowings incurred by a company, acknowledged in writing, and normally carrying a fixed rate of interest and secured against assets owned by the company.

Term	Description
Depreciation	Allocation of the depreciable amount of an asset over its useful economic life.
Directors' report	Commentary on the financial performance for the period, required by CA 85 to be included with the financial statements in the annual report.
Elements of financial statements	The Framework identifies five elements, the classes of items that financial statements comprise: assets, liabilities, equity interest, income and expenses.
Equity accounting	The accounting method used to incorporate an associate into the consolidated accounts.
Extended trial balance	Working sheet in which the trial balance is analysed into the income statement and balance sheet of the business.
Fair value	Amount the asset could be exchanged for between willing parties in an arms length transaction.
Financing activities	Activities that result in changes in the size and composition of the contributed equity and borrowings of the entity.
First in, first out	FIFO assumes that the inventories in hand represent the latest purchases or production.
Gearing ratios	Ratios that measure the dependence on non-equity funds.
Goodwill	Difference between the cost of shares acquired and the fair value of net assets acquired.
Group accounts	Accounts prepared for a group.
Group of companies	A parent company together with its subsidiaries.
Impairment	Reduction in the recoverable amount of a non-current asset below its carrying amount.
Income statement	Accounting statement showing an entity's financial performance over a particular period of time (under UK standards this was referred to as Profit and Loss account).
Intangible non-current assets	An identifiable non-monetary asset without physical substance. Examples are purchased goodwill and deferred development costs.
Inventories	Assets held for sale in the ordinary course of business, or in the process of production for sale, or in the form of materials or supplies.
Investing activities	Acquisition and disposal of long-term assets and other investments not included in cash equivalents.
Investment property	Property held to earn rentals or for capital appreciation or both.
Limited company	Business structure in which the shareholders are not legally responsible for the debts owed by their company. A limited company is a distinct 'person' in law so can sue or be sued in its own name.
Liquidity ratios	Ratios that measure short term solvency.

Term	Description
Minority interest	The stake in a subsidiary not owned by the parent company. For example, if P Ltd owns 80% of S Ltd, then there is a 20% minority interest.
Net realisable value	Estimated selling price less all costs to completion and all selling costs.
Operating activities	Principal revenue-producing activities of the entity.
Ordinary shares	The normal type of share. Dividends vary in size according to the profits available.
Parent company	A company that controls another company (its subsidiary), normally by owning more than half of that company's ordinary share capital.
Post-acquisition reserves	Reserves of a subsidiary that have been earned subsequent to acquisition by a parent company.
Pre-acquisition reserves	Reserves of a subsidiary at the date of acquisition by a parent company.
Preference shares	An unusual type of share. A fixed dividend is paid, in priority to any ordinary dividends.
Profitability ratios	Ratios that measure profitability.
Property, plant and equipment	Tangible items that are held for use in the production or supply of goods, for rental to others or for administrative purposes and are expected to be used for more than one period.
Qualitative characteristics	The Framework identifies four characteristics that make financial information useful: relevance, reliability, comparability and understandability.
Recoverable amount	Higher of an asset's fair value less costs to sell and its value in use.
Risk	In this context, risk is the danger that a business will be unable to meet its financial objectives (in particular dividends to shareholders) because of excessive interest payments on debt.
Share premium	Amount for which a share is issued over and above its nominal value.
Summary financial statements	Simplified set of statements that shareholders of listed companies can choose to receive rather than a full set of accounts.
Trial balance	List of the balances on all the ledger accounts at a particular date. The total debit balances should equal the total credit balances.

KAPLAN PUBLISHING FOULKS LYNCH

AAT Order Form

Swift House, Market Place, Wokingham, Berkshire RG40 1AP, UK.
Tel: +44 (0) 118 989 0629   Fax: +44 (0) 118 979 7455
Order online: www.kaplanfoulkslynch.com
Email: publishing@kaplanfoulkslynch.com

To order books, please indicate quantity required in the relevant box, calculate the amount(s) in the column provided, and add postage to determine the amount due. Please clearly fill in your details plus method of payment in the boxes provided and return your completed form with payment attached.

For assessments in 2006/07		Study Text		Workbook		Pocket Notes		Total
Unit		Price £	Order	Price £	Order	Price £	Order	£
30	Introductory accounting	21.00	☐	21.00	☐	8.00	☐	
1, 2 & 3	Receipts, payments and an initial trial balance	21.00	☐	21.00	☐			
		Study Text & Workbook				8.00	☐	
Unit		Price £	Order					
4	Supplying information for management control	16.00	☐					
5	Maintaining financial records and preparing accounts	16.00	☐					
6	Recording and evaluating costs and revenues	21.00	☐			8.00	☐	
7	Preparing reports and returns	21.00	☐			8.00	☐	
8 & 9	Performance management, enhancement of value and planning & control of resources	21.00	☐			8.00	☐ ☐	
10	Managing systems and people in the accounting environment	21.00	☐			8.00	☐	
11	Drafting financial statements	21.00	☐			8.00	☐	
15	Cash management and credit control	16.00	☐			8.00	☐	
17	Implementing auditing procedures	21.00	☐			6.00	☐	
18	Business taxation (FA05)	15.00	☐					
18	Business taxation (FA06)	21.00	☐			8.00	☐	
19	Personal taxation (FA05)	15.00	☐			6.00		
19	Personal taxation (FA06)	16.00	☐			8.00		
21, 22&23	Working with computers, personal effectiveness and health & safety	16.00	☐			8.00	☐	
31	Accounting work skills	16.00	☐			8.00	☐	
32	Professional ethics	16.00	☐			8.00	☐	
33	Management accounting	16.00	☐			8.00	☐	
							TOTAL	

Postage, Packaging and Delivery (per item):   **Note:** Maximum postage charged for UK orders is £15

Study Texts and Workbooks	First	Each	Pocket Notes		First	Each Extra
UK	£5.00	£2.00	UK		£2.00	£1.00
Europe (incl Republic of Ireland	£7.00	£4.00	Europe (incl Republic of Ireland and		£3.00	£2.00
Rest of World	£22.00	£8.00	Rest of World		£8.00	£5.00

Product Sub Total £................   Postage & Packaging £................   Order Total £.....................   (Payments in UK £ Sterling)

Customer Details

☐ Mr   ☐ Mrs   ☐ Ms   ☐ Miss   Other

....

Initials:................................ Surname:

....

Address:

....

....

....

Delivery Address – if different from above

Address:

....

....

..

Delivery please allow:-	United Kingdom	- 5 working days
	Europe	- 8 working days

Payment

1 I enclose Cheque/Postal Order/Bankers Draft for £................
  Please make cheques payable to **'FTC Kaplan Limited'**.

2 Charge MasterCard/Visa/Switch/Delta no:

▭▭▭ ▭▭▭ ▭▭▭ ▭▭▭ ▭▭▭

Valid from: ▭▭▭   Expiry date: ▭▭▭

Issue no: (Switch only) ▭▭▭   3-digit security code on back of card ▭▭▭

Declaration

I agree to pay as indicated on this form and understand that FTC Kaplan Limiteds Terms and Conditions apply (available on request).

Signature: ....   Date: ....

Notes: All orders over 1kg will be fully tracked & insured. Signature required on receipt of order. Delivery times subject to stock availability. A telephone number or email address is required for orders that are to be delivered to a PO Box number

STUDY TEXT/WORKBOOK REVIEW FORM
AAT Unit 11

Thank you for choosing this Kaplan Publishing Study Text/Workbook for your AAT qualification. As we are constantly striving to improve our products, we would be grateful if you could provide us with feedback about how useful you found this publication.

Name: ....

Address: ....

....

Email: ....

Why did you decide to purchase this Study Text/Workbook?

Have used them in the past ☐

Recommended by lecturer ☐

Recommended by friend ☐

Saw advertising ☐

Other (please specify) ....

....

How do you study?

At a college ☐

On a Distance Learning Course ☐

Home study ☐

Other (please specify) ....

....

Within our AAT range we also offer Distance Learning Courses and Pocket Notes. Is there any other type of service/publication that you would like to see as part of the range?

CD Rom with additional questions and answers ☐

A booklet that would help you master exam skills and techniques ☐

Space on our website that would answer your technical questions and queries ☐

Other (please specify) ....

During the past six month do you recall seeing/receiving any of the following?

Our advertisement in Accounting Technician magazine? ☐

Our leaflet/brochure or a letter through the post? ☐

Other (please specify) ....

Overall opinion of this Study Text/Workbook

	Excellent	Adequate	Poor
Introductory pages	☐	☐	☐
Standards coverage	☐	☐	☐
Clarity of explanations	☐	☐	☐
Clarity of definitions and key terms	☐	☐	☐
Diagrams	☐	☐	☐
Activities	☐	☐	☐
Quick quiz questions	☐	☐	☐
Key technique questions	☐	☐	☐
Answers to key technique questions	☐	☐	☐
Mock exams/skills tests	☐	☐	☐
Layout	☐	☐	☐
Index	☐	☐	☐

If you have further comments/suggestions or have spotted any errors, please write them on the bottom of the next page.
Please return this form to: Briony Wastell, Kaplan Publishing Foulks Lynch, FREEPOST NAT 17540, Wokingham RG40 1BR

Other comments/suggestions and errors

. . . .
. . . .
. . . .
. . . .
. . . .
. . . .
. . . .
. . . .
. . . .
. . . .
. . . .
. . . .
. . . .